Forging the American Nation, 1787–1791

Shlomo Slonim

Forging the American Nation, 1787–1791

James Madison and the Federalist Revolution

Shlomo Slonim
Hebrew University of Jerusalem
Jerusalem
Israel

ISBN 978-1-349-95747-7   ISBN 978-1-349-95163-5 (eBook)
DOI 10.1057/978-1-349-95163-5

© The Editor(s) (if applicable) and The Author(s) 2017
Softcover reprint of the hardcover 1st edition 2017
This work is subject to copyright. All rights are solely and exclusively licensed by the Publisher, whether the whole or part of the material is concerned, specifically the rights of translation, reprinting, reuse of illustrations, recitation, broadcasting, reproduction on microfilms or in any other physical way, and transmission or information storage and retrieval, electronic adaptation, computer software, or by similar or dissimilar methodology now known or hereafter developed.
The use of general descriptive names, registered names, trademarks, service marks, etc. in this publication does not imply, even in the absence of a specific statement, that such names are exempt from the relevant protective laws and regulations and therefore free for general use.
The publisher, the authors and the editors are safe to assume that the advice and information in this book are believed to be true and accurate at the date of publication. Neither the publisher nor the authors or the editors give a warranty, express or implied, with respect to the material contained herein or for any errors or omissions that may have been made. The publisher remains neutral with regard to jurisdictional claims in published maps and institutional affiliations.

Cover illustration: © Andrey Kuzmin/Alamy Stock Photo
Cover design by Samantha Johnson

Printed on acid-free paper

This Palgrave Macmillan imprint is published by Springer Nature
The registered company is Nature America Inc.
The registered company address is: 1 New York Plaza, New York, NY 10004, U.S.A.

*To the memory of two devoted friends
who together introduced me to
American constitutional law and history*

*JACOB W. LANDYNSKI
Scholar and generous colleague*

and

*GERALD GUNTHER
Master of the Law and mentor*

Happily for America, happily we trust for the whole human race, they [the Founders] pursued a new and more noble course. They accomplished a revolution which has no parallel in the annals of human society. They reared the fabric of governments which have no model on the face of the globe.

James Madison, *Federalist* #14, November 30, 1787

The Public Mind cannot be occupied about a nobler Object than the proposed Plan of Government. It appears to be admirably calculated to cement all America in affection and Interest as one great Nation.

John Adams to Secretary of State John Jay, December 16, 1787, The Works of John Adams (Boston, MA: Little, Brown, 1856), VIII: 467

No one can rejoice more than I do at every step taken by the People of this great Country to preserve the Union—establish good order and government—and to render the Nation happy at home & respected abroad. No Country upon Earth ever had more in its power to attain these blessings than United America.

George Washington to Benjamin Lincoln, June 29, 1788
GWP: Confederation Series, 6:365

Acknowledgements

The gestation of this work has taken a long time, in the course of which I have incurred many debts to people and institutions. First and foremost, I wish to thank my host institution, the Hebrew University of Jerusalem at Mt. Scopus, for the privilege of an office after retirement, and its extensive collection of original documentary material—*The Documentary History of the Constitution*, and the Papers of James Madison, George Washington, Thomas Jefferson, Alexander Hamilton, George Mason, and the numerous volumes of the *Documentary History of the Ratification of the Constitution*—all of which were essential for the original research upon which this book is based. The staff members at various university libraries in Israel and the United States were universally gracious in providing me with books and materials that I required, and I wish to thank them for their courteous service. Likewise I wish to thank the Israel Science Foundation for a generous grant that enabled me to pursue the research.

Turning to individuals, it is a pleasure to express my appreciation to Shlomo Goldberg, Director of the lending division at the National & Hebrew University Library, for his help over many years. The staff of the Bloomfield Library at the Mt. Scopus campus, headed by Karen Sitton, and later by Naomi Alshech, were most helpful in producing required materials, as was Dafna Mizrahi-Melcer, of the library administration. The members of the Hebrew University Law Library staff, including, in particular, Lorraine Epand, Miriam Shatz-Sharon, and Chana Tal, were equally attentive to my needs and were very accommodating in tracing electronic materials when needed. In the United States, I enjoyed working at the McKeldin Library of the University of Maryland, College Park campus, which had every item I could need. Ralph Amelan of the US Center in Jerusalem was always available to assist in time of need, and I owe him a special note of thanks.

Several scholars read the manuscript from beginning to end, and others read parts of it. They include Professors Henry Abraham of the University of Virginia; Herman Belz of the University of Maryland; Louis Fisher, Scholar in

Residence at the Constitution Project and Visiting Scholar at the William and Mary Law School; Charles F. Hobson of the University of William and Mary and Editor of the James Madison Papers; Mark R. Killenbeck of the University of Alabama, Sanford Levinson of the University of Texas; Peter Onuf of the University of Virginia, and Michael Stokes Paulsen of the University of Minnesota and, more recently, of St Thomas University in Minneapolis. I am profoundly grateful for their helpful comments, which saved me from many an error, and in general helped to improve the manuscript. Of course, the usual disclaimer applies: I alone am responsible for the thesis presented.

I wish to thank my excellent assistants, Moriah Freeman, Daniel Gross, and Tal Oriana Rogoff, for their devoted work. Editorial review was completed by Jill Rogoff, who helped in more ways than I can describe. The task of finishing the manuscript in reasonable time would never have been accomplished without her contribution. I am also greatly indebted to Dr. Charles Siegman, economist, who read the work from cover to cover and made valuable suggestions for revision. I very much appreciate his keen insights.

I am grateful to Cambridge University Press for allowing me to quote from my article: "Securing States' Interests at the 1787 Constitutional Convention: A Reassessment," which appeared in *Studies in American Political Development* in 2000.

My thanks also to the editors of the *University of St. Thomas Law Journal* for permission to quote from my article on the New Federalism, which they published in 2015.

And, finally, I am ever grateful to my wife, Professor Michla Pomerance, an international legal scholar in her own right, who reviewed every word in this manuscript and improved its content, style, and clarity.

The editorial staff at Palgrave Macmillan, publishers, were all considerate and patient with my preparation of the manuscript. and helped in a variety of ways to produce an estimable volume. They include Kristin Purdy, Michelle Smith, and Jessie Wheeler.

The book is dedicated to the memory of two great scholars of American constitutional law and history who were instrumental in my joining those who labor in the vineyard of the Founding period of US history.

Contents

1	America's First Constitution: State Over Nation	1
2	The Road to Philadelphia: Nationalists in Search of Energy and Supremacy	15
3	The Constitutional Convention: Nation Over State Within a Federal Framework	31
	Federalizing the National Legislature	33
	Federalizing the Choice of a National Executive	39
	Senate Advice and Consent	41
4	Delimiting the Scope of National Authority	59
	Enumerating Congressional Powers	59
	Vetoing the National Legislative Veto	66
	Constitutional Flexibility	72
5	Three Dissenting Fathers: The First Salvo in the Antifederalist Campaign	85
6	The Antifederalist Drive to Reinstitute State Over Nation	105
	Stage 1: The Constitution Faulted for Lack of a Bill of Rights	106
	Stage 2: The Federalist Response	108
	Stage 3: The Antifederalist Rejoinder to the Wilsonian Thesis	110

xii CONTENTS

7	Three Ratification Contests: The Fate of the Union in the Balance	127
	Massachusetts: "The Conciliatory Resolutions that Saved the Constitution"	127
	Virginia: "The Battle Royal." Where Lies Dominion?	134
	New York: "Convinced by Circumstances." Antifederalists Come Face to Face with Reality	143
8	Madison and the Threat of a Second Constitutional Convention	163
9	The Bill of Rights in Congress: Madison's Race Against Time	179
10	The Tenth Amendment: Nation Over State Preserved	195
11	Postscript: Federalism Tested: Madison v. Marshall and the Antifederalist Revival	205
	Madison's Embrace of Antifederalist Ideology	206
	The Tenability of Madison's Legal Theses	208
	The Creation of the Democratic-Republican Party	214
	Antifederalists: Co-founders of the Constitution?	218
	Marshall's Federalism, Dual Federalism, and the New Federalism	219

Chronology	229
Appendix 1: The Constitution of the United States of America 1787	233
Appendix 2: The Bill of Rights	243
Bibliography	245
Index	257

ABBREVIATIONS

AHP	*The Papers of Alexander Hamilton.* Edited by Harold C. Syrett and Jacob E. Cooke. 27 vols. New York: Columbia Univ. Press, 1961–1979
Bailyn, *Debate*	Bailyn, Bernard (ed.), *The Debate on the Constitution: Federalist and Antifederalist Speeches, Articles and Letters During the Struggle over Ratification*, Parts I and II. New York: Library of America, 1993
DHC	*Documentary History of the Constitution of the United States of America 1786–1870.* 5 vols. Washington, DC: Dept. of State, 1894–1905
DHRC	Jensen, Merrill, John P. Kaminski, and Gaspare J. Saladino (eds.). *The Documentary History of the Ratification of the Constitution.* 27 vols. to date. Madison, WI: State Historical Society of Wisconsin, 1976–
Elliot's Debates	Elliot, Jonathan (ed.), *The Debates of the Several State Conventions on the Adoption of the Federal Constitution in 1787.* 5 vols. Philadelphia, PA: Lippincott, 1836
Farrand, *Records*	Max Farrand (ed.), *The Records of the Federal Convention of 1787.* Revised edition, 4 vols. New Haven, CT: Yale University Press 1911, 1937
Federalist	Alexander Hamilton, James Madison, and John Jay, *The Federalist.* Edited by Jacob E. Cooke. Middletown, CT: Wesleyan University Press, 1982. All references to *The Federalist* are to the Cooke edition.
GMP	*The Papers of George Mason, 1725–1792.* Edited by Robert Allen Rutland. 3 vols. [Chapel Hill]: University of North Carolina Press, 1970
GWP	*The Papers of George Washington, Confederation Series.* Edited by Dorothy Twohig et al. 6 vols. Charlottesville: University Press of Virginia, 1987–

JMP	*The Papers of James Madison.* Edited by William T. Hutchinson, William M. E. Rachal, Robert A. Rutland, Charles F. Hobson et al. 17 vols. to date. Vols. 1–10: Chicago: University of Chicago Press, 1962–77; Vols. 11–: Charlottesville: University of Virginia Press, 1978–
Storing, *Antifederalist*	Storing, Herbert J. (ed.), *The Complete Anti-Federalist.* 7 vols. Chicago: University of Chicago Press, 1981
Tansill, *Documents*	Tansill, Charles C. *Documents Illustrative of the Formation of the Union of the American States.* Sewanee, TN: Spencer Judd, 1984
TJP	*The Papers of Thomas Jefferson.* Edited by Julian P. Boyd et al. 27 vols. to date. Princeton, NJ: Princeton University Press, 1950–

Introduction

The American nation was forged in the crucible of the Convention that met in Philadelphia in the summer of 1787 and produced the Constitution. It was there that this second phase of the American Revolution, justly labeled the Federalist Revolution, was launched. A new instrument of government, undertaken without specific authorization of the national authority or the state legislatures, converted thirteen disparate states into one body politic. Upon the adoption of the Bill of Rights, the nascent state overcame the centrifugal forces that threatened to pull the republic asunder again.

This study focuses on the manner by which the original scheme of James Madison for a highly centralized and powerful national government, as reflected in the Virginia Plan which he largely drafted, was systematically modified and federalized, until a federal design emerged from the Philadelphia conclave. Moreover, in tracing the federalization process, it delineates the stages by which the Federalist Revolution was completed. It highlights the importance of the last stage, which encompassed the ratification struggles in key states and culminated in the adoption of the Bill of Rights. A better understanding of the forces that brought about the federal scheme has continuing implications—not least, perhaps, for recent Supreme Court jurisprudence.[1]

Contrary to common belief (including that of Justices on the US Supreme Court), federalism did not form an integral part of the scheme presented to the Constitutional Convention by Madison and his colleagues. It was forced upon them at Philadelphia, primarily by the smaller and slave states. While the role of the smaller states in the federalization process is well known, the critical contribution of the slave states to the federal framework has been scarcely noticed heretofore.

The new light shed upon the birth of American federalism emerges from an examination of the relevant documentation that, to date, has not been adequately appreciated. In place of the usual reliance on the *Federalist Papers*, which were essentially designed to sway the wavering electorate in the state of

New York, the present study is based on a close reading of the minutes of the Constitutional Convention, as recorded by Madison and others, and as conveniently published by Max Farrand in *The Records of the Federal Convention of 1787*.[2] With this review, the federal character of the Constitution assumes an entirely novel perspective.

An original feature of this study lies in its focus on the doctrine of implied powers as a central factor linking the three foundational documents—the Articles of Confederation, the Constitution, and the Bill of Rights. Viewing the documents through the prism of implied powers enables us to appreciate why and how each document was adopted to replace or supplement its predecessor. The absence of a doctrine of implied powers in the Articles of Confederation condemned them to failure; the presence of the doctrine in the Constitution aroused fears that a national government with unlimited powers would create a consolidated nation in which the states would be cast into oblivion; the Bill of Rights was adopted to assuage such fears.

It is well recognized that the rigidity of the Articles of Confederation defeated every attempt to create an effective national government. In particular, Article II, by preserving "the sovereignty, freedom and independence" of each state and restricting the national authority to the powers "expressly delegated," frustrated every move to apply and expand even those powers that were delegated to the United States. This provision was responsible for precluding the development of a doctrine of implied powers. A primary aim of the Framers was to alter that situation by eclipsing state independence and sovereignty. As Gouverneur Morris said at the Convention: "State attachments, and State importance have been the bane of this country. We cannot annihilate; but we may perhaps take out the teeth of the serpents."[3] It was in this spirit that the Framers presented a plan to the plenum that would institute a highly centralized and powerful national government under which the states would be completely subordinate—indeed, mere ciphers. The story of the Convention is how this drastic scheme was itself revised in the face of small-state and slave-state demands. Federalism, which had been barred from entry through the front door, now reappeared through the back door.

The first and most critical concession of the Framers was in the composition of the national legislature where they were compelled to concede equal representation for each state in the upper house, and the three-fifths rule in the lower house. This was followed by the federalization of the system for the election of a President by means of the Electoral College, which again granted the smaller and slave states inordinate influence in the choice. And by imposing an enumeration of the powers of Congress, the slave states succeeded in curbing the previously accepted, almost unlimited, scope of national authority. The states emerged from the Constitutional Convention with their independence preserved and, beyond that, with an effective role in the functioning of the national government. In short, the aim of eliminating federalism was defeated, and federalism became a mainstay of the national system of government.

At the same time, national domination was assured by means of several provisions. The necessary and proper clause at the end of the enumeration of the powers of Congress in Article 1, Section 8, paved the way for implementation of a doctrine of implied powers by the federal government; and the supremacy clause in Article 6, Section 2, made it clear that state interference with federal legislation would be ruled out. Thus, even within a federal framework, national predominance was manifest. The Federalists had lost the battle, but they had won the war. Thanks to the inclusion of these two clauses, the national government, even with a restricted list of powers, was free of dependence on the states for its operation.

However, fears arising from the combined operation of these two provisions proved to be the greatest obstacle to ratification of the Constitution in several states. Antifederalists contended that the "sweeping clause," as the necessary and proper clause became known, opened up vast avenues for increasing and expanding the powers of Congress. Anything that Congress deemed "necessary and proper" could be enacted into law, and the supremacy clause would ensure its overriding any contrary state legislation. There was no restriction on the power of Congress to create new areas of authority even if they invaded state prerogatives. With congressional powers open-ended and elastic, the states could be faced with a consolidated Leviathan threatening their independence. To avoid such an eventuality, the Antifederalists in several states vigorously promoted an Article II-type amendment limiting the federal government to the powers *expressly* enumerated. At a later stage, they sought to organize a second Constitutional Convention to attain their avowed goal of restoring sovereign state authority.

All this alarmed Madison, who viewed these proposals as transparent attempts to undermine the constitutional system formulated at Philadelphia. He moved swiftly to derail the Antifederalist drive by hastening through Congress a draft bill of rights that would protect civil liberties but leave intact the federal equation instituted under the Constitution. In order to confirm and preserve that equation, he formulated an innocent reserved powers clause that would stipulate that all powers not granted the federal government remained with the states or the people. This, of course, was implicit in the construction of the Constitution in any case, but Madison felt it did no harm to make the principle more explicit. He firmly rejected every attempt to introduce a formulation that would limit the federal government to the powers *expressly* conveyed and foreclose thereby the emergence of a doctrine of implied powers. The reserved powers clause, which became the Tenth Amendment, sealed at once, both the Bill of Rights and the Constitution. But it is important to appreciate that it was a two-way street. As much as that Amendment ensured that those powers not conveyed to the national government inhered to the states, it also affirmed that the full scope of powers assigned to the federal government, including implied powers, continued to reside with the national government.

In sum, while the Articles represented state over nation, the Constitution reversed that equation and established nation over state. The Bill of Rights overcame Antifederalist efforts to restore the original equation of state over nation. Beyond that, a bill of rights presumed that there would be judicial review to determine the constitutionality of legislation, national and state.

The Bill of Rights was the price paid by the Federalists to the Antifederalists for ratification of the Constitution, and Madison's version of the Tenth Amendment was the price paid by the Antifederalists to the Federalists for a bill of rights. The Bill of Rights saved the Constitution, and the Tenth Amendment saved them both.

By successfully defeating the Antifederalist attempt to turn back the clock and neuter the necessary and proper clause, Madison provides ample reason for labeling him the Father of the Constitution. His earlier achievements at the Constitutional Convention hardly justified a claim of paternity, since his proposal for a powerful nationalist constitution, premised on popular majorities, was denied by the small state/slave state combination. In fact, Madison regarded the final document as a failure because it omitted the federal veto over state legislation for which he had incessantly campaigned. But in facing up to the Antifederalist challenge in the struggle over ratification, he proved to be a supreme strategist, whose role was crucial. It is to his credit that the Federalist Revolution was crowned with success, with the Constitution in place, untrammeled by restrictive amendments that would have destroyed national cohesion and unity.

While the Constitution that emerged from Philadelphia was not the one the Federalists had anticipated, the decrepit federal design of the Articles of Confederation had been radically altered and the American nation was now safely anchored. The national government would be equipped with an array of powers that could be effectively implemented by means of a doctrine of implied powers, and with a supremacy clause to ensure state compliance. Of course, implementation was not automatic. It would depend on the actions of the new government, and particularly its judicial arm. The Constitution provided the blueprint, and it was left to John Marshall and his Court to bring the Federalist Revolution to its subsequent fruition. This was achieved in the celebrated case *McCulloch v. Maryland*,[4] which determined the constitutional balance between the federal and state governments. The full scope of national authority was predicated on a broad interpretation of the necessary and proper clause operating in conjunction with the supremacy clause. The federal government was empowered to create a national bank, and the states were not permitted to block its operation by means of taxation. While the states were acknowledged as essential elements in the federal-state nexus, they were not at liberty to challenge or undermine the preeminent status of the nation.

Of late, the meaning and scope of this seminal case has come under renewed scrutiny from a conservative majority of the Supreme Court. In particular, the Court has invested the reserved powers clause, the Tenth Amendment, with new and dispositive authority. This, in turn, is employed to sustain a jurisprudence of Dual Federalism in adjudicating nation-state relations. It remains to be seen what impact this fresh jurisprudence, entitled the New Federalism, will have on welfare legislation as it has emerged over the course of more than three-quarters of a century. Moreover, there is room to question how consistent this New Federalism is with originalist interpretation of the Constitution, as promoted by this same Court majority.

The final section of this work, entitled "Federalism Tested," examines Madison's abandonment of the Federalist camp and his adoption of Antifederalist ideology in opposition to the economic policies proposed by the Washington/Hamilton administration. Madison's objections to the creation of a national bank stunned colleagues and is deemed an about-face by most of his biographers. In place of nation over state, Madison was now advocating restoration of state over nation to the extent that the Constitution permitted it. The legal thesis devised by Madison to rationalize his reversal of policy is critically examined. Chief Justice Marshall's opinion in *McCulloch v. Maryland*, based on a broad interpretation of the necessary and proper clause, confirmed a doctrine of implied powers for the United States. Nonetheless, Madison and his successors in the White House continued to apply a narrow, restrictive approach to congressional schemes of national development, invariably applying a veto. Moreover, Chief Justice Taney devised Dual Federalism, according to which national and state levels of government were equally sovereign and independent. The task of the Court was to prevent invasions of the other's prerogative. Adoption of the New Deal in the 1930s in favor of new welfare programs reflected a revival of Marshall's jurisprudence. Of late, espousers of Antifederalist ideology have even propounded a theory that the Antifederalists, who had vigorously opposed ratification of the Constitution, were actually co-founders of the federal republic. Such ideological innovation confirms the popularity of the Constitution, even as it stretches historical imagination.

The entire constitutional saga was aptly described by Charles Warren, who remarked: "It is only when the strength of the opposition to the Constitution, as framed, is duly understood that one can begin to appreciate the greatness of the triumph of the Constitution over its opponents... [It] was a triumph of the determination ... to achieve Union."[5]

NOTES

1. In some respects, the title Federalist Revolution is a misnomer, since it aimed to expand national power and curb state power. Understandably, the Antifederalists claimed that they were the true Federalists, since they promoted state sovereignty. History, however, has reserved the name Federalists for those who engineered the revolution that endowed the United States with the Constitution.
2. Farrand, *Records*.
3. Ibid., 1:530.

4. 17 US (4 Wheat.) 315 (1819).
5. Charles Warren, *The Making of the Constitution* (Boston, MA: Little, Brown, 1928), 745, 780.

The work by Mary Sarah Bilder, *Madison's Hand: Revising the Constitutional Convention* (Cambridge, MA: Harvard Univ. Press, 2015) reached me too late to incorporate valuable notes into my own work. I have perused the Bilder work carefully, and found it to be a remarkable study of Madison's attempt to revise his minutes, to make himself appear less nationalistic than he was at the Philadelphia Convention. As Bilder demonstrates, his efforts were in vain, since he could not disguise the nationalist stance he had adopted throughout the Convention.

CHAPTER 1

America's First Constitution: State Over Nation

There is nothing more common than to confound the terms of the American revolution with those of the late American war. The American war is over: but this is far from being the case with the American revolution. On the contrary, nothing but the first act of the great drama is closed. It remains yet to establish and perfect our new forms of government; and to prepare the principles, morals, and manners of our citizens, for these forms of government, after they are established and brought to perfection.
Benjamin Rush, 1786[1]

It is to this [requirement of] unanimous consent, [that] the depressed situation of the Union is undoubtedly owing ... To this weak, this absurd part of the Government, may all our distresses be fairly attributed.
Charles Pinckney, 1787[2]

It is well recognized that in the space of the first 11 years of its existence, the United States experienced not one, but two revolutions. The first was the political revolution of 1776 that severed the bond between the 13 colonies and Great Britain and proclaimed, in the Declaration of Independence, the sovereignty of the United States. But it was only in the second, 1787 revolution, that the states were welded into one nation under a central governing authority by means of the Constitution.

The defects that marked the initial political system established under the Articles of Confederation were legion. As analyzed by Alexander Hamilton in *Federalist* #15 and successive numbers of the *Federalist Papers*, they included primarily such matters as the inability of the Confederation Congress to levy taxes directly on individuals and its dependence for revenue on the oft-unfulfilled requisitions leveled against the states; the disarray in interstate and foreign commerce due to conflicting state policies and imposts; the undermining of the confederation's foreign relations by the states' pursuit of independent foreign policies and concomitant frequent serious breaches of treaties; and the fact that, in the absence of a national executive, judiciary, or legislature competent to bind individuals, the observance of federal law was illusory.

In 1786, in advance of the Constitutional Convention, James Madison had penned a private memorandum entitled "Vices of the Political System of the United States." At that point in his career, Madison, barely 35 years old, had already amassed considerable political and governmental experience on both the state and national levels. A Princeton graduate, he had been elected to the state legislature and contributed to drafting the state Constitution and its Declaration of Rights. From 1780 to 1783, he had represented Virginia in the Confederation Congress, during which period he had advocated reforms in the system of government to strengthen national government. Now, in his memorandum, he explicated 12 major flaws of the Articles of Confederation.[3] Of those (to be discussed in detail below), perhaps the most crucial was the absence of an effective sanction to ensure the observance of federal laws. "A sanction," he averred, "is essential to the idea of law, as coercion is to that of Government,"[4] and the present federal system, "being destitute of both, wants the great vital principles of a Political Constitution." It was "in fact nothing more than a treaty of amity of commerce and of alliance, between so many independent and Sovereign States." "From what cause," he then asked, "could so fatal an omission [of a sanction] have happened in the articles of Confederation?" The key, to his mind, lay in noble impulses unaccompanied by adequate understanding of human nature:

> From a mistaken confidence that the justice, the good faith, the honor, the sound policy, of the several [state] legislative assemblies would render superfluous any appeal to the ordinary motives by which laws secure the obedience of individuals: a confidence which does honor to the enthusiastic virtue of the compilers, as much as the inexperience of the crisis apologizes for their errors.[5]

His own emphatic conclusion was that it could "no longer [be] doubted that a unanimous and punctual obedience of 13 independent bodies, to the acts of the federal Government, ought not be calculated on."[6] This last comment helps explain a crucial matter that figured as a sharply controversial issue in the ratification debate: Why did the Framers at Philadelphia find it necessary to completely abandon the Articles and draft an entirely new instrument of government? After all, the resolution of the Confederal Congress calling for the Convention to assemble in Philadelphia had specified that it should meet "for the sole and express purpose of revising the Articles of Confederation and reporting to Congress and the several legislatures such alterations and provisions therein as shall when agreed to in Congress and confirmed by the states render the federal constitution adequate to the exigencies of Government & the preservation of the Union."[7]

Andrew C. McLaughlin, in his classic study *A Constitutional History of the United States*,[8] entitles one chapter "The Tribulations of the Confederate Period: The Chief Problem of the Time." In his view, "the failure of the states to abide by their obligations" was the primary culprit; it was "the *chief problem of the day*."[9] This was indubitably a crucial failing, since the inability of the national government to exercise supremacy over the states enabled them to evade every obligation to which they were subject, thus enfeebling the federal government. The latter lacked both energy, to take initiatives and carry them out, and supremacy, to prevent the states from undermining the decisions taken. Nevertheless, had there been a means of rectifying this central defect the Articles might have survived. What condemned them beyond reprieve was indeed the failing that Madison underscored. The Articles provided no viable method for modification and adaptation—whether by formal amendment or binding judicial interpretation.

Two provisions sealed the fate of the Articles of Confederation. "Each state," according to Article II, "retains its sovereignty, freedom and independence, and every Power, Jurisdiction and right, which is not by this confederation expressly delegated to the United States, in Congress assembled." And on the amendment process, Article XIII read: "The Articles of this confederation shall be inviolably observed by every State, and the union shall be perpetual; nor shall any alteration at any time hereafter be made in any of them; unless such alteration be agreed to in a congress of the united states, and be afterwards confirmed by the Legislatures of every State."

By limiting national powers to those "expressly delegated," Article II precluded the rise of a doctrine of implied powers. The crippling effect that this had on federal affairs is well illustrated by a dispute that arose between the Confederal Congress and the state of Virginia in 1782.[10] The Articles of Capitulation that followed the 1781 British surrender at Yorktown had stipulated that British traders could sell and remove their property. On this basis, Congress authorized its Secretary to issue passports (i.e. licenses) to British merchants to receive a consignment of tobacco from Virginia. But when the ships arrived in Virginia, the Governor, Benjamin Harrison, refused to recognize the passports and referred the matter to the state legislature and its Attorney-General, Edmund Randolph. Virginia's lower house adopted a resolution stating that only the states had authority to issue passports. Randolph disagreed, contending that Congress possessed the necessary competence by virtue of the war power. The Governor remained steadfast in his refusal, and upon notification of Virginia's action, Congress delegated representatives to travel to Virginia and persuade it to relent. In the meantime, Virginia's upper house amended the resolution of the lower house, thus putting an end to the dispute. But by highlighting the difficulty of asserting congressional power in the absence of an express grant, this incident well illustrated the harmful effects of Article II. As John Murrin said of the provision, "States' Rights thus triumphed over national aspirations."[11]

Article XIII, with its unanimity requirement for amendments, was even more crippling. It meant that it would be well-nigh impossible to rectify the revealed flaws of the Articles and that the federal government would continue to lack both the energy and supremacy that would permit it to govern effectively.

Salvation would have to come through the adoption of a new instrument of government.[12]

Indeed, the very process of formulating and ratifying the Articles of Confederation demonstrated that the drafters had been overly optimistic in requiring the consent of every state before the Articles could enter into force or be amended. It took over a year for Congress to complete the draft and nearly 4 more years to secure the consent of all the states. Congress had agreed upon the text of the Articles on November 15, 1777, but the Articles did not enter into force until March 1, 1781, when the last state, Maryland, finally ratified.[13] This extraordinary delay took place because Maryland had conditioned its ratification on prior renunciation by Virginia of its claims to western territories. Only after Virginia complied with this demand did the Maryland legislature give its assent to the Articles.

This episode foreshadowed future deadlocks and graphically revealed how difficult it was to secure the affirmative vote of every single state. Any state could at any time and for any reason—however extraneous—derail a Congressional proposal for modifying a provision in the Articles to meet new exigencies. The door was left wide open to caprice, willful obstructionism, and total insensitivity to national needs. Repeated attempts to amend the Articles amply confirmed the extent to which the document was critically flawed from the outset.

Thus, for example, the national government proved unable to resolve the financial crisis, the most immediate issue demanding attention. As noted earlier, the central government was totally dependent for its income on the states; but their payments were haphazard, and rarely matched the amounts levied on them. The sum total collected was not nearly enough to cover the government's operating expenses and the interest on the national debt. The major creditors of the United States included foreign states, namely France and Holland, as well as domestic sources. Besides the embarrassment of failing to pay the interest due, not to speak of part of the principal, there was the danger that the creditors would refuse to extend further funds.[14] Proposals for alleviating the national financial situation focused on methods of compelling the states to contribute the amount assessed and also on empowering the national government to collect a modest customs duty. In each instance, the attempt to revise the Articles failed owing to the recalcitrance of one or two states. As Peter Onuf has written: "The very fact that the drafting process lasted so many years – and that reformers began campaigning for amendments immediately thereafter – made the Articles seem provisional at best."[15]

The first suggestion to bolster federal finances emanated from the states and was put forward even before the Articles had formally entered into force. In November 1780, delegations of New York and the New England states met at Hartford, Connecticut, and submitted proposals for coercing delinquent states to meet their obligations.[16] This approach was premised on the assumption of the New York delegates that such powers "necessarily existed in Congress, and we cannot suppose that they should want [lack] the Power of compelling the several States to their Duty and thereby enabling the Confederacy to expel the common Enemy."[17] Accordingly, it was proposed that the commander-in-chief be granted power to enforce requisitions on defaulting states. Additionally, it was recommended that the states authorize Congress to levy a duty on imports so as to provide revenue to pay the interest on the public debt.[18]

It may well have been the Hartford Convention that inspired Madison to join with others in Congress to propose an amendment to the Articles of Confederation empowering the United States to use force to compel a delinquent state to comply with a requisition levied against it. Significantly, this was the first time that the notion of implied powers as a basis for congressional action was publicly posited. Congress had appointed a three-man committee, composed of James Duane, James Mitchell, and Madison, to consider ways "to invest the United States ... with full and explicit powers for effectually carrying into execution in the several states" the decisions of Congress.[19] The report of the committee, delivered on March 16, 1781, and largely inspired by Madison, noted that since Article 13 of the Confederation explicitly obliged each state to "abide by the determinations" of Congress, this Article vested "a general and implied power ... in the United States ... to enforce and carry into effect" its decisions against any state failing to fulfill its obligation.[20] But since this power was not spelled out, the committee recommended the adoption of an amendment to confirm the implicit interpretation.[21] The draft amendment declared that Congress "was authorized to employ the force of the United States as well by sea as by land to compel ... States to fulfill their federal engagements."[22] In a letter to Jefferson, dated April 16, 1781, Madison explained what was entailed in the reference to "land and sea." "The situation of most of the States is such, that two or three vessels of force employed against their trade will make it their interest to yield prompt obidience to all just requisitions on them." Landlocked states would have their inland trade interdicted. Madison's letter elaborated on the need for such an amendment. Without it, he said, "the whole confederacy may be insulted and the most salutary measures frustrated by the most inconsiderable State in the Union." Interestingly, Madison concluded his letter with what the editor describes as a "sectionalist" argument. "A Navy so formed and under the orders of the general Council of the States, would not only be a guard against aggression & insults from abroad; but without it what is to protect the Southern States for many years to come against the insults & aggressions of their N. Bretheren."[23]

Not surprisingly, the suggestions to coerce delinquent states to fulfill their obligations were stillborn. The idea that the federal government apply force against the states was utterly abhorrent to the members of the Continental Congress.[24] Ultimately, of course, the Constitutional Convention devised the scheme of subjecting citizens directly to federal authority for tax and other purposes, without resort to state intervention, and thus the notion of coercing states became moot.[25]

In the meantime, more realistic reforms in Congress centered on proposals of an economic nature relating to revenue and trade. Thus, in February 1781, in the wake of the Hartford Convention, Congress requested the states to approve an amendment that would empower the federal government to levy a 5% duty on imports, to be devoted to reducing the national debt.[26] New York immediately approved this impost.[27] Eleven other states also endorsed the request of Congress. However, while Congress was busy beseeching each of the states to approve the impost amendment, Rhode Island's representatives in Congress were feverishly advising the state legislature to disapprove the measure: "The object of a seven years war has been to preserve the Liberties of this Country, and not to assume into our own hands the power of governing tyrannically."[28] As a result, the Rhode Island legislature unanimously rejected the proposal. Providing a permanent revenue for the national government, it was said, would make Congress "independent of their constituents; and so the proposed impost is repugnant to the liberty of the United States."[29] In the absence of the general consent of the states, the impost scheme collapsed. David Howell, Rhode Island's representative in Congress, added insult to injury when he sought to justify his state's rejection of the measure. "It derogated from the Sovereignty and Independence of the State for the Ud. Ss. to draw a Revenue for their benefit out of our State and to collect it by their officers."[30]

It is commonly, but incorrectly, assumed that it was Rhode Island's refusal alone which doomed the impost amendment. In fact, Congress had delegated a commission to proceed to Rhode Island in order to persuade that state's legislature to join the other states in ratifying the amendment. After setting out, the three-member delegation became aware that Virginia had retracted its ratification and that Maryland was about to do so as well.[31] In the absence of unanimous state support for the impost, the journey to Rhode Island seemed purposeless, and the delegation returned to Philadelphia, where Congress was sitting.

The Virginian Legislature's retraction, which deeply chagrined Madison,[32] had been engineered by Richard Henry Lee. It demonstrated well the nature of the struggle confronting all those intent on strengthening the federal government, whether by way of amendment or by the holding of a constitutional convention. Lee's arguments, like those of the Rhode Island representatives, reflected a parochial and insular outlook, coupled with a profound concern for preserving what were deemed to be essential individual rights and true liberty.

Lee, born in Virginia in 1732, was an outstanding American patriot who, early on, had become associated with Patrick Henry and Thomas Jefferson, two other young radicals intent on making the break with Great Britain permanent. It was Lee who, in June 1776, introduced a resolution in the Continental Congress to proclaim American independence—a step taken on July 4. He had also authored the resolution calling for the creation of a confederation. Although he was subsequently chosen as a delegate from Virginia to the Constitutional Convention, he declined to serve since, he explained, as a member of the Confederation Congress, it would be his duty to review and react to the handiwork of the Convention, and there was, therefore, a clash of interests.[33] Now, in a series of letters to various colleagues, Lee expounded on the considerations which had led him to move to repeal the Virginia legislature's approval of the impost. The impost would tend to "strangle" Virginia's "infant commerce"; it would make Virginia pay more than its "proportion"; and it would sacrifice the state to its "northern brethren." But the primary consideration for opposing the impost was "the danger to liberty that it threatens."[34] The emphasis on liberty was also highlighted by Lee in a subsequent letter, dated July 1, 1783, to General William Whipple:

> To me it [the 5 percent impost] seems ... too early and too strong an attempt to over leap those fences, established by the Confederation to secure the liberties of the respective States. Where the possession of power creates as it too frequently does, a thirst for more, plausible arguments are seldom wanting to persuade acquiescence... For, give the purse, & the sword will follow, and with these the wheel of rotation so much relied on, will presently be trashed ... and that liberty which we love and now deserve, will become an empty Name. Let us be cautious how we introduce such radical defects into our system.[35]

And in a letter to Samuel Adams, the old Massachusetts revolutionary, Lee wrote:

> So we have a constant cry... That Congress must have more power – That we cannot be secure & happy until Congress command implicitly both purse & sword. So that our confederation must be perpetually changing to answer sinister views in the greater part, until every fence is thrown down that was designed to protect & cover the rights of Mankind... I think Sir that the first maxim of a man who loves liberty should be, never to grant to Rulers an atom of power that is not most clearly & indispensably necessary for the safety and well being of Society.[36]

Clearly, opposition to the enhancement of federal power was prompted by sectional fears of being placed at a disadvantage; but for Lee and others like him, these particularistic concerns were only part of the story and not necessarily even the major part. The same ideological grounds that underlay their embrace of the American Revolution in the first place—resistance to concentrated power and solicitude for guarding cherished liberties—led them now to reject attempts to increase the powers of the center at the expense of the states. In their eyes, endorsement of the proposed concessions was akin to forfeiting to a new, remote, and alien center the hard-won fruits of liberation from the British Crown. Liberty was the banner that needed to be constantly raised, and it trumped all else. Yet, by denying the center the essential authority needed to govern effectively, would this not lead to anarchy—which, as Hamilton warned, was no less a danger to liberty than despotism?[37]

Surprisingly, New York, one of the first states to approve the 1781 impost proposal, decided in 1783 to repeal its earlier endorsement and join the dissenters. By then the 1781 proposal was dead anyway, so what prompted the New York legislature to keep flogging a dead horse? The answer, it appears, relates to the changed fortune of the state during the course of the War of Independence and following the conclusion of the peace treaty. According to

John Kaminski, New York probably suffered more than any other state during the course of the conflict.[38] Parts of the state were occupied for lengthy periods by British forces, and devastation was rampant. As a result, New York desperately looked to Congress to come to its aid; but given the paucity of its resources, the latter was unable to be of much assistance. This prompted New York's Governor Clinton to propose to Congress, in September 1780, "that in all Matters which relate to the war, their Requisitions may be peremptory."[39] And the state legislature soon afterward instructed its delegates to the Hartford Convention to move that Congress, by virtue of an implied power, should "exercise every Power which they may deem necessary for an effectual Prosecution of the war," including the application of force to extract requisitions from delinquent states.[40]

With the cessation of hostilities and the evacuation of British forces in 1783, the attitude of New York State underwent a radical change, and there was no longer any interest in strengthening national authority or surrendering sources of revenue to Congress. As Jackson Turner Main observed: "By 1783 the situation had changed in every respect, and New York was preparing her own financial arrangements based partly upon import taxes. Thereafter she had every selfish economic reason to reject the grant to Congress."[41] In Kaminski's words, "The state impost was to be the cornerstone of the Clintonian financial system, and as such, it could not be given up for federal use."[42] Henceforth, New York was intent on looking after itself and had no need, or desire, to bolster national power. Apparently, the New York legislature was concerned that the impost proposal might yet be resurrected. In order to drive an additional nail into its coffin, it was decided to repeal the initial New York endorsement of the 1781 impost proposal.

The action of the New York legislature in repealing its earlier approval of the 1781 impost amendment forms the essential backdrop to understanding New York's adamant and isolated opposition to a new congressional proposal for an impost in 1783. The new financial program differed in essential ways from that of 1781.[43] To help cover the federal debt, the states were requested to grant Congress the power to tax imports for the limited period of 25 years. Furthermore, the states would contribute supplemental funds amounting to one and a half million dollars annually for the same period and purpose. And finally, the method of assessing the contributions of states would be changed from value of land to size of population.

By the spring of 1786, New York was the only state holding out against approving the impost. In May of that year the New York legislature, recognizing that it had to appear more flexible, ratified the impost amendment, subject to certain conditions.[44] It demanded the right to pay the impost in the recently approved state paper money; it also insisted that the collectors of the national tax be under state, rather than national, control. Not surprisingly, Congress found the New York formula unacceptable and, in its response of August 11, requested Governor Clinton to urgently convene a special session of the state legislature to reconsider the matter.[45] This Clinton declined to do, contending that the state Constitution permitted him to summon the legislature only on "extraordinary occasions"; in this instance, the legislature had just decided the issue. A second appeal from Congress for the Governor to treat this as an "extraordinary occasion" elicited no more positive response. Only in January 1787, when the New York legislature convened in regular session, was the matter taken up for fresh consideration. An attempt to censure the Governor for his inaction on the congressional request was overwhelmingly defeated. As one member of Congress said, this amounted to giving "Congress a Slap in the face."[46] Nor was the state legislature inclined to modify its substantive position. In the words of James Madison, by this act New York had put "a definitive veto on the Impost."[47] In a letter in his later years, Madison wrote:

> He [Robert Yates] & his colleague [Lansing] were the Representatives [in the Philadelphia Convention] of the dominant party in N. York, which was opposed to the Convention & the object of it, which was averse to any essential change in the Articles of Confederation, which had inflexibly refused to grant even a duty of 5 per Ct. on imports for the urgent debt of the Revolution, which was availing itself, of the peculiar situation of New York, for taxing the consumption of her neighbours, and which forsaw that a primary aim of the Convention wd. be to transfer from the States to the Common authority, the entire regulation of foreign Commerce.[48]

Congress had shifted its focus by early 1787. It was formulating a resolution for holding a convention in Philadelphia in the summer, and several states had already moved to appoint delegates. The experience with state obstructionism in relation to proposed amendments to the Articles of Confederation would not be lost on the delegates to the Constitutional Convention. No amendment to the Articles had been approved and proposals failed repeatedly, owing to the recalcitrance of a single state. The unanimity requirement of the Articles had proved to be the bane of every plan to strengthen the national government and impart to Congress the necessary powers to govern effectively. It was clear that some method of overcoming the unanimity hurdle would need to be devised. The creation of a special category of amendments to be subject to less than unanimous consent was one possibility; another was to discard the Articles entirely and draft a new constitution permitting a more flexible method of adopting amendments. The Convention, quite logically, opted for the second option.

At the same time, Madison and others were beginning to appreciate that constitutional flexibility required more than just a revised method for adopting formal amendments. The initial abortive impost proposals, put forward by the Hartford Convention and Madison,[49] had illuminated a new, less formal, alternative method for expanding national authority: reliance on a doctrine of implied powers.[50] Admittedly, in Madison's suggestion about the 5% impost, such an interpretation had not been considered sufficient in itself to arm the national government with power to coerce the states to abide by the decisions of Congress. Upon their return from the Hartford Convention, he and his two colleagues recommended that Congress adopt an amendment to the Articles to make explicit what was implicit. Their proposal was stillborn. But the very mention of implied powers foreshadowed the creation of a fully fledged thesis according to which every grant of power automatically incorporated within itself the implied authority to implement the grant. This thesis was to serve as a fundamental plank in the formulation of the new Constitution, as reflected in the adoption of the necessary and proper clause. The basic principle was subsequently enunciated by Madison in *Federalist*, #44: "No axiom is more clearly established in law, or in reason, than that wherever the end is required, the means are authorised; wherever a general power to do a thing is given, every particular power necessary for doing it, is included."[51] As will be seen, Madison's thesis on implied powers served as a critical point of contention between the Federalists and the Antifederalists in the struggle over ratification of the Constitution, and lay behind the campaign for the adoption of a bill of rights. Thus, the absence or presence of the implied powers doctrine linked the three foundational documents: the Articles, the Constitution, and the Bill of Rights. The subsequent development of the doctrine of implied powers was to become a fundamental and central theme in the constitutional history of the United States, since the scope of the doctrine inevitably defines the nature of American federalism.

In sum, experience with the Articles of Confederation had revealed two fundamental flaws: the requirement of unanimous consent of the states for amendments; and limiting the exercise of national authority to express powers without allowing a doctrine of implied powers to develop.

Notes

1. Benjamin Rush, "Address to the American People," June 3, 1786; *DHRC*, 13: 46. Also in: Colleen A. Sheehan and Gary L. McDowell (eds.), *Friends of the Constitution: Writings of the "Other" Federalists 1787–1788* (Indianapolis, IN: Liberty Fund, 1998), 1. Cited by Jack N. Rakove, "From One Agenda to Another: The Condition of American Federalism, 1783–1787" in Jack Greene (ed.), *The American Revolution: Its Character and Limits* (New York: New York University Press, 1987), 80.

    For an excellent survey of the constitutional development of the United States from the Revolution to the adoption of the Constitution, see Leonard W. Levy, "Introduction: American Constitutional History, 1776–1789" in Leonard W. Levy and Dennis J. Mahoney (eds.), *The Framing and Ratification of the Constitution* (New York: Macmillan, 1987), 1–18. The 21 articles assembled in this volume comprise perhaps the best collection to have appeared on the occasion of the 1987 Bicentennial. Each article was written by a foremost authority in the field and summarizes succinctly and expertly the significance of the specific topic in relation to the adoption of the Constitution.

2. Charles Pinckney, "Observations on the Plan of Government…" (1787). Reprinted in Farrand, *Records*, 3: 120–121.

3. *JMP*, 9: 348–358; and see editor's comment, ibid., 345–348.
4. Ibid., 9: 351.
5. Ibid.
6. Ibid.
7. Tansill, *Documents*, 46.
8. Andrew C. McLaughlin, *A Constitutional History of the United States* (New York: Appleton-Century-Crofts, 1935).
9. Ibid., 146.
10. This account of the crisis that arose as a result of the passport episode is drawn from Randolph's letter to Madison, dated May 21, 1782, in which Randolph describes his argument with Virginia's lower house. *JMP*, 4: 263–264. The matter arose frequently in the debates at Virginia's Ratification Convention in 1788. See, for instance, Randolph's remarks, June 4, 1788. "Congress was reduced to the humiliating condition of being obliged to send deputies to Virginia to solicit a passport." *DHRC*, 9: 936 and n. 19.
11. John M. Murrin, "1787: The Invention of American Federalism" in John M. Murrin et al. (eds.), *Essays on Liberty and Federalism: The Shaping of the U.S. Constitution* (College Station: Texas A& M University Press, 1988), 34. See also the comprehensive work by Alpheus Thomas Mason, *The States Rights Debate: Antifederalism and the Constitution* (Englewood Cliffs, NJ: Prentice-Hall, 1964), Chap. 1. The Mason work presents an excellent analysis of the tension surrounding the adoption of the Constitution and the Bill of Rights.
12. Even Merrill Jensen, who believed the Articles of Confederation were operating effectively, conceded: "The great political mistake made by the supporters of this strictly federal [as against national] government was that any changes in it had to be approved by all the states." *The Making of the American Constitution* (Malabar, FL: Krieger, 1979), 28.
13. Tansill, *Documents*, 27, n. 1, citing the Journals of the Continental Congress.
14. On the financial crisis, see Calvin H. Johnson, *Righteous Anger at the Wicked States: The Meaning of the Founders' Constitution* (New York: Cambridge University Press, 2005), 15–39.
15. Peter S. Onuf, "The First Federal Constitution: The Articles of Confederation" in Levy and Mahoney, *Framing and Ratification*, 97.
16. Edmund Cody Burnett, *The Continental Congress* (New York: Macmillan, 1941), 484–485.
17. Cited in Jack N. Rakove, *The Beginnings of National Politics: An Interpretive History of the Continental Congress* (New York: Knopf, 1979), 281; and see John P. Kaminski, "New York: The Reluctant Pillar" in Stephen L. Schechter (ed.), *The Reluctant Pillar: New York and the Adoption of the Federal Constitution* (New York: Russell Sage College, 1985), 50–51.
18. For proceedings of the Hartford Convention, see message to Governor Jefferson, *TJP*, 4: 138–141.
19. *JMP*, 3: 19, n. 1.
20. *JMP*, 3: 17 and see *TJP*, 4: 138–141. Note the comment of the editor of the *Madison Papers* on Madison's reference to implied powers. "This is believed to be JM's first use of a phrase of great moment in the constitutional history of the United States." *JMP*, 3: 19, n. 3. The editor of the *Jefferson Papers* likewise notes that Madison and his fellow member of Congress, Joseph Jones, were both intent on eliciting Jefferson's support for their claim that the Articles incorporated a doctrine

of implied powers. See *TJP*, 5: 471. Madison's advocacy to Jefferson seems to have borne fruit. In a letter to Carrington in 1787, Jefferson argued that Congress was implicitly empowered to compel a delinquent state to pay its requisition. His very formulation of the argument echoed Madison. See below Chap. 2, in text at n. 9.

As will be seen, the notion that Congress was vested with implied powers had already been canvassed by Hamilton in a letter to Madison's fellow committee member, James Duane. But as Hamilton noted, the doctrine of implied powers stood little chance of acceptance under the Confederation when the powers of the national legislature were restricted to those "expressly" enumerated in the Articles of Confederation.

21. Burnett, *Continental Congress*, 504–505.
22. *Journals of Congress*, 20: 469–471.
23. *JMP*, 3: 71–72; see also *TJP*, 5: 471, 474. Burnett, *Continental Congress*, 507. Acknowledging "the delicacy and importance of the subject," Madison requested Jefferson's "judgment" on the proposal. But see the critical comments on the notion by a foremost member of the Progressive school of historiography, Merrill Jensen: "The Idea of a National Government During the American Revolution," *Political Science Quarterly*, 58 (1943): 372–373. In his view, the proposal was part of the nationalists' design to gain "the power of coercion over the states and their citizens." It was all part of a giant plot to subordinate the states to the national government. According to Jensen's interpretation of the Founding in this article and his other writings, the Articles of Confederation were operating successfully, and the Constitutional Convention represented a *coup d'état* by a group of aristocrats intent on suppressing the democratic spirit that the Revolution had spawned. However, his approach differs from that of Charles Beard, who, while labeling the Convention a *coup d'état*, had regarded it as a necessary positive step in the capitalist development of the United States. Gordon Wood appears to accept, in principle, the Jensen analysis. See his article, "Interests and Disinterestedness in the Making of the Constitution" in Richard Beeman, Stephen Botein, and Edward C. Carter II (eds.), *Beyond Confederation: Origins of the Constitution and American National Identity*. (Chapel Hill: University of North Carolina Press, 1987), 69–112.
24. The notion of applying force against delinquent states derived from the Hartford Convention, and when broached, it aroused immediate opposition. See Burnett, *Continental Congress*, 485–487, 507–508; Rakove, *Beginnings*, 281.
25. Whether the federal government can require states to implement federal programs is an issue that divides majority from minority opinion in the US Supreme Court. See discussion of the New Federalism in Shlomo Slonim, "The Scheme of Enumeration: A Critical Analysis of the New Federalism in the U.S. Supreme Court," *University of St Thomas Law Review*, 12 (2015): 178–227.
26. Burnett, *Continental Congress*, 480–481.
27. Kaminski, *New York*, 51.
28. Burnett, *Continental Congress*, 532.
29. Richard Leffler, "The Constitution of the United States: The End of the Revolution" in Schechter, *Reluctant Pillar*, 30.
30. Cited in Rakove, *Beginnings*, 315.
31. Burnett, *Continental Congress*, 533; and Leffler, *Constitution*, 30–31.
32. See letter to Randolph, Dec. 30, 1782, *JMP*, 5:472–473.
33. See Oliver Perry Chitwood, *Richard Henry Lee: Statesman of the Revolution*. (Morgantown: West Virginia University Library, 1967), 166. For an excellent

analysis of Lee's philosophy, see Gary L. McDowell, "Richard Henry Lee and the Quest for Constitutional Liberty" in Ralph A. Rossum and Gary L. McDowell (eds.), *The American Founding.* (Port Washington, NY: Kennikat Press, 1981), 80–93.
34. James Curtis Ballagh (ed.), *The Letters of Richard Henry Lee.* (New York: Macmillan, 1914), 2: 282.
35. Ibid., 284.
36. March 14, 1785. Ibid., 343–344.
37. See his article, "The Continentalist," No. 1, July 12, 1781, *AHP*, 2: 651.
38. Kaminski, *New York*, 50.
39. Ibid.
40. Ibid. See also Leffler, *Constitution*, 29.
41. Jackson Turner Main, *Political Parties before the Constitution.* (Chapel Hill: University of North Carolina Press, 1973), 139. For an analysis of New York's change of heart, see, in particular, David E. Narrett, "A Zeal for Liberty: The Anti-Federalist Case against the Constitution in New York" in Murrin et al., *Essays*, 69–71.
42. Kaminski, *New York*, 52.
43. Burnett, *Continental Congress*, 71–72; Leffler, *Constitution*, 31–33; Kaminski, *New York*, 52; Rakove, *Beginnings*, 337–338.
44. Kaminski, *New York*, 56–57.
45. Ibid., 57.
46. Cited ibid.
47. *JMP*, 9: 285, cited in Kaminski, *New York*, 58.
48. Farrand, *Records*, 3: 530.
49. See text at nn. 16–23, above.
50. As noted, Hamilton had raised the subject of implied powers earlier, in a letter to James Duane, but Madison's suggestion was the first public expression of the doctrine. On Hamilton's suggestion see below, Chap. 3.
51. James Madison, *The Federalist*, #44.

CHAPTER 2

The Road to Philadelphia: Nationalists in Search of Energy and Supremacy

I do not conceive we can exist long as a nation, without having lodged somewhere a power which will pervade the whole union in as energetic a manner, as the authority of the different state governments extends over the several States. To be fearful of investing Congress, constituted as that body is, with ample authorities for national purposes, appears to me the very climax of popular absurdity and madness.
George Washington[1]

Energy in Government is essential to that security against external and internal danger, and to that prompt and salutary execution of the laws, which enter into the very definition of good Government.
James Madison[2]

In every proceeding of the Convention where the question of paramountship in the laws of the Union could be involved, the necessity of it appears to have been taken for granted.
James Madison[3]

Alexander Hamilton was probably the first to suggest that a convention be held to adopt a new charter of government to replace the Articles of Confederation. In September 1780, Hamilton wrote a remarkably prescient letter on the subject to James Madison's colleague, James Duane, New York delegate to the Continental Congress.[4] Duane had written to Hamilton asking him to outline the defects in the present system of government and what changes he recommended. Hamilton was at that time barely 23 years old and was serving as aide-de-camp to General Washington. Born in the British West Indies in 1757 and orphaned at an early age, he was recognized as a child prodigy and sent by friends to a preparatory school in Elizabethtown, New Jersey. From there he proceeded to King's College (subsequently Columbia University), where he again revealed extraordinary brilliance as a student. The revolutionary movement interrupted his studies and he began to produce a series of anonymous pamphlets justifying the rupture with Great Britain. The pamphlets, written when he was not yet 20, were so mature and sophisticated that they were initially attributed to John Adams or John Jay. Hamilton's response to Duane was a tour de force, in which he spelled out the shortcomings of the federal Union and what needed to be done to provide the United States with a sound system of government.

"The fundamental defect," he wrote, "is a want of power in Congress." The feebleness of the Union was a result "of an uncontrolable sovereignty in each state." Hamilton cited as an example the influence of the states in the affairs of the army. "They should have nothing to do with it," he declared. Failure to detach the army from state influence, he warned, would have dire consequences. He also recommended granting Congress an independent source of revenue through taxation and imposts to be laid on commerce. "Another defect in our system," he said, "is want of method and energy in the administration." To remedy this, an executive should be created which would be free of unnecessary congressional interference in the details of administration. The attempt by Congress to administer by boards was flawed, since "their decisions were slower their energy less their responsibility more diffused" than necessary. Individuals should be appointed to direct the executive departments. "As these men will be ... at all times under the direction of Congress, we shall blend the advantages of a monarchy and republic in our constitution." Hamilton also recommended the establishment of a professional army to be financed and supplied exclusively by the federal government rather than by individual states. While the internal policing of the states could be safely left to the state legislatures, he felt that the federal government should have exclusive control over all matters of war and peace, foreign affairs, trade, finance, coining money, and banking.

Hamilton recommended two possible solutions to the national predicament. The first was to summon a national convention to draft a new constitution. Since it was impossible to support "the contest [with Great Britain] on its present footing," it was urgent to meet within two months. It was also necessary, he thought, to arm the delegates with "plenipotentiary authority" that would allow them "to conclude finally upon a general confederation" without need to refer the Constitution back to the states for ratification. "The business [of a constitution] may suffer no delay in the execution"; and "the measure of a Convention would revive the hopes of the people and give a new direction to their passions."[5]

Hamilton's alternative solution would have had Congress assert "the discretionary powers" which, he claimed, Congress rightly possessed all along as an integral part of its sovereignty. Rejecting the view that Congress was limited to making recommendations, he stated:

> The manner in which Congress was appointed would warrant, and the public good required, that they should have considered themselves as vested with full power *to preserve the republic from harm*. They have done many of the highest acts of sovereignty, which were always cheerfully submitted to – the declaration of independence, the declaration of war, the levying of an army, creating a navy, emitting money, making alliances with foreign powers, appointing a dictator &c. &c. – all these implications of a complete sovereignty were never disputed, and ought to have been a standard for the whole conduct of Administration. Undefined powers are discretionary powers, limited only by the object for which they were given – in the present case, the independence and freedom of America.[6]

In short, Hamilton contended that Congress, in fact, already possessed every power necessary to dominate and command the Confederation. Implicitly, it was endowed with all the attributes of sovereignty and therefore could take all the measures required to conduct the war and lead the country to victory.

Here was an outstanding exposition of the doctrine of implied powers which, Hamilton argued, would enable the country to dispense with the need for a constitutional convention. He recognized, however, that this alternative stood very little chance of adoption. "I expect [it] will be thought too bold an expedient by the generality of Congress," since "their practice hitherto has so rivetted the opinion of their want of power, that the success of this experiment may very well be doubted."[7] But his analysis is of historical importance. Those who assume that the doctrine of implied powers was first pronounced by Hamilton in his debate with Jefferson over the constitutionality of the Bank of America might note that Hamilton had already expounded the thesis in the early days of the republic—and that he was consistent in his constitutional line of interpretation. Not surprisingly, James Madison—during the period in which he was still Hamilton's nationalist colleague—was led to enunciate a very similar thesis on implied powers, as noted above in Chap. 1,[8] and as analyzed further below in relation to the Federalist–Antifederalist contest over ratification. What is perhaps surprising is that Jefferson himself, at this period, endorsed a form of implied powers to compel the states to fulfill their requisition payments. In a letter from Paris to Edward Carrington, dated August 4, 1787 (when the Constitutional Convention was sitting), he wrote:

> It has been so often said, as to be generally believed, that Congress have no power by the confederation to enforce any thing, e.g. contributions of money. It was not necessary to give them that power expressly; they have it by the law of nature. When two nations make a compact, there results to each a power of compelling the other to execute it. Compulsion was never so easy as in our case, where a single frigate would soon levy on the commerce of any state the deficiency of its contributions.[9]

But all of this, of course, was well before the political ferment of the 1790s when Jefferson and Madison vigorously opposed Hamilton's economic schemes based on a broad interpretation of the provisions of the Constitution.[10]

It is not clear how great an effect Hamilton's letter to Duane had at the time, but his suggestion for a convention to draft a constitution seems to have borne fruit at a later date. Edmund C. Burnett, a foremost commentator on the Founding, described its importance in the following terms: "It was a long way from 1780 to 1787, but it would seem to have been directly, perhaps chiefly, from this implantation by Hamilton that the Federal Convention of 1787 eventually grew."[11]

In 1781, Hamilton followed up his earlier letter with a series of articles written under the pseudonym *The Continentalist*,[12] in which he called for a strengthening of the Articles of Confederation. (The Articles of Confederation had finally entered into force earlier that year with ratification by the thirteenth state, Maryland.) Hamilton deplored the "WANT OF POWER IN CONGRESS." He reminded his countrymen that "as too much power leads to despotism, too little leads to anarchy, and both eventually to the ruin of the people."[13] The key weakness of the federal government lay in its total lack of independent sources of income. Unless Congress were granted the authority to raise funds by means of taxes and to regulate trade, the federal government would fall prey to the separate state governments, leading ultimately to the dissolution of the Union. Not only would the United States be unable to prosecute successfully the Revolutionary War, then still in progress, but rivalry between the states would intensify and lead ultimately to war between them. "Political societies in close neighbourhood, must either be strongly united under one government, or there will infallibly exist emulations and quarrels. This is in human nature; and we have no reason to think ourselves wiser, or better, than other men."[14] In conclusion, Hamilton issued a dramatic appeal to his countrymen to rise to the occasion:

> There is something noble and magnificent in the perspective of a great Foederal Republic, closely linked in the pursuit of a common interest, tranquil and prosperous at home, respectable abroad; but there is something proportionably diminutive and contemptible in the prospect of a number of petty states, with the appearance only of union, jarring, jealous and perverse, without any determined direction, fluctuating and unhappy at home, weak and insignificant by their dissentions, in the eyes of other nations. Happy America! if those, to whom thou hast intrusted the guardianship of thy infancy, know how to provide for thy future repose; but miserable and undone, if their negligence or ignorance permits the spirit of discord to erect her banners on the ruins of thy tranquillity![15]

The Continentalist series apparently inspired the New York state legislature to adopt a resolution on July 20, 1782, calling for a convention of the states "to revise and amend the Articles of Confederation." Together with his father-in-law and close political ally Philip Schuyler (then serving as a member of the committee of the whole), Hamilton had urged the state legislature to take this step.[16]

In a letter to Governor George Clinton dated February 24, 1783, Hamilton reverted once again to a doctrine of implied powers that would confirm the power of Congress to impose taxes upon the states. "One thing only is now certain that Congress having the discretionary power of determining the quantum of money to be paid into the general treasury towards defraying the common expenses, have in effect the constitutional power of general taxation."[17] He recognized, however, that the majority in Congress were not amenable to such an interpretation.

Hamilton's argument, that failure to unite would inevitably lead to discord and strife between the states, was a theme that he regularly expounded upon in his drive to replace the Articles of Confederation with a new constitution. He resorted to the argument at the Constitutional Convention, elaborated upon it in several numbers of *The Federalist*, and lectured on it at the New York Ratifying Convention. The theme was not exclusive to Hamilton, however. As will be seen below, Madison, Gouverneur Morris, and other Federalists buttressed their case by warning of the danger of the Europeanization of the American continent if the states did not unite.

While Hamilton was bent on pursuing the path of a constitutional convention as the best means of overcoming the deficiencies of the Articles of Confederation, at this point James Madison seemed resolved to pursue the path of reform. Thus, Madison did not endorse the notion of a convention in 1782, as advocated by Hamilton, nor did he support a Massachusetts suggestion in 1785 for the calling of a constitutional convention.[18] In the words of the editor of the *Madison Papers*, "Madison was consistently lukewarm to the convention approach as a remedy for the ills of the national government."[19] When Richard Henry Lee inquired of Madison in 1784 how he felt about a convention, Madison replied very guardedly that, before answering, he would need to know more "of the temper & views of the different States." Since "the perpetuity & efficacy of the present system can not be confided on," he said, "the question therefore is, in what mode & at what moment the experiment for supplying the defects ought to be made."[20] At that time, it should be noted, Madison was no less a nationalist than Hamilton; but given the existing jealousy and divisiveness that marked national affairs, he considered wholesale revision of the Articles to be an unattainable goal. Better, then, in Madison's view, to concentrate on securing the sequential adoption of specific, but essential, changes in the Articles.

As national affairs steadily deteriorated during the 1780s, with states failing to fulfill their requisitions, and rivalry and dissonance in matters of trade producing a chaotic situation, the opportunity presented itself for holding a convention to draw up national regulations in the sphere of commerce.[21] The inspiration for this move came from an earlier successful endeavor between Virginia and Maryland. In 1785, delegates from these two states had held a conference at Mount Vernon and had agreed on regulations for administering traffic on Chesapeake Bay and the Potomac River. The cooperative spirit evinced at Mount Vernon induced members of the Virginia legislature to propose, in January 1786, that a convention be held at Annapolis, Maryland, to explore the possibility of adopting a uniform system in the commercial regulations of the states "to their common Interest and their permanent Harmony."[22] Madison was initially somewhat skeptical regarding this initiative and suspected that it may have been "patronized by half-hearted localists" intent on disarming nationalist aspirations.[23] In a letter to Jefferson, he wrote: "Considering that the States must first agree to the proposition for sending deputies – that these must agree in a plan to be sent back to the States, and that these again must agree unanimously in a ratification of it[,] I almost despair of success."[24] But after eight states responded to the invitation of Virginia's Governor Patrick Henry and appointed delegates to the convention, Madison became more optimistic; and he began to envision the possibility of the Annapolis Convention serving as a stepping stone to something more ambitious. In a letter to Jefferson, dated August 12, 1786, he wrote: "Many Gentlemen both within & without Congs. wish to make this Meeting subservient to a Plenipotentiary Convention for amending the Confederation."[25]

Madison's initial suspicion that the Annapolis Convention would be poorly attended was fully vindicated. While nine states appointed delegates, only the representatives of five states turned up at Annapolis on September 11, 1786 for the opening meeting. Two further sessions were held on September 13 and 14, but no new faces appeared. With less than a majority of states represented, the participants considered it pointless to proceed with "the business of their mission." However, taking a cue from the terms of reference of the New Jersey delegation, which was empowered to consider more than just commercial regulations, the delegates unanimously addressed a report to their respective legislatures, proposing that a convention meet in Philadelphia in May 1787 for the purpose of devising provisions "to render the constitution of the Foederal Government adequate to the exigencies of the Union." "From motives of respect," copies of the report were also transmitted to Congress and the executives of the other states.[26]

Since interstate and sectional rivalries had in no way abated by then, it is not clear why this Address from Annapolis should have evoked a warmer response than all the previous calls for remedial action. But as fortune would have it, a crisis in Massachusetts in the fall of 1786 alarmed nationalists and localists alike, prompting them to support the move to strengthen the federal government so as to enable it to cope with the "exigencies" confronting the Union. In the aftermath of the Revolutionary War, a depressed economic situation in New England led to disorders in Massachusetts. Widespread vigorous protests were staged by farmers who, unable to meet payments on their debts, faced foreclosure on their lands. The protests soon assumed the character of a "rebellion," particularly after they came under the control of Daniel Shays, a former army captain. By force of arms, he prevented the courts from issuing edicts of eviction. Men of property became alarmed by these developments and saw in the disturbances yet another sign of civic post-Revolutionary breakdown of law and order. Although Shays' Rebellion was quickly subdued by the state authorities, the episode helped convince many people that only a firm, powerful, central government could save the United States from anarchy and dismemberment. These sentiments are reflected in the contemporary correspondence of George Washington and other leading figures, including Madison.

Thus, in his report to Washington concerning the outbreak of the disorders, General Henry Knox of Massachusetts observed:

> Our political machine constituted of thirteen independent sovereignties, have been constantly operating against each other, and against the federal head, ever since the peace – The powers of Congress are utterly inadequate to preserve the balance between the respective States, and oblige them to do those things which are essential to their own welfare, and for the general good. The human mind in the local legislatures seems to be exerted, to prevent the federal constitution from having any beneficial effects. The machine works inversly [*sic*] to the public good in all its parts. Not only is State, against State, and all against the federal head, but the States within themselves possess the name only, without having the essential concomitant of government, the power of preserving the peace; the protection of the liberty and property of the citizens.[27]

The "insurgents" who had rallied to Shays' banner were, to his mind, a band of "desperate & unprincipled men ... determined to annihilate all debts public and private and have agrarian Laws" instituted. "This dreadful situation," he continued, "has alarmed every man of principle and property in New England – They start as from a dream, and ask what has been the Cause of our delusion? What is to afford us security against the violence of lawless men?" His answer was categorical: "Our government must be braced, changed, or altered to secure our lives and property."[28]

In a letter to Madison after he had received the communication from Knox, Washington lamented the absence of power in the federal government:

> Fain would I hope, that the great & most important of all objects, – the foederal governmnt. – may be considered with that calm & deliberate attention which the magnitude of it so loudly calls for at this critical moment. Let prejudices, unreasonable jealousies, and local interest yield to reason and liberality. Let us look to our National character, and to things beyond the present period. No morn ever dawned more favourable than ours did – and no day was ever more clouded than the present! Wisdom, & good examples are necessary at this time to rescue the political machine from the impending storm.

This led Washington to declare: "Without some alteration in our political creed, the superstructure we have been seven years raising, at the expence of much blood and treasure, must fall. We are fast verging to anarchy & confusion!"[29]

Citing the disturbances in Massachusetts, Washington summarized the perils America faced:

What stronger evidence can be given of the want of energy in our governments than these disorders? If there exists not a power to check them, what security has a man of life, liberty, or property?... The consequences of a lax, or inefficient government, are too obvious to be dwelt on. Thirteen Sovereignties pulling against each other, and all tugging at the foederal head, will soon bring ruin on the whole; whereas a liberal, and energetic Constitution, well guarded, & closely watched, to prevent incroachments, might restore us to that degree of respectability & consequence, to which we had a fair claim, & the brightest prospect of attaining.[30]

John Jay's comments on the impact of the recent events, as described in a letter of October 27, 1786, to Thomas Jefferson serving as Ambassador in Paris, are also illuminating:

The inefficacy of our government becomes daily more and more apparent. Our treasury and our credit are in a sad situation; ... A spirit of licentiousness has infected Massachusetts, which appears more formidable than some at first apprehended. Whether similar symptoms will not soon mark a like disease in several other States is very problematical, ... If faction should long bear down law and government, tyranny may raise its head, or the more sober part of the people may even think of a king. In short, my dear sir, we are in a very unpleasant situation. Changes are necessary; but what they ought to be, what they will be, and how and when to be produced, are arduous questions.[31]

James Madison similarly viewed Shays' Rebellion as a reflection of a deeper malaise affecting the Confederacy. There was a breakdown of authority that was threatening government generally. Only a major revision of the constitutional arrangements governing the nation, including a decided shift in power to the center, could save the country from catastrophe. However, he was hopeful that the events in Massachusetts had worked a change in the views of many people. In replying to a letter from Washington, he noted that his information about the disorders was even gloomier than that conveyed by Knox. "If the lessons which it inculcates should not work the proper impressions on the American Public, it will be a proof that our case is desperate. Judging from the present temper and apparent views of our [Virginia] Assembly, I have some ground for leaning to the side of Hope."[32] Just 2 days earlier, in response to the Annapolis Address, the Virginia legislature had, at Madison's urging, unanimously adopted a resolution calling for "a general revision of the federal system" and had provided for the appointment of its delegates to the proposed Philadelphia convention.[33] The resolution even went so far as to proclaim that "the crisis is arrived" and that "the good people of America are to decide the solemn question" of their future form of government. Nothing could better capture the radical change of mood that had set in as a result of the events in Massachusetts. The same Virginia Assembly that, barely a few months earlier, had refused to sanction a federal impost, was now prepared to take the initiative and make Virginia the first state to endorse a constitutional convention to meet in Philadelphia for "devising ... alterations ... to render the federal Constitution adequate to the exigences of the Union."³⁴ In a letter to Jefferson, Madison commented on the magnitude of what had transpired: "The evidence of dangerous defects in the Confederation has at length proselyted the most obstinate adversaries to a reform. The unanimous sanction given by the Assembly to the [resolution] ... marks sufficiently the revolution of sentiment which the experience of one year has affected in this Country."³⁵ The impact of this episode is aptly summed up by Paul A. Rahe: "Had it not been for Shays' Rebellion ... the state legislatures and the Continental Congress might have ignored the request of the ... delegates to the abortive Annapolis Commercial Convention that a federal convention be called to amend the Articles of Confederation."³⁶

The events in Massachusetts, it is clear, also had a profound impact on Madison's own thoughts on government. He was no longer content with effecting one or two reforms via the Confederation Congress; his mind was now set on revamping the entire system so as to endow the national government with close to absolute authority over the states. The locus of sovereign power would be shifted. Unlike the current situation in which the states ruled over the Congress, the states would be subordinate to a central authority.

If anything further was needed to convince him of the need for a radical revision in national–state relations, it was furnished by the distressing condition of America's foreign affairs.³⁷ For one thing, the need for national implementation of the 1783 Peace Treaty with Great Britain raised acute problems that could not be resolved under existing federal arrangements. The states simply refused to abide by the terms of the Treaty, and as a result, England refused to fulfill its own commitments under the Treaty. The manner in which loyalists and their properties were handled by the states prompted severe retaliation by the British who, inter alia, refused to evacuate the Western posts. Congress was totally impotent either to compel the states to adjust their legislation to conform with the terms of the Treaty or to oblige the British to desist from their discriminatory conduct. In a letter to John Jay, Secretary for Foreign Affairs, Washington remarked: "If you tell the Legislatures they have violated the treaty of peace and invaded the prerogatives of the confederacy they will laugh in your face."³⁸ For his part, Jay lamented the situation in his communication to John Adams, then US Ambassador to the Court of St James:

> The result of my inquiries into the conduct of the States relative to the treaty, is, that there has not been a single day since it took effect, on which it has not been violated in America, by one or other of the States. ... Our affairs are in a very unpleasant situation, and changes become necessary, and in some little degree probable. When government, either from defects in its construction or administration, ceases to assert its rights, or is too feeble to afford security, inspire confidence, and overawe the ambitious and licentious, the best citizens naturally grow uneasy and look to other systems.... I suspect that our posterity will read the history of our last four years with much regret.³⁹

Another issue in foreign relations that exercised Madison greatly was Jay's abortive effort to barter away America's untrammeled right of passage on the Mississippi river. This episode revealed to Madison how close the United States was to dismemberment as a result of sectional tensions. In 1785, the Confederation Congress had authorized Secretary Jay to engage in negotiations with the Spanish chargé d'affaires, Diego de Gardoqui, regarding the boundaries between the Spanish and American territories. Jay was instructed to insist upon America's right of free navigation on the Mississippi river to the Gulf of Mexico. In August 1786, by a vote of 7:5, Congress removed the latter requirement in order to facilitate conclusion of a favorable bilateral trade agreement with Spain. This development, dispensing with the right of free navigation on the Mississippi, aroused considerable ire in Virginia and the South generally; it was viewed as a sign of how readily the North would be prepared to sacrifice southern interests in return for marginal commercial benefits. Settlers in the West were particularly resentful at the suggestion that their line of communication with the outside world was dispensable.[40]

Madison realized that this development, so pregnant with sectional antagonism, endangered the prospect of persuading a national convention to agree to establish a powerful federal government.[41] He acted, therefore, to short-circuit the congressional decision that allowed Jay to relent on unimpeded American passage on the river. Although he did not induce Congress to reinstate the original instruction to Jay to insist upon freedom of passage, he did manage to remove the issue from center stage. His battle to quash the notion that the United States was prepared to forego such a vital line of communication impressed itself on all the sectional parties involved, and "the obnoxious project" was sidelined.[42] His success in this matter was critically important for achieving his goal of creating a strong national federation which would simultaneously protect the rights of the component parts. This did not prevent Antifederalists in Virginia, particularly Patrick Henry, from subsequently citing the Mississippi affair as an illustration of the dangers inherent in ratifying the Constitution and setting up a national government.[43]

On February 21, 1787, the Confederation Congress finally endorsed the suggestion of the Annapolis Convention for the states to appoint delegates to a constitutional convention that would meet in Philadelphia in May 1787. In view of the pending meeting, Madison was spurred to complete and summarize his research of "Ancient & Modern Confederacies," which he had commenced in 1784.[44] It was a compendium of the outstanding features of various confederacies throughout history and of the reasons for their disintegration. In all, the study filled 42 notebook pages in Madison's handwriting. He had had no opportunity to utilize any of this material at Annapolis, but it later served him valiantly in debates at the Constitutional Convention, in the struggle over ratification, and in the preparation of several numbers of *The Federalist Papers*. The fundamental lesson that Madison drew from his study was, in the words of the editor of the *Madison Papers*, "that confederacies were fragile creations, continually tending toward dissolution or impotency."[45] The most fatal feature of the various confederacies, he concluded, was their lack of a strong central authority to prevent the periphery from tearing the union apart.[46] This led Madison to strive to invest the national legislature with a veto that would allow it to cancel any state law of which it disapproved. Central authority would thus be dominant, and the Union effectively bound together and united.

If Annapolis helped produce the study on confederacies, ancient and modern, the proposed Constitutional Convention impelled Madison to analyze the failings of the current American Confederation. As noted earlier,[47] on the eve of the Convention, he had detailed, in a private memorandum, twelve "Vices of the Political System of the United States."[48] They were:

1. Failure of states to comply with requisitions.
2. Encroachments by states on federal authority.
3. State violations of the law of nations and treaties.
4. Trespasses of states on rights of each other.
5. Want of concert where required.
6. Want of guarantees to states for internal security.
7. Want of sanction to federal laws.
8. Want of popular ratification of Articles of Confederation.
9. Multiplicity of state laws.
10. Mutability of state laws.
11. Injustice of state laws.
12. Impotence of state laws.

As can be seen, the last four "vices" related to the state governments, while the first eight focused on the confederal government and its total dependence on the states for its proper functioning. Madison elaborated upon each of the vices, except the last. In the commentary, he illustrated in each case how experience under the Articles had failed to provide answers to the failings of the Confederation. Above all, he highlighted the impotence of the central authority, which could issue directives to the states but was incapable of enforcing implementation. In the memorandum, Madison did not yet spell out his suggested remedies, but in his contemporary private correspondence with close Virginian associates—Washington, Randolph, and Jefferson—he proceeded to develop a radical plan for vesting sovereignty in the new central authority.

In a letter to Thomas Jefferson, dated March 19, 1787, Madison noted several key points for inclusion in the proposed Constitution.[49] To ensure the federal government of being "clearly paramount to their [the states'] Legislative authorities," it was necessary that "the new system receive ratification by the people." Secondly, he recommended:

> Over & above the positive power of regulating trade and sundry other matters in which uniformity is proper, to arm the federal head with a negative *in all cases whatsoever* on the local Legislatures. Without this defensive power experience and

reflection have satisfied me that however ample the federal powers may be made, or however clearly their boundaries may be delineated, on paper, they will be easily and continually baffled by the Legislative sovereignties of the States. The effects of this provision would be not only to guard the national rights and interests against invasion, but also to restrain the States from thwarting and molesting each other, and even from oppressing the minority within themselves by paper money and other unrighteous measures which favor the interest of the majority.[50]

Thirdly, representation in the national legislature, he felt, must be based on size of population and could no longer remain, as under the Articles, equal as between large and small states. "The Eastern States" would welcome this change "by the actual superiority of their populousness" and the Southern States would be attracted to it "by their expected superiority" in the future.[51] Fourthly, while increasing the powers of the central government, the new Constitution should be so organized as to ensure adherence to the principle of the separation of powers at federal level. "The limited powers now vested in Congs. are frequently mismanaged from the want of such a distribution of them."[52]

Madison elaborated on many of these points in letters to Edmund Randolph and George Washington.[53] No partial revision of the Articles, he continually stressed, would be sufficient. His "ideas" of "reform," he said, "strike so deeply at the old Confederation" as to lead to "a systematic change." On the matter of national supremacy he was quite categorical:

> I hold it for a fundamental point that an individual independence of the States, is utterly irreconcileable with the idea of an aggregate sovereignty. I think at the same time that a consolidation of the States into one simple republic is not less unattainable than it would be inexpedient. Let it be tried then whether any middle ground can be taken which will at once support a due supremacy of the national authority, and leave in force the local authorities so far as they can be subordinately useful.[54]

Besides emphasizing national supremacy in the legislature, Madison now advocated extending this supremacy to the judiciary as well:

> If those who are to expound & apply the laws, are connected by their interests & their oaths with the particular States wholly, and not with the Union, the participation of the Union in the making of the laws may be possibly rendered unavailing. It seems at least necessary that the oaths of the Judges should include a fidelity to the general as well as local constitution, and that an appeal should lie to some national tribunals in all cases to which foreigners or inhabitants of other States may be parties.[55]

Madison was not yet decided, in these letters, on the shape or nature of the executive. He recommended a two-house legislature, with the upper house composed of a smaller number of representatives and going out in rotation.

"As a further check," Madison suggested the institution of a "council of revision" to review all laws.⁵⁶ Guarantees for the tranquility of the states against internal and external dangers should be inserted in the constitutional document. Ratification of the final document by the people, he pointed out to Washington, would impart both "validity and energy" to the whole system.⁵⁷

But even while he was planning and outlining his ideas about a new constitution, Madison was far from sanguine about the outcome at Philadelphia. In a letter of April 22, 1787 to the distinguished Virginian judge Edmund Pendleton, he noted the obstacles that had to be overcome and the supreme difficulty—that of making federal law paramount to state law:

> The nearer the crisis approaches, the more I tremble for the issue. The necessity of gaining the concurrence of the Convention in some system that will answer the purpose, the subsequent approbation of Congress, and the final sanction of the States, presents a series of chances, which would inspire despair in any case where the alternative was less formidable. The difficulty too is not a little increased by the necessity which will be produced by encroachments on the State Constitutions, of obtaining not merely the assent of the Legislatures, but the ratification of the people themselves.⁵⁸

Such ratification was essential, Madison stated, since "a higher Sanction than the Legislative authority would be necessary to render the laws of the Confederacy paramount to the Acts of its members."⁵⁹

His correspondence with leading Virginian personalities enabled Madison to crystallize his own ideas on how to establish an effective national government; it also laid the groundwork for galvanizing, among his state's delegates to Philadelphia, the necessary support for his ambitious constitutional scheme. The result was the Virginia Plan with its complete reversal of the existing national-state nexus. It was presented to the Convention on May 29 by Virginia's young Governor, Edmund Randolph.⁶⁰

NOTES

1. George Washington to John Jay, Aug. 1, 1786. *DHRC*, 4: 19. Reprinted in *GWP*, 4: 212, with slight grammatical differences and dated Aug. 15.
2. *The Federalist*, #37.
3. James Madison to W.C. Rives, Oct. 21, 1833. Farrand, *Records*, 3: 523.
4. *AHP*, 2: 400–418. For discussion of the Hamilton letter, see Andrew C. McLaughlin, *The Confederation and the Constitution 1783–1789* (New York: Macmillan, 1962), 120.
5. *AHP*, 2: 407, 417.
6. Ibid., 2: 401. Emphasis in original.
7. Ibid., 2; 407.
8. In text at n. 20.
9. *TJP*, 11: 678.

10. It is interesting to note that at the same time that Madison was advocating the use of force against delinquent states on the basis of an implied power, he opposed the creation of a national bank on the ground that the Articles of Confederation did not provide for such a measure. Robert Morris, as the Superintendent of Finance, had requested that the Congress provide a charter for the Bank of North America. Although Madison recognized the urgent necessity of such an institution for the war effort, he insisted that it be chartered by each state rather than by the Congress. Subsequently, he apparently "acquiesced" rather than voting affirmatively for the proposal, which the Congress adopted by an overwhelming majority. To ensure state acquiescence, the states were also urged to give the bank licence to operate within their jurisdictions. In a letter to Edmund Pendleton, he described the latter recommendation, as "a tacit admission of a defect of power" and hoped that "it will be an antidote against the poisonous tendency of precedents of usurpation." See *JMP*, 4: 22–24.

    Madison's "acquiescence" has been interpreted by some writers as a positive vote. See the comment of Max Farrand: *The Framing of the Constitution of the United States* (New Haven, CT: Yale University Press, 1913), 46 and the discussion in Kevin R.C. Gutzman, *James Madison and the Making of America*. (New York: St Martin's Press, 2012), 29–30. At any event, it is not an easy matter to reconcile Madison's conflicting views on a doctrine of implied powers. See further below, Postscript.

11. Edmund Cody Burnett, *The Continental Congress*. (New York: Macmillan, 1941), 487.
12. The series, which amounted to six articles, appeared in the *New York Packet*. See *AHP*, 2: 649 ff., and 3: 75 and 99 ff.
13. Ibid., 2: 651.
14. Ibid., 2: 660.
15. Ibid., 3: 106.
16. Ibid., 3: 110–113.
17. Ibid., 3: 269.
18. See editorial note, *JMP*, 8: 406–409.
19. Ibid., 8: 406.
20. Ibid., 8: 201.
21. For a vivid description of the clashing commercial policies of the states, see Madison's letter to Jefferson, dated March 18, 1786. Ibid., 8: 502.
22. Ibid., 8: 471. A note in the *Madison Papers* traces the origin of this call for a convention to an initiative, presumably by Hamilton, in the New York Legislature in 1782. Ibid., 294, n. 4.

    For discussion of the legal significance of the Mount Vernon Conference and the Annapolis Convention, as progressive steps toward the Constitutional Convention, see Bruce Ackerman and Neal Katyal, "Our Unconventional Founding." *University of Chicago Law Review*, 62 (1995): 492–498.

23. Editorial Note, *JMP*, 8: 470–471. See also Madison's letter of March 14, 1786 to James Monroe, then serving in Congress. Ibid., 498.
24. March 18, 1786. Ibid., 8: 503.
25. Ibid., 9: 96. For an example of the desire to see the Annapolis Convention "comprehend all the grievances of the Union," see the letter of William Grayson to Madison, dated May 28, 1786. Ibid., 64.

26. The text is reprinted in *AHP*, 3: 686–689. Madison subsequently stated (and his version is generally accepted) that it was Hamilton who drafted the text of the Address. See editorial comment, ibid., 686, n. 1.
27. Oct. 23, 1786, *GWP*, 4: 299. The editor of the *Madison Papers* notes that Knox and Henry Lee, both of whom wrote grim reports of Shays' uprising, were among those who yearned for "energetic government" and helped turn the Shays affair "into a powerful propaganda vehicle" toward that end. *JMP*, 9: 167, n. 1.
28. *GWP*, 4: 300–301.
29. Nov. 5, 1786. Ibid., 4: 331; also in *JMP*, 9: 161.
30. *GWP*, 4: 332; *JMP*, 9: 162.
31. *JJP*, 3: 213.
32. Nov. 8, 1786. *JMP*, 9: 166; *GWP*, 4: 344.
33. For the text of the resolution, see *JMP*, 9: 163–164.
34. Ibid., 9: 164.
35. Dec. 4, 1786. Ibid., 9: 189.
36. Paul A. Rahe, *Republics Ancient and Modern: Classical Republicanism and the American Revolution* (Chapel Hill: University of North Carolina Press, 1992), 579.
37. As the editor of the *Madison Papers* writes: "Although he hardly needed convincing of the weaknesses of the Confederation, the report [by Secretary for Foreign Affairs John Jay to Congress] provided him with damning evidence of one of its more outstanding faults." *JMP*, 9: 264.
38. Aug. 15, 1786. *GWP*, 4: 213.
39. Nov. 1, 1786. John Jay, *The Correspondence and Public Papers of John Jay*. Edited by Henry P. Johnston (New York: G. P. Putnam's, 1890–1895), 3: 214–215.
40. See Madison's letter to Jefferson, March 19, 1787, *JMP*, 9: 319–320, and the editorial comment on the topic generally, ibid., 264–266.
41. Ibid., 9: 320.
42. See letter of Madison to Jefferson, April 23, 1787. Ibid., 9: 400.
43. See below, Chap. 7, at nn. 93–95.
44. For the text, see *JMP*, 9: 4–24.
45. Ibid., 9: 4.
46. Thus, in connection with one republic that he analyzes, Madison writes: "A striking proof of the want of authority in the whole over its parts." Ibid., 9: 11.
47. See Chap. 1, at nn. 3–6.
48. *JMP*, 9: 348–357.
49. Ibid., 9: 317–322.
50. Ibid., 9: 318. Emphasis in original.
51. Ibid., 9: 318–319.
52. Ibid., 9: 319.
53. Madison to Randolph, April 8, 1787, ibid., 9: 368–371; Madison to Washington, April 16, 1787, ibid., 382–387.
54. Ibid., 9: 369; repeated nearly verbatim, ibid., 383.
55. Madison to Washington, April 16, 1787. Ibid., 9: 384. Madison also recommended that the admiralty jurisdiction be vested exclusively in the hands of the national government. Ibid.
56. Ibid., 9: 384–385.
57. Ibid., 9: 385.
58. Ibid., 9: 395.
59. Ibid.

60. Randolph, at thirty-two, was one of the youngest delegates to the Convention. "Character Sketches of Delegates to the Federal Convention," by William Pierce, Farrand, *Records*, 3: 95. Twenty-four-year-old Charles Pinckney of South Carolina was the youngest. Ibid., 96.

CHAPTER 3

The Constitutional Convention: Nation Over State Within a Federal Framework

> *Give N. Jersey an equal vote, and she will dismiss her scruples, and concur in the Natil. system.*
> Charles Pinckney[1]

"Federalism," Herbert Wechsler remarked, "was the means and price of the formation of the Union."[2] History confirms that federalism has been both the fabric and tension of the American system of government.

No person was as instrumental as James Madison in securing a new constitution for the United States. He was actively involved in promoting and organizing the Constitutional Convention; preparing studies in advance of the conclave; formulating the outline of the Virginia Plan which served as the major working paper of the Convention; participating in the drafting of the constitutional provisions at Philadelphia; authoring major parts of the *Federalist Papers*; and managing the process of state ratification. Indisputably, he deserves the title of Father of the Constitution.

Yet there is an element of irony in applying this appellation to Madison, since the final document was not the Constitution he had planned and for which he had fought. In fact, he thought the Convention had been a failure and wrote as much to Jefferson after leaving Philadelphia, as noted below. His original scheme was not accepted by the Convention. Instead of an all-powerful national government, under which the states would be reduced to the status of counties, a federal system of government emerged in which the national government, while clearly superior, had to acknowledge and accept the sovereignty of the states. Moreover, the desires of the states would be regularly factored into the composition of the national government itself, by means of their equal state representation in the upper house of the legislature and their selecting the members to serve there; the disproportionate representation accorded the South in the lower house; the definition and enumeration of the powers of Congress; and the role of the states in the presidential election process. This chapter, and the next, chart the process whereby Madison's highly centralized and powerful national system of government was federalized as a result of the demands of the smaller and slave states.

Madison's Papers, it might be noted, do not contain a copy of any formal plan by Madison for presentation to the Convention. But as was seen earlier,[3] in his letters to his colleagues he had articulated the goal of having an entirely new constitution adopted, one that would categorically establish national paramountcy over the states. He wished at all costs to avoid the kind of shared power system that had doomed the Articles of Confederation to dismal failure. At this point in his career, the attempt of some historians to portray a different picture notwithstanding,[4] Madison was a supreme nationalist. His study of federations in history had taught him one lesson: fundamental federations had regularly fallen apart owing to the inroads of the separate units against the national authority. There was only one way that national authority could survive—if it was truly independent of, and dominant over, the separate units. For one thing, the states, as such, would have to be precluded from any role in the governing structure of the national authority, and secondly, the authority would be empowered to exercise a supervisory veto over state legislation. This, of course, was a total reversal of the present governing system. But as noted, his plan to have the Convention guarantee absolute supremacy of the federal government was unable to command a Convention majority, and a federal arrangement was adopted in its stead. The predominance of the central government was fully confirmed, but in a modified form. At the same time, various provisions incorporated in the Constitution endowed it with a crucial element of flexibility—most notably, the necessary and proper clause that sanctioned implied powers, and Article V that allowed formal amendments by less than unanimity.

Madison's preoccupation with the twin goals of energy and supremacy was reflected very early in the deliberations at Philadelphia. The Convention had been scheduled to get underway on May 14, but as a result of bad weather, the delegates were slow in arriving and a quorum was only assembled on May 25. The Virginia delegation, composed of George Washington, Edmund Randolph, John Blair, James Madison, George Mason, George Wythe, and James McClurg, all of whom arrived early, took advantage of the interval to "meet and confer together two or three hours every day, in order to form a proper correspondence of sentiments."[5] These discussions gave birth to the Virginia Plan, which Edmund Randolph, as Governor of Virginia was deputed to present to the plenum on May 29 on behalf of his state's delegation, although he was the youngest member of that delegation. The Plan bore Madison's stamp in all its particulars. The unequivocal dominance of the central government was reflected in the draft provisions on the composition of the legislature, the scope of federal powers accorded the legislature, and relations with the states.[6]

In Randolph's "long speech" on the Plan, "he pointed out the various defects of the federal system, [and] the necessity of transforming it into a national efficient Government."[7] The confederation, he said, was "incompetent to any *one* object for which it was instituted." It was incapable of producing "certain blessings," among which were "the establishment of great national works—the improvement of inland navigation—agriculture—manufactures—a freer intercourse among the citizens."[8] By conferring energy and supremacy upon the national government, the Virginia Plan would effect a remedy for the deficiencies of the Articles of Confederation.[9] The federal government would be independent of the states in its mode of election, term of office, and means of support. No longer would the national government be beholden to the state governments for its existence and daily operation. Federal law would be fiat and would override contrary state law. The full measure of national authority was reflected in the provisions on the composition of the legislature and the powers it would dispose of. The strongly national design of the Virginia Plan was confirmed by its designation of the three branches of government as a *National* Legislature, a *National* Executive, and a *National* Judiciary. Bernard Bailyn has vividly summed up the design of the Virginia Plan as follows: It proposed the creation of a "*Machtstaat*, a central national power that involved armed force, the aggressive management of international relations, and, potentially at least, the regulation of vital aspects of everyday life by a government dominant over all other, lesser governments."[10]

Federalizing the National Legislature

In Madison's view, a prime flaw in the Articles of Confederation lay in the composition of the Confederal Congress. Each of the thirteen states represented in the single house legislature was entitled to one vote, regardless of the size of its population or its wealth. Important decisions required a majority vote of nine for adoption (i.e. two-thirds) and amendments to the Articles, as noted earlier, necessitated unanimous approval by the states. A primary goal of the Virginia Plan was to end this dependency on the states by abolishing the state-dominated formula for the composition of the national legislature and replacing it with popular control to secure absolute freedom in the national council. The legislature would consist of two houses and suffrage would be proportioned according to "the number of free inhabitants" or according to "the Quotas of contribution," depending upon the circumstances in each case. The members of the lower house would be elected by "the people of the several States" and those of the upper house would be elected by the lower house from candidates nominated by the state legislatures. In both cases the independence of the representatives from state control was assured since they would vote as individuals and not as members of a state delegation.

When the Committee of the Whole reported to the plenum 2 weeks later, on June 13, the provision on representation was little changed, except that members of the second house would be chosen by the state legislatures.

However, representation in both houses would remain as before, proportional to size of population. Salaries of the representatives would be paid out of the national treasury, something that would further ensure their independence. One other change was recorded, namely, that in addition to counting white citizens for purposes of representation, "three fifths of all other persons," where relevant, would be added to a state's representation in the lower house.[11] Outright popular representation was already slipping.

On June 15, William Patterson presented the New Jersey Plan to the Convention on behalf of the smaller states, calling for retention of the one-house legislature that operated under the Articles of Confederation in which each state exercised one vote.[12] In fact, the Plan made no reference to representation or the composition of the legislature at all. It simply proceeded on the assumption that the previous arrangement under the Articles, with each state enjoying one vote only, would continue unchanged. As explained in a footnote in Madison's minutes, the smaller states were against the scheme for proportional representation. For weeks they had been demanding that at least the upper house provide for an equal vote for all the states. The New Jersey Plan was their ultimatum.

The primary tactic of the Federalists was to warn of the danger of disunity and the inevitable Europeanization of America if the smaller states remained obdurate and refused to accept the principle of proportional representation in both houses of the national legislature. If the Union was sundered, the smaller states faced the prospect of continuous tension and conflict. Thus Madison said: "The same causes which have rendered the old world the Theatre of incessant wars, & have banished liberty from the face of it, wd. soon produce the same effects here. The weakness & jealousy of the small States wd. quickly introduce some regular military force agst. sudden danger from their powerful neighbours. The example wd. be followed by others, and wd. soon become universal."[13]

Hamilton stressed that great power intervention in America would work in both directions—to involve the powers in America's affairs and to embroil the American states in European conflicts.

> Alliances will immediately be formed with different rival & hostile nations of Europes [*sic*], who will foment disturbances among ourselves, and make us parties to all their own quarrels... It is a miracle that we were now here exercising our tranquil & free deliberations on the subject. It would be madness to trust to future miracles.[14]

Gouverneur Morris was more blunt than his Federalist colleagues. "This country must be united. If persuasion does not unite it, the sword will. He begged that this consideration might have its due weight. The scenes of horror attending civil commotion can not be described … and the Gallows & Halter will finish the work of the sword." The history of Germany, Morris said, illustrated "the melancholy picture" of "foreign intrusions" which served as "a standing lesson to other nations."[15] "State attachments, and State importance have been the bane of this Country. We cannot annihilate; but we may perhaps take out the teeth of the serpents." On another occasion Gouverneur Morris resorted to a biblical episode to describe the sort of argument used in the effort to persuade the smaller states of the necessity of union: "If Aaron's rod could not swallow the rods of the Magicians, their rods would swallow his."[16]

The smaller states remained unmoved by the terrible scenarios predicted by the Federalists. References to the calamitous consequences of the Europeanization of the American scene did not frighten them. Equality had been the hallmark of the confederation of the states and there was no reason to abandon that principle now that a more national government was to be formed. Fear of some remote contingency could not match the immediate fear of large state paramountcy.

John Dickinson of Delaware is reported to have said to Madison:

> You see the consequence of pushing things too far. Some of the members from the small States wish for two branches in the General Legislature, and are friends to a good National Government; but we would sooner submit to a foreign power, than submit to be deprived of an equality of suffrage, in both branches of the legislature, and thereby be thrown under the domination of the large States.[17]

While Dickinson's warning was uttered in a private conversation, Gunning Bedford of Delaware did not shy away from more brazenly issuing a public threat in the plenum itself: "The Large States," he declared, "dare not dissolve the confederation. If they do the small ones will find some foreign ally of more honor and good faith who will take them by the hand and do them justice."[18] Representatives of the larger states complained about the unfairness of the smaller states' dictat. James Wilson protested that the principle of equality in the Confederal legislature at the birth of the Union had been imposed on the larger states out of necessity, not choice:

> There are other instances of their yielding from the same motive to the unreasonable measures of the small states. The situation of things is now a little altered. He insisted that a jealousy would exist between the State Legislature & the General Legislature: observing that the members of the former would have views & feelings very distinct in this respect from their constituents. A private citizen of a State is indifferent whether power be exercised by the Genl. or State Legislatures, provided it be exercised most for his happiness.[19]

Gouverneur Morris echoed the same argument:

> On the declaration of Independence, a Governnt. was to be formed. The small States aware of the necessity of preventing anarchy, and taking advantage of the moment, extorted from the large ones an equality of votes. Standing now on that ground, they demand under the new system greater rights as men, than their fellow Citizens of the large States. The proper answer to them is that the same

necessity of which they formerly took advantage does not now exist, and that the large States are at liberty now to consider what is right, rather than what may be expedient.[20]

These were brave words, and no doubt some delegates from the larger states were prepared to call the bluff of the smaller states' ultimatum. The debate extended for over 3 weeks, but in the end, the larger states relented. The critical vote took place on July 16, and the vote was 5:4 with one state divided.[21] There was little choice. As Rutledge of South Carolina put it: "He could see no chance of a compromise. The little States were fixt. They had repeatedly & solemnly declared themselves to be so. All that the large States then had to do, was to decide whether they would yield or not."[22] Yield they did. As Charles Pinckney subsequently said: "Nothing but the prudence and forbearance of the large States saved the Union."[23] Virginia's Randolph, for one, conceded openly. "He was far from thinking the large States could subsist of themselves any more than the small; an avulsion would involve the whole in ruin, and he was determined to pursue such a scheme of Government as would secure us agst. such a calamity."[24] On the morrow of the critical vote to accept the Connecticut Compromise, Madison reports that the large state representatives held a rather desultory discussion.[25] In an editorial comment in his Minutes, Madison notes that opinion amongst these members was divided whether to "inflexibly" oppose the Compromise since such opposition risked "a failure of any general act of the Convention." Such a division of opinion ensured large-state acquiescence. Equality was fixed for the upper house and national domination was henceforth compromised. It was not going to be a totally national system of government in which the states would simply function as the maidservants of the central government. It was a federal system in which the states would preserve their sovereignty alongside a sovereign federal government.

The irony was that the smaller states had succeeded in bouncing the ball back into the Federalists' court. If dissension was fatal to the Union, then the larger states, as Gunning Bedford bluntly stated, could not afford to dismiss the smaller states and seek to set up a larger-state union. This, more than anything else, would produce small-state wandering afield and usher in foreign intervention. The prospect of disunity and civil war was too menacing a threat to dismiss lightly. The Federalists were hoisted by their own petard.

The importance of the Federalist argument regarding the danger of the Europeanization of the American scene as a factor in promoting compromise at the Convention has not, until fairly recently, been fully appreciated. Hamilton's warning, in his letter to James Duane, that the United States was no different from other loose groups of states that invariably fell apart and began to compete with one another and become beset with strife, violence, and ultimately war, was well recognized. Failure of the American states to unite and create a powerful central government was a prescription for disaster, Hamilton said.[26] In his publications on the subject, Peter Onuf of the University of Virginia has highlighted this neglected facet of the Founding and pointed out how central this line of argument was in the Federalist campaign to secure the ratification of the Constitution. The Federalists hammered away at the danger of disunity and the anarchy that would result. Both in his book, *The Origins of the Federal Republic*, and several articles, most especially, "Anarchy and the Crisis of the Union," Onuf elaborated on the threat of the internationalization of state rivalry and the dire consequences that would ensue, as argued by the Federalists.[27] Ironically enough, use of the disunity argument, it becomes clear, served as a two-edged sword. In the campaign for ratification, the argument impressed sufficient delegates in sufficient states to help ensure ratification; but at the Constitutional Convention, as noted, the force of this argument acted as a boomerang, and caused the Federalists to concede. Moreover, the argument played a role not only with respect to the composition of the Senate, but also regarding the question of slavery.[28]

The slavery issue effected another dent in the scheme for a powerful national government and made certain that the method for selecting an executive would also reflect the now federal character of the Union. In fact, the northern states were compelled to make substantial concessions in numerous areas that bore on the practice of slavery. They abandoned completely any thought of curbing the scope of the institution of slavery, that "accursed plague," in the South. Time and again delegates from the northern states condemned the evil system, but failed to take a stand in opposition. Perhaps the most outspoken foes of the institution were Rufus King of Massachusetts, George Mason of Virginia, and Gouverneur Morris of Pennsylvania. When the provision for representation in the House of Representatives came up for consideration, it was tied, as noted, to direct taxation, three-fifths for slaves in both cases.[29] "The admission of slaves," said King, "was a most grating circumstance to his mind, & he believed would be so to a great part of the people of America." The hands of the legislature "were absolutely tied" with regard to two matters—the importation of slaves and a ban on taxing exports. "Is this reasonable?" he asked. Slavery was an invitation to internal uprisings. "If slaves are to be imported shall not the exports produced by their labor, supply a revenue the better to enable the Genl. Gov. to defend their Masters?" Although a Virginia plantation owner himself, George Mason vigorously condemned the practice of slavery. "Every master of slaves is born a petty tyrant. They bring the judgment of heaven on a Country. As nations can not be rewarded or punished in the next world they must be in this. By an inevitable chain of causes & effects providence punishes national sins, by national calamities."[30] Gouverneur Morris was severely condemnatory. He formally proposed an amendment to restrict representation to "free inhabitants."[31] Slavery, he declared, was "the curse of heaven on the States where it prevailed." He demanded to know why slaves were computed in the representation. If they were men, "then make them Citizens & let them vote." If they were property, "why then is no other property included?" The admission of slaves into the scale of representation amounted to this, he said: That the person who "goes to the coast of Africa, and in defiance of the most sacred laws of humanity tears away his fellow creatures from their dearest connections & dam[n]s them to the most cruel bondages, shall have more votes in a Govt. instituted for protection of the rights of mankind, than the Citizen of Pa. or N. Jersey who views with a laudable horror, so nefarious a practice."[32]

In conclusion, said Morris: "He would sooner submit himself to a tax for all the Negroes in the U. States, than saddle posterity with such a Constitution." Jonathan Dayton of New Jersey seconded the Morris motion.[33] But it was all in vain. In the dispute over the composition of the upper house of the legislature the battle had lasted for some 4 weeks; but over slavery there was no contest. The North surrendered wholesale. The vote was 1:10, with only New Jersey voting in favor of the Morris motion.[34] Roger Sherman of Connecticut summed it up: The slave trade, he said, was "iniquitous; but the point of representation having been Settled ... he did not think himself bound to make opposition."[35] In the New York Ratifying Convention, Hamilton candidly stated: "The regulation complained of [the three-fifths rule] was one result of the spirit of accommodation which governed the Convention; and without this indulgence no union could possibly have been formed."[36]

Slavery was a fact of life for the South, and any suggestion that it be barred and totally eliminated from the Union aroused immediate threats to withdraw from the Convention completely. Only continuation of the importation of slaves was an issue, because Virginia—with an oversupply of slaves—was opposed, while the Deep South, South Carolina and Georgia, were pressing for an unlimited right to import. In the end, the matter was settled by one of the more notorious deals between North and (Deep) South. The South agreed to abandon the requirement of a two-thirds majority for navigation (trade) laws, while the North accepted that the importation of Negroes would be permitted until 1800 (subsequently extended to 1808).[37]

Northerners not only accepted slavery, they conceded numerous concessions to the South that gave those states precious advantages in the operation of the federal system. First and foremost was the three-fifths rule that increased a slave state's representation in the House of Representatives by three-fifths of the state's slave population. Of course, slaves did not vote, but the number of Representatives available to a state's white electorate was three-fifths larger than it was to a comparable northern state, so that overall, the South's representation in the House was artificially increased by three-fifths. This increment had an impact, not only with reference to legislation, but also in the Electoral College, which was a mirror image of the Congress. As history would prove, southern candidates would have a built-in advantage in the race for the presidency. But the Constitution buttressed the system of slavery in numerous ways. Paul Finkelman enumerates in an important and comprehensive article some fifteen clauses in the Constitution that, directly or indirectly, sustained slavery in the United States.[38] As noted, the importation of new slaves was permitted for 20 years, until 1808. Export taxes by either state or federal governments were prohibited, thus ensuring that staple products produced by slaves would not be burdened. The federal government was committed to coming to the aid of a state subjected to domestic violence, which implicitly included slave revolts. Federal courts were obliged to return fugitive slaves to their owners. In these and other ways, the Constitution not only recognized, but facilitated, the continuance of slavery. Any attempt to ban and abolish slavery by amendment would run into a double hurdle—a two-thirds requirement in both houses of Congress, and a three-quarters requirement for state ratifications.

It is noteworthy that the two major controversies that engaged the Constitutional Convention related to the composition of the national legislature, the heart of the national/federal structure. Whatever nationalist design was envisaged for the legislature was radically modified by the demands of the two groups of states—the smaller states and the slave states. The end result was that, in place of the nationalist Virginia Plan, the Constitution emerged as a national system of government but within a federal framework. The smaller states succeeded in their demand for equal representation for states in the upper house, in contrast to size of population, which operated in the lower house. The slave states prevailed in having their slave population counted for purposes of representation in the lower house. The three-fifths rule was the concession that they extracted. Those who opposed these concessions realized that obduracy on their part would lead to a break-up of the Convention and a shattering of the Union. They were not prepared to accept the consequences of such a disruption. With regard to the three-fifths rule, Bernard Bailyn has summed it up accurately: "Most of the Revolutionary leaders hated slavery—not one of them ever publicly praised it—but they valued the preservation of the Union more."[39] Unity had to be preserved at all costs and so they felt compelled to yield to the respective demands of these two groups of states, even though this meant that the national design to which they aspired would be materially compromised. This becomes clear when the debate on the formula for electing a President is carefully analyzed.

Federalizing the Choice of a National Executive

As Max Farrand explained, the formulation of the provisions of the Constitution was greatly influenced by the experience of the states under their own constitutions.[40] In most of the state governments the choice of chief executive was made by the state legislature. Unsurprisingly, therefore, Article 7 of the Virginia Plan provided for the National Executive to be selected by the National Legislature. For various reasons, however, this proposal was found to be problematic. First of all, it violated the principle of the separation of powers which called for independent means of electing each branch of government. Secondly, it might too readily lead to a situation in which a sitting President would conspire with members of the legislature to ensure his reelection. So if the choice were to be made by the legislature, many delegates felt the executive would have to be limited to one term of office, preferably a long one. Initially, therefore, the Convention resolved that the executive be elected by the legislature for a 7-year term and be ineligible for reelection.[41] But this formula was deemed deficient because it eliminated a vital incentive for effective administration—the right to stand for reelection. And so, although the delegates reverted frequently to the legislative formula in their search for a suitable procedure for electing a chief executive, they just as often abandoned this arrangement on the grounds that it penalized a successful executive by barring his reelection.[42]

In the meantime, the Convention became embroiled in a critical 3-week debate over the composition of the upper house of the legislature. Ultimately the matter was resolved on July 17 with acceptance of the Connecticut Compromise. But the equality granted the states in the upper chamber meant that the smaller states would now exercise a disproportionate influence in the selection of an executive. Upon acceptance of the Compromise, therefore, representatives of the larger states moved that the choice of executive be moved from the legislature to the public at large.[43] Predictably, this method was resisted by the smaller states, since they were no more willing to sanction large-state domination of the executive selection process than they had been prepared to concede large-state control of the national legislature.[44]

The representatives of the slave states likewise objected to a popular election. As a result of the compromise on slaves, these states enjoyed a three-fifths increase in representation in the House of Representatives based on the number of slaves each state possessed. But this increment only applied to a state's representation in the legislature; it would have no bearing on a straight-out vote by the white population in a popular election.[45] Thus, both the smaller states and slave states resisted any suggestion that the choice be removed from the legislature—the former, because of their special status in the Senate, the latter because of their enhanced status in the House.

When the Convention, toward its final stages, took up for consideration the steps necessary for putting the government into operation, it became clear that the delegates had still not settled on a definite formula for the selection of an executive. This was one of several unresolved issues conveyed to the Brearley Committee on Unfinished Parts for decision.[46] All draft items not yet finally formulated were referred to this Committee, named after its chairman and composed of one representative from each state.[47]

After 4 days of deliberation, the Committee presented its solution to the Convention: the Electoral College. It was remarkable for having combined the good points of all the proposals that had surfaced on the subject, while overcoming their deficiencies. It removed the choice from Congress and conveyed it instead to a body that was, in terms of its composition, a mirror image of Congress. Each state received the same representation in the Electoral College as it was entitled to in Congress, so neither the smaller states nor the slave states had any cause to object. The independence of the President was assured, and his reelection was freed from congressional interference. Since the electors met but once, in their respective state capitals, there was no danger of cabal or corruption. And with each elector voting for two candidates, one of whom had to be from a state other than his own, there was no fear that the larger states would overwhelm the process.[48]

The entire Electoral College scheme was assuredly an ingenious device for satisfying state demands for equality in the selection of a President. It underscored the influence exerted by the two groups of states on the draftsmen. In essence, the Electoral College scheme represented but stage two of the Connecticut Compromise. As noted, the advantages that the smaller states and slave states had secured in the real Congress were faithfully preserved in the congress away from home, the Electoral College. Furthermore, electors would be selected as the state legislatures prescribed. This meant that a state legislature could, if it wished, select the electors itself. And the final concessions to state influence were reflected in the contingency arrangements. If no candidate secured a majority in the Electoral College, the Senate—in the final version, the House of Representatives, voting as states—would make the choice from the top five. The designation of top five was deliberately designed to offer greater opportunity to a candidate from a smaller state to be selected. And the requirement that voting in the House take place by state, rather than by individual Representatives, meant that the last word, and not merely the first, was reserved for the states in the selection of a chief executive for the United States.[49]

Paradoxically, then, the federal character of the Constitution was in large measure shaped, not by delegates concerned with state rights, but by two groups of states with special interests—the smaller states and the slave states. On their own, those few delegates bent on preserving state sovereignty did not stand a chance of restraining the nationalist juggernaut as reflected in the Virginia Plan. Only the emergence of the two special interest groups succeeded in imposing a federal constitution in place of the nationalist one originally envisaged. As noted earlier, this was clearly reflected in the formation of the legislature and in the adoption of the Electoral College scheme for the selection of a President. These same two groups of states also insisted that presidential appointments and treaties would require the approval of the Senate, and Senate only, for confirmation. They zealously guarded this role for the body that represented the states where they had due influence and refused to grant any role to the popularly elected House of Representatives, which was dominated by the larger states. Step by step the federalist stamp was grafted onto the Virginia Plan, and the scheme for a powerful central government was gradually revised.

SENATE ADVICE AND CONSENT

Two topics are encompassed under this heading: appointments and treaties. Article 2, Section 2, Clause 2 of the Constitution reads:

> He [the President] shall have Power, by and with the Advice and Consent of the Senate, to make Treaties, provided two-thirds of the Senators present concur; and he shall nominate, and by and with the Advice and Consent of the Senate, shall

appoint Ambassadors, other public Ministers and Consuls, Judges of the supreme Court, and all other Officers of the United States, whose Appointments are not herein otherwise provided for and which shall be established by Law; but the Congress may by Law vest the Appointment of such inferior Offices, as they think proper, in the President alone, in the Courts of Law, or in the Heads of Departments.

Several facets of this provision call for explanation: (1) Why treaties and appointments require the joint operation of two branches of government, both President and Senate "in unique combination," for entry into force; (2) why the House of Representatives is denied a role with respect to both matters; and (3) why there is a difference in the size of the stipulated Senate majority, with treaties requiring a two-thirds vote and appointments a simple majority.[50]

In order to trace the formulation of the provision at the Constitutional Convention it is first necessary to examine the relevant provision in the Articles of Confederation. Under the Articles, both functions, the treaty power and the power to appoint ambassadors, resided in "the united states in congress assembled." Appointments required a majority vote, while treaties needed the approval of nine out of the 13 states.[51] The Virginia Plan, presented to the Convention on May 29, made no reference to either treaties or appointments, except for the appointment of judges "by the National Legislature."[52] In effect, then, both matters would continue to devolve on the Congress, as under the Articles of Confederation.[53]

In debate, on June 5, Madison objected to the election of judges by the whole legislature "or any numerous body." "Besides the danger of intrigue and partiality," he said, "many of the members were not judges of the requisite qualifications." Nor did he favor lodging the appointment of judges in the executive:

> He rather inclined to give it to the Senatorial branch, as numerous eno' to be confided in – as not so numerous as to be governed by the motives of the other branch; and as being sufficiently stable and independent to follow their deliberative judgments.[54]

On June 13, Madison's formal proposal for lodging the appointment of judges in the Senate was carried unanimously.[55] At this point, the Senate to which Madison and the Convention referred was that outlined in the Virginia Plan (essentially drafted by Madison) in which representation would be proportional to population, as in the lower house.[56]

The New Jersey Plan, first presented to the plenum on June 15, provided for the appointment of judges to the Supreme Court by the executive acting alone.[57] This may ring strange in a plan devoted to according the states, and particularly the smaller states, a greater role in the operation of the federal government. However, two things should be borne in mind. First, the New Jersey Plan endorsed a plural executive; and second, the national executive was subject to the control of state executives who could apply to Congress for his removal. Consequently, a restraining feature was built into the appointment process, and there was no need for additional restraint by another branch of government. The New Jersey Plan made no reference to the adoption of treaties, and presumably under its scheme the power to make treaties would continue to reside in the one-House, state-controlled Congress that operated under the Articles of Confederation.

On June 19, the Convention opted for the Virginia Plan in preference to the New Jersey Plan.[58] This, of course, did not put an end to small-state agitation for equality in at least one house of the national legislature.[59] The matter was only resolved with finality when the Connecticut Compromise was adopted on July 16, granting all states equality in the Senate.[60] The previously adopted formula, according to which the Senate alone made judicial appointments, was now significantly weighted in favor of the smaller states. This fact was not lost on the delegates of the larger states when the judicial appointments provision was once again taken up for debate on July 18.

Randolph was quite candid in noting the objections raised against leaving appointments in the new Senate. "It is true," he said, "that when the appt. of the Judges was vested in the 2d. branch an equality of votes had not been given to it." Nonetheless, he preferred leaving that power in the Senate rather than transferring it to the executive as other delegates desired.[61] Among the latter was James Wilson, who made a formal proposal to that effect.[62] Gunning Bedford of Delaware demurred, since "it would put it in his [the executive's] power to gain over the larger States, by gratifying them with a preference of their Citizens."[63] Nathaniel Ghorum of Massachusetts submitted a motion to accept the formula practiced in his own state, according to which the executive appointed with the advice and consent of the second branch of the legislature.[64] Neither Wilson's nor Ghorum's suggestion was accepted by the Convention.[65]

Although Madison had been instrumental in getting the Convention to lodge the appointment power in the Senate exclusively, following the change in circumstances he moved to have that formula revised.[66] His first suggestion was for appointment by the executive "with the concurrence of {1/3 at least} of the 2d. branch." "This," he said, "would unite the advantage of responsibility in the Executive with the security afforded in the 2d. branch agst. any incautious or corrupt nomination." The failure of Ghorum's proposal to be accepted led Madison to move that judges be nominated by the executive, which appointments should enter into force unless "disagreed to within—days by 2\3 of the 2d. branch."[67] The negative formulation and stipulation of a high percentage for disapproval would, of course, preclude a veto by the smaller states.

Madison candidly revealed the considerations that led him to make his proposal:

> As the 2d. b. was very differently constituted when the appointment of the Judges was formerly referred to it, and was now to be composed of equal votes from all the States, the principle of compromise which had prevailed in other instances

required in this that their [*sic*] shd. be a concurrence of two authorities, in one of which the people, in the other states, should be represented. The Executive Magistrate wd be considered as a national officer, acting for and equally sympathising with every part of the U. States.[68]

If the 2d branch alone should have this power, [of appointment] the Judges might be appointed by a minority of the people, tho' by a majority, of the States, which could not be justified on any principle as their proceedings were to relate to the people, rather than to the States; and as it would moreover throw the appointments entirely into the hands of ye Nthern States, a perpetual ground of jealousy & discontent would be furnished to the Southern States.[69]

Concerned with the implications of the proposal for the status of the states, Elbridge Gerry of Massachusetts objected to Madison's proposal[70]: "The appointment of the Judges like every other part of the Constitution shd. be so modeled as to give satisfaction both to the people and to the States"; but "the mode under consideration will give satisfaction to neither." He also disagreed with the suggestion that a two-thirds vote in the Senate be required to reject a nomination. Whereupon Madison revised his proposal to allow Senate disapproval by simple majority.[71] Even with this revision, however, Madison's motion failed, by a vote of 3:6.[72]

It is noteworthy that the only states favoring Madison's proposal were the three large states—Massachusetts, Pennsylvania, and Virginia. In a separate vote, with the same three large states opposed, the Convention immediately confirmed that judges were to be appointed by the Senate alone.[73] This formula on judicial appointments became part of the clause on Senate powers incorporated in the outline of a constitution prepared by the Committee of Detail. In the meantime, several delegates were becoming alarmed at the inordinate concentration of powers in the Senate. Thus, in a discussion on August 15, George Mason strongly protested the fact that the treaty power was lodged in the Senate alone. "The Senate by means of [a] treaty might alienate territory &c. without legislative sanction. ... [It] might by treaty dismember the Union."[74]

On August 23, the Convention considered the draft provision on Senate powers which read: "The Senate of the United States shall have power to make treaties, and to appoint Ambassadors, and Judges of the supreme Court."[75] Gouverneur Morris argued against Senate appointment of officials. "He considered the body as too numerous for the purpose; as subject to cabal; and as devoid of responsibility."[76] He was supported in this stand by his colleague from Pennsylvania, James Wilson.

Madison spoke out against granting the Senate exclusive control over treaty-making. "The Senate represented the States alone," he said, "and ... for this as well as other obvious reasons it was proper that the President should be an agent in Treaties."[77] Madison's comment reflected both a more "national" perspective on the foreign affairs power and the dissatisfaction of the larger states with the disproportionate influence the smaller states would now be wielding in the Senate. Hence his suggestion that the President, the only truly national figure in the structure of government, be brought into the picture.

Gouverneur Morris was skeptical about according the Senate any role in treaty-making but, as a minimum, he suggested that no treaty bind the United States unless "ratified by a law."[78] This meant that the House of Representatives, the repository of large-state influence, would be involved in the treaty-making process. The implications of the Morris amendment were spelled out by Mr. Dickinson of Delaware. He "concurred in the amendment, as most safe and proper, tho' he was sensible it was unfavorable to the little States; which would otherwise have an *equal* share in making Treaties."[79] But Gouverneur Morris's motion was rejected, with only his own state, Pennsylvania, voting in favor.[80] Obviously, the states, and particularly the smaller states, were not disposed to share foreign affairs power with the lower house of the national legislature, in which the larger states would exercise predominant influence.[81]

At this point, therefore, the treaty power remained lodged in the Senate exclusively. Madison, however, had reservations regarding this arrangement and "hinted for consideration, whether a distinction might not be made between different sorts of Treaties—Allowing the President & Senate to make Treaties eventual and of Alliance for limited terms—and requiring the concurrence of the whole Legislature in other Treaties."[82] Many delegates were apparently not fully satisfied with the treaty provision as it stood, and the whole draft provision on Senate powers was therefore unanimously conveyed to the Brearley Committee on Unfinished Parts.

Both Madison and Gouverneur Morris served on the Committee which introduced significant changes in the draft clause. For one thing, Madison's suggestion for presidential involvement in the treaty-making process was accepted, as was a presidential role in appointments. Senate approval of both treaties and appointments was stipulated, but the Senate was no longer the referent; it was the President. Both by formulation and location—in Article 2 "the powers were confirmed as essentially presidential in nature." And finally, the vote required for Senate approval for treaties was raised to two-thirds.

The clause now read:

> The President by and with the advice and Consent of the Senate, shall have power to make Treaties; and he shall nominate and by and with the advice and consent of the Senate shall appoint Ambassadors, and other public Ministers, Judges of the Supreme Court, and all other Officers of the U. S. whose appointments are not otherwise herein provided for. But no Treaty shall be made without the consent of two thirds of the members present.[83]

The Committee of Style and Arrangement reformulated the provision, without introducing any substantive change, into its present form in the Constitution.

Clearly, tension between the large and small states contributed significantly to the formulation of the provision on treaties and appointments. As happened in the compromise on the composition of the national legislature, both groups of states gained a measure of control and some of their desiderata; and the small-state gains were significant. The small states strove to have treaties and appointments lodged in the Senate alone, where they had gained a privileged position, while the larger states fought for the involvement of the President, representative of the national will and more beholden to the wishes of the larger states.[84] The House of Representatives was excluded from the whole process, not only because it was more numerous and therefore less guarded in relation to secret affairs, but because its involvement would dilute the dominant influence which the smaller states sought to exercise through the Senate.

The remarks of William Richardson Davie in the North Carolina Ratifying Convention testify to the tenacity of the smaller states in these matters. The power of making treaties, he noted, had in all countries been placed in the executive department, and the United States Constitution would also have followed this practice. The President, "being elected by the people ... at large, will have their general interest at heart," he said. However,

> the extreme jealousy of the little states, and between the commercial states and the non-importing states, produced the necessity of giving an equality of suffrage to the Senate. The same causes made it indispensable to give to the senators, as representatives of states, the power of making, or ratifying, treaties ... The small states would not consent to confederate without an equal voice in the formation of treaties. Without the equality, they apprehended that their interest would be neglected or sacrificed in negotiations. This difficulty could not be got over ... [Because] of the inflexibility of the little states in this point it ... became necessary to give them an absolute equality in making treaties ... The necessity of their interfering in the appointment of officers resulted from the same reason ... The small states would not agree that the House of Representatives should have a voice in the appointment to offices; and the extreme jealousy of all the states would not give it to the President alone.[85]

Explaining the roots of Senate involvement does not, however, tell the full story. Why was a special majority deemed necessary for approving treaties? The considerations which prompted the Brearley Committee to raise the vote required in the Senate to two-thirds are not readily apparent, since that Committee's deliberations were not preserved, and the Convention itself approved the revised treaty clause "with surprising unanimity and surprisingly little debate."[86] It would seem, however, that sectional interests, that other perennial factor at the Convention, influenced the delegates to raise the vote required for treaties from simple majority to two-thirds.[87] The size of the majority required for Senate advice and consent for treaties became caught up in one of the more famous, or infamous, compromise settlements of the Convention.[88]

Throughout the Convention, the adoption of navigation laws had been made dependent on a qualified majority of two-thirds in Congress.[89] This reflected southern concerns that the North might promote legislation restricting the shipment of goods to American ships, thus disadvantaging the South by making the importation of goods and the exportation of staples more expensive than if a free choice of available ships were allowed.[90] As the end of the Convention approached, North–South differences over the issue of navigation laws,[91] and two other issues, the right of the South (really the Deep South) to continue the importation of slaves,[92] and a ban on export taxes,[93] became the subject of a compromise. In return for abolishing the two-thirds requirement for navigation laws, the North relented on the importation of slaves for a further 12 (ultimately 20) years and all export taxes were banned.[94] In conjunction with that compromise, the majority required for Senate advice and consent for treaties was raised to two-thirds. While navigation laws affected the southern staple states only, the treaty power bore both on the South as well as on the fishing rights of the North. Confirmation for this interpretation of the turn of events is provided by the remarks of George Mason at the Virginia Ratifying Convention:

> Mr. Chairman – With respect to commerce and navigation ... I will give you, to the best of my recollection, the history of that affair. This business was discussed at Philadelphia for four months, during which time the subject of commerce and navigation was often under consideration; and I assert, that eight states out of twelve, for more than three months, voted for requiring two-thirds of the members present in each house to pass commercial and navigation laws. True it is, that afterwards it was carried by a majority, as it stands. If I am right, there was a great majority for requiring two-thirds of the states in this business, till a compromise took place between the northern and southern states; the northern states agreeing to the temporary importation of slaves, and the southern states conceding, in return, that navigation and commercial laws should be on the footing on which they now stand. ... The Newfoundland fisheries will require that kind of security which we are now in want of: the Eastern states therefore agreed at length, that treaties should require the consent of two-thirds of the members present in the senate.[95]

Thus, the mutual fear of both East and South regarding possible adverse effects of commercial treaties on their respective interests had prompted raising the vote required for treaties from simple majority to two-thirds.

Attempts by Madison to except peace treaties from the two-thirds requirement and permit their endorsement by simple majority were initially accepted but then rejected,[96] once it became clear to the delegates that peace treaties could serve as a means by which the United States could concede shipping, fishing, and other rights to foreign countries.[97] The memory of Jay's recent attempt under the Continental Congress to bargain away US rights of passage on the Mississippi to Spain for a period of 25 years in return for certain commercial rights that would benefit the North spurred the southern delegates to insist that all treaties, peace treaties included, be made subject to the advice and consent of a two-thirds vote in the Senate.[98]

When the treaty-making clause came up for discussion in the Convention on September 7 and 8, the delegates overwhelmingly rejected two proposals submitted by James Wilson to modify the details of the treaty provision. The first would have included the House in the treaty-making process,[99] and the second would have eliminated the two-thirds requirement.[100] Thus, the power to approve treaties remained the prerogative of the Senate, the bastion of the states, and the two-thirds requirement was sacrosanct, serving as it did to protect sectional interests.

The significance of the Mississippi episode in prompting the South to institute the two-thirds requirement is highlighted by the following account of the Convention discussions given by Hugh Williamson, delegate of North Carolina, in a letter to Madison:

> It is said that some antifed in Maryland on the last Winter fastened on the Ear of Genl Wilkinson who was accidentally there and persuaded him that in case of a new Govt. the Navigation of the Mississippi would infallibly by given up. Your Recollection must certainly enable you to say that there is a Proviso in the new Sistem which was inserted for the express purpose of preventing a majority of the Senate or of the States which is considered as the same thing from giving up the Mississippi. It is provided that two thirds of the Members present in the senate shall be required to concur in making Treaties and if the southern states attend to their Duty, this will imply 2\3. of the States in the Union together with the President, a security rather better than the present 9 States especially as Vermont & the Province of Main may be added to the Eastern Interest and you may recollect that when a Member, Mr. Willson objected to this Proviso, saying that in all Govts. the Majority should govern it was replyed that the Navigation of the Mississippi after what had already happened in Congress was not to be risqued in the Hands of a meer Majority and the Objection was withdrawn.[101]

It might also be noted that consideration of the treaty-making clause in the state ratifying conventions evoked criticism, as Charles Warren has noted, primarily because of the ease with which treaties could be adopted and the vulnerability of critical sectional interests.[102] Several states proposed amendments to tighten the treaty-making procedure. The following draft amendment, submitted by the Virginia Ratifying Convention for adoption by the first Congress, embraced all the specific interests noted above—commercial interests, territorial rights, fishing, and navigation of the Mississippi. It also called for a qualified majority in both Houses in certain instances:

> That no commercial treaty shall be ratified without the concurrence of two-thirds of the whole number of the Members of the Senate; and no treaty, ceding, contracting, restraining or suspending, the territorial rights or claims of the United States, or any of them, or their, or any of their rights or claims to fishing in the American seas, or navigating the American rivers shall be made, but in cases of the most urgent and extreme necessity, nor shall any such treaty be ratified without the concurrence of three fourths of the whole number of the Members of both Houses respectively.[103]

The considerations of the Convention in its drafting of the treaty provision are also noted by President Washington in his message to the House of Representatives in relation to the Jay Treaty.[104]

Explaining his refusal to convey the background papers to the House, Washington stressed that the function of advice and consent for treaties had been vested exclusively in the Senate, because in that body large and small states had equal representation. "For, on the equal participation of those powers [of the Senate], the sovereignty and political safety of the smaller States were deemed essentially to depend."[105] A proposal to include the House in the treaty-making process was explicitly rejected by the Convention, Washington noted.

In sum, formulation of the treaty-making clause at the Constitutional Convention proceeded through three stages. With the establishment of the Senate as the repository of state power, the smaller states, intent on ensuring an equal role, restricted the treaty-making power to the Senate, the counterpart of the Congress under the Confederation. For their part, representatives of the larger states, the dissatisfied nationalists, succeeded in reserving for the President—the only truly national figure in government—a central role in the process. Finally, sectional interests, from both the Northeast and the South, operated to raise the voting requirement from simple majority to two-thirds. The influence of each of these three groups—small states, nationalists, and sectional interests—is reflected in the composite compromise that was the final product of the Constitutional Convention in its formulation of the treaty-making power.

Drafting the provision on Senate advice and consent demonstrated that there was no gainsaying the pressure of the smaller states in the formulation of each and every one of the provisions of the Constitution. Both this provision and the one regarding the Electoral College were only resolved in the final stages of the Convention. Madison's national scheme provided the foundation, but the drive to federalize that scheme meant that the smaller states would not be ostracized in the operation of the federal government. Their voice would be heard in its deliberations.

The decision of the Convention to accede to the demand of the smaller states for an equal vote in the second house, it has been said, was the crucial act defining the nature of American federalism in the political system. Herbert Wechsler and Jesse Choper have each presented a thesis that the interests and concerns of the states were meant to be satisfied by means of the representation that they extracted at Philadelphia.[106] In other words, the national institutions of government were deliberatedly designed to give voice and influence to the states to allow them to participate in formulating policies and reaching decisions in the conduct of the federal government. As we have seen, the states gained an effective role in each of the three branches of government—in the national legislature by means of the Senate, in the selection of a President by means of the Electoral College, and in the choice of judges by requiring federal judges to receive the approval of the state-dominated Senate. Judicial review was not expected to serve as the primary means of protecting the states from federal aggrandizement, since the organization of the federal government itself, in which they had meaningful representation, offered them adequate means of expressing their policy preferences and securing their vital interests.

In support of his thesis, Wechsler cites a letter written by Madison in 1830. Madison lists three constitutional features that would serve "as a security of the rights and powers of the states" against federal encroachment: (1) "The responsibility of the Senators and Representatives in the Legislature of the U.S."; (2) "The responsibility of the President to the people of the U. States"; and (3) "The liability of the Ex[ecutive] And Judiciary functionaries of the U.S. to impeachment."[107] It is noteworthy, says Wechsler, that Madison did not emphasize the function of the Court as an instrument for restraining the federal branch of the government. Judicial review in relation to federalism, Wechsler maintains, was primarily intended as a means of ensuring national supremacy "against nullification or usurpation by the individual states, the national government having no part in their composition or their councils." This, he says, is made clear by the fact that judicial review replaced the national legislative veto over state legislation, so vehemently supported by Madison. He concludes, therefore, that "the national political process in the United States—and especially the role of the states in the composition and selection of the central government—is intrinsically well adapted" to restraining federal intrusions. Consequently, when the Court opposes federal legislation it is interposing in a process to which the representatives of the states have acquiesced and perhaps even initiated: "Federal intervention as against the states is thus primarily a matter for congressional determination in our system,"[108] with judicial review only as a rare and ultimate resort.

Nearly half a century after Wechsler's piece appeared, Larry D. Kramer published a major article endorsing Wechsler's thesis on the political safeguards of federalism and sharply attacking the US Supreme Court for repeatedly intervening in the name of federalism to protect the states from alleged congressional aggrandizement.[109] Kramer agrees with Wechsler that the primary line of defense for the states was their representation in both houses of Congress. Thus, in his headnote one reads: "The Founders believed that any attempt by Congress to usurp state power could and would be thwarted by state officials' mounting popular appeals."[110] Wechsler was correct, says Kramer, in pointing to state representation in both houses of Congress as the primary line of defense assigned by the Framers for securing the sovereignty and interests of the states. However, the development of political parties in the United States very much eroded the protective role of a state's representation in Congress, since members of Congress became beholden to the overriding influence of national politics. But the new form of politics brought about close ties between politicians on the national and state levels and this served to protect state interests. "The key feature of this new federalism was the unique American system of decentralized national political parties, which linked the fortunes of federal officeholders to state politicians and parties and in this way assured respect for state sovereignty."[111] For this reason, Kramer contends, the active role adopted by the Supreme Court in recent years to shield the states from federal assertiveness is both misguided and destructive of national needs. The Framers, Kramer declares, never intended to make the Court a guardian of state sovereignty. It was not part of the original design, nor is it consistent with more than two centuries of practice. The present conduct of the Court represents "a radical experiment in judicial activism" that is "reckless in the extreme—irresponsibly so."[112] Kramer calls on the Court to return to the standard practice of the New Deal era, "applying rational basis scrutiny to questions regarding the limits of Congress's power under Article 1" of the Constitution.

This interpretation of the federal character of the Constitution is of particular significance, given the latest trend of the Supreme Court to act vigorously to protect state sovereignty and independence, as will be seen below in the Postscript.

NOTES

1. Farrand, *Records*, 1: 255. In writing this chapter I have relied in part on my journal article: "Securing States' Interests at the 1787 Constitutional Convention: A Reassessment," *Studies in American Political Development*, 14 (2000): 1–19. I am grateful to the editors of the journal for permission to quote extracts from that article.
2. Herbert Wechsler, "The Political Safeguards of Federalism; The Role of the States in the Composition and Selection of the National Government" in *Principles, Politics, and Fundamental Law* (Cambridge, MA: Harvard University Press, 1961), 49.
3. See above, Chap. 2.
4. See, especially, the views of Lance Banning, as expressed in various articles and in his magnum opus, *The Sacred Fire of Liberty: James Madison and the Founding of the Federal Republic* (Ithaca, NY: Cornell University Press, 1995). At the same time, his survey of the drafting of the Constitution presents a splendid summary of the key issues at the Convention. See Lance Banning, "The Constitutional Convention" in Leonard W. Levy and Dennis J. Mahoney (eds.), *The Framing and Ratification of the Constitution* (New York: Macmillan, 1987), 112–131.
5. Letter of George Mason to his son on the eve of the convention, May 20, 1787. Farrand, *Records*, 3: 23.
6. Robert Yates's notes include the following comment regarding the Virginia Plan: "He [Randolph] candidly confessed that they [the resolutions] were not intended for a federal government—he meant a strong *consolidated* union, in which the idea of states should be nearly annihilated." Ibid., 1: 24. Subsequently, in 1833, John Tyler, in describing the Virginia Plan, said: "The design of this plan, it is obvious, was to render the States nothing more than the provinces of a great government to rear upon the ruins of the old Confederacy a consolidated Government, one and indivisible." Cited in a draft reply letter (never sent) by Madison to John Tyler. Ibid., 3: 524.
7. Ibid., 1: 18, n. 1.

8. Minutes of James McHenry of Maryland, May 29, 1787. Ibid., 1: 26.
9. Minutes of Robert Yates of New York. Ibid., 1: 24.
10. *The Ideological Origins of the American Revolution*, enlarged ed. (Cambridge, MA: Belknap Press, 1992), *Postscript*, "Fulfillment: A Commentary on the Constitution," 325.
11. James Wilson of Pennsylvania explained that this "was the rule in the Act of [the Confederal] Congress agreed to by eleven States, for apportioning quotas of revenue on the States." Farrand, *Records*, 1: 201. Several northern delegates vigorously objected to this artificial increase in southern representation, and wanted to know why slaves were different from any other species of property in calculating a state's representation. See debate, ibid., 1: 561, 580–583, 587–588. The three-fifths rule was adopted on July 13, by a vote of nine to zero, with one state divided. In northern state ratification conventions this rule was justified on the ground that representation and taxation was made to go hand in hand, as the Constitution prescribed. See ibid., 3: 255, 400, 429–430.
12. Ibid., 1: 242.
13. Ibid., 1: 464–465.
14. Ibid., 1: 466–467.
15. Ibid., 1: 530.
16. Letter by Gouverneur Morris to Robert Walsh, Feb. 5, 1811. Cited in ibid., 3: 419.
17. Ibid., note.
18. Ibid., 1: 492.
19. Ibid., 343–344.
20. Ibid., 552.
21. Ibid., 2: 15–16.
22. Ibid., 19.
23. Ibid., 3: 441. Pinckney was addressing the House of Representatives, Feb. 14, 1820.
24. Ibid., 1: 515.
25. Ibid., 3: 19–20.
26. See above, Chap. 2, text at nn. 14–15.
27. Onuf first enunciated his thesis in *The Origins of the Federal Republic: Jurisdictional Controversies in the United States, 1775–1787* (Philadelphia: University of Pennsylvania Press, 1983) and elaborated upon it in his outstanding article, "Anarchy and the Crisis of the Union" in Herman Belz et al. (eds.), *To Form a More Perfect Union* (Charlottesville: University Press of Virginia, 1992), 272–302. Two younger scholars, protégés of Onuf, have written books describing in greater detail the impact of the disunity argument employed by the Federalists. David C. Hendrickson's work, *Peace Pact: The Lost World of the American Founding* (Lawrence: University Press of Kansas, 2003), presents a grand thesis according to which the Constitution's greatest achievement lay in forestalling conflict between the states by ushering in a procedure for the peaceful resolution of interstate disputes. He likens this development to the great historic peace settlements that defined relations between the European states, and subsequently throughout the world, as for instance the Paris Peace Conference of 1919 and the San Francisco Conference of 1945. While the thesis is summed up in the title of the work, the study has implications for an appreciation of the Constitutional Convention from diplomatic and international perspectives, and not only constitutional law.

Max M. Edling's book, *A Revolution in Favor of Government: Origins of the US Constitution and the Making of the American State* (New York: Oxford University Press, 2003), links the adoption of the Constitution to the emergence in Europe of the "fiscal-military state" in the eighteenth century. War-making was transferred from the separate states to the national government and, as a result, that government appeared as a colossus that threatened the liberties of American citizens. To mollify the fears emanating from the states, the system of government was carefully designed to grant extraordinary powers in time of crisis but apply minimal imposition on the citizens at all other times. Both books are valuable adjuncts to Onuf's original work.

28. The present focus is not directed to the general subject of slavery at the Constitutional Convention, which is a vast one. The aim is strictly to examine how the federal character of the Constitution was also shaped by the slavery issue. In particular, the discussion reviews how the slave states joined with the smaller states to effect changes in the grand scheme of the larger states for an all-powerful national government in which the states, as states, would barely survive. However, as will be seen, the change effected in the scope of national power was essentially a product of slave-state fears, not that of the smaller states. Once the smaller states secured equality in the institutions of government, they were content with the enhancement of national power.
29. Farrand, *Records*, 2: 220.
30. Ibid., 2: 370.
31. Ibid., 2: 221.
32. Ibid., 2: 223.
33. Ibid., 2: 224.
34. Ibid.
35. Ibid., 2: 220–221. For a critical review of the role of the Founders in relation to slavery, see John P. Kaminski (ed.), *A Necessary Evil? Slavery and the Debate Over the Constitution* (Madison, WI: Madison House Publishers, 1995) and William M. Wiecek, "The Witch at the Christening: Slavery and the Constitution's Origins" in Levy and Mahoney, *Framing and Ratification*, 167–184.
36. Farrand, *Records*, 3: 333.
37. Farrand, *Framing*, 149–151.
38. Paul Finkelman, "Slavery and the Constitutional Convention: Making a Covenant with Death", in Richard Beeman, Stephen Botein, and Edward C. Carter II (eds.), *Beyond Confederation: Origins of the Constitution and American National Identity*. (Chapel Hill: University of North Carolina Press, 1987), 188–225. See also Finkelman, *Slavery and the Founders: Race and Liberty in the Age of Jefferson*. 2nd ed. (New York: E. M. Sharpe, 2001). In his article "The Witch" (op. cit., 168), William M. Wiecek indicates that the Constitution supported slavery in no fewer than ten clauses. His shorter list obviously refers only to explicit clauses touching on slavery.
39. Bernard Bailyn, *Faces of Revolution: Personalities and Themes in the Struggle for American Independence* (New York: Knopf, 1990), 223.
40. Farrand, *Framing*, 204.
41. Farrand, *Records*, 1: 77–78, 81, 88.
42. Ibid., 2: 23, 33.
43. Ibid., 2: 22, 29.
44. Ibid., 2: 29–30.

45. See the comment of Hugh Williamson of Virginia, ibid., 2: 32.
46. Ibid., 2: 472–473, 480–481.
47. Ibid., 2: 473, 481.
48. Gouverneur Morris was given the task of explaining the committee's decision to the plenum of the Convention. Ibid., 2: 500.
49. For a more complete analysis of this topic, see Shlomo Slonim, "The Electoral College at Philadelphia: The Evolution of an Ad Hoc Congress for the Selection of a President," *Journal of American History*, 73 (1986): 35–58. Republished in Slonim, *Framers' Construction/Beardian Deconstruction: Essays on the Constitutional Design of 1787* (New York: Peter Lang, 2001), Chap. 1.
50. See Louis Henkin, *Foreign Affairs and the Constitution* (New York: Norton, 1975), 127.
51. Art. IX of the Articles of Confederation.
52. Resolution 9, Farrand, *Records*, 1: 21.
53. See Resolution 6 in Report of the Committee of the Whole on the Virginia Plan on June 13 (ibid., 1: 236). In debate, Madison moved that the executive be empowered "to appoint to offices in cases not otherwise provided for" (ibid., 1: 67). His motion was accepted, and the provision appeared in that form in the Report of the Committee of the Whole (ibid., 1: 236).
54. Ibid., 1: 120.
55. Ibid., 1: 232–233.
56. At the time, Hamilton made a proposal that was little noticed. (There is no reference to it in Madison's minutes. It is noted only in Pierce's record.) Hamilton suggested that the executive nominate and the Senate have "the right of rejecting or approving" appointments (ibid., 1: 128). When Hamilton presented his own Plan to the Convention on June 18 in a major address (recorded in Madison's minutes), he proposed that the executive have the power to make all treaties "with the advice and approbation of the Senate;" "to have the sole appointment of the heads or chief officers of the departments of Finance, War, and Foreign Affairs;" and to nominate all other officers, including ambassadors, "subject to the approbation or rejection of the Senate" (ibid., 1: 292).
57. Ibid., 1: 244.
58. Ibid., 1: 313, 322.
59. See, for example, Forrest McDonald, *Novus Ordo Seclorum: The Intellectual Origins of the Constitution*. (Lawrence: University Press of Kansas, 1985), 227–233; McLaughlin, *Constitutional History*, 76–78.
60. Farrand, *Records*, 2: 14, 15.
61. Ibid., 2: 43.
62. Ibid., 2: 37, 41.
63. Ibid., 2: 43.
64. Ibid., 2: 38, 41, 44.
65. Ibid., 2: 37, 38, 44.
66. Ibid., 2: 42–43.
67. Ibid., 2: 38, 44.
68. Ibid., 2: 80–81.
69. Ibid., 2: 81.
70. Ibid., 2: 82.
71. Ibid., 2: 71–72, 82.
72. Ibid., 2: 72, 83.

73. Ibid.
74. Ibid., 2: 297–298.
75. Ibid., 2: 183, 389, n. 8. The Committee of Detail had apparently, on its own, added the appointment of ambassadors to the powers of the Senate.
76. Ibid., 2: 389.
77. Ibid., 2: 392.
78. Ibid.
79. Ibid., 2: 393 (emphasis in original).
80. Ibid., 2: 382–383, 394. However, the term "and other public ministers" was inserted after the word "Ambassadors."
81. No doubt other factors, including the transient nature of House membership resulting from biannual elections and the larger size of the body, in which secrets would be preserved with difficulty, also militated against giving the House of Representatives a role in the adoption of treaties. See, in this regard, John Jay, *Federalist*, #64. But the debate makes clear that the crucial factor for the smaller states was the desire to retain the treaty power in the chamber in which they had secured an advantage in terms of representation.
82. Farrand, *Records*, 2: 394.
83. Ibid., 2: 495, 498–499. The provision was affirmed in the Convention on September 7, with the word "consuls" being added to the appointments clause (ibid., 2: 533, 539–540).
84. Arthur Bestor, in a lengthy article, "Respective Roles of Senate and President in the Making and Abrogation of Treaties The Original Intent of the Framers of the Constitution Historically Examined." *Washington Law Review*, 55 (1979), 1–135, contends that the introduction of the executive into the treaty-making process was only intended to make the President the "agent" of the Senate, not to endow him with independent, initiating powers in the sphere of foreign relations. Jack N. Rakove takes issue with this assumption both in an article, "Solving a Constitutional Puzzle: The Treatymaking Clause as a Case Study," *Perspectives in American History*, New Series 1 (1984): 233–281, and in his Pulitzer prize-winning book, *Original Meanings: Politics and Ideas in the Making of the Constitution* (New York: Alfred A. Knopf, 1996), 240–242, 250–251, 266–267. The fact that the treatymaking power was lodged in Article 2, coupled with the comment of Gouverneur Morris in reference to treaties, that the President represented "the general Guardian of the National interests," (Farrand, *Records*, 2: 540–541) would seem to confirm that the President was to serve as more than merely a "Senate agent" in this connection.
85. Jonathan Elliot, (ed.), *The Debates of the Several State Conventions on the Adoption of the Federal Constitution in 1787*, 5 vols. (Philadelphia, PA: Lippincott, 1836), 4: 119–122. Reprinted also in Farrand, *Records*, 3: 348.
86. Farrand, *Framing*, 171.
87. The background to the two-thirds requirement for treaties is traced in a short article by R. Earl McClendon, "Origin of the Two-Thirds Rule in Senate Action Upon Treaties," *American Historical Review*, 36 (1931): 768–772. The present discussion is based largely on McClendon's note except that McClendon does not discuss navigation laws. See also S. Slonim, "Congressional–Executive Agreements," *Columbia Journal of Transnational Law*, 14 (1975): 434–450. Strangely enough, neither Bestor nor Rakove cites the McClendon article in discussing the two-thirds requirement for treaties.

88. Andrew C. McLaughlin, *The Confederation and the Constitution, 1783–1789* (New York: Macmillan, 1905), 84–86, 260–262; Farrand, *Framing*, 147–152; and Warren, *Making of Constitution*, 579–586.
89. See Committee of Detail, Farrand, *Records*, 2: 169, 183.
90. See Farrand, *Framing*, 147–148. Interestingly, during the course of the debate it apparently occurred to George Mason that Senate adoption of treaties by majority vote posed as much danger to the interests of the South as did the adoption of navigation laws by Congress. There was need, therefore, to require a two-thirds vote in both cases (Farrand, *Records*, 4: 52–53). Mason does not seem to have submitted any formal proposal to this effect. It is ironic to note that, in the end, treaties gained the security of a special majority while navigation laws lost it. In the one case the issue of fisheries was also involved; in the other it was not.
91. See Farrand, *Records*, 2: 374–375.
92. Ibid., 2: 364–365, 369–374.
93. Ibid., 2: 359–364.
94. Ibid., 2: 396, 400; and see 449–453.
95. John P. Kaminski and Gaspare J. Saladino (eds.), (Merrill Jensen, Founding Editor), *Documentary History of the Ratification of the Constitution: Virginia*, 18 vols. (1993), 10: 1488. Repr. in Farrand, *Records*, 3: 334–335, and cited in McClendon, "Origin of Two-Thirds Rule," 772. See also Warren, *Making of Constitution*, 584, for a statement made subsequently by Mason to Jefferson summarizing his remarks at the Virginia Convention.
96. Farrand, *Records*, 2: 533, 540.
97. Ibid., 2: 534, 543, 544, 547, 548–549.
    Madison also moved to empower two-thirds of the Senate "to make treaties of peace without the concurrence of the President." The President, Madison argued, "would necessarily derive so much power and importance from a state of war that he might be tempted, if authorized, to impede a treaty of peace" (ibid.). His proposal was seconded by Butler of South Carolina, who "was strenuous for the motion, as a necessary security against ambitious & corrupt Presidents" (ibid., 2: 541). The motion was rejected by a vote of three to eight (ibid., 2: 533, 541).
98. For further discussion of this episode, known as the Jay–Gardoqui negotiations, see Samuel Flagg Bemis, *Pinckney's Treaty*. (Baltimore, MD: Johns Hopkins University Press, 1926); Bemis, *A Diplomatic History of the United States*, 5th ed. (New York: Holt, Rinehart and Winston, 1965), 78–80; McLaughlin, *Confederation and Constitution*, 94–101; Frank Monaghan, *John Jay: Defender of Liberty*. (New York: Bobbs-Merrill, 1935), 255–261; Warren, *Making of Constitution*, 24–30; Rakove, "Solving a Constitutional Puzzle," 272–274; and Banning, *Sacred Fire of Liberty*, 66–70.
99. Farrand, *Records*, 2: 532, 538. Wilson contended that the need for secrecy was not sufficient reason to exclude the House from sharing in the treaty-making power. "As treaties ... are to have the operation of laws, they ought to have the sanction of laws also." In response, Sherman of Connecticut argued that "the necessity of secrecy in the case of treaties forbade a reference of them to the whole Legislature" (ibid., 2: 538). The vote was 1:10, with only Pennsylvania, Wilson's own state, voting in favor.
100. "Mr. Wilson thought it objectionable to require the concurrence of 2/3 which puts it in the power of a minority to controul the will of the majority" (ibid., 2: 540). Of

course, this is precisely what these states wanted to achieve. The vote was 1:9 with one state divided (ibid., 2: 549).
101. Ibid., 3: 306–307. The letter, dated June 2, 1788, is also quoted in McClendon, "Origin of Two-Thirds Rule," 771–772, and Warren, *Making of Constitution*, 657–658.
102. Ibid., 658, 773–774.
103. Elliot, Debates 3: 660; repr. in Tansill, *Documents*, 1029–1030.
104. *Annals of Congress*, 5: 760 [1789–1824].
105. Ibid., 5: 761.
106. Wechsler, *Political Safeguards*, and Jesse H. Choper, *Judicial Review and the National Political Process* (Chicago: University of Chicago Press, 1980). See also Henry Paul Monaghan, "We the People[s], Original Understanding, and Constitutional Amendment," *Columbia Law Review*, 96 (1996): 121, who highlights "the crucial role reserved for the states in the newly established constitutional order."
107. Wechsler, *Political Safeguards*, 79.
108. Ibid., 81.
109. Larry D. Kramer, "Putting the Politics Back Into the Political Safeguards of Federalism." *Columbia Law Review*, 100 (2000): 215–293.
110. Ibid., 100: 215.
111. Ibid., 100: 276.
112. Ibid., 100: 291.

CHAPTER 4

Delimiting the Scope of National Authority

The introduction of federalism into the draft constitution disrupted Madison's scheme for an all-powerful central government that would convert the country into one national entity. The demands of the smaller states and the slave states for an augmented status in the national institutions of government frustrated his basic plan to revamp the previous regime by barring any statal role in the operation of the national government. The states' control of the national government had been the bane of the government's independence under the Articles of Confederation, and only the complete elimination of any station for the states in the national institutions could remedy this situation. Madison's plan had a dual purpose—to keep the states out of the national government and to impose the national authority on the state governments—by making them subject to a national legislative veto. This was to reverse the federal arrangements with a vengeance. Every bicameral state legislature would, in effect, have a third house attached which was qualified to veto any and all legislation. Only by this double arrangement, Madison felt, would the new consolidated system of government be stable and secure. Chapter 3 analyzed how the states got back into the picture. This chapter captures the manner in which the general powers of Congress were crimped and the legislative veto over the states totally rejected. The effective role of the states was also confirmed in the procedure instituted to provide for the flexibility of the Constitution. Thus, while the Constitution permitted the adoption of amendments, changes could be instituted only with the sanction of the states.

ENUMERATING CONGRESSIONAL POWERS

Article 6 of the Virginia Plan spelled out the full scope of national authority:

> Resolved … that the National Legislature ought to be impowered to enjoy the Legislative Rights vested in Congress by the Confederation & moreover to legislate in all cases to which the separate States are incompetent, or in which the

harmony of the United States may be interrupted by the exercise of individual Legislation; to negative all laws passed by the several States, contravening in the opinion of the National Legislature the articles of Union; and to call forth the force of the Union agst. any member of the Union failing to fulfill its duty under the articles thereof.[1]

Draft Article 6, it might be said, encompassed three topics: federal power, federal supremacy, and federal coercion of recalcitrant states. As will be seen, while confirming national energy and supremacy, the Convention progressively modified Madison's expansive formulation of these attributes. It quickly abandoned the third clause of Article 6, which entertained the notion of applying force against delinquent states. This idea derived from Madison's experience in the Confederal Congress, where he advocated applying a blockade or some other form of coercion against states that were delinquent in requisition payments. But as the debate proceeded in the Convention, Madison obviously had second thoughts and moved that consideration of the clause be postponed. "The use of force agst. a State, would look more like a declaration of war, than an infliction of punishment ... He hoped that such a system would be framed as might render the recourse unnecessary." "The more he reflected on the use of force, the more he doubted the practicability, the justice and the efficacy of it when applied to people collectively and not individually."[2] In these last words he spelled out the solution that was ultimately devised. Once federal law, and especially federal tax law, was applied directly against the individual citizen, the whole question of imposing requisitions against states would be deemed immaterial.[3]

By proposing in Article 6 that in addition to the powers enjoyed by Congress under the Articles the national legislature be qualified "to legislate in all cases to which the separate States are incompetent, or in which the harmony of the United States may be interrupted by the exercise of individual [state] Legislation," the Virginia Plan was setting forth a formula for virtually open-ended federal governmental power. Unlike the Articles of Confederation, the provision referred to heads of power rather than specified, enumerated powers. Any subject that the legislature deemed national in scope or impact would now come within the exclusive purview of federal legislation, rendering states automatically "incompetent" to adopt their own laws on the matter, since these might well "interrupt the harmony of the United States." In any area in which the federal government sought to ensure national uniformity, the states would be left powerless.[4] Clearly, a government endowed with such sweeping powers would have no need to resort to any doctrine of implied powers or a supremacy clause; in the context of Article 6, such provisions would be irrelevant and superfluous.

The Virginia formula on powers was discussed by the Convention no fewer than three times. On each occasion, the extremely broad formulation of national power provoked critical comment, even from some noted nationalists.

The first discussion took place on May 31 in the Committee of the Whole, and the following colloquy ensued:

> Mr. Butler [of South Carolina] apprehended that the taking so many powers out of the hands of the States as was proposed, tended to destroy all that balance {and security} of interests among the States which it was necessary to preserve; and called on Mr. Randolph the mover of the propositions, to explain the extent of his ideas...[5]
>
> Mr. Pinkney & Mr. Rutledge [both from South Carolina] objected to the vagueness of the term *incompetent*, and said they could not well decide how to vote until they should see an exact enumeration of the powers comprehended by this definition.[6]
>
> Mr. Butler repeated his fears that we were running into an extreme in taking away the powers of the States, and called on Mr. Randolp[h] for the extent of his meaning.

In response, Mr Randolph [of Virginia] "disclaimed any intention to give indefinite powers to the national Legislature." He declared "that he was entirely opposed to such an inroad on the State jurisdictions, and that he did not think any considerations whatever could ever change his determination. His opinion was fixed on this point."[7]

> Mr. Madison said that he had brought with him into the Convention a strong bias in favor of an enumeration and definition of the powers necessary to be exercised by the national Legislature; but had also brought doubts concerning the practicability.[8] His wishes remained unaltered; but his doubts had become stronger. What his opinion might ultimately be he could not yet tell. But he should shrink from nothing which should be found essential to such a form of Govt. as would provide for the safety, liberty and happiness of the Community. This being the end of all our deliberations, all the necessary means for attaining it must, however reluctantly, be submitted to.[9]

The vote to grant powers in cases "to which the States are incompetent" was nine in favor, with none opposed and one divided; and the other clause, giving powers "necessary to preserve harmony among the States" was agreed to unanimously.[10] The report of the Committee of the Whole, submitted to the Convention on June 13, endorsed the formulation of Article 6 of the Virginia Plan on powers.[11]

It is to be noted that those delegates objecting to the broad heads of power and calling for enumeration and definition were all from the Deep South. Very clearly, they saw danger to the institution of slavery in the sweeping heads of power assigned to Congress. They knew how despised slavery was in the North, and they were concerned that a day may come when Congress might seek to emancipate the slaves or interfere in some other way with the institution of slavery. Substituting defined powers in place of broad heads of power would preclude such a possibility. On July 12, when the Convention debated the demand of the southern states for expanded representation in the lower house of Congress by reference to its slave population, the fears of their delegates once again came to the fore. General Pinckney was led to say: "Property in slaves should not be exposed to danger under a Govt. instituted for the protection of property."[12] The next day, Butler remarked: "The security the Southn. States want is that their negroes may not be taken from them which some gentlemen within or without doors, have a very good mind to do."[13] One form of security was enshrined in the inflated representation that the three-fifths rule would impart to them in the lower house. Likewise, enumeration of specific powers would forestall congressional forays into matters of slavery.

Once the Convention in mid-July settled on the Connecticut Compromise for equal representation of the states in the upper house of the legislature, discussion was resumed on various provisions, including Article 6, assigning broad heads of power to Congress. Butler once again rose to object to the extraordinary scope of the powers granted. He called for "some explanation of the extent of this [legislative] power; particularly of the word *incompetent*." "The vagueness of the terms," he said, "rendered it impossible for any precise judgment to be formed."[14] In response, Mr. Gorham of Massachusetts sought to allay Butler's fears by explaining that "the vagueness of the terms constitutes the propriety of them. We are now establishing general principles, to be extended hereafter into details which will be precise & explicit."[15] This explanation left Rutledge less than satisfied. If details were to be supplied, he wanted them to be supplied here and now. He "moved that the clause should be committed [to committee,] to the end that a specification of the powers comprised in the general terms, might be reported."[16] But the vote on his motion failed, the delegates being equally divided, 5:5.[17]

The division between the states on defining the powers of Congress was very revealing about the motives of those favoring and opposing the delimitation of national power. All the smaller states, except for Connecticut, voted against enumeration and were in favor of retention of Article 6 in its pristine form, while all the slave states, except for North Carolina, voted for enumeration. This confirms what Charles Pinckney said: "Give New Jersey an equal vote, and she will dismiss her scruples, and concur in the Natil. system."[18] Once the smaller states secured equality in the upper house they were prepared to enhance national power, since now they were part of the government. They had influence in the legislature and executive and every increase in national power was, willy nilly, a reflection of their own authority. The heads of power allowing Congress to legislate wherever the individual states were incompetent or where separate state legislation would upset national harmony, posed no threat to them since now they shared in the exercise of authority. The slave states, however, were thinking ahead, and the possibility of some administration in the future exercising the unlimited authority that Article 6 conferred represented a menace which they felt compelled to inhibit by a revision of the formula provided. As the plenum prepared to convey the resolutions that had been adopted to a Committee of Detail for formulation in a draft constitution, southern agitation for protection of slavery arose once again: "Genl. Pinkney reminded the Convention that if the Committee should fail to insert some security to the Southern States agst. an emancipation of slaves, and taxes on exports, he shd. be bound by duty to his State to vote agst. their Report."[19]

While the southern delegates were demanding specification of powers, some northerners were concerned that the division of powers between national and state authorities was not clearly defined, and this might lead to controversy. Thus on July 17, Roger Sherman of Connecticut "observed that it would be difficult to draw the line between the powers of the Genl. Legislatures, and those to be left with the States; that he did not like the definition contained in the Resolution." He therefore proposed that the following clause be inserted in the provision on powers:

> To make laws binding on the people of the United States in all cases (which may concern the common interests of the Union); but not to interfere with the {government of the individual States in any matters of internal police which respect the Govt. of such States only, and wherein the General} welfare of the United States is not concerned.[20]

Sherman's amendment, surprisingly perhaps, was seconded by nationalist James Wilson "as better expressing the general principle."[21] In this vein, he had earlier stressed that "all interference between the general and local Governmnts. should be obviated as much as possible."[22] However, Wilson's nationalist colleague from Pennsylvania, Gouverneur Morris, took exception to the proposed amendment. He found nothing wrong in infringing "the internal police" power of the states when they were guilty of committing "tricks" affecting the "Citizens" of other states, "as in the case of paper money."[23] Mr Sherman attempted to assuage Morris's concern about national authority by reading "an enumeration of powers, including the power of levying taxes on trade."[24] In response, Morris noted that the power of levying "*direct taxation*" was omitted from Sherman's enumeration. "It must have been the meaning of Mr. Sherman," said Morris, "that the Genl. Govt. should recur to quotas & requisitions, which are subversive of the idea of Govt."[25] Sherman acknowledged that provision would have to be made "for supplying the deficiency of other taxation," but as yet "he had not formed any" proposal. While Sherman's amendment evoked a positive response from some delegates, failure to include provision for a national power of direct taxation undermined the wider support necessary for adoption. As a result, his proposal failed by a vote of 2:8.[26]

Thereupon, Gunning Bedford of Delaware sought to save the first part of Sherman's amendment, which linked federal legislation with "the general interests of the Union."[27] If Bedford's amendment would be accepted, this part of the sixth resolution with the addition in italics, would now read:

{and moreover} to legislate in all cases *for the general interests of the Union*, and also in those to which the States are separately incompetent, {or in which the harmony of the U. States may be interrupted by the exercise of individual Legislation.}

By omitting the second half of Sherman's proposal, the scope of federal power was expanded, rather than curtailed.[28] Bedford's motion was seconded by Gouverneur Morris, but it prompted the following exchange:

> Mr. Randolph. This is a formidable idea indeed. It involves the power of violating all the laws and constitutions of the States, and of intermeddling with their police. The last member [part] of the sentence is {also} superfluous, being included in the first.
>
> Mr. Bedford. It is not more extensive or formidable than the clause as it stands; *no state* being *separately* competent to legislate for the *general interest* of the Union.[29]

Bedford's formulation of the clause was endorsed by a vote of 6:4, and in this form it was conveyed, a week later on July 24, to the Committee of Detail.[30]

The debate over the formulation of the powers of the national legislature demonstrated that while the South was solidly committed to scuttling the broad heads of power, there were also some delegates who wished to define more precisely the powers of the national government and to delineate the demarcation line between national and state authority. It is noteworthy that two of this group were members of the nationalist camp—James Wilson of Pennsylvania and Edmund Randolph of Virginia. Their stand assumes particular significance, since both men were selected to serve in the five-member Committee of Detail which was charged with preparing the outline of a constitution on the basis of the resolutions adopted.[31] Two other members were Nathaniel Gorham of Massachusetts, who had acknowledged that enumeration was warranted, and Oliver Ellsworth of Connecticut, a principal proponent of the idea of state equality in the upper chamber of the legislature, and a colleague of Roger Sherman, who had proposed a formula for defining the line between state and federal power. But most significantly, John Rutledge of South Carolina was selected as chairman of the Committee of Detail. Throughout the plenum debate he had led the charge on behalf of the southern states to condemn the broad heads of power. His drive for enumeration had been stymied by a tied vote. Now, as chairman of the committee charged with formulation of the provisions of the draft constitution, it was relatively simple—given the desire of other members of the Committee for a more precise division of powers between state and national authorities—to ram through the proposal he wanted.

Little wonder, therefore, that one of the first acts of the Committee was to revise the wording of the Virginia Plan and enumerate a detailed list of powers that would appertain to the national legislature. In a very early Committee draft (found among the papers of George Mason), the Virginia formula was replaced by a rudimentary list of powers, subject to exceptions and limitations in various cases.[32] A second draft incorporated, practically verbatim, the clauses on powers in the Articles of Confederation and the New Jersey Plan, as Farrand notes in his monograph on the drafting of the Constitution.[33] When the Committee of Detail completed its labor and presented its ultimate formulation to the plenum on August 6, the draft constitution contained a detailed list of federal powers closely resembling the list contained in Article 1, Section 8, of the final Constitution.[34] Southern fears had won out where small-state concern was negligible or even non-existent. In sum, while the smaller states were instrumental in introducing federalism into the Constitution through their demand for a controlling role in the national institutions of government, the slave states succeeded in modifying national power by insisting on an enumeration of defined powers in place of heads of power. True it is that the slave states alone would not have had sufficient votes to revise Article 6; they needed the support of other delegates, such as James Wilson and Roger Sherman, who sought to define the division between federal and state authority more precisely. But it is equally true that, without persistent slave state pressure to rewrite Article 6, and the fortuitous circumstance of Rutledge's chairmanship of the Committee of Detail, the provision granting the national government near-absolute national power would most likely have remained as drafted and as endorsed repeatedly by the plenum majority. As part of the Convention's concessions to the slave states, the change effected in the clause on congressional power represented, without doubt, a most significant reduction in overall national authority in the federal structure of the Constitution.

Curiously, the events enumerated above relating to the origins of federalism in the Constitution have gone largely unnoticed in the literature. One writer, however, has charged that the five members of the Committee of Detail totally transformed the Convention's resolutions to produce a much more weakened national government than was intended by the Convention plenary. John C. Hueston, in a Note that appeared in the *Yale Law Journal*,[35] condemns the conduct of the Committee as a usurpation of the plenary will. He writes: "This note suggests that rather than simply elaborating upon the existing resolutions, the Committee actually redefined the constitutional balance of state and federal powers by enhancing the rights of states at the expense of sweeping central powers."[36] According to Hueston, scholars and judges should recognize that the Committee's version was "second choice" and "should redefine" accordingly the intent of the Convention in constitutional interpretation. In making his charge, Hueston does not refer or link the issue to the slavery question.

In an article that I published in 2000,[37] I discounted Hueston's conspiratorial interpretation of the work of the Committee of Detail, primarily for one reason: When the Committee submitted its report to the Convention, there was not even a murmur of protest about the change that had replaced heads of power with defined and enumerated powers. I assumed that the delegates were satisfied that the change helped prevent clashes between the central and state governments. Undoubtedly, this was a factor with some delegates; but upon closer reading of the Minutes, it became clear—as shown in the text—that the prime consideration for enumeration was the demand of the slave states to ensure that the federal government not be empowered to interfere with the system of slavery. Rutledge of South Carolina was chairman of the Committee of Detail, and from the earliest days of the Convention he kept calling for an enumeration of powers.[38] Now, with a committee sympathetic to his concern, he rammed this through and presented it to the Convention as a fait accompli. Thus, the reason for the silence of the delegates was apparently because they recognized that this was a vital plank in the pro-slavery program and no one was prepared to oppose it, just as they did not oppose other elements in that program. What emerges is that the scheme for an all-powerful national government was revised to eclipse the scope and number of federal powers in order to accommodate the slave states.[39]

Southern delegates subsequently highlighted the manner in which slavery was now made immune from federal intervention. General Pinckney, in 1788, speaking on ratification in the South Carolina legislature, said:

> We have a security that the general government can never emancipate them, for no such authority is granted; and it is admitted, on all hands, that the general government has no powers but what are expressly granted by the Constitution, and that all rights not expressed were reserved by the several states.[40]

Most significantly, when the draft constitution of the Committee of Detail was taken up for debate by the Convention, the radical change effected in defining federal powers evoked no comment. Delegates discussed the details of the provision on powers without a single reference to the major change that had been introduced. Apparently, the delegates were aware that this was one further concession to the slave states that they had to accept, and there was no point in debating the issue again. Perhaps the inclusion of the necessary and proper clause, with its promise of a doctrine of implied powers, reassured the nationalists that the central government would still be qualified to exercise broad national authority. Regardless, the process of minimizing federal intervention in strictly state affairs emerges also from the Convention's handling of the issue of the legislative veto.

Vetoing the National Legislative Veto

As noted, Article 6 of the Virginia Plan also proposed endowing the national legislature with the right "to negative all laws passed by the several States, contravening in the opinion of the National Legislature the articles of Union." Madison's original legislative veto idea, from which this clause derived, had been even more ambitious.

In his March 19, 1787 letter to Thomas Jefferson, it will be recalled,[41] Madison had highlighted the need "to arm the federal head with a negative *in all cases whatsoever* on the local Legislatures."⁴² He persisted in this vein in his letter of April 16, 1787, to George Washington, in which he wrote:

> A negative *in all cases whatsoever* on the legislative acts of the States, as heretofore exercised by the Kingly prerogative, appears to me to be absolutely necessary, and to be the least possible encroachment on the State jurisdictions. Without this defensive power, every positive power that can be given on paper will be evaded & defeated. The States will continue to invade the national jurisdiction, to violate treaties and the law of nations & to harass each other with rival and spiteful measures dictated by mistaken views of interest. Another happy effect of this prerogative would be its controul on the internal vicissitudes of State policy; and the aggressions of interested majorities on the rights of minorities and of individuals.⁴³

Madison's emphasis of the term "in all cases whatsoever" and his reference to the "Kingly prerogative" accurately reflected his conception of the legislative veto as an absolute instrument with which to control the state governments.⁴⁴ In the Virginia Plan, the veto was significantly, if subtly, modified. It was to extend only to such state laws as the National Legislature deemed to be "contravening ... the articles of the Union." While resolved to tilt the balance of governmental powers towards the central government, Virginia's Convention delegates had no desire to cripple state governments by interfering in their purely domestic affairs. The expansion of national authority did not, in their view, require the extreme denial of state sovereignty envisaged by Madison. So long as state action did not invade the prerogatives of the national government, there was no justification for the exercise of a national legislative veto.

Despite the setback he had sustained in the Virginia caucus, Madison continued to raise the issue of an absolute legislative veto several times during the Convention.⁴⁵ On May 31, the limited veto formula of the Virginia Plan was accepted by the Committee of the Whole without "debate or dissent."⁴⁶ A week later, on June 8, Charles Pinckney of South Carolina, acting obviously in concert with Madison, moved that the legislative veto extend to "all Laws which they [members of the national legislature] shd. judge to be improper."⁴⁷ "A universality of the power," he said, "was indispensably necessary to render it effectual." "The States must be kept in due subordination to the nation; that if the States were left to act of themselves ... it wd. be impossible to defend the national prerogatives, however extensive they might be on paper; that the acts of Congress had been defeated by this means."

Madison seconded Pinckney's motion:

> [A]n indefinite power to negative legislative acts of the States ... [was] absolutely necessary to a perfect system. Experience had evinced a constant tendency in the States to encroach on the federal authority; to violate national Treaties, to infringe the rights & interests of each other; to oppress the weaker party within their respective jurisdictions... Should no such precaution be engrafted, the only remedy wd. lie in an appeal to coercion... The negative wd. render the use of force

unnecessary. The States cd. of themselves then pass no operative act, any more than one branch of a Legislature where there are two branches, can proceed without the other... In a word, to recur to the illustrations borrowed from the planetary System, This prerogative of the General Govt. is the great pervading principle that must controul the centrifugal tendency of the States; which, without it, will continually fly out of their proper orbits and destroy the order & harmony of the political system.[48]

The Pinckney–Madison proposal for a comprehensive legislative veto was vigorously attacked. "The Natl. Legislature with such a power," declared Elbridge Gerry of Massachusetts, "may enslave the States. Such an idea as this will never be acceded to."[49] Gunning Bedford of Delaware voiced the fears of the smaller states:

> [He] would refer ... to the smallness of his own State which may be injured at pleasure without redress. It was meant ... to strip the small States of their equal right of suffrage. In this case Delaware would have about 1/90 {for its} share in the General Councils, whilst Pa. & Va. would possess 1/3 of the whole. Is there no difference of interests, no rivalship of commerce, of manufactures? Will not these large States crush the small ones whenever they stand in the way of their ambitions or interested views. This shows the impossibility of adopting such a system as that on the table... It seems as if Pa. & Va. by the conduct of their deputies wished to provide a system in which they would have an enormous & monstrous influence.[50]

Bedford also raised practical considerations that he considered insuperable. "Are the laws of the States to be suspended in the most urgent cases until they can be sent seven or eight hundred miles, and undergo the deliberations of a body who may be incapable of Judging them? Is the National Legislature too to sit continually in order to revise the laws of the States?"[51] Madison attempted to resolve the practical difficulties by suggesting procedures for implementing the comprehensive negative,[52] but his scheme was dismissed by Pierce Butler of South Carolina "as cutting off all hope of equal justice to the distant States." "The people there," he was sure, "would not ... [even] give it a hearing."[53] The suggestion to broaden the national legislative veto was voted down by a 3:7:1 majority.[54] The Report of the Committee of the Whole adhered to the pattern of the Virginia Plan in limiting the legislative veto to instances of unconstitutional state action.[55]

The issue of the national legislative veto was taken up again on July 17, immediately after the question of the composition of the second house was settled. The right of the national legislature to nullify state laws that, in its view, violated the Constitution, was vigorously criticized.[56] Gouverneur Morris, a foremost nationalist, opposed the power "as likely to be terrible to the States, and not necessary, if sufficient Legislative authority should be given to the Genl. Government." Roger Sherman of Connecticut "thought it unnecessary, as the Courts of the States would not consider as valid any law contravening the

Authority of the Union." Luther Martin of Maryland "considered the power as improper & inadmissable." "Shall all the laws of the States be sent up to the Genl. Legislature before they shall be permitted to operate?" he asked.

This criticism prompted Madison once again to expound on the essentiality of the veto "to the efficacy & security of the Genl. Govt." "A power of negativing the improper laws of the States is at once the most mild & certain means of preserving the harmony of the system." He adverted to the British example where "harmony & subordination of the various parts of the empire" were maintained thanks to "the prerogative by which means the Crown, stifles in the birth every Act of every part tending to discord or encroachment."[57]

As the debate wore on, Gouverneur Morris indicated that he was "more & more opposed to the negative." It would, he declared, "disgust all the States. A law that ought to be negatived will be set aside in the Judiciary departmt. and if that security should fail; may be repealed by a Nationl. law."[58] The opposition to the legislative veto was sufficiently strong to lead to its complete elimination from the draft constitution by a vote of 7:3.[59] The three states voting in favor of the legislative veto were Massachusetts, Virginia, and North Carolina—all large or relatively large states. All the smaller states voted with the majority to eliminate the legislative veto entirely.

With the elimination of any authority qualified to umpire federal-state relations, Luther Martin of Maryland now moved the adoption of a supremacy clause binding "the Judiciaries of the several States" to treat federal legislation as "the supreme law of the respective States" "any thing in the respective laws of the individual States to the contrary notwithstanding."[60] Martin's proposal was accepted unanimously.[61] Later, the provision was revised to include a reference to the Constitution itself, so as to make it and the laws of the United States "the supreme Law of the Land"—and not merely of the states.[62] This clause, derived, as noted earlier, from the New Jersey Plan, was intended to substitute the court for the legislature in ensuring that national laws were not disregarded by the states (as they had been under the Articles of Confederation) and that in the event of a federal-state clash, the laws of the federal government would prevail in its area of jurisdiction. The supremacy clause was thus the basis for the judicial review of state legislation, without which, as Justice Holmes declared, "the Union would be imperiled."[63] (In *Marbury v. Madison*, Chief Justice Marshall would later invoke the supremacy clause to justify establishing the principle of judicial review over federal legislation as well.)

Even as the Convention was drawing to a close, a last-minute attempt was made to institute some form of national legislative veto. The various federalizing changes made in the draft constitution made it more imperative than ever that a legislative veto be on hand to bind the nation. On August 23, Pinckney moved that Congress, by a vote of two-thirds of both houses, be empowered to cancel state laws that interfered "with the General interests and harmony of the Union." Pinckney stressed that the smaller states would not be disadvantaged by this form of the legislative veto. "The objection drawn from the predominance of the large {States} had been removed by the equality established in the

Senate."[64] Madison proposed that the issue be taken up by a committee.[65] Even James Wilson, who had endorsed enumeration of federal powers, supported Pinckney's veto proposal "as the key-stone wanted to compleat the wide arch of Government" being raised. "The power of self-defence had been urged as necessary for the State Governments—It was equally necessary for the General Government."[66]

Emphasizing the practical difficulties of administering such a veto, George Mason queried: "Is no road nor bridge to be established without the Sanction of the General Legislature? Is this to sit constantly in order to receive & revise the State Laws?"[67] John Rutledge, Pinckney's fellow delegate from South Carolina who had served as chairman of the Committee of Detail, was clearly outraged by the proposal. "If nothing else, this alone would damn and ought to damn the Constitution," he said, adding: "Will any State ever agree to be bound hand & foot in this manner."[68] Ellsworth of Connecticut condemned the proposal as possibly implying that "the State Executives should be appointed by the Genl Government, and have a controul over the State laws."[69] John Langdon of New Hampshire highlighted the matter at issue. It was "resolvable," he said, "into the question whether the extent of the National Constitution was to be judged of by the Genl or the State Governments."[70] In this, he differed from Roger Sherman of Connecticut who thought the motion "unnecessary; the laws of the General Government being Supreme & paramount to the State laws."[71] Though Pinckney's proposal represented a significant concession to the smaller states by requiring a two-thirds majority in both houses, it failed, by a 5:6 vote, to be sent to committee.[72]

The foregoing review confirms that, while the Convention was determined to establish federal supremacy, it was equally led to carefully confine this supremacy to the essential requirements of the Union. These requirements were spelled out in the Constitution in both positive and negative terms—in the enumeration of federal powers in Article 1, Section 8, and in the imposition of prohibitions on the states in Article 1, Section 10. The purpose of both provisions was to restrict federal power to the national sphere while excluding state encroachment on that sphere. Matters deemed inherently national were completely removed from state competence so as to avoid any cause for friction. Thus coinage, for example, was listed as a federal power and was also explicitly denied to the states. At the same time, the Convention spurned the idea of ongoing federal involvement in the exclusively internal affairs of the states. As summed up by Gouverneur Morris: "Within the State itself a majority must rule, whatever may be the mischief done among themselves."[73]

The debate had underscored the extreme divergence between Madison, who campaigned vigorously for a blanket legislative veto, and the majority, who opposed any national legislative role in disallowing state laws, even those deemed manifestly unconstitutional. That task would be handled by the courts, not by the national legislature. State autonomy was to be preserved even while the federal government was strengthened and accorded paramountcy.

4 DELIMITING THE SCOPE OF NATIONAL AUTHORITY 71

The Convention's handling of the entire subject of national powers and a legislative veto is neatly summarized by Madison in his letter of October 24, 1787 to Jefferson:

> The second object, the due partition of power, between the General & local Governments, was perhaps of all, the most nice and difficult. A few contended for an entire abolition of the States; some for indefinite power of Legislation in the Congress, with a negative on the laws of the States: some for such a power without a negative: some for a limited power of legislation, with such a negative: the majority finally for a limited power without the negative.[74]

Madison had favored the second proposition: "indefinite power of Legislation in the Congress, with a negative on the laws of the States"[75]; but the majority endorsed "limited power without the negative." In short, Madison's scheme for open-ended heads of power for the national legislature, as outlined in the Virginia Plan, was rejected—thanks to slave states' concern—in favor of a list of defined powers carefully enumerated, following the pattern of the Articles of Confederation and the New Jersey Plan. And even the qualified legislative veto of the Virginia Plan, restricted to nullifying unconstitutional state laws, was totally abandoned, thanks largely to the concerns of the small states. Federal powers were to be enhanced, and national supremacy confirmed, but not at the expense of every semblance of state sovereignty.

The consequences of abandoning Article 6 of the Virginia Plan were far-reaching and impressive. In place of an all-powerful legislature, the United States received a Congress of limited, defined powers directed strictly to the fulfillment of national needs, with no authority to intervene in state affairs on an ongoing basis or to meddle in strictly state concerns. In particular, slavery was out of bounds for federal legislation. Instead of being totally submerged and subordinated components of the national government, the states would survive as independent, sovereign political entities exercising governmental control at the local level and with notable representation and influence in the national institutions of government. Moreover, quite significantly, the courts emerged as the umpire of federal-state relations. A constitutional system in which Congress would have possessed the power to veto state legislation would not likely have encompassed judicial review as we know it—whether in respect of state or federal laws. Judicial review was thus a direct by-product of the replacement of the clause in the Virginia Plan on broad heads of power with the format of defined powers, coupled with the introduction of the supremacy clause, as a natural concomitant of the abandonment of legislative supervision of the federal-state constitutional nexus.

In sum, parochial state pressure groups with special interests succeeded in introducing federalism into the new system of government, and one of the groups also worked to whittle down the range of national power. The Constitutional Convention was instrumental in producing a nation at Philadelphia, but it was a different being from that originally envisaged by the

Federalist architects. Federal supremacy was ensured, but only within the range of the enumerated powers. Moreover, Congress was not authorized to decide for itself what it could or could not do. If the judiciary deemed the proposed action to fall within the scope of one of the enumerated powers, the government could act; if not, it could not. While national supremacy and energy were preserved in the final draft, they were restrained by force of the federal framework superimposed on the national design by the demands of the smaller and slave states.

The Convention had confirmed the creation of the nation, but not at the price of obliterating the states. If the aim of the Founding Fathers was to revise the division of powers between center and periphery, they had succeeded admirably. The states survived and the national government was not all-powerful, but it was paramount. How paramount was a matter for judicial determination.

This interpretation of the federal character of the Constitution is of particular significance, given the latest trend of the Supreme Court to act vigorously in protecting what it deems to be state sovereignty and independence, as will be seen below in the Postscript.

Constitutional Flexibility

The revamping of both parts of Article 6 of the Virginia Plan—the section on powers and that on the legislative veto—signified more than just the mutation of Madison's radical plan of nearly unlimited national governmental power. Above all, it reflected the federalization of the Constitution and rejection of the drive to superimpose the national government on the states. Energy and supremacy for the central government would be preserved, but the states would be endowed with a significant role in the functioning of the federal system. Thus, the demands of states-minded delegates—especially from the smaller states and slave states—would be met in this sphere, even as they were accommodated with respect to the composition of the upper house, the process for selecting a national executive, and the scope of federal power.

However, this dramatic change in the pattern of the federal government naturally aroused concern among the Federalists, who worried that the calamitous mistakes and rigidity of the Articles of Confederation might be replicated in the new constitutional framework. To ensure the desired flexibility, they strove to have the Constitution incorporate a doctrine of implied powers and a procedure for amendments by less than unanimity. This is the background to the addition to the Constitution of both the necessary and proper clause and Article V.

Had Article 1 of the Constitution been limited to an enumeration of specific powers, it might well have been subjected to the kind of restrictive interpretation that hobbled the Confederal Congress. Even without a provision corresponding to Article II of the Articles of Confederation that confined the legislature to the powers expressly granted, the constitutional grant of powers might have been deemed finite, and any attempt to extrapolate additional subsidiary powers from those enumerated might have been perceived as an illegitimate attempt to aggrandize federal power at the expense of the states. Evidently, it was to obviate any such possibility that the Committee of Detail decided to add the necessary and proper clause as the final number in the list of eighteen clauses enumerating the powers conferred on the national legislature under Article 1, Section 8. Congress was now empowered "to make all Laws which shall be necessary and proper for carrying into Execution the foregoing Powers, and all other Powers vested by this Constitution in the Government of the United States, or in any Department or Officer thereof." No one objected to the inclusion of this clause among the defined powers of Congress. Thereby the doctrine of implied powers became an integral part of the Constitution.[76] Apparently, the slave states did not regard the "sweeping" clause as an open-ended avenue for the expansion of national power. Only in the ratification contest did the clause become the focus of dispute. As Leonard Levy observed, "That 'necessary and proper' clause was the most formidable in the array of national powers, therefore the most controversial, and the one most responsible later for the demand for a bill of rights to ensure that the United States did not violate the rights of the people or of the states."[77]

The background to the adoption of Article V of the Constitution on formal amendments also attests to the determination of the Federalists to remove the shackles of the Articles by allowing the new instrument of government to adjust to changing circumstances. Amendments would require something less than unanimous consent to enter into force.

> On amendments, the Virginia Plan contained the following paragraph (Resolution 13):
>
> Res[olve]d. that provision ought to be made for the amendment of the Articles of Union whensoever it shall seem necessary, and that the assent of the National Legislature ought not to be required thereto.[78]

The logic behind the draft, and especially that of the last clause, was provided by George Mason in the plenum debate:

> The plan now to be formed will certainly be defective, as the Confederation has been found on trial to be. Amendments therefore will be necessary, and it will be better to provide for them, in an easy, regular and Constitutional way than to trust to chance and violence. It would be improper to require the consent of the Natl. Legislature, because they may abuse their power, and refuse their consent on that very account.[79]

In accordance with this logic, the report of the Committee of Detail, delivered on August 6, contained the following draft passage, which appears to have originated with James Wilson:

> On the application of the Legislatures of two thirds of the States in the Union, for an amendment of this Constitution, the Legislature of the United States shall call a Convention for that purpose.[80]

Under this scheme, the role of Congress was limited to calling a convention. The term "shall" was peremptory, leaving no room for congressional discretion or abuse. Later, at the suggestion of Gouverneur Morris, the legislature was also given the power to summon a convention without prior application from the states.[81] However, when the provision came up for reconsideration on September 10, there was no reference in the draft provision to the possibility of a national legislative initiative to call a convention; and certainly the legislature was not empowered to propose amendments itself. Gouverneur Morris's suggestion had somehow been lost in the shuffle.[82] This explains why Hamilton now expressed reservations about relying on the states exclusively for the adoption of amendments.[83] The Articles of Confederation had suffered from a lack of an easy method of introducing amendments, he said, and the new System should not suffer from the same shortcoming." "The mode proposed was not adequate. The State Legislatures will not apply for alterations but with a view to increase their own powers." He therefore suggested that the National Legislature also be empowered to summon a convention whenever it saw fit. "The National Legislature will be the first to perceive and will be most sensible to the necessity of amendments."

In the meantime, it appears that Madison had become skeptical about the idea of entrusting amendments to conventions. No doubt the experience with the Constitutional Convention itself—which had abandoned all pretense of adhering to the instructions that the states and Congress had stipulated—induced him to modify his earlier views and to waver:

> Mr Madison remarked on the vagueness of the terms, "call a Convention for the purpose." as sufficient reason for reconsidering the article. How was a Convention to be formed? by what rule decide? ... what the force of its acts?[84]

Roger Sherman then proposed that the National Legislature also be empowered to propose amendments, subject to state approval. It was decided that the approval be conditioned on the acquiescence of three-quarters of the states.[85] Thus, at this point, the amendment provision allowed for Congress to propose draft amendments and for the states to propose a convention. Not content with the provision as then formulated, Madison submitted, and Hamilton seconded, a new draft provision that discarded any reference to a convention.[86] Instead, two-thirds of the Legislature would be qualified to initiate an amendment or endorse one requested by two-thirds of the states. Approval by three-quarters of the state legislatures or state conventions would be required for the amendment to enter into force. The plenum accepted the formula, which was incorporated as clause XIX in the draft constitution submitted to the Committee of Style.[87]

This formula was noteworthy for having abandoned the whole notion of a free-floating convention competent to draft amendments on its own.[88]

In the final reading of the draft constitution on September 15, 2 days before the Convention was to rise, George Mason, now thoroughly disillusioned with the Constitution, expressed his dissatisfaction with the formula of Article V, the provision on amendments. It was, he said, "exceptionable & dangerous." As now formulated, congressional approval was required either "immediately" or "ultimately" for amendments. He reiterated his fear of congressional obstructionism: "No amendments of the proper kind would ever be obtained by the people, if the Government should become oppressive, as he verily believed would be the case."[89] Intent on soothing ruffled feathers as the Convention was drawing to a close, and hoping thereby to encourage all delegates to sign the completed document, Gouverneur Morris proposed that the congressional method of adopting amendments be supplemented with a convention route, when two-thirds of the states apply for it.[90] Madison, reflecting his deep suspicion of conventions, "did not see why Congress would not be as much bound to propose amendments applied for by two thirds of the States as to call a Convention on the like application." He was not opposed, he said, to the idea of a convention, but the issue raised difficult technical questions regarding "the form, the quorum &c."[91] Madison's reservations notwithstanding, the Convention unanimously approved the Morris amendment,[92] and in this form it was published in the completed Constitution.[93]

In sum, the amendment procedure was one that was perceived by the delegates to be neither too easy nor too difficult and cumbersome. A broad, but nevertheless attainable, consensus would need to underlie the adoption of constitutional amendments. As noted by Madison in *Federalist* #43,[94] the procedure "guards equally against that extreme facility, which would render the Constitution too mutable; and that extreme difficulty which might perpetuate its discovered faults." Moreover, it enables both national and state governments to originate amendments "as they may be pointed out by the experience on one side or the other." The limitations on the amendment power represented "a palladium to the residuary sovereignty of the States."

At the same time, a doctrine of implied powers was assured by means of an express clause in the provision on congressional powers. In lieu of Madison's scheme for an all-powerful national government, under which reference to implied powers would have been superfluous, the Convention opted for a federal system of government in which powers and authority would be shared between center and periphery. There was no question that the national government would be armed with all requisite energy and supremacy, far removed from the "imbecilic" legislature of the era of the Confederation. The Convention successfully drafted a vibrant instrument of government that would allow for national domination of the states, but not for their obliteration. Energy and supremacy were balanced within a flexible federal framework. The task of the Federalists was now to convince the nation that these arrangements would promote, not threaten, the welfare of the American people.

As noted earlier, Madison, however, was convinced that the Constitutional Convention had failed, that the Federalist Revolution had been stymied. He had envisaged an all-powerful national government that would suppress the states—in short, a system of government that would be devoid of federalism in any meaningful sense. Instead, while the Constitution created a national government armed with a supremacy clause, it did so within a federal framework. Federalism permeated all spheres of effective government—the composition of the national legislature, the range of national powers, the system for selecting a chief executive, and the method for amending the Constitution. Given Madison's obsession with the legislative veto, little wonder that he was deeply disappointed that it had not been incorporated in the Constitution. He gave voice to his distress in two letters to Jefferson. In the first, dated September 6, even before the Convention rose, he wrote: "I hazard an opinion ... that the *plan should* it *be adopted* will neither effectually *answer* its *national object* nor prevent the local *mischiefs* which every where *excite disgusts* agst. the *state governments*. The grounds of this opinion will be the subject of a future letter."[95] The follow-up letter, dated October 24, 1787, was a lengthy essay in which Madison analyzed the results of the Convention. In it he explained in detail why, in his view, the national legislative veto was critically important to the successful operation of the federal system and to the protection of individual rights within the states.[96]

> Wthout such a check in the whole over the parts, our system involves the evil of imperia in imperio [divided government]. If a compleat supremacy some where is not necessary in every Society, a controuling power at least is so, by which the general authority may be defended against encroachments of the subordinate authorities, and by which the latter may be restrained from encroachments on each other ... without the royal negative or some equivalent controul, the unity of the [British] system would be destroyed. The want of some such provision seems to have been mortal to the antient Confederacies, and to be the disease of the modern... Still more to the purpose is our own experience both during the war and since the peace. Encroachments of the States on the general authority, sacrifices of national to local interests, interferences of the measures of different States, form a great part of the history of our political system... It may be said that the Judicial authority under our new system will keep the States within their proper limits, and supply the place of a negative on their laws. The answer is, that it is more convenient to prevent the passage of a law, than to declare it void after it is passed.[97]

In the second paragraph of his lengthy epistle, Madison contended that, without the legislative veto, individual rights in the states would be in danger:

> The evils issuing from these sources [in the states] contributed more to that uneasiness which produced the Convention, and prepared the public mind for a general reform, than those which accrued to our national character and interest from the inadequacy of the Confederation to its immediate objects. A reform

therefore which does not make provision for private rights, must be materially defective.[98]

Madison quickly overcame his forebodings about the survivability of the Union under the Constitution, notwithstanding his conviction that the omission of an all-embracing federal veto was a fatal error. He actively promoted the ratification of the Constitution by expounding its virtues in the series of *Federalist Papers*, which he published in conjunction with Alexander Hamilton and John Jay. For the cause of the Federalist Revolution in which Madison and the other delegates were engaged, it is perhaps most fortunate that the strongly nationalist position advocated by Madison on federal energy (powers) and supremacy was not accepted by the Convention majority. The adoption of Madison's legislative veto might so have diminished the prospects of ratification as to doom the entire constitutional enterprise. As Clinton Rossiter has said, "The whole of clause 6 of the Virginia Plan [on national powers and a legislative veto] would have been too large a dose of nationalism for most Americans to swallow."[99] Notwithstanding Madison's pessimistic assessment, the Federalists had succeeded brilliantly in creating a federal government endowed with primary powers and manifestly superior in its jurisdiction to the states. The twin essentials of energy and supremacy were safely enshrined in the Constitution. On the other hand, it would be the aim of the Antifederalists to demonstrate that the inordinate measure of energy and supremacy with which the federal government was now armed would endanger individual liberty within the states and undermine the federal character of the Union. The ratification debates would very much revolve around this one issue, and ultimately they would generate the impulse leading to the adoption of a bill of rights.

Notes

1. Farrand, *Records*, 1: 21.
2. Ibid., 54. Given the strong objections that such a suggestion evoked regarding the possible use of force against any of the states, it is surprising that Madison included such a clause in the Virginia Plan, and even more surprising that the Virginia delegates adopted the proviso for inclusion in the Plan.
3. In this regard, see the following comments. Edmund Randolph: "The true question is whether we shall adhere to the federal plan, or introduce the national plan." The former, of necessity, had to rely on the application of force. "We must resort therefore to a national *Legislation over individuals.*" Ibid., 1: 255–256. Emphasis in original. Oliver Ellsworth in the Connecticut Ratifying Convention, January 7, 1788: "The only question is, Shall it be a coercion of law, or a coercion of arms?... I am for coercion by law—that coercion which acts only upon delinquent individuals. This Constitution does not attempt to coerce sovereign bodies, states, in their political capacity." Ibid., 3: 241. Nonetheless, several state ratifying conventions called for requisitions upon states to be instituted before taxes were imposed directly on individuals, and they proposed the adoption of an amendment to this effect. Requisitions, are pre-eminently impositions on the states, as such. The first state to

propose such a draft amendment was Massachusetts, in its ratification of the Constitution on February 6, 1788. Congress would first notify each state of the amount of its requisition, and upon payment by the state, no direct tax on individuals would be imposed. Failure to pay would allow Congress to impose a penalty at the rate of 6% per annum. See Tansill, *Documents*, 1019. South Carolina, New Hampshire, Virginia, New York, North Carolina, and Rhode Island all followed suit. Ibid., 1023, 1025, 1031, 1039, 1048, 1057.

4. "This proposal, had it been allowed to stand, would have given Congress vast authority of a vague and undefined character, inconsistent with the very nature of a federal state." Alfred H. Kelly and Winfred A. Harbison, *The American Constitution: Its Origin and Development*, 3rd ed. (New York: Norton, 1955), 143.
5. Farrand, *Records*, 1: 51.
6. Ibid., 1: 53. The queries of the South Carolina delegates regarding the scope of national powers under the Virginia Plan clearly reflected concern about the possibility of national interference with the system of slavery.
7. Ibid., 1: 53.
8. Irving Brant, who saw Madison's original minute, indicates that the phrase read "grave doubts" but that Madison subsequently crossed out "grave," leaving it as in the text. See Irving Brant, *James Madison, Father of the Constitution: 1787–1800* (Indianapolis, IN: Bobbs-Merrill, 1950), 36.
9. Farrand, *Records*, 1: 51, 53. William Pierce of Georgia records Madison's remarks as follows: "Mr. Maddison said he had brought with him a strong prepossession for the defining of the limits and powers of the federal Legislature, but he brought with him some doubts about the practicability of doing it:—at present he was convinced it could not be done." Ibid., 1: 60. Many years later, in 1833, Madison sought to convey the impression that the broad formulation of powers in the Virginia Plan was never intended to be adopted as is. He wrote: "It can not be supposed that these descriptive phrases were to be left in their indefinite extent to Legislative discretion. A selection & definition of the cases embraced by them was to be the task of the Convention. If there could be any doubt that this was intended, & so understood by the Convention, it would be removed by the course of proceeding on them as recorded, in its Journal. many of the propositions made in the Convention, fall within this remark: being, as is not unusual general in their phrase, but if adopted to be reduced to their proper shape & specification." Ibid., 3: 526–527. This interpretation does not seem to coincide with the views he expressed at the Convention, as indicated in the text and in Pierce's minutes. Nor does it coincide with the description of the debate on powers he subsequently conveyed to Jefferson, as will be seen below. See text at n. 74. See also Charles Warren, *The Making of the Constitution* (Boston, MA: Little, Brown, 1928), 164.
10. Farrand, *Records*, 1: 47, 54.
11. Ibid., 1: 229, 236.
12. Ibid., 1: 594.
13. Ibid., 1: 605.
14. Ibid., 2: 17. Emphasis in original.
15. Ibid.
16. Ibid.
17. Ibid.
18. Ibid., 1: 255.
19. Ibid., 2: 95.

20. Ibid., 2: 25.
21. Ibid., 2: 26.
22. Ibid., 1: 49. See also the following remarks by Wilson: "By a Natl. Govt. he did not mean one that would swallow up the state Govts. as seemed to be wished by some gentlemen. He thought… that they might {not} only subsist but subsist on friendly terms with the former." Ibid., 322. "If security is necessary to preserve the one, it is equally so to preserve the other…. [L]et us try to designate the powers of each, and then no danger can be apprehended nor can the general government be possessed of any ambitious views to encroach on the state rights." Ibid., 363.
23. Ibid., 2: 26.
24. Ibid.
25. Ibid., Emphasis in original.
26. Ibid.
27. Ibid.
28. It may seem strange that Bedford, from the small state of Delaware, should have presented a motion that tended to expand national power—the more so since he had earlier warned the larger states that denial of state equality in at least one branch of the legislature would prompt the smaller states to "find some foreign ally … who will take them by the hand and do them justice." Ibid., 1: 492. Bedford, however, was apparently not averse to expansion of national power so long as state equality was assured. What was needed, from his perspective, was "Enlarging the federal powers not annihilating the federal system." Ibid.
29. Ibid., 2: 26–27, Emphasis in original. (Additions in curved brackets are in original; those in square brackets are by the author).
30. Ibid., 85, 95. For the text of the provision as conveyed to the Committee of Detail, see ibid., 2: 131–132.
31. Ibid., 2: 97, 106.
32. Committee of Detail, IV, ibid., 2: 142–144.
33. Committee of Detail, VII, ibid., 2: 157. The very next draft constitution, IX, presents an enumeration of powers. Ibid., 2: 167–168. It is instructive to note the following observations by Farrand:
    > In tracing the work of the committee [of Detail] through its various stages a number of interesting and important things are noticeable. The first of these is that the document which proved to be of the most service to the committee was the articles of confederation… The provisions for the powers of congress, the prohibitions placed upon state action, … were taken directly from the articles… It is not too much to say that the articles of confederation were at the basis of the new constitution… the next most useful documents were the New Jersey and Pinckney plans. These were used… more for the purpose of assistance in wording various sections and clauses.

    Max Farrand, *The Framing of the Constitution of the United States* (New Haven, CT: Yale University Press, 1913), 127–128.
34. Jack N. Rakove maintains that replacement of the original open-ended formula of the Virginia Plan with a finite list of powers was probably intended from the beginning. *Original Meanings: Politics and Ideas in the Making of the Constitution* (New York: Knopf, 1996), 84, 178. Lance Banning, going even further, declares categorically that Madison, and the Convention generally, never entertained the

thought of leaving the powers of Congress unenumerated. *The Sacred Fire of Liberty: James Madison and the Founding of the Federal Republic* (Ithaca, NY: Cornell University Press, 1995), 159. In this he concurs with Michael P. Zuckert, "Federalism and the Founding: Toward A Reinterpretation of the Constitutional Convention," *Review of Politics*, 48 (1986): 178–180. As noted, however, this conclusion would seem not to accord with Madison's summation on the subject of powers in his letter to Jefferson, as cited below in text at n. 74. The interpretation presented above in n. 9 coincides with that reached by Irving Brant, *James Madison: Father of the Constitution 1787–1800* (Indianapolis, IN: Bobbs-Merrill, 1950), 35–36. However, Brant does not cite Madison's letter to Jefferson.
35. John C. Hueston, "Note: Altering the Course of the Constitutional Convention: The Role of the Committee of Detail in Establishing the Balance of State and Federal Powers," *Yale Law Journal*, 100 (1990–1991: 765–783.
36. Ibid., 766.
37. See Shlomo Slonim, "Securing States' Interests at the 1787 Constitutional Convention: A Reassessment," *Studies in American Political Development*, 14 (2000): 1–19.
38. See Farrand, *Records*, 1: 53.
39. In listing the concessions which the slave states extracted from the northern states, Paul Finkelman notes that "Congress's powers were limited and could never reach the slaveowner." In support, he cites the statement of General Pinckney at the South Carolina ratifying convention, noted in the text. "The Constitution and the Intentions of the Framers: The Limits of Historical Analysis," *University of Pittsburgh Law Review*, 50 (1988–1989): 349 at 381.
40. Farrand, *Records*, 3: 254. In 1820, Charles Pinckney, addressing the House of Representatives, said:
> It was an agreed point, a solemnly understood compact, that, on the Southern States consenting to shut their ports against the importation of Africans, no power was to be delegated to Congress, nor were they ever to be authorized to touch the question of slavery. Ibid., 3: 443.
41. See discussion above, Chap. 2, text at n. 49. Emphasis added.
42. *JMP*, 9: 318. Emphasis in original. Jefferson, it should be noted, objected to the veto proposal. "It fails in an essential character, that the hole & the patch should be commensurate. But this proposes to mend a small hole by covering the whole garment." Ibid., 10: 64 (June 20, 1787). In place of a legislative veto, Jefferson suggested a federal judicial veto for controlling unconstitutional state legislation. "Would not an appeal from the state judicatures to a federal court, in all cases where the act of Confederation controuled the question, be as effectual a remedy, & exactly commensurate to the defect."
43. Ibid., 9: 383–384. Emphasis in original. See also Madison's letter to Randolph, April 8, 1787, ibid., 368–371.
44. During discussion of the legislative veto at the Convention, Madison stated that it would make the national legislature "an essential branch of the State Legislatures." Farrand, *Records*, 1: 447. Charles F. Hobson, the author of a pathbreaking article on the subject, concluded that "Madison proposed nothing less than an organic union of the general and state governments." "The Negative on State Laws: James

Madison, the Constitution, and the Crisis of Republican Government," *William and Mary Quarterly*, 36, Third Series (1979): 219. Michael P. Zuckert presents a different perspective on the national character of Madison's scheme. He writes: "There is no hint that Madison favored granting the legislature of the general government plenary or full legislative power." See Michael P. Zuckert, "A System Without Precedent: Federalism in the American Constitution" in Leonard W. Levy and Dennis J. Mahoney (eds.), *The Framing and Ratification of the Constitution* (New York: Macmillan, 1987), 145. However, Article 6 of the Virginia Plan did provide for the national legislature to legislate wherever the separate states are incompetent or where national harmony would be affected—a provision which broadens the scope of legislation immeasurably. Also cf. Edward J. Erler, "The Constitution and the Separation of Powers," ibid., 162.
45. Farrand, *Records*, 1: 318, 447; 2: 440, 589.
46. Ibid., 1: 47, 54. At the suggestion of Benjamin Franklin, the legislative veto was extended to cover also state laws violating treaties.
47. Ibid., 1: 164. In this regard, it might be noted that an outline of what has been described as the Pinckney Plan, submitted to the Convention on May 29, contained the following clause: "No Bill of the Legislature of any State shall become a law till it shall have been laid before S. & H.D. in C. assembled and received their Approbation." Ibid., 2: 135, and 3: 607.
48. Ibid., 1: 164–165.
49. Ibid., 1: 165–166.
50. Ibid., 1: 167.
51. Ibid., 1: 167–168.
52. Ibid., 1: 168. For the purpose of affirming urgent state legislation, Madison suggested the possibility of "some emanation of the power from the Natl. Govt. into each State so far as to give a temporary assent at least."
53. Ibid.
54. Ibid., 1: 162–163, 168.
55. Ibid., 1: 225, 229.
56. Ibid., 2: 27–28.
57. Ibid. In his later years, Madison discussed the notion that lay behind the suggestion for a legislative veto, and said: "In every proceeding of the Convention where the question of paramountship in the laws of the Union could be involved, the necessity of it appears to have been taken for granted." Ibid., 3: 523. See also ibid., 549.
58. Ibid., 2: 28.
59. Ibid.
60. Ibid., 2: 28–29. It is somewhat curious that Martin, of all people, was the one who moved the resolution on the supremacy clause. For his explanation of his initiative, see the citations in Farrand, Records, 2: 29, n. 12.
61. Ibid., 2: 22, 29.
62. Ibid., 2: 389, 603. It was apparently at the initiative of John Rutledge that the express reference to the Constitution was added.
63. Oliver W. Holmes, "Law and the Court," *Collected Legal Papers* (New York: Harcourt Brace, 1921), 295. On the role assumed by the judiciary in the constitutional system, see two outstanding articles, Ralph A. Rossum, "The Courts and the Judicial Power" and Charles A. Lofgren, "War Powers, Treaties, and the Constitution" in Levy and Mahoney, *Framing and Ratification*, 222–241 and 242–258.

64. Farrand, Records, 2: 390.
65. Ibid., 2: 390.
66. Ibid., 2: 391.
67. Ibid., 2: 390.
68. Ibid., 2: 391.
69. Ibid. Interestingly enough, Pinckney, in reply, indeed recommended that "State Executives ought to be so appointed." Ibid.
70. Ibid.
71. Ibid., 2: 390.
72. Ibid., 2: 382, 391.
73. Ibid., 2: 439.
74. *JMP*, 10: 209.
75. For Madison's initial concept of the role of the states in relation to the national government, see his letter to Randolph, cited above in text, Chap. 2 at n. 54.
76. There is no indication of the origin of the clause—who first composed it and submitted it to the rest of the committee members for inclusion in the provision on powers. However, given the presence on the Committee of James Wilson, a foremost legal scholar and subsequent Justice of the Supreme Court, it is reasonable to assume that he was the author of this vital clause rejecting any implication of an Article II interpretation of the enumerated powers.
77. Leonard W. Levy, "Bill of Rights" in Leonard W. Levy (ed.), *Essays on the Making of the Constitution*, 2nd ed. (New York: Oxford University Press, 1987), 262. Akhil Reed Amar has said that "the Tenth Amendment beautifully sums up many of the themes of prior amendments—and it is wholly unsurprising that, alone among the successful amendments, the Tenth was the only one proposed by every one of the state ratifying conventions that proposed amendments." Akhil Reed Amar, *The Bill of Rights: Creation and Reconstruction* (New Haven, CT: Yale University Press, 1998), 123. Cited in Mark R. Killenbeck (ed.), *The Tenth Amendment and State Sovereignty: Constitutional History and Contemporary Issue*s. (Lanham, MD: Rowman & Littlefield, 2002), 104.
78. Farrand, *Records*, 1: 22.

    For an overview of Madison's thinking in relation to the adoption of amendments, see Sanford Levinson, "'Veneration' and Constitutional Change: James Madison Confronts the Possibility of Constitutional Amendment," *Texas Tech Law Review*, 21 (1990): 2443–2460.
79. Ibid., 1: 202–203. Although the Virginia Plan was, in the main, a direct product of Madison's workmanship, this remark by Mason leads one to suspect that the amendment clause in the Virginia Plan may have originated with him. That clause, as noted, had suggested that congressional approval for amendments not be required. That would seem to accord very much with Mason's comments at this stage in the debate. In contrast, Madison seems to have opposed the convention method from the beginning. See further discussion below.
80. Ibid., 2: 188. For the attribution to Wilson, see Richard B. Bernstein and Jerome Agel, *Amending America* (New York: Random House, 1993), 15.
81. Farrand, *Records*, 2: 468.
82. See text of draft provision in Gerry's remarks. Ibid., 2: 557.
83. Ibid., 2: 558.
84. Ibid.

85. Ibid., 2: 558–559.
86. Ibid., 2: 559.
87. Ibid., 2: 578.
88. At the insistence of John Rutledge of South Carolina, a proviso was added to the amendment provision precluding any change in the clause that permitted the importation of slaves for 20 years, that is, until 1808. Ibid., 2: 559. For his part, Roger Sherman of Connecticut later moved that the provision providing for equal representation for all states in the Senate be no less immune from amendment. Ibid., 2: 629–630. A proposal to this effect by Gouverneur Morris was adopted unanimously. Ibid., 2: 631.

    Sherman had sought to protect state sovereignty by a further proviso, in accordance with which "no State should be affected in its internal police." Ibid., 2: 630. To this Madison voiced strong objection. "Begin with these special provisos," he warned, "and every State will insist on them, for their boundaries, exports etc." After this proposal was rejected, Sherman attempted to get the entire clause on amendments struck out, thereby ensuring that no amendment affecting state sovereignty could ever be adopted. But this move too was rejected. Ibid., 630. At that point, Gouverneur Morris, sensing an element of crisis because of small-state fears, proposed adoption of Sherman's proviso that no state be deprived of its equal vote in the Senate, and, as noted, it was unanimously approved. Ibid., 631.

89. Ibid., 2: 629.
90. Ibid., 629–630. The following "anecdote," recorded in Farrand, confirms that it was Mason who all along fought to institute a convention method that would bypass Congress, for the adoption of amendments. The extract is from the Jefferson Papers and in the handwriting of Jefferson, who recorded what Mason had reported to him:

    > the constn. as agreed at first was that amendments might be proposed either by Congr. or the [state] legislatures a comm[itt]ee was appointed to digest & redraw. Go[u]v[erneur]. Morris & King were of the comm[itt]ee. one morng. Gov. M. moved an instr[uctio]n for certain alter[atio]ns (not 1/2 the members yet come in) in a hurry & without understanding it was agreed to. the Comm[itt]ee reported so that Congr. shd have the exclusive power of proposg. amendmts. G. Mason observed it on the report & opposed it. King denied the constr[uctio]n. Mason demonstrated it, & asked the Comm[itt]ee by what authority they had varied what had been agreed. G. Morris then impudently got up & said by authority of the convention & produced the blind instruction beforementd. which was unknown by 1/2 of the house & not till then understood by the other. they then restored it as it stood originally.

    Farrand, *Records*, 3: 367–368.

91. Ibid., 2: 629–630. For an alternative discussion of the adoption of the amendment procedure, not emphasizing Madison's reluctance to provide for a convention method, see the major work by David E. Kyvig, *Explicit and Authentic Acts: Amending the U.S. Constitution, 1776–1995* (Lawrence: University Press of Kansas, 1996), 56–60.

92. Farrand, *Records*, 2:630.
93. Ibid., 2: 662–663. The text of Article V, reads as follows:
    The Congress, whenever two thirds of both Houses shall deem it necessary, shall propose Amendments to this Constitution, or, on the Application of the Legislatures of two thirds of the several States, shall call a Convention for proposing Amendments, which, in either Case, shall be valid to all Intents and Purposes, as Part of this Constitution, when ratified by the Legislatures of three fourths of the several States, or by Conventions in three fourths thereof, as the one or the other Mode of Ratification may be proposed by the Congress; Provided that no Amendment which may be made prior to the Year One thousand eight hundred and eight shall in any Manner affect the first and fourth Clauses in the Ninth Section of the first Article; and that no State, without its Consent, shall be deprived of it's [*sic*] equal Suffrage in the Senate.
94. Cooke, *Federalist*, 296.
95. *JMP*, 10: 163–164.
96. Ibid., 10: 209–214.
97. Ibid., 209–211.
98. Ibid., 212.
99. Clinton Rossiter, *1787: The Grand Convention* (New York: Norton, 1966), 264.

CHAPTER 5

Three Dissenting Fathers: The First Salvo in the Antifederalist Campaign

No satisfactory answer has been given to explain why, for the initial three and a half months during which the Constitutional Convention deliberated, no one mentioned the topic of a bill of rights.[1] None of the four schemes which had at different stages been presented to the Convention—the Virginia, New Jersey, Pinckney, and Hamilton Plans—provided for a bill of rights, and this deficiency had not been noted in the debates.[2] Only on September 12, less than a week before the Convention was to close, did George Mason of Virginia raise the issue and propose that the Constitution be "prefaced with a Bill of Rights."[3] It would, he said, "give quiet to the people; and with the aid of the State declarations, a bill might be prepared in a few hours." Elbridge Gerry of Massachusetts, Mason's dissenting colleague, then proposed the creation of a committee to prepare a bill of rights, and Mason hastened to second the motion.[4] The minutes record only one response: "Mr. Sherman [of Connecticut] was for securing the rights of the people where requisite. The State Declaration of Rights are not repealed by this Constitution; and being in force are sufficient." Mason retorted: "The Laws of the U.S. are to be paramount to State Bills of Rights." His comment, however, had no impact on the delegates, and Gerry's proposal was roundly defeated.[5]

Undoubtedly, by then the delegates were worn out by months of debate and repeated reformulations of draft constitutional provisions, and they were most reluctant to extend their stay for the additional weeks that composition of yet another document might entail. Few had dreamt, when they first arrived in Philadelphia in May, that the constitutional project would engage them up to mid-September. Their desire to depart for home without further ado was understandable. Events were to show, however, that by omitting a bill of rights, the Federalists had committed a near-fatal error, since the issue was to haunt them throughout the ratification process and threaten to capsize the entire constitutional enterprise.

Mason's role on this occasion was quite natural, since in 1776 he had authored Virginia's Declaration of Rights, a historic document that served as a prototype for all the other state and federal bills of rights that were to follow.[6] Born in 1725, George Mason, at 62 years old, was one of the oldest delegates at the Constitutional Convention. The respect he engendered in that conclave, however, derived not only from his seniority but also from his achievements, both on a personal and national level. Although he had not practiced law, nor received any training in the field, he was known as an outstanding constitutionalist.[7] He had extensively read the legal treatises of the time. This was thanks to his uncle, John Mercer, a prominent lawyer who helped educate and guide young George from the tender age of 10, when he lost his father. His mother, a hardy woman who assumed the management of her husband's vast estate in the Northern Neck of Virginia, succeeded in conveying to her son the key elements of sound administration—personal attention to detail, wise planning, careful scrutiny of labor in progress, and an appreciation of frugality. These virtues he carried with him for life, and they marked his career as a prosperous Virginian plantation owner who, dispensing with the need for a manager or steward, personally administered his estate (with its workforce of some 500 slaves). His manor, Gunston Hall, rested on the shores of the Potomac River, and his nearest neighbor, at Mount Vernon, was another gentleman-farmer, George Washington. The two maintained close contact and frequently exchanged notes on husbandry and farming.

With his wide knowledge in matters of law, commerce, and realty, Mason was well equipped to assume a leading and creative role in political affairs when relations between England and America began to deteriorate in the 1770s. In 1774, he drafted what became known as the Fairfax Resolves,[8] in which he spelled out the reasons for American discontent with British authority. "The fundamental principle" of the British Constitution, he wrote, was that "people should not be governed by any laws other than those to which they have given their consent." Anything else would constitute tyranny. In the absence of representation, there was no place for British taxation. He proposed that the American colonies appoint a Congress "to concert a general and uniform plan for the defense and preservation of our common rights." His draft was accepted by the Fairfax county meeting, chaired by George Washington.

When the break finally came in 1776, George Mason was exceptionally well placed to draw up a draft Declaration of Rights for the nascent state of Virginia, detailing those natural rights of American citizens which, it was charged, the British Crown had so wantonly violated. The appearance of this charter preceded by 3 weeks the proclamation of the American Declaration of Independence and would appear to have significantly contributed to Jefferson's thoughts in formulating the Declaration.[9] In fact, it has been said that Virginia's Declaration of Rights authored by Mason captures, and indeed reflects, nineteenth-century political philosophy even more successfully than does the Declaration of Independence. Clearly, the liberal spirit of that philosophy informed Mason's stance at the Constitutional Convention.

The first item to engage the delegates was the proposal in the Virginia Plan for members of the lower house in the national legislature to be chosen in direct popular elections. Several delegates spoke out forcefully against this idea, since democracy, in their view, was the bane of the country and the source of all its ills. Mason, equally forcefully, defended the right of the people to choose their own representatives:

> He admitted that we had been too democratic but was afraid we s[houl]d. incautiously run into the opposite extreme. We ought to attend to the rights of every class of the people. He had often wondered at the indifference of the superior classes of society to this dictate of humanity & policy, considering that however affluent their circumstances, or elevated their situations, might be, the course of a few years, not only might but certainly would, distribute their posterity throughout the lowest classes of Society. Every selfish motive therefore, every family attachment, ought to recommend such a system of policy as would provide no less carefully for the rights – and happiness of the lowest than of the highest orders of Citizens.[10]

Mason also opposed a property qualification for exercising the right of suffrage:

> I think every person of full age and who can give evidence of common interest with the community shd. be an Elector – under this definition has a Freeholder alone ys [this] common Interest –? I think the Father of a Family has this interest – his Children will remain…[11]

He also objected to granting the Senate the right to originate money bills. "The Senate did not represent the *people*, but the *States* in their political character. It was improper that it should tax the people… The pursestrings should be in the hands of the Representatives of the people."[12]

These excerpts of Mason's comments at the Constitutional Convention amply confirm the assessment of two noted constitutional scholars that Mason was "an outstanding liberal of eighteenth-century America … [who] was far ahead of his time in his democratic social philosophy."[13] Given his liberal philosophy, it is not surprising that Mason should have been the first to suggest adding a bill of rights to the Constitution. What is surprising, however, is that it took him so long to broach the subject. Moreover, given the powerful sentiment that subsequently emerged for adding a bill of rights to the Constitution, why did no delegate draw attention prior to the final week of the Convention's deliberations to the absence of such a charter? The most reasonable explanation is that throughout the Convention the delegates did not perceive the federal government as a threat to the rights of citizens under any circumstances. The Articles of Confederation contained no bill of rights and no one had deemed the Articles wanting for that reason. Admittedly, the new Constitution would establish a far more powerful national government. Yet it would remain a government of delegated and enumerated powers, giving little scope, at first glance, for interference with individual rights. It was only as the plan of government began to jell and as the extent of the powers to be granted the federal government loomed larger and larger, that Mason and one or two others began to express alarm at the absence of a bill of rights. Mason's concern was heightened by an episode in which he had more than a casual interest.

In the early years of the Confederation, Mason had been wary of any effort to expand federal power. A set of Instructions delivered by the County of Fairfax to their delegates in the state assembly in 1783, and almost certainly drafted by Mason, called upon the delegates "strenuously to oppose all encroachments of the American [Confederal] Congress upon the sovereignty and jurisdiction of the separate States; and every assumption of power, not expressly vested in them, by the Articles of Confederation."[14] In particular, they were to oppose any attempts made by Congress "to obtain a perpetual revenue, or the appointment of revenue officers." Such powers, it was said, would render the Articles and the state constitutions "mere parchment bulwarks to American liberty."[15]

That same year Madison bore witness to the nature of Mason's opinions at the time. After visiting Mason at Gunston Hall, Madison wrote to Jefferson of Mason's "heterodoxy," which "lay chiefly in being too little impressed with either the necessity or the proper means of preserving the Confederacy."[16]

During the course of the intervening 4 years, Mason's outlook underwent a radical change. No doubt, the renewal of his contact with his neighbor George Washington, who had since retired from the army, helped convince him of the necessity of a strengthened federal government.[17] By the spring of 1787, Madison was able to write Jefferson that Mason "is renouncing his errors on the subject of the Confederation, and means to take an active part in the amendment of it" at the forthcoming Convention.[18] How far Mason had gone in revising his views can be gleaned from a letter he wrote his son shortly after he arrived in Philadelphia, expressing the hope "that we may be able to concert effectual means of preserving our country from the evils which threaten us."

> The most prevalent idea... seems to be a total alteration of the present federal system, and substituting a great national council or parliament, consisting of two branches... with full legislative powers upon all the subjects of the Union; and an executive: and to make the several State legislatures subordinate to the national, by giving the latter the power of a negative upon all such laws as they shall judge contrary to the interest of the federal Union.[19]

Throughout the Convention, Mason was an active participant in the debates and contributed significantly and substantively to the formulation of the provisions of the Constitution. Even when his ideas failed to impress his colleagues, he abided by the majority opinion and relented. Nonetheless, he harbored a continuous fear that the interests of the South might suffer at the hands of the North and East in the national councils.[20] For this reason, he advocated a multiple executive:

> If the Executive is vested in three persons, one chosen from the Northern, one from the Middle, and one from the Southern States, will it not contribute to quiet the minds of the people and convince them that there will be proper attention paid to their respective concerns?[21]

Even more important to Mason was the need to make navigation laws (laws governing matters of trade, shipping, tariffs, etc.) dependent on approval by a two-thirds majority of Congress. England had enacted Navigation Acts which put America at a disadvantage by restricting shipment of goods to British vessels, and this, in fact, had been one of the factors which led to the Revolution. Under the Articles of Confederation, the Congress was powerless to impose navigation laws on the states. Mason was now intent on making sure that the new Constitution would not permit the adoption of such laws without southern consent. Since the southern economy was built on the export of staples, it was vital, in his view, that it not be at the mercy of New England shipping interests for carrying its cargo abroad. The requirement of a two-thirds majority for navigation acts would provide for a southern veto and enable the South to ship its goods by the cheapest service available. A provision stipulating that a two-thirds majority was required for navigation acts was incorporated in the draft constitution produced by the Committee of Detail on August 6.[22] But on August 24 it was proposed that the provision be struck out, leaving navigation laws to be adopted by the same simple majority as all other legislation. It appears clear that the two-thirds requirement for navigation laws got caught up in a deal that was struck over the importation of slaves.

In the draft constitution of the Committee of Detail it was stipulated that "the emigration or Importation of such persons as the several States shall think proper to admit" should neither be prohibited nor subject to taxation.[23] This open-ended permit to import slaves encountered serious opposition.[24] On the other hand, delegates from the Carolinas and Georgia warned that any interference with the right to import slaves would doom the Constitution in their respective states.[25] It was, therefore, suggested that the two issues—navigation and slavery—be conveyed to a committee. In the words of Gouverneur Morris: "These things may form a bargain among the Northern & Southern States."[26] A committee representing each of the states was designated, and within 2 days a bargain was struck. In its report, the committee recommended permitting the importation of slaves until 1800, subject to normal import duties, and the elimination of the two-thirds requirement for navigation laws.[27] The delegates from the Deep South were obviously more concerned to preserve the right of importing slaves (albeit for a limited time) than they were to shield themselves from exorbitant shipping rates or skewed customs duties. As Farrand noted, "This was one of the conspicuous and important compromises of the convention."[28] In Mason's eyes, it was also a distinctly nefarious compromise—in fact, a double tragedy, since he opposed *both* parts of the deal.

Although he was a plantation owner with numerous slaves, Mason regarded the practice of slavery as a calamity for all involved. In the words of one writer:

"No other institution was ever the object of such passionate or consistent opposition on Mason's part as slavery."[29] As early as 1765, Mason lamented the economic effect of slavery on America's development and condemned its "ill effect ... upon the Morals & Manners of our People."[30] In 1774, in the Fairfax Resolves which Mason authored, calling for a boycott of British goods, Mason expressed the hope that "an entire Stop" might be put to the "wicked cruel and unnatural" slave trade."[31] At the Constitutional Convention, Mason had occasion to express himself in the most forceful terms on the subject. "This infernal traffic," he declared, "originated in the avarice of British Merchants. The British Govt. constantly checked the attempts of Virginia to put a stop to it. The present question concerns not the importing States alone but the whole Union."[32] And in words reminiscent of an ancient Hebrew prophet, he warned:

> Every master of slaves is born a petty tyrant. They bring the judgment of heaven on a Country. As nations can not be rewarded or punished in the next world they must be in this. By an inevitable chain of causes & effects providence punishes national sins, by national calamities... He held it essential in every point of view, that the Genl. Govt. should have power to prevent the increase of slavery.[33]

Mason's plea was not heeded, and the Convention proceeded to adopt the provision permitting the importation of slaves until 1808 (changed from 1800, the original date proposed).[34] Since both Mason and Madison objected to the provision, Virginia voted against its adoption, but it was outvoted. Mason was apparently unaware of the deal that linked the slavery question with the elimination of a qualified majority for navigation laws; and when the latter issue arose several days later (August 29), he strongly supported a move by Charles Pinckney of South Carolina to retain the two-thirds requirement[35]:

> If the Govt. is to be lasting, it must be founded in the confidence & affections of the people, and must be so constructed as to obtain these. The *Majority* will be governed by their interests. The Southern States are the *minority* in both Houses. Is it to be expected that they will deliver themselves bound hand & foot to the Eastern States, and enable them to exclaim in the words of Cromwell on a certain occasion – "the lord hath delivered them into our hands."[36]

His Virginia colleague, Edmund Randolph, also warned of dire consequences if the Pinckney proposal was not accepted:

> There were features so odious in the Constitution as it now stands, that he doubted whether he should be able to agree to it. A rejection of the [Pinckney] motion would compleat the deformity of the system.[37]

But the effort was doomed. Once the states of the Deep South had resolved to equate navigation laws to general legislation for adoption by simple majority, there was no way that the Pinckney proposal could survive. This episode, it is clear, had a direct and major impact on Mason's thinking. It served to intensify his fears regarding the scope of federal power under the new Constitution. The significance of this event for Mason, is best revealed in an account he subsequently gave to Thomas Jefferson:

> The const[itutio]n as agreed to till a fortnight before the convention rose was such a one as he w[oul]d have set his hand & heart to ... [it required] a vote of 2/3 in the legislature on particular subjects, & expressly on that of navig[atio]n. the 3. new Engl[an]d. states were constantly with us in all questions ... so that it was these 3. states with the 5. Southern ones against Penns[yl]va[nia] Jersey & Delaware. with respect to the import[atio]n of slaves it was left to Congress. this disturbed the 2 Southernmost states who knew that Congress would immediately suppress the import[atio]n of slaves. those 2 states therefore struck up a bargain with the 3. N[ew]. Engl[an]d. states, if they would join to admit slaves for some years, the 2 Southernmost states w[oul]d join in changing the clause which required 2/3 of the legislature in any vote. it was done. these articles were changed accordingly, & from that moment the two S[outhern]. states and the 3 Northern ones joined Pen[nsylvania]. Jers[ey]. & Del[aware]. & made the majority 8. to 3. against us instead of 8. to 3. for us as it had been thro' the whole Convention. under this coalition the great principles of the Const[itutio]n were changed in the last days of the Convention.[38]

As the Convention entered into the final stretch early in September, Mason's earlier deep concern about an all-powerful national government grew appreciably. He saw a colossus emerging before his eyes that would bestride the highways of freedom throughout the land. He was anxious to institute restraints which would ensure the preservation of the states and safeguard the liberties of individual citizens. These were the considerations that prompted him to raise the issue of a bill of rights on September 12. For their part, the weary delegates, after three and a half months of debate, were determined to wind up the Convention as quickly as possible. The last thing they wanted at that stage, on the eve of winter, was to become mired in a vast new exercise that would likely delay their departure for many more days, if not weeks.

Mason's colleague in dissent was Elbridge Gerry who, in many ways, presented a sharp contrast to the Virginian plantation owner.[39] Gerry, a Northerner from Massachusetts, had made his money from successful shipping and business ventures. While Virginia's vulnerability as a producer of staples troubled Mason, the North's vulnerability in relation to fishing and shipping was Gerry's concern. On the need for a bill of rights, the two men were united, but their purposes diverged. Mason, the author of Virginia's Declaration of Rights, was intent on *protecting* democracy; Gerry was intent on restraining it. Shays' Rebellion, more than anything else, had propelled Gerry to Philadelphia.

Gerry was a study in paradoxes. He was for republicanism but against democracy; he endorsed elitism but opposed aristocracy; he advocated energetic government but rejected centralization; he believed that the power of government derived from the people but was frightened by what the masses could do. In the eyes of many, Gerry was "constant only in his inconsistency."[40]

He was said to have acted at the Convention as "a man of sense, but a Grumbletonian … objecting to every thing he did not propose."[41]

Elbridge Gerry was born in Marblehead, Massachusetts, in 1744 to a prosperous merchant engaged in the shipping trade. He was educated at Harvard College and even wrote an MA thesis justifying the refusal of Americans to pay British-imposed prohibitory duties. Upon his return to Marblehead, he entered the family business and helped to propel it to new heights. The revolutionary atmosphere that gripped Massachusetts in the 1770s led him to join a group of young activists that included Richard Henry Lee and Thomas Jefferson. He came under the influence of Samuel Adams in Boston and worked closely with him in organizing Marblehead, Salem, and adjoining towns as centers of resistance. It was at this juncture that Gerry developed the unique political philosophy that was to serve as his lodestar through life and that was to give rise to seeming contradictions. Gerry strove to secure republican virtue in America which, he felt, had been undermined in England by venal corruption. Virtue required that the individual be willing to sacrifice for the public good. America could be sustained as a virtuous republic only if the citizenry was committed to this ideal. For him, true republicanism was even more important than Americanism. The quest for virtue and republicanism prompted him to rebel against tyranny from above and to oppose the threat of anarchy arising from below. Monarchy and mobocracy were, to his mind, equally destructive forces and needed to be equally combated. His struggle against tyranny ingrained in him an absolute aversion to a standing army, and his fear of the masses imbued him with a dread of democratic control of government. He thought that government should be administered on behalf of the people—and if by the people, by the right kind of people! His central concern was to control the exercise of power, and he believed that the wider the distribution of power, the better for all concerned.

These principles guided him in his service in the Continental Congress and beyond. He was one of the signatories of the Declaration of Independence and was equally energetic in proposing the immediate establishment of state governments so as to forestall disintegration of public order at the local level. He was one of the principal framers of the Articles of Confederation that granted the federal government only as much power as was deemed absolutely essential and safe. He fully endorsed the provision in the Articles that confirmed that each state retained "its sovereignty, freedom, and independence" (Article II). He described the Articles of Confederation as "the finishing Stroke of our independence." But American liberties, he hastened to say, "could only be assured by the people's virtue and not by any proclamation in a document."[42]

During his lengthy service on behalf of Massachusetts in the Confederal Congress, Gerry regularly opposed any attempt to expand federal power. He remained extremely suspicious of a professional army and championed the cause of state militias, which he saw as the only safe guarantee for American freedoms.[43] But if he harbored "a lifelong distrust of militarism,"[44] he was no less jealous of the power of the purse and rejected every effort to grant Congress an independent means of revenue. He opposed the notion of a federal impost and even doubted whether Congress could be trusted with the power to control foreign commerce.[45]

Given Gerry's inordinate suspicion of national power and his lack of faith in human nature, it is possible that, had there been no Shays' Rebellion, he would not have joined the Philadelphia conclave at all. But the turbulent events of the winter of 1786–1787, occurring, as they did, in his own state of Massachusetts, clearly stirred him to the core. The threat of public disorder now loomed larger for him than his fear of despotic aristocracy. Echoes of the impact of Shays' Rebellion can be discerned in his comments at the Constitutional Convention on popular control of government:

> The evils we experience flow from the excess of democracy. The people do not want [lack] virtue; but are the dupes of pretended patriots... He had ... been too republican heretofore: he was still however republican, but had been taught by experience the danger of the levilling [sic] spirit.[46]

At another point in the debate, his sense of elitism came to the fore when he proposed indirect elections by the people. While it was necessary "that the people should appoint one branch of the Govt. in order to inspire them with the necessary confidence," he wished the election "to be so modified as to secure more effectually a just preference of merit."[47] This could be accomplished by the people nominating candidates from whom the state legislature would make the appointment. On the other hand, Gerry "was as much principled as ever agst. aristocracy and monarchy."[48] He wished to promote a "republicanism" that assured social stability and would occupy "the middle ground between the ... extremes of anarchy and despotism."[49]

While the mainspring of Gerry's support for a bill of rights differed from that of Mason, who was inspired by a profoundly liberal democratic spirit, the aims of the two men converged. Both Mason and Gerry became alarmed by the enormous range of powers with which the national government was now to be endowed, and the inclusion of a bill of rights was seen as a means of limiting power and shielding citizens from its abuse. The defeat of Mason's September 12 proposal for a bill of rights did not deter the two men from suggesting, together or separately, a variety of measures to inhibit the exercise of federal power or, at least, provide the citizenry with some safeguards of their rights.

Thus, on September 14, in the final week of the Convention, Mason sought to amend the clause on the militia in Article 1, Section 8, by adding words that would deprecate the need for a standing army.[50] He acknowledged that an absolute prohibition on standing armies in time of peace was unwise and unsafe. But, "wishing at the same time to insert something pointing out and guarding against the danger of them" he moved to preface the clause "To provide for organizing and disciplining the Militia etc." with the words: "And that the liberties of the people may be better secured against the danger of standing armies in time of peace." Mason's motion was seconded by Edmund Randolph and supported by James Madison. It was defeated, however, by a vote of 2:9. The prevailing sentiment was probably reflected in the words of Gouverneur Morris, who objected to the proposal "as setting a dishonorable mark of distinction on the military class of Citizens."[51] The same day, Pinckney and Gerry moved to insert a declaration "that the liberty of the Press should be inviolably observed."[52] Once again, Sherman countered with the argument he had adduced to defeat the proposal for a bill of rights: "It is unnecessary—The power of Congress does not extend to the Press." The Pinckney–Gerry resolution was rejected by a vote of 4:7.[53]

Mason and Gerry garnered sufficient support to get one of their proposals adopted unanimously—a draft resolution requiring "that an Account of the public expenditures should be annually published."[54] However, there were no supporters for an initiative by Gerry to include a constitutional bar to federal impairment of the obligation of contracts, parallel to the prohibition imposed on the states in Article 1, Section 10.[55] Likewise, an effort by Edmund Randolph to preclude presidential pardons in cases of treason also failed of adoption.[56] Randolph had argued that "the prerogative of pardon in these cases was too great a trust. The President himself may be guilty. The Traytors may be his own instruments." Implicitly, the power of pardon in cases of treason, under his proposal, would be left with the legislature. The vote was 2:8:1 against. An attempt by Pinckney and Gerry to provide for trial by jury in civil no less than in criminal cases, as presently prescribed by the Constitution, was unanimously rejected. It was pointed out that jury trial for civil cases was not standard in all states, and a federal requirement would thus raise complications.[57]

The amendment provision, as noted earlier, also occasioned a fierce attack by Mason. He regarded it as "exceptional and dangerous" since it would depend, "immediately" or "ultimately," on Congress. In a margin of his copy of the draft constitution Mason referred to this as "a doctrine utterly subversive of the fundamental principles of the rights and liberties of the people."[58] In response, as noted, a proposal by Gouverneur Morris and Gerry to enable the states to require Congress to call a convention for considering amendments was unanimously adopted.[59]

Up to the last minute, Mason, Gerry, and Randolph strove to introduce changes into the text of the draft constitution that would provide better safeguards for the liberties of the people. In some cases they were successful; in most, not. Mason, still smarting from the defeat of a permanent two-thirds requirement for navigation laws, suggested on September 15 that a temporary two-thirds requirement—until 1808—be adopted to match the revised date set for the importation of slaves. His proposal read: "that no law in nature of a navigation act be passed before the year 1808, without the consent of 2/3 of each branch of the Legislature." It failed by a vote of 3:7:1.[60] This was apparently the final straw for Mason and Randolph. Both Virginians announced that they would be unable to sign the Constitution as completed. Randolph drew attention to "the indefinite and dangerous power given by the Constitution to Congress."[61] Expressing pain "at differing from the body of the

Convention, on the close of the great & awful subject of their labours," Randolph presented a motion for summoning a second convention to consider amendments to the Constitution as may be proposed by the state conventions. If his proposal fell, it would be impossible for him to attach his signature to the instrument. He made clear, however, that he was not categorically rejecting the Constitution. He left open the possibility of reversing his stand at the Virginia ratifying convention.

In contrast, both Mason and Gerry announced that their opposition to the draft constitution was absolute and final.[62] Both endorsed Randolph's idea of a second convention that would serve to eliminate the errors that had crept into the present document. Referring to "the dangerous power and structure of the government," Mason expressed his belief that it would end up as either a "monarchy or a corrupt, tyrannical aristocracy." He bitingly complained that the Constitution "had been formed without the knowledge or idea of the people" (although he made no attempt to explain why it had taken him so long to wake up to this fact). A second convention would be better able to judge "the sense of the people," he said:

> As the Constitution now stands, he could neither give it his support or vote in Virginia; and he could not sign here what he could not support there. With the expedient of another Convention as proposed, he could sign.[63]

Although both Mason and Gerry had fought for a bill of rights in the Convention, when they enumerated their respective reasons for not signing, it is interesting to note that only Mason expressly alluded to the absence of a bill of rights as a consideration. It was listed first among his objections to the Constitution.[64] As Madison wrote, for Mason, "the want of a Bill of Rights [was] a fatal objection."[65] The danger posed to the rights of the individual citizen concerned Mason greatly. The Senate, he declared, not being composed of "the representatives of the people or amenable to them," could "accomplish what [ever] usurpations they please upon the rights and liberties of the people."[66] Likewise, the judiciary was "so constructed and extended, as to absorb and destroy the judiciaries of the several states." As a result, law was rendered "tedious, intricate and expensive" so that justice was "unattainable," "enabling the rich to oppress and ruin the poor."[67] These were but a few of the reservations, reflective of his liberal philosophy, that he registered in a lengthy memorandum of dissent, which was later published in pamphlet form and fairly widely distributed.[68]

On the last day of the Convention Benjamin Franklin turned to the three dissenters to lay their complaints aside and join their colleagues in signing the final document of the Constitution.[69] Mason, although present at the final signing ceremony, did not respond. Gerry described his "painful feelings" at declining Franklin's invitation.[70] His decision not to sign, he said, arose from fears "that a Civil war may result from the present crisis of the U.S.—In Massachusetts ... there are two parties, one devoted to Democracy, the worst he thought of all political evils, the other as violent in the opposite extreme. From the collision of these in opposing and resisting the Constitution, confusion was greatly to be feared."

Randolph likewise apologized for refusing to sign the Constitution, "notwithstanding the vast majority & venerable names that would give sanction to its wisdom and its worth."[71] His refusal, he said, did not mean that he would necessarily "oppose the Constitution without doors." "He meant only to keep himself free to be governed by his duty as it should be prescribed by his future judgment." He was convinced that the plan would not be ratified by the necessary nine states "and confusion must ensue." There would be "anarchy and civil convulsions." He recognized that he was taking a step "which might be the most awful of his life," but it was "dictated by his conscience." Unlike Mason and Gerry, Randolph made no attempt to enumerate and publicize specific objections to the Constitution. He indicated clearly that his decision was revocable; he might give his assent at a later date (as indeed he did).

An explanation for Randolph's conduct must be sought in the morass of Virginia's politics. He had been elected Governor of the state of Virginia barely a year earlier to succeed Patrick Henry. Prior to that he had served as Attorney-General of the state and had also completed a 3 year stint as a delegate to the Continental Congress. The race for Governor (elected annually by the Virginia legislature) had been a three-cornered contest, and Randolph had managed to demonstrate his popularity over Richard Henry Lee and Theodorick Bland. His continuance in office would depend crucially on the reception Virginia would accord the new federal Constitution. There were good grounds to suspect that Patrick Henry and Richard Henry Lee would oppose it. The foreign affairs power, in relation to such questions as passage on the Mississippi and the majority required for navigation acts, would undoubtedly stir up considerable controversy, and Randolph was intent on keeping his options open. He had, or hoped he had, a promising and extended political career ahead of him, and he was not intent on antagonizing critical sectors of his supporters in the state legislature. Born in 1753, he was, at 34, the youngest member of the Virginia delegation at the Constitutional Convention. During the Revolutionary War he had served as aide-de-camp to General Washington, only to return to Virginia after the death of his uncle and patron, the distinguished lawyer, Peyton Randolph. Upon his return home, he became the youngest member of the Virginia Convention that drew up the state Constitution. He was also elected Mayor of the town of Williamsburg. His subsequent service as State Attorney-General and as Governor gave him a keen sense of the political realities operating in his home state. He was thus not prone to risk his political future at that point on a gamble, even one so worthy as the adoption of a federal constitution to which he had contributed so much.[72]

The dissent of Mason, Gerry, and Randolph foreshadowed many of the key issues that would arise during the struggle over ratification. One of these—which all three of the dissenters had noted with alarm—was the scope of the necessary and proper clause. As expressed by Mason: "Under their own construction of the general clause, at the end of the enumerated powers, the Congress may ... extend their powers as far as they shall think proper; so that the State legislatures have no security for the powers now presumed to remain to them, or the people for their rights."[73]

In the last stages of the debate, the Dissenting Fathers,[74] as noted, had also raised a demand for a second constitutional convention. The present document would thus be relegated to the status of preliminary draft while a succeeding convention would serve as the determinative and final decision-making body. The states would be given the opportunity to introduce whatever changes they deemed necessary. This idea was anathema to the delegates who had labored so hard to produce a new constitution for the United States. All the compromises that had been woven into the text would now unravel and the great achievement of the Federalist Revolution—energy and supremacy in the national government—would be wantonly undone. It is hardly surprising that the suggestion for a second convention was rejected outright by the delegates of all the states. The dread of a second convention movement arose seriously only after New York, as the eleventh state to ratify, in a round-robin letter to the other states proposed such a conclave. As will be seen, it took all the genius and stratagem of Madison to outmaneuver the fateful proposition. For the moment, however, it was the issue of a bill of rights that would pose the gravest threat to the process of ratification.

While Mason, Gerry, and Randolph revealed their displeasure with the Constitution at the closing ceremony by refusing to sign, there were other delegates to the Philadelphia Convention who had left earlier and subsequently joined the opposition. The first to retire from the Convention were two of the three New York delegates, Robert Yates and John Lansing. These 2 men had been selected as delegates by the New York state legislature majority that was under the strong influence of Governor Clinton, known for his antipathy to any attempt to expand national power.[75] Alexander Hamilton was sufficiently prominent that he was added to the state delegation although his strong nationalist views were well known. Hamilton was 30 years old and, besides practicing law, was serving as a state Assemblyman. Yates, 49 years old, was a judge on the New York Supreme Court, while Lansing, aged 33, practiced law and was Mayor of Albany. He had served several terms in the state Assembly and had also represented his state in the Confederation Congress. The two men left Philadelphia on July 10 when it became clear to them, as they said, that the majority was bent on adopting "a system of consolidated government" under which their state government would be deprived of the "most essential rights of sovereignty." They were confronted with the choice of "exceeding the powers delegated" to them or acquiescing in measures they conceived would be destructive "to the political happiness of the citizens of the United States."[76] Once Yates and Lansing departed, the state of New York was deprived of a vote in the Convention, since Hamilton alone could not represent the state. Subsequently, as will be seen, in the New York State Ratifying Convention, Lansing was very active in combating the federalist arguments for ratification, while Yates barely said a word.[77] Incidentally, this is ample reason in itself to doubt that Yates was the author of the brilliantly sharp essays criticizing the Constitution that appeared in New York under the pseudonym of Brutus, as some have suggested.[78]

Luther Martin, delegate from Maryland, left the Convention in mid-August, apparently in disgust at what he regarded was the extreme national character of the emerging Constitution. Martin was Attorney-General of the state of Maryland and regarded it as his sacred task to save his state, and the other states as well, from the national avalanche that was sweeping all before it. If anyone at the Convention can be classified as a states' righter it was Luther Martin. He spoke out at every opportunity to criticize the grand and expansive pattern of the provisions of the Constitution which, he said, would lead to a consolidated national system of government in which the states would be annihilated. State sovereignty was crucial to him as it was to Lansing and Yates. "At the separation from the British Empire," said Martin, "the people of America preferred the Establishment of themselves into thirteen separate sovereignties instead of incorporating themselves onto one." They now objected to "granting powers unnecessarily" lest state sovereignty be endangered.[79]

On more than one occasion Martin's address was one long tirade that left his audience tired and vexed, querying what he was getting at. As William Pierce described him: "This Gentleman possesses a good deal of information, but he has a very bad delivery, and so extremely prolix, that he never speaks without tiring the patience of all who hear him."[80] Upon returning to Maryland, Martin delivered a long, exhaustive, and rambling report to the Maryland House of Representatives on November 29, regarding the discussions that transpired at Philadelphia, in an effort to demonstrate how intent the majority was on instituting a consolidating government.[81] The report was expanded and subsequently published as the 60-page *Genuine Information*,[82] in which Martin described in great detail the attempts of the larger states to abolish state equality in any part of the national legislature, a proposal, he claimed, that was designed to bring about a near total eclipse of sovereign state authority. The creation of the Senate did not appease him; nor did the federal character of the Electoral College. He regretted the inclusion of a provision in the Constitution declaring that no religious test should be required for anyone holding office under the United States. In conclusion, he declared that the present system was "so destructive to the happiness" of his "country," Maryland, that he would be prepared to reduce himself to indigence if it would help in rejecting "those chains which are forged for it." Not only would the small states suffer, the Union itself would be destroyed. As summed up by Peter Onuf, Martin charged that "the federal Constitution, notwithstanding its declared intention of creating a 'more perfect union,' violated the fundamental principles of union by demolishing state rights and capitulating to the ambitions of the large states."[83]

It is interesting to observe that Martin's long and tedious *Genuine Information* had practically no impact on the Maryland delegates who expeditiously ratified the Constitution on April 28, by the overwhelming majority of

63:11. As a result, his bitter opposition to the Constitution was like a lone voice crying in the wilderness. In contrast to the opposition of the three dissenting delegates who refused to sign the Constitution at the closing ceremony, his criticism failed to make any serious impression on his audience, and for good reason. Maryland, in common with the other smaller states, appreciated that they had extracted at Philadelphia the most they could ever hope to attain from the larger states. From an initial extreme national proposal they had secured a truly federal system of national government, in which the smaller states had gained disproportionate representation, and they were not going to jeopardize this achievement by striking out for more. As Peter Onuf sums it up: "Only in a 'true federal Republic' could Maryland enjoy true equality. Disunion surely meant annihilation, for then the radical imbalance of state power would tell against small states such as Maryland."[84] The result was that Maryland joined five other smaller states in hastening to ratify. It is to be noted that neither Lansing-Yates nor Martin made an issue of the absence of a bill of rights in the Constitution. In the words of Pauline Maier, their objections "were fundamental and could not be met by amendments to the Constitution."[85] The smaller states were simply not exercised by the absence of a bill of rights. They were too pleased to note such "triviality." None of them proposed a list of amendments for they had no desire to undermine the ratification process with extraneous issues.[86] In the larger states, however, this was to be the key issue, and it nearly caused the ship of ratification to capsize.

NOTES

1. See Robert Allen Rutland, *The Birth of the Bill of Rights, 1776–1791* (Boston, MA: Northeastern University Press, 1983), 120. Alpheus Mason writes: "It seems that the Antifederalist drive for a bill of rights arose only as they slowly awakened to the 'consolidating' implications" of the Constitution. Alpheus Thomas Mason, *The States Rights Debate: Antifederalism and the Constitution* (Englewood Cliffs, NJ: Prentice-Hall, 1964), 76.
2. But cf. Farrand, *Records*, op. cit., 3: 122 and 609.
3. Ibid., 2: 587–588.
4. Ibid., 2: 588.
5. Ibid. The vote was 10: 0, with one state absent. Voting at the convention, of course, was by state delegations en bloc and not by individual delegates.
6. See Rutland, *Birth of Bill of Rights*, 33–34.
7. Mason was a vigorous opponent of paper money which, he maintained, was "contrary to every principle of … Justice" and corrupted "Manners and Morals." In a letter to Thomas Jefferson, he described how he had succeeded in obtaining the adoption of a resolution in the Virginia Assembly banning any such currency. Adoption of the resolution, he hoped, "has given that iniquitous Project it's [*sic*] Death's-Wound." May 26, 1788, *TJP*, 13: 206.
8. Robert Rutland, *George Mason: Reluctant Statesman* (Charlottesville: University Press of Virginia, 1961), 39–40; and see Rutland, *Birth of Bill of Rights*, 35.

See also, the more recent biography by Jeff Broadwater, *George Mason: Forgotten Founder* (Chapel Hill: University of North Carolina Press, 2006), 65–76.
9. Rutland, *Birth of Bill of Rights*, 36.
10. Farrand, *Records*, 1: 48–49.
11. Ibid., 2: 207–208.
12. Ibid., 2: 273–274. Emphasis in original.
13. Alfred, H. Kelly and Winfred A. Harbison, *The American Constitution: Its Origin and Development*, 3rd ed. (New York: Norton, 1955), 120. See also S. Slonim, "The Philosophy of a Dissenting Father: George Mason at the Constitutional Convention of 1787" in *Framers' Construction/Beardian Deconstruction: Essays on the Constitutional Design of 1787* (New York: Peter Lang, 2001), 213–230.
14. May 30, 1783, *GMP*, 2: 781.
15. Ibid.
16. Dec. 10, 1783, *JMP*, 7: 401.
17. See Helen Hill, *George Mason: Constitutionalist* (Gloucester, MA: Peter Smith, 1966), 185.
18. Apr. 23, 1787, *JMP*, 9: 401.
19. Farrand, *Records*, 3: 23.
20. On this topic, see Robert Allen Rutland, *The Ordeal of the Constitution: The Antifederalists and the Ratification Struggle of 1787–1788* (Norman: University of Oklahoma Press, 1966), 12ff.
21. Farrand, *Records*, 1: 113.
22. Ibid., 2: 143, 169, 183.
23. Ibid., 2: 169, 183.
24. Ibid., 2: 364–374.
25. See remarks of Rutledge, ibid., 2: 373.
26. Ibid., 2: 374.
27. Ibid., 2: 396, 400.
28. Farrand, *Framing*, 151.

    Robert Rutland, in an editorial note to the Mason Papers (*GMP*, 3: 990), states that Mason "had served on the special committee (appointed 18 Aug.) which made its report on 24 Aug. that permitted slave importations until 1800 (later 1808), but struck the ban on navigation acts." Rutland confuses the committee appointed on August 18 to settle the issue of federal assumption of state debts with the compromise committee, appointed on August 22. Mason was a member of the former but not of the latter. In the compromise committee, it was Madison, not Mason, who represented Virginia. See Farrand, *Records*, 2: 326–328 and 374–375. From all indications, it was only subsequently that Mason stumbled on the deal between the northern and deep southern states on the importation of slaves.
29. Hill, *George Mason*, 216.
30. *GMP*, 1: 61.
31. Ibid., 1: 207.
32. Farrand, *Records*, 2: 370; *GMP*, 3: 965–966.
33. Ibid.
34. Farrand, *Records*, 2: 416. Virginia had a surplus of slaves while the Deep South required more and more. This explains their differences over the importation of further slaves.

35. Ibid., 2: 446, 449. Pinckney himself either did not know of the bargain to which other members of his South Carolina delegation had committed themselves; or, if he did know, he disapproved of it.
36. Ibid., 2: 451. Emphasis in original.
37. Ibid., 2: 452.
38. Ibid., 3: 367. See also Mason's remarks at the Virginia Ratifying Convention, ibid., 334–335.
39. The classic biography of Elbridge Gerry is that by George Athan Billias, *Elbridge Gerry: Founding Father and Republican Statesman* (New York: McGraw Hill, 1976). Most of the biographical material presented here is drawn from this source.
40. Ibid., 1.
41. Letter to Jefferson, Oct. 11, 1787, Farrand, *Records*, 3: 104. Author of letter unknown.
42. Billias, *Gerry*, 85.
43. Ibid., 107.
44. Ibid. At the Constitutional Convention, Gerry suggested that, except when the country was at war, the army should be limited to 3000 soldiers. Farrand, *Records*, 2: 329. Reportedly, this elicited from George Washington a wry counter-proposal: that the Convention include also an amendment stating that "no foreign enemy should invade the United States at any time, with more than three thousand troops." Cited ibid., 191; and in James Hutson, *Supplement to Max Farrand's The Records of the Federal Convention of 1787*, vol. 4 (New Haven, CT: Yale University Press, 1987), 229.
45. Billias, *Gerry*, 113–114, 116.
46. Farrand, *Records*, 1: 48.
47. Ibid., 1: 132.
48. Ibid.
49. Billias, *Gerry*, 155.
50. Farrand, *Records*, 2: 616–617.
51. Ibid.
52. Ibid.
53. Ibid., 2: 618.
54. Ibid., 2: 618–619.
55. Ibid., 2: 619.
56. Ibid., 2: 626.
57. Ibid., 2: 628. The Seventh Amendment to the Constitution confirmed the right of jury trial in civil cases.
58. Ibid., 2: 629, n. 8.
59. Ibid., 2: 629–630.
60. Ibid., 2: 631.
61. Ibid.
62. Ibid., 2: 631–632.
63. Ibid., 2: 632.
64. "Objections to this Constitution of Government," ibid., 2: 637.
65. Ibid., 3: 136.
66. Ibid., 2: 638.
67. Ibid.
68. Ibid., 2: 637–640.

69. Ibid., 2: 641–643. Franklin's remarks were read by fellow-delegate from Pennsylvania, James Wilson.
70. Ibid., 2: 646–647.
71. Ibid., 2: 644–646.
72. "He is said to be afraid of the democracy & Patrick Henry." Robert Milligan to William Tilgham, Sept. 20, 1787, *DHRC*, 13: 219, cited in Henry Mayer, *A Son of Thunder: Patrick Henry and the American Republic* (Charlottesville: Univ. Press of Virginia, 1991), 384.
73. Farrand, *Records*, 2: 640. For Randolph's objection on this score, see ibid., 563–564; and for that of Gerry, see ibid., 635.
74. The title "Dissenting Fathers" is warranted since, despite their refusal to sign, all three dissenters had contributed significantly to the formulation of the Constitution in its final form.
75. See the letter of the French chargé d'affaires, dated July 25, 1787, cited ibid., 3: 63.
76. Letter (undated) of Yates and Lansing to George Clinton, Governor of New York, ibid., 3: 245; *DHRC*, 19: 457.
77. For background discussion of the role of Yates and Lansing at the Constitutional Convention and during the State Ratifying Convention, and the clash between Hamilton and Clinton, see the comprehensive essay:, John P. Kaminski, "New York: The Reluctant Pillar" in Stephen L. Schechter (ed.), *The Reluctant Pillar: New York and the Adoption of the Federal Constitution* (New York: Russell Sage College,1987), 48–117 and the essay by Cecil L. Eubanks, "New York: Federalism and the Political Economy of Union" in Michael Allen Gillespie and Michael Lienesch (eds.), *Ratifying the Constitution* (Lawrence: University Press of Kansas, 1989). See also editor's comment, *DHRC*, 19: 454–456.
78. See discussion in Storing, *Complete Anti-Federalist*, 2: 358 and n. 8, as also in *DHRC*, 19: 103.
79. Farrand, *Records*, 1: 340–341. Earlier the same day Lansing had argued: "It could not be expected that those possessing sovereignty could ever voluntarily part with it. It was not to be expected from any one State, much less from thirteen." Ibid., 336–337. For a review of the contending arguments on sovereignty at the Convention, see Thornton Anderson, *Creating the Constitution: The Convention of 1787 and the First Congress* (University Park: Pennsylvania State University Press, 1993), 54–58.
80. Farrand, *Records*, 3: 93. For background to the Maryland Ratification Convention, see the informative summary presented in Gregory Stiverson, "Necessity, the Mother of Union: Maryland and the Constitution, 1785–1789" in Patrick T. Conley and John P. Kaminski, (eds.), *The Constitution and the States: The Role of the Original Thirteen in the Framing and Adoption of the Federal Constitution* (Madison, WI: Madison House, 1988), 131–152.
81. Farrand, *Records*, 3: 151–159.
82. Ibid., 3: 172–232.
83. Peter Onuf, "Maryland: The Small Republic in the New Nation" in Gillespie and Lienesch, *Ratifying the Constitution*, 183. Onuf expertly surveys the Maryland ratification campaign while explaining why Maryland's past contention with neighboring Virginia over western lands was not allowed to affect the positive outcome. Onuf also analyzes very carefully Martin's contribution to the debate and shows why his critical opinion of the Constitution was not seriously entertained.
84. Ibid., 194. In her classical work on ratification, Pauline Maier does not analyze the Maryland Ratification Convention. As explained in her introduction, the relevant

documents for the Maryland Convention had not yet appeared in *The Documentary History of the Ratification of the Constitution* when she was completing her book. The Maryland chapter was, in any case, a side-show, so it was not crucial to the saga she was portraying in great detail. She does make some penetrating comments, however, about Luther Martin. She notes that Martin "explicitly dissociated himself" from George Mason and Elbridge Gerry, because throughout the Convention they "tended to give the *large states power* over the *smaller*," and only belatedly abandoned the Constitution. In contrast, Maier points out, Martin "felt a political kinship" with New York delegates Yates and Lansing who left the Constitutional Convention early because they felt it was betraying the trust with which they had been charged. Pauline Maier, *Ratification: The People Debate the Constitution 1787–1788* (New York: Simon & Schuster, 2010), 91.
85. Ibid., 92.
86. The Antifederalists in Maryland attempted to secure the state Convention's endorsement of thirteen draft amendments for adoption by the First Congress. The Federalists rejected the whole package and ratified the Constitution without any attachments. See Richard Beeman, *Plain Honest Men: The Making of the American Constitution* (New York: Random House, 2009), 392–393.

CHAPTER 6

The Antifederalist Drive to Reinstitute State Over Nation

Of all the complaints lodged by the Antifederalists in their campaign to defeat ratification of the Constitution, the failure to attach a bill of rights emerged as the leading and most formidable one.[1] Indeed, this omission came very close to dooming the prospects of ratification.

The debate over the absence of a bill of rights revolved chiefly around the question of whether the Constitution was imbued with a doctrine of implied powers. Was the list of congressional powers enumerated in Article 1, Section 8 of the Constitution complete, or could it be supplemented by means of the concluding, necessary, and proper clause? Did that clause connote that new categories of congressional powers could be implied at will? If so, contended the Antifederalists, then it was wide open for the national government to dominate the states totally, to the point of national consolidation. The states would be obliterated as sovereign political entities, and the rights of individuals would also be severely jeopardized. There were only two ways, they argued, in which the inherent danger of unlimited federal power could be averted—by adopting a provision which, like Article II of the Articles of Confederation, would limit the number of federal powers to those specifically enumerated in the Constitution; or by adding a Bill of Rights protecting the liberties of citizens. Implicitly, judicial review would be the necessary corollary for safeguarding specific constitutional rights. In this regard, it is worth recalling Leonard Levy's comment about the significance of the necessary and proper clause:

> That clause was the most formidable in the array of national powers, therefore the most controversial, and the one most responsible later for the demand for a bill of rights to ensure that the United States did not violate the rights of the people or of the states.[2]

Ironically, as the debate progressed through its various stages, the Federalists—hard-pressed to answer the Antifederalist charges—felt impelled to deny that the Constitution was imbued with a doctrine of implied powers.

Stage 1: The Constitution Faulted for Lack of a Bill of Rights

The first confrontation between Federalists and Antifederalists over the absence of a bill of rights in the Constitution took place in Pennsylvania.[3] Immediately after the Constitutional Convention had completed its labors in Philadelphia on September 17, 1787 and issued the text of the Constitution for ratification by the states, the Federalist majority in the Pennsylvania Assembly hastened to arrange for elections to a state ratifying convention, as provided for in Article VII of the Constitution.[4] The Assembly majority refused to wait for formal notification from the Confederation Congress sitting in New York before initiating the ratification process. And when members of the opposition absented themselves from the session—wishing to forestall what they viewed as precipitate summoning of a ratifying convention—the majority gave instructions to forcibly haul enough dissenters into Constitution Hall so that a quorum would be present and a vote could be taken. A resolution was then rushed through the Assembly, scheduling the elections for November 6, with the ratifying convention to open on November 20.[5]

Such overbearing maneuvers for expediting the ratification process naturally aroused resentment at what was justifiably construed as a transparent stratagem to prevent public consideration of the strengths and weaknesses of the Constitution. The most immediate reaction came on October 2, in an *Address* to constituents by sixteen seceding members of the Pennsylvania Assembly, explaining their reasons for absenting themselves in the final days of the Assembly session.[6]

They accused the majority of "attempting to surprise" the people of Pennsylvania into ratifying the Constitution without proper deliberation, and they urged the state's citizens to "look over" the Constitution carefully, "that you may be enabled to think for yourselves."[7]

Beyond inveighing against the strong-arm tactics of the state assembly majority, the seceding members impugned the behavior of the Constitutional Convention itself. They argued that the adoption of an entirely new constitution "which annihilate[d] the present Confederation," was an ultra vires act.[8] And they proceeded to delineate, in telegraphic fashion, many of the issues that the Antifederalists would subsequently highlight in their campaign to defeat the Constitution. Thus, they warned that the vast expansion of federal power would threaten the rights of citizens. It was up to the people to "judge whether the liberty of the press may be considered as a blessing or a curse in a free government, and whether a declaration for the preservation of it is necessary, or whether in a plan of government any declaration of rights should be prefixed or inserted?" They also asked their constituents to ponder whether the Constitution ought not to provide against a standing army in time of peace and whether jury trial in civil cases should not be assured.

The refrain of the seceders was taken up by the Pennsylvanian Antifederalist, Samuel Bryan, in his first essay published in the *Centinel* series on October 5.[9]

In that essay he charged that the Constitution provided neither a balanced system of government, as recommended by John Adams, nor the type of responsible government reflected, for example, in the Pennsylvania constitution. The framers of the new Constitution had been "actuated by the true spirit of such a government, which ever abominates and suppresses all free enquiry and discussion," and they therefore "made no provision for the *liberty of the press*, that grand *palladium of freedom*, and *scourge of tyrants*; but observed a total silence on that head." He also noted "that there is no declaration of personal rights, premised in most free constitutions; and that trial by *jury* in *civil* cases is taken away."[10] These sins of omission were coupled with sins of commission. The Constitution permitted "a standing army in time of peace, that grand engine of oppression." And not content with "absolute controul over the commerce of the United States" and all external sources of revenue, the federal government would be invested "with every species of *internal* taxation."[11]

> Whatever taxes, duties and excises that they may deem requisite for the *general welfare*, may be imposed on the citizens of these states, levied by the officers of Congress, distributed through every district in America; and the collection would be enforced by the standing army, however grievous or improper they may be.[12]

The Supremacy Clause, the sixth Article of the Constitution, "put the omnipotency of Congress over the state government and judicatories out of all doubt."[13] In conclusion, he suggested that "a future general Convention being in possession of the objections [to the Constitution], will be better enabled to plan a suitable government."[14]

Centinel's comments in this very first essay, coming on the heels of the debate in the Pennsylvania Assembly and the *Address* of the seceders, made clear that the omission of a bill of rights in the Constitution would be a critical issue in the ratification struggle. Before long it was recognized as the Antifederalists' primary grievance.[15] As Robert Rutland observed: "The Antifederalists stumbled upon one oversight in the Constitution that bore the appearance of an Achilles' heel." They "assiduously promoted the idea that the failure to include a bill of rights was not an oversight, but a studied bit of Federalist deception."[16]

For most critics, supplementing the Constitution with a bill of rights was seen as an effective safeguard of the individual rights now threatened by the extraordinary range of power accorded the federal government under the Constitution. The absence of a bill of rights had underscored the danger posed by the new instrument of government; but the shortcoming was remediable. On the other hand, for the ideological Antifederalists—the states' righters—the issue of a bill of rights furnished a useful springboard for getting the entire constitutional design jettisoned, or at least drastically transformed.[17] To achieve the latter, they would seek to insert substantive amendments that would allow the states to regain much of the power that the Constitution had transferred to the national government. The basic aim was to revise the federal balance by restoring the states to their former primacy.

STAGE 2: THE FEDERALIST RESPONSE

To counter the Antifederalist onslaught regarding the absence of a bill of rights, there were various options open to the Federalists. They could acknowledge that it was an error—as they ultimately did—and promise to remedy the situation with the adoption of amendments to the Constitution. They might have tried arguing that the state bills of rights were unaffected and citizens were therefore fully protected under them. This, after all, was the argument that had been used by Roger Sherman at Philadelphia to dismiss George Mason's call for a bill of rights.[18] James Wilson, however, declined to follow either of these courses. Instead, he challenged the challengers by asserting that a bill of rights was uncalled for in a constitution of defined and delegated powers. The federal government could not legislate on matters affecting rights since these were beyond the scope of its power. In fact, to enumerate rights would dangerously imply that the government did possess legislative authority that had been denied to it. Moreover, enumeration of rights might be interpreted as leaving unprotected those rights that were excluded from the list.

A day after the appearance of the first *Centinel* essay, James Wilson delivered a major speech in the State House Yard. In the course of his campaign to gain election to the Pennsylvania state ratifying convention, he explained and defended the fundamental principles of the new Constitution.[19] While it is not clear that he was already responding to the charges published only the previous day, he seems to have been clearly reacting to the earlier arguments presented by the sixteen seceders in their *Address*. Wilson's comment is important, not only because he was "present at the creation" and was, in fact, one of the major architects of the Constitution, but because this widely disseminated speech was regarded by most Federalists as the best case that could be made to justify the omission of a bill of rights from the Constitution. They repeatedly adopted Wilson's line of argument throughout the ratification campaign to explain away the oversight—which they claimed had not been an oversight at all![20] Thus, at the Virginia ratifying convention, Madison resorted to Wilson's thesis[21]; and in Federalist #84, Hamilton elaborated on Wilson's constitutional analysis.

Wilson distinguished between the state governments, where every power not reserved to the people inhered in the government, and the federal government, where everything not conferred would be automatically reserved to the state governments or the people:

> This distinction being recognized, will furnish an answer to those who think the omission of a bill of rights, a defect in the proposed Constitution: for it would have been superfluous and absurd to have stipulated with a federal body of our own creation, that we should enjoy those privileges, of which we are not divested either by the intention or the act, that has brought that body into existence. For instance,

the liberty of the press, which has been a copious source of declamation and opposition, what control can proceed from the federal government to shackle or destroy that sacred palladium of national freedom?[22]

Wilson also sought to refute various other Antifederalist charges. The Constitution did not guarantee jury trial in civil cases, he said, because of the different rules on the subject in the various states. It was therefore "impractical" to have made "a general rule." Likewise, he rejected the contention that the Constitution had "a pernicious tendency" because it allowed the maintenance of a standing army in time of peace. How else, asked Wilson, could the security of the nation be preserved? Was it necessary to inform the enemy of a declaration of war before the government could prepare to defend the country? "The consequence is too obvious to require any further delineation."[23]

As a delegate to the state ratifying convention that assembled in Philadelphia on November 20, Wilson found himself, for a second time, called upon to explicate the thesis he had enunciated in the State House Yard. Time and again he argued that there was no room for a bill of rights in a government of limited powers:

> There are two kinds of government; that where general power is intended to be given to the legislature and that where the powers are particularly enumerated. In the last case, the implied result is, that nothing more is intended to be given, than what is so enumerated, unless it results from the nature of the government itself... [I]n a government like the proposed one, there can be no necessity for a bill of rights. For ... the people never part with their power.[24] ... We are told, that there is no security for the rights of conscience. I ask ... what part of this system puts it in the power of Congress to attack those rights? When there is no power to attack, it is idle to prepare the means of defense.[25]

The underlying principle of the new constitution, Wilson contended, was that "the supreme power resides in the people." The opening words of the Preamble to the Constitution, "We the people," was "tantamount to a volume and contains the essence of all the bills of rights that have been or can be devised; for it establishes, at once, that in the great article of government, the people have a right to do what they please."[26] "The fee simple of freedom and government is declared to be in the people, and it is an inheritance with which they will not part."[27] Wilson went on to say that the difference between him and those demanding a bill of rights revolved around different concepts of the locus of sovereignty. For them, "the sovereign power resides in the state governments; mine is that it resides in the *people*... In a general government there is no necessity of a bill of rights, for in my opinion all rights are in the people"[28] (Thus, Wilson was presenting the argument that Chief Justice Marshall subsequently made famous in *McCulloch v. Maryland*—that the Constitution was the creation of the people, not of the states).[29]

The serious challenge on the subject of a bill of rights led other Pennsylvania Federalists at the state-ratifying convention to reiterate Wilson's thesis in denying that the Constitution was critically flawed.

Thus, in addressing the convention, Justice Thomas McKean said:

> This system proposes a union of thirteen sovereign and independent states in order to give dignity and energy to the transaction of their common concerns. It would be idle, therefore to countenance the idea that any other powers were delegated to the general government than those specified in the Constitution itself.[30]

If a person possessed of 1000 acres decides to convey 250 acres, "is it necessary to reserve the 750?" he asked.[31] "The whole plan of government [of the Constitution] is nothing more than a bill of rights—a declaration of the people in what manner they choose to be governed."[32] "It seems," he said, "that the honorable members are so afraid the Congress will do some mischief that they are determined to deny the power to do any good."[33] In conclusion, he exhorted the delegates to ratify the Constitution, despite any deficiencies:

> But sir, perfection is not to be expected in the business of this life; and it is so ordered by the wisdom of Providence that as our stay in this world seldom exceeds three score and ten years, we may not become too reluctant to part with its enjoyments, but by reflecting upon the imperfections of the present, learn in time to prepare for the perfection of a future state. Let us, then, Mr. President, be content to accept this system as the best which can be obtained.[34]

Perhaps the high point in arguing for a constitution minus a bill of rights was reached in the remark of delegate Dr Benjamin Rush, when he said: "Sir, I consider it as an honor to the late Convention that this system has not been disgraced with a bill of rights."[35]

STAGE 3: THE ANTIFEDERALIST REJOINDER TO THE WILSONIAN THESIS

Wilson's argument, that a bill of rights was uncalled for in a constitution of enumerated powers, was subjected to severe criticism on various grounds. Basically, his thesis reflected two axioms that were one: First, that since the federal government possessed only the powers enumerated, it could not threaten rights; second, the scope or number of the enumerated powers could not be increased by means of constitutional interpretation. It fell to the Antifederalists to demonstrate that neither axiom was valid. The number of powers to which Congress could lay claim was not finite, and this was evident from the terms of the Constitution itself. Since Congress could dispose of unenumerated powers, it was in a position to curtail, or even deny essential rights. Only the adoption of a bill of rights would provide security; but if so, it followed that the courts would have to disqualify laws infringing upon constitutional rights. In effect, therefore, judicial review was the essential complement of the Antifederalist argument that the Constitution incorporated a doctrine of implied powers.

The Absence of an Express Clause Limiting Congress to the Powers Enumerated

Wilson's line of argument possessed a fundamental flaw, which was quickly exposed. If federal authority was indeed restricted to enumerated powers, why was that principle not spelled out in the Constitution as it had been in the Articles of Confederation? Obviously, in their desire to free Congress from the shackles under which its predecessor had operated, the Framers had intentionally omitted, in Article I, Section 8, a provision corresponding to Article II of the Articles of Confederation. They had felt it vital to preserve in the Constitution an implied powers gloss. Thus, when Thomas Jefferson, then in Paris, was apprised of Wilson's argument, he dismissed it out of hand as "gratis dictum," that is, gratuitous, and "opposed by strong inferences from the body of the instrument." In a letter to Madison he pointed out that, in contrast to the Articles of Confederation, the Constitution contained no clause to the effect that "every power ... not ... expressly delegated to the United States in Congress" was retained by the states. "A bill of rights," he wrote, "is what the people are entitled to against every government on earth, general or particular [i.e. national or state], and what no just government should refuse, or rest on inference."[36]

Countless essays, appearing in newspapers throughout the nation, echoed Jefferson's complaint. Perhaps the first, chronologically, was that published in the *Pennsylvania Herald* on October 17 and signed "A Democratic Federalist." Wilson's arguments, it declared, "although extremely ingenious and the best that could be adduced in support of so bad a cause, are yet extremely futile, and will not stand the test of investigation." Why, it was asked, was there no constitutional provision corresponding to Article II of the Articles of Confederation? "If this doctrine is true [that the federal government disposes only of delegated powers] and since it is the only security that we are to have for our natural rights, it ought at least to have been clearly expressed in the plan of government."[37]

An Old Whig published a second article on October 17, challenging the validity of the Wilsonian thesis. "There is nothing in the new constitution which either in form or substance bears the least resemblance to the second article of the confederation... So far from the reservation of all powers that are not expressly given, *the future Congress will be fully authorised to assume all such powers as they in their wisdom or wickedness, according as the one or the other may happen to prevail, shall from time to time think proper to assume*."[38]

In the Massachusetts Convention the issue was summed up by General Samuel Thompson with a quotation from the biblical volume Job. "Gentlemen say ... that all power is retained which is not given. But where is the bill of rights which shall check the power of this Congress, which shall say, *thus far shall ye come and no farther*. The safety of the people depends on a bill of rights."[39]

The absence of a clause in the Constitution restricting the federal government to the enumerated powers was a focus of sharp criticism in the Virginia ratifying convention by such Antifederalists as George Mason, Patrick Henry, and James Monroe. Thus, Mason thought "there ought to be some express declaration in the Constitution, asserting that rights not given to the General Government, were retained by the States. He apprehended that unless this was done, many valuable and important rights would be concluded to be given up by implication."[40] And Patrick Henry felt that without an Article II-type provision, "you ... by a natural and unavoidable implication, give up your rights to the General Government."[41] After citing the necessary and proper clause which, he said, provided "no limits," Monroe proposed that "our great unalienable rights ought to be secured from being destroyed by such unlimited powers, either by a Bill of Rights, or by an express provision in the body of the Constitution. It is immaterial in which of these two modes rights are secured."[42] Monroe's comment effectively dismissed the argument, made by Madison and other Federalists, that since the Articles of Confederation had contained no bill of rights, there was no reason to demand one in the Constitution.[43] Besides the fact that the Constitution conferred far more power to interfere in the lives of citizens than the Articles ever did, it was Monroe's contention that Article II had served as a comprehensive limitation on national power, so that a bill of rights spelling out detailed rights had been unnecessary. However, the Constitution contained neither a clause limiting the exercise of powers nor a bill of rights: This was intolerable.

The Enumeration of Certain Rights in the Constitution

If Congress disposed only of those powers enumerated in Article 1, Section 8, and therefore could not threaten rights, then why did the Constitution stipulate certain rights, such as no suspension of the writ of habeas corpus, no ex post facto laws, no bills of attainder, and no requirement of a religious test for holding office? If Congress lacked power to enact laws dealing with such topics, since they were not referred to in the Article 1 list, why the need to proscribe such legislation in the first place? Obviously, the Framers must have felt that even without a specific constitutional grant of authority, Congress might feel free to suspend habeas corpus, adopt *ex post facto* laws, adopt bills of attainder, or grant titles of nobility—all of which confirmed that the list of powers in Article 1 was not exhaustive.

In the Pennsylvania ratifying convention, Robert Whitehill pointed to the contradictions which arose from the enumeration of some rights and the absence of others:

> No satisfactory reason has yet been offered for the omission of a bill of rights; but, on the contrary, the honorable members are defeated in the only pretext which they have been able to assign, that every thing which is not given is excepted, for we have shown that there are two articles expressly reserved, the writ of *habeas*

corpus and the trial by jury in criminal cases; and we have called upon them in vain, to reconcile this reservation with the tenor of their favorite proposition.[44]

The Federal Farmer noted that "the distinction, in itself just, that all powers not given are reserved, is in effect destroyed by this very constitution."[45] In support, he referred to the express prohibition on titles of nobility and suspension of habeas corpus. Silence with reference to other rights, he stressed, might be taken to indicate acquiescence. He illustrated this with regard to enforced quartering of soldiers.

> The constitution will give congress general powers to raise and support armies. General powers carry with them incidental ones, and the means necessary to the end. In the exercise of these powers, is there any provision in the constitution to prevent the quartering of soldiers on the inhabitants? you will answer, there is not. This may sometimes be deemed a necessary measure in the support of armies; on what principle can the people claim the right to be exempt from this burden?[46]

At one point in the Pennsylvania ratifying convention, Wilson promised to offer an explanation at a later stage in the debate of why the Constitution enumerated certain rights even though, as he contended, the federal government could never threaten those rights.[47] The promise remained unfulfilled; but two other Federalists tried their hand at explaining the discrepancy. Thomas Hartley suggested that "Some articles indeed, from their preeminence in the scale of political security, deserve to be particularly specified, and these have not been omitted in the system before us."[48] And Jasper Yeates remarked, somewhat inscrutably, that some rights were singled out "merely as a reservation on the part of the people and a restriction on the part of their rulers."[49] Such flimsy rationalizations merely lent greater weight to the Antifederalist assault on Wilson's "delegated powers" thesis.

Thus, the Federal Farmer argued that if certain rights were listed in the Constitution "from very great caution," this in itself "implies a doubt, at least, that it is necessary."[50] In writing a constitution, he said, precision was essential.

> The rights reserved must be indisputably so, and in their nature defined; the powers delegated to the government, must be precisely defined by the words that convey them, and clearly be of such extent and nature as that, by no reasonable construction, they can be made to invade the rights and prerogatives intended to be left in the people.[51]

Under the circumstances, he declared, there was no alternative to adding to the Constitution both a bill of rights and a clause paralleling Article II of the Articles of Confederation.

In the Virginia ratifying convention, Patrick Henry lamented the fact that the restrictions on Congress in favor of rights were "so feeble and few." He cited the ban on suspension of the writ of habeas corpus to demonstrate that without such a prohibition "they could suspend it in all cases whatsoever." This, Henry claimed, was the reverse of the thesis "that every thing is retained which is not given up."[52]

Henry also pointed to the provision in the Constitution (Article 1, Section 9) that prevented Congress from interfering with the slave trade until 1808. Even absent the provision, wherefrom, he asked, would Congress, have been able to draw such power? "The power not having been expressly delegated, must be obtained by implication."[53] "My mind," he concluded, "will not be quieted till I see something substantial come forth in the shape of a Bill of Rights."[54]

Edmund Randolph, then Governor of Virginia, attempted to dismiss the evidence regarding implied powers which Henry and the other Antifederalists had adduced from the enumeration of certain rights in the Constitution.[55] "Every exception here mentioned, is an exception not from general powers, but from the particular powers therein vested." The temporary restriction with regard to the slave trade, Randolph said, was an exception from the power to regulate commerce; and habeas corpus was an exception from the congressional power to regulate courts. The ban on bills of attainder and ex post facto laws constituted an exception to the "criminal jurisdiction" vested in Congress. In addition, the restriction on awarding titles of nobility represented an exception to the power of creating military and civil offices.

Randolph's explanation, it would seem, failed because it explained too much. If every constitutional restriction could be deemed to be an exception to one or another of the long list of enumerated powers, then those powers evidently lent themselves to a very broad interpretation indeed. Hence, the implied powers granted to Congress were obviously almost unlimited—even without reference to the "sweeping" necessary and proper clause which the opposition claimed added powers exponentially to those that the Constitution conferred explicitly.[56] It does not appear that Henry (or any of his colleagues) attempted to answer Randolph. Perhaps the fact that the two had had a sharp altercation earlier at the convention, with Henry being compelled to apologize for his remarks, led to his restraint on this occasion.[57]

Freedom of the Press

Of all the rights whose omission the Antifederalists deplored, none was more consequential for them than freedom of the press. Illustrative of the importance they attached to it was the accusation in the first essay of *Centinel*, cited earlier. The framers, the writer charged, were "actuated by the true spirit of such a government, which ever abominates and suppresses all free enquiry and discussion." Therefore, they "made no provision for the *liberty of the press*, that grand *palladium of freedom*, and *scourge of tyrants*; but observed a total silence on that head."[58]

Wilson responded to this complaint in similar fashion to his argument on a bill of rights generally—a government of enumerated powers was unable to interfere with freedom of the press and thus there was no need to stipulate such a right in the Constitution.[59] In their rejoinder, the Antifederalists sought to demonstrate that many of the enumerated powers of Congress could be utilized to curb freedom of the press, and therefore it was essential that this right be spelled out.

Thus, in the Pennsylvania ratifying convention, Whitehill referred to the power of Congress to authorize copyrights.

> They have a power to secure to authors the right of their writings. Under this they may license the press, *no doubt*; and under licensing they may suppress it... Tho it is not declared that Congress have a power to destroy the liberty of the press; yet, in effect, they will have it.[60]

The same point was made in an article written by A Republican. Did not the Constitution provide for granting an "exclusive right" for "*writings* and discoveries" for a limited time?

> I do not mean to call in question the propriety of this provision, but I would ask, whether under it the press may not be considered subject to the *influence* and controul of this government? – Will it be denied that this power includes in it (in some measure) *that of regulating literary publications*?[61]

If Congress passed a law requiring printers to be licensed and a printer was denied a license, to whom, An Old Whig queried, could he turn for relief? Reliance on a state's guarantee of freedom of the press would avail him very little, he stressed, since the state judge, by virtue of the supremacy clause, would be bound by the federal statute.[62]

The Federal Farmer referred to the national taxing power to illustrate the vulnerability of the press to federal suppression. Although he confessed that he did not see "in what cases the congress can, with any pretence of right, make a law to suppress the freedom of the press," nonetheless, Congress does not appear "restrained from laying any duties [taxes] whatever on printing."[63] "Printing, like all other business, must cease when taxed beyond its profits." And in a sentence reminiscent of what Chief Justice Marshall would pronounce in 1819 in the case of *McCulloch v. Maryland*, the Federal Farmer declared: "A power to tax the press at discretion, is a power to destroy or restrain the freedom of it."[64]

In the absence of a constitutional guarantee of press freedom, George Mason cautioned at the Virginia ratifying convention, Congress might act to restrict such freedom by relying on its power to provide for the general welfare:

> Now suppose oppressions should arise under this Government, and any writer should dare to stand forth and expose to the community at large, the abuses of those powers. Could not Congress, under the idea of providing for the general welfare, and under their own construction, say, that this was destroying the general peace, encouraging sedition, and poisoning the minds of people? And could they not, in order to provide against this, lay a dangerous restriction on the press?[65]

For his part, Patrick Henry remarked: "Is it necessary for your liberty," he asked, "that you should abandon those great rights by the adoption of this system? Is the relinquishment of the trial by jury, and the liberty of the press, necessary for your liberty?"⁶⁶

The Treaty Power

In their argument that the national government disposed of more powers than those explicitly enumerated in Article 1 of the Constitution, the Antifederalists pointed to the treaty-making power of the federal government. They also noted that, by the terms of the supremacy clause, treaties would rank as "the supreme law of the land" and override contrary state law. Was not the treaty clause thus an open-ended instrument for expanding federal power? Could not the treaty power be employed to expand federal authority at the expense of the states and to undermine citizens' rights?

An Old Whig, in his third number, published on October 20, illustrated the dangerous use to which the treaty power might be applied:

> If Great Britain, for instance, were willing to enter into a treaty with us, upon terms which would be inconsistent with the liberties of the people and destructive of the very being of a Republic, the consent of our president for the time being, and of two thirds of the senators present, even though the senators present should be but a very small part of the senate, will give such a treaty the validity of a law. What power will there be to prevent this? – None.⁶⁷

Similarly, Brutus, writing in early November, reached the conclusion that the broad scope of the treaty power made a bill of rights imperative:

> I do not find any limitation, or restriction, to the exercise of this [treaty] power. The most important article in any constitution may therefore be repealed, even without a legislative act. Ought not a government vested with such extensive and indefinite authority, to have been restricted by a declaration of rights? It certainly ought.⁶⁸

These points were summarized by the minority in their *Dissent*, issued upon the conclusion of the Pennsylvania ratifying convention. The Senate, acting in conjunction with the President, it said, "form treaties with foreign nations, that may controul and abrogate the constitutions and laws of the several states. Indeed, there is no power, privilege or liberty of the state governments, or of the people, but what may be affected by virtue of this power. For all treaties, made by them, are to be the 'supreme law of the land.'"⁶⁹

Patrick Henry voiced the same complaint:

> No cession of territory is binding on the nation [England] unless it be fortified by an act of Parliament. Will it be so in your American Government? – No – They will tell you that they are omnipotent as to this point… Will the Gentleman … say, that

this power is only paramount to the State laws only? Is it not paramount to the Constitution, and every thing? – Can any thing be paramount to what is paramount?[70]

He demanded that the treaty power be reined in: "We wish to guard against the temporary suspension of our great national rights. We wish some qualification of this dangerous power. We wish to modify it."[71]

The Necessary and Proper Clause Combined with the Supremacy Clause

Of all the evidence adduced by the Antifederalists to refute Wilson's thesis and to establish that an implied powers gloss was inherent in the Constitution, none was more persuasive than their reference to the necessary and proper clause as conjoined with the supremacy clause.

At the Constitutional Convention, George Mason had already inveighed against the privilege of auto-interpretation that the necessary and proper clause apparently bestowed upon Congress:

> Under their own construction of the general clause, at the end of the enumerated powers, the Congress may grant monopolies in trade and commerce, constitute new crimes, inflict unusual and severe punishments, and extend their powers {power} as far as they shall think proper; so that the State legislatures have no security for the powers now presumed to remain to them, or the people for their rights.[72]

Accurately reflecting Antifederalist sentiment, A Republican Federalist labeled the necessary and proper clause an "omnipotent" provision that will enable "an artful and arbitrary legislature" to "*stretch* their powers."[73] Patrick Henry referred to it as the "sweeping" clause[74]; and *Centinel* warned that "every law of the states may be controuled" by it. "The legislative power," he said, "so unlimited in its nature, may be so comprehensive and boundless in its exercise, that this alone would be amply sufficient to carry the coup de grace to the state governments, to swallow them up in the grand vortex of general empire."[75]

Brutus warned that the clause might be applied "to effect an entire consolidation of the whole into one general government." The powers given by this article are very general and comprehensive, and it may receive a construction to justify the passing almost any law," even to abolishing "the state legislatures."[76] It "amounts to a power to make laws at discretion. No terms can be found more indefinite than these, and it is obvious, that the legislature alone must judge what laws are proper and necessary for the purpose."[77] The provision "leaves the legislature at liberty, to do every thing, which in their judgment is best."[78]

He then addressed the argument presented in Federalist #33 (by Hamilton) and in #44 (by Madison), that the necessary and proper clause merely states a truism, and does not expand or increase powers[79]:

> It is said, I know, that this clause confers no power on the legislature, which they would not have had without it – though I believe this is not the fact, yet admitting it to be, it implies that the constitution is not to receive an explanation strictly, according to its letter; but more power is implied than is expressed.[80]

At the Virginia ratifying convention, Patrick Henry cited the necessary and proper clause, cautioning: "Implication is dangerous, because it is unbounded: If it be admitted at all, and no limits be prescribed, it admits of the utmost extension. They say that every thing that is not given is retained. The reverse of the proposition is true by implication." A bill of rights was "indispensably necessary." Furthermore, "a general positive provision should be inserted in the new system, securing to the States and the people, every right which was not conceded to the General Government; and that every implication should be done away."[81]

Such arguments were repeated by An Old Whig, who took the matter a step further. If the charter of rights were to serve as a barrier to federal encroachment on the rights of citizens, it would have to be supplemented by the power of *judicial review*. In rebutting Wilson, he asked what value could be attached to the fact that the powers of Congress were supposedly delegated and enumerated, if the necessary and proper clause conferred "*undefined, unbounded and immense power*" on Congress.

> Under such a clause as this can any thing be said to be reserved and kept back from Congress? ... So far from the reservation of all powers that are not expressly given, *the future Congress will be fully authorised to assume all such powers as they in their wisdom or wickedness, according as the one or the other may happen to prevail, shall from time to time think proper to assume.*[82] ... It is not of a farthing consequence whether they really are of opinion that the law is necessary and proper, or only *pretend to think so*; for who can overrule their pretensions?—No one; unless we had a bill of rights to which we might appeal, and under which we might contend against any assumption of undue power and appeal to the judicial branch of the government to protect us by their judgements.[83]

In conclusion, An Old Whig pointed to the supremacy clause to clinch his argument about the unbridled power of the federal government in the absence of a bill of rights. As if it were determined that no doubt should remain, "by the sixth article" of the Constitution it was confirmed that the Congress would be "vested with the supreme legislative power, without controul. In giving such immense, such unlimited powers, was there no necessity of a bill of rights to secure to the people their liberties?" he asked.[84]

The foregoing review demonstrates the manner in which the debate over the omission of a bill of rights from the Constitution gave rise to a discussion about the scope of federal power and, in particular, whether the Constitution was imbued with an unbridled doctrine of implied powers. Wilson's claim that a constitution of enumerated powers ipso facto precluded federal interference in matters affecting the rights of American citizens was subjected to withering Antifederalist criticism on several grounds.

If the federal government disposed only of the powers enumerated, why was there no clause in the Constitution stating this fact, as there had been in the Articles of Confederation? If rights could not be threatened, why did the Framers find it necessary to specify certain rights in the Constitution? Given the numerous powers assigned to Congress, could one say that freedom of the press was under no threat of control or restriction? And did not the treaty-making power offer the federal government a convenient means of multiplying the number of powers already at its disposal? Finally, was not the "necessary and proper" clause an open-ended invitation to Congress to extend federal powers into any area it wished to reach?

All of these arguments, the Antifederalists contended, revealed that the doctrine of implied powers was part and parcel of the Constitution, enabling the federal government to operate in totally unexpected spheres with the result that the national government could create a consolidated regime in which the states would be reduced to precincts and the liberties of American citizens could be threatened. Consequently, a bill of rights—or alternatively a provision corresponding to Article II of the Articles of Confederation—was essential in order to preclude the expansion of Congressional powers at the expense of the states and encroachment upon individual liberties. And as the indispensable guarantee against such usurpation, there would need to be an acceptance of judicial review. Significantly, judicial review was an implicit element in the Antifederalist drive for a bill of rights.

In a word, the contest over ratification became a struggle over a bill of rights, and the struggle over a bill of rights became a dispute over the presence or absence of a doctrine of implied powers under the Constitution. The Federalists were led to deny that the Constitution was endowed with an unlimited doctrine of implied powers, while the Antifederalists sought to demonstrate that such a doctrine was a fundamental part of the constitutional system launched at Philadelphia.

Concern over the absence of a bill of rights was genuine and widespread; but, as noted earlier, some critics of the Constitution worried less about the danger to individual rights than about the threat posed to state rights. Patrick Henry and the other ideological Antifederalists wished, above all, to restore to the states much of the power and sovereignty that the Constitution had transferred to the national government. They hoped that the drive for a bill of rights would serve as the medium for either defeating the Constitution or for drastically revising the federal equation that it encompassed. For most of the Constitution's critics, the adoption of a bill of rights was the goal; and Madison's task in the ratification contest became to separate them from the ideologues, by producing a bill of rights that confirmed federal power even as it offered greater protection for individual rights.

Notes

1. As George Lee Turbeville wrote to James Madison shortly after the Constitution was published: "The principal objection that the opponents bring forward against this Constitution, is the total want of a Bill of Rights." December 11, 1787. *DHRC*, 8: 232.
2. Leonard W. Levy, "Bill of Rights," first published in Jack P. Greene (ed.), *Encyclopedia of American Political History* (New York: Charles Scribner's Sons, 1984), 2: 106; reprinted in Leonard W. Levy (ed.), *Essays on the Making of the Constitution*, 2nd ed. (New York: Oxford University Press, 1987), 262.

    For a succinct and outstanding review of Antifederalist strategy, see Murray Dry, "The Case Against Ratification: Anti-Federalist Constitutional Thought" in Levy and Mahoney (eds.), *Framing and Ratification of Constitution*, 271–291. For a comprehensive discussion of Antifederalist political thought, see Storing, *AntiFederalist*, vol. 1, and Cecelia M. Kenyon, *The Antifederalists* (Indianapolis, IN: Bobbs-Merrill, 1966), Introduction.
3. For an enlightening description of the events in Pennsylvania, see *DHRC*, 2: 30–35, 54–56. See also Storing, 3: 3–6, 11. Pauline Maier discusses the Pennsylvania contest in detail in Chap. 4 of her book: *Ratification: The People Debate the Constitution, 1787–1788* (New York: Simon & Schuster, 2010).
4. Federalist strategy generally aimed to secure as many ratifications as possible in quick order so that any state tempted to dissent would be confronted with an overwhelming majority in favor of the Constitution. The question then would be not whether sufficient states will ratify, but rather whether the dissenting state will choose to remain outside the Union. The following extract of a letter from Edward Carrington to Thomas Jefferson in Paris reflects this strategy:

    > The long postponement [of the Virginia ratifying convention] was occasioned by unfriendly intentions toward it [the Constitution], but I apprehend the rapidity of the movements of the other States in the business, will, by that time, have brought so many into the adoption, that even its enemies will see the *necessity* of joining.

    TJP, 12: 336.

    Opponents of the Constitution warned against the Federalist aim of "stampeding" the states into ratifying. Thus, Luther Martin of Maryland declared at the Constitutional Convention: "The people … would not ratify it unless hurried into it by surprize." Farrand, *Records*, 2: 478. See, generally, Robert Allen Rutland, *The Ordeal of the Constitution: The Antifederalists and the Ratification Struggle of 1787–1788* (Norman: University of Oklahoma Press, 1966), 19–23.

    In Maryland, Samuel Chase, writing in early October under the pseudonym of CAUTION, suggested to the inhabitants of Baltimore that "an attempt to *surprise* you into an *public* measure, ought to meet your indignation and contempt." The "haste" with which a decision on the matter is urged leads one to suspect, Chase said, that the motives of those pushing for early ratification are "improper" and that they wish to preclude a "dispassionate and most deliberate consideration." Paul Leicester Ford (ed.), *Essays on the Constitution of the United States: Published During Its Discussion by the People, 1787–1788* (Brooklyn, NY: Historical Printing Club, 1892) 325–328. (See Storing, *Antifederalist*, 5:80, n.2.)

5. *DHRC*, 2: 95–111.
6. Ibid., 112–117; Storing, *AntiFederalist*, 3.2.3–7.
   DHRC, 2: 113–115; Storing, 3.2.4.
7. Centinel II condemned the Federalist tactics in the Pennsylvania Assembly:
   > Are Mr. W[ilso]*n*, and many of his coadjutors ... the disinterested patriots they would have us believe? ... View them, preventing investigation and discussion, and in the most despotic manner endeavouring to compel its adoption by the people, with such precipitancy as to preclude the possibility of a due consideration, and then say whether the motives of these men can be pure.

   DHRC, 13: 468
   > In a letter to Elbridge Gerry dated October 20, 1787, George Mason deplored "the precipitation with which the City of Philadelphia, & that party in their Legislature, are attempting to force the new Government upon the People ... they dread a thorough Knowledge & public Discussion of the Subject, & wish to hurry it down, during the short & raging Fever of Approbation." *GMP*, 3: 1006.
8. *DHRC*, 2: 115; Storing, 3.2.4–7.
9. Storing, 2.7.1–27; *DHRC*, 2: 158–167; ibid., 13: 328–336. For background to the appearance of Centinel, see ibid., 326–328; Storing, 2: 130–135.
10. Ibid., 2.7.25. Published in the *Independent Gazetteer*.
11. Ibid., 2.7.11.
12. Ibid.
13. Ibid., 2.7.15.
14. Ibid., 2.7.27.
15. Saul Cornell, in his comprehensive study of the Antifederalists, lists nine issues that repeatedly appeared in Antifederal writings, with the omission of a bill of rights only appearing as item number six. *The Other Founders: Anti-Federalism and the Dissenting Tradition in America, 1788–1828* (Chapel Hill: University of North Carolina Press, 1999), 30–31. His enumeration may have held initially, but within a short while the failure to include a bill of rights in the Constitution figured as item number one in nearly every Antifederalist set of charges against the Constitution. Thus, the *Dissent* of the minority in the Pennsylvania ratifying convention, issued on December 18, states: "The first consideration that this review [of the Constitution] suggests is the omission of a BILL of RIGHTS." Storing, 3.11.32; *DHRC*, 2: 630. See also the quotation from George Lee Turbeville in his letter to Madison, cited in n. 1 above; and his subsequent letter to Madison dated April 16, 1788, in which he refers to the demand for the adoption of a bill of rights as "the favorite Topic of the ablest Antifoederal declamers." *JMP*, 11: 23. James Wilson, at one point, referred to the complaint over the omission of a bill of rights as "this [subject] so violently supported out of doors." *DHRC*, 2: 469–470. It may also be noted that John P. Kaminski, editor of the series, *The Documentary History of the Ratification of the Constitution*, writes: "Throughout the ratification debate (1787–1788), the lack of a federal bill of rights remained the single most important issue." "Restoring

the Grand Security: The Debate Over a Federal Bill of Rights, 1787–1792," *Santa Clara Law Review*, 33 (1993): 891. See also Leonard W. Levy, *Origins of the Bill of Rights* (New Haven, CT: Yale University Press, 1999), 30. "The single issue that united Anti-Federalists throughout the country was the lack of a bill of rights."

16. Rutland, *Ordeal of Constitution*, 32–33.
17. As Levy noted: "The omission of a bill of rights became an Antifederalist mace with which to smash the Constitution." Bill of Rights, 105.
18. See Chap. 5, above, at n. 4. Sherman had stated: "The State Declarations of Rights are not repealed by this Constitution; and being in force are sufficient." Farrand, *Records*, 2: 588.

    Brutus, in his second number, dismisses the argument based on the rights preserved in state constitutions. By force of the supremacy clause, he contends, "the different state constitutions are repealed and entirely done away, so far as they are inconsistent with this [Constitution]; ... of what avail will the constitutions of the respective states be to preserve the rights of its citizens? should they be plead, the answer would be, the constitution of the United States, and the laws made in pursuance thereof, is the supreme law." *DHRC*, 13: 528–529. See also text at n. 77 below.

    For a review of the Federalists' arguments on behalf of ratification, see David F. Epstein, "The Case for Ratification: Federalist Constitutional Thought" in Levy and Mahoney (eds.), *Framing and Ratification of Constitution*, 292–304.

19. Oct. 6, 1787, *DHRC*, 2: 167–168.
20. See, for example, the comment of Cassius II: "As Congress can exercise no power, except such as are expressly given to them by the people, a bill of rights is, not only, unnecessary, but, would be, highly dangerous. Because, if an enumeration was made, it might, then be supposed, that every right was given up, but what was reserved." Ibid., 9: 715.
21. Ibid., 10: 1501–1502, 1507. In *Federalist* #38, Madison simply contented himself with noting that under the Confederation there was also no bill of rights.

    Bernard Schwartz refers to Wilson's theory of reserved powers as the "official" Federalist explanation for the absence of a bill of rights.

    Bernard Schwartz, *The Bill of Rights: A Documentary History*, 2 vols. (New York: McGraw Hill, 1971), 1: 572. Kaminski endorses Schwartz's assessment. Restoring the Grand Security, 896.

22. *DHRC*, 2: 167–168; also reproduced ibid., 13: 339–340. For discussion of Wilson's presentation and the reaction to it, see ibid., 13: 337–339.
23. Ibid., 2: 168–169; 13: 341. Wilson's response regarding a standing army is reminiscent of George Washington's reported reaction at the Constitutional Convention to a proposal by Elbridge Gerry to limit the army to 3000 men. See above, Chap. 5, n. 44.
24. Dec. 4, *DHRC*, 2: 470.
25. Ibid., 471.
26. Nov. 28, *DHRC*, 2: 383–384. Cf. Hamilton's comment in *Federalist* #84: "Here [in "We the people"] is a better recognition of popular rights than volumes of those aphorisms which make the principal figure in several of our state bills of rights, and which would sound much better in a treatise of ethics than in a constitution of government."

27. *DHRC*, ibid.
28. Dec. 4, ibid., 485. No one has more effectively analyzed the debate over sovereignty between Antifederalists and Federalists than Gordon S. Wood, *The Creation of the American Republic, 1776-1787* (New York: Norton, 1972), Chap. XIII, "The Federalist Persuasion," particularly 524–536. See also, in connection with the debate over sovereignty, Charles A. Lofgren, "The Origins of the Tenth Amendment: History, Sovereignty, and the Problem of Constitutional Intention" in *Constitutional Government in America* (Durham: Carolina Academic Press, 1980), 331–357; Akhil Reed Amar, "Of Sovereignty and Federalism," *Yale Law Journal*, 96 (1987): 1425–1520, and Jack N. Rakove, "Making a Hash of Sovereignty, Parts 1 and 2," *Green Bag*, 2d (1998): 2: 35 and 51.
29. During the debate, Wilson indicated it was more dangerous to err in enumerating the rights of the people than to err in enumerating the powers of the federal government. Nov. 28,1787, *DHRC*, 2: 388.

    For a favorable appreciation of the Federalist position as enunciated by Wilson, see Hadley Arkes, *Beyond the Constitution* (Princeton, NJ: Princeton University Press, 1990), Chap. 4, "On the Dangers of a Bill of Rights: Restating the Federalist Argument."
30. Nov. 28, *DHRC*, 2: 412.
31. Dec. 10, ibid., 546–547.
32. Nov. 28, ibid., 387.
33. Ibid., 414.
34. Ibid., 418.
35. Nov. 30, ibid., 434.
36. Letter of Dec. 12, 1787, *TJP*, 12: 440. Jefferson also took issue with Wilson's attempted justification of the Convention's failure to institute jury trial in civil cases because it had been cancelled in several states. He wrote: "It was a hard conclusion to say because ... some [states] have been so incautious as to abandon this mode of trial, therefore the more prudent states shall be reduced to the same level of calamity. It would have been much more just and wise to have concluded the other way that as most of the states had judiciously preserved this palladium, those who had wandered should be brought back to it, and to have established general right instead of general wrong."
37. *DHRC*, 13: 387; Storing, 3: 58–59. The essay also attacked Wilson's argument in support of a standing army, according to which it was "necessary to maintain the appearance of strength even in times of the most profound tranquility." This contention, the writer said, was "a thread-bare hackneyed argument, which has been answered over and over in different ages, and does not deserve even the smallest consideration." It was a product of the "advocates of tyranny" since a standing army was "that *great support of tyrants*." *DHRC*, 13: 390; Storing, 3: 61–62. Emphasis in original.

    This opening broadside by A Democratic Federalist against Wilson's thesis confirms the comment by David Epstein: "James Wilson offered an argument widely praised on one side and widely ridiculed on the other." "The Case for Ratification: Federalist Constitutional Thought", in Levy and Mahoney, *Framing and Ratification*, 299.
38. *DHRC*, 13: 400–401. Emphasis in original.
39. Cited in Alpheus Thomas Mason (ed.), *The states Rights Debate: Antifederalism and the Constitution* (New York: Oxford University Press, 1972), 299.

40. *DHRC*, 10: 1328. See also ibid., 1325–1326.
41. Ibid., 10: 1329.
42. Ibid., 9: 1112. On Monroe's appearance at the ratifying convention as an opponent of the Constitution, see ibid., 9: 844–846.
43. See n. 21 above.
44. *DHRC*, 2: 427.
45. Storing, 2:8.197.
46. Ibid., 2.8.202.
47. *DHRC*, 2: 471.
48. Ibid., 2: 430.
49. Ibid., 2: 437.
50. Storing, 2.8.198.
51. Ibid., 197.
52. *DHRC*, 10: 1345.
53. Ibid., 10: 1341. Earlier in the debate, this argument was made by John Tyler: "This temporary *restriction* on Congress [with regard to the slave trade] militated, in his opinion, against the arguments of Gentlemen on the other side, that what was not given up was retained by the States... The power of prohibiting it, was not expressly delegated to them; yet they would have had it by implication, if this restraint had not been provided." Ibid., 1339–1340.

    The assumption of Tyler and Henry that it was only by means of an implied power that Congress would have been able to prohibit the slave trade is not easy to understand. Express congressional authority under Article 1, Section 8, to regulate trade, would seem to have provided ample scope to act. This point was made by Edmund Randolph in the Virginia ratifying convention in his endeavor to dismiss the Antifederalist arguments on behalf of a bill of rights. See ibid., 1348, and see text immediately below.
54. Ibid., 10: 1347.
55. Ibid., 10: 1348–1350.
56. Randolph acknowledged that the "necessary and proper" clause was ambiguous and that "that ambiguity may injure the states." His fear was that "it will by gradual accessions gather to a dangerous length." Ibid., 10: 1353. Nonetheless, as will be seen, he advocated ratification of the Constitution.
57. Ibid., 9: 1081–1082, 1087 n. 1.
58. Storing, 2.7.25; *DHRC*, 2: 166. Emphasis in original. See above, text following n. 8, and see comment of Patrick Henry, *DHRC*, 10: 1345.
59. See text at n. 22 above; also *DHRC*, 2: 454–455.
60. Ibid., 2: 454. Emphasis in original.
61. Ibid., 13: 479. Emphasis in original.
62. Storing, 3.3.15; *DHRC*, 13: 426.
63. Storing, 2.8.56.
64. Ibid., 2.8.203. Hamilton, in a lengthy footnote in *Federalist* #84, specifically challenged the logic of this argument according to which freedom of speech is threatened by the power of taxation. "It would be quite as significant to declare that government ought to be free, that taxes ought not to be excessive, &c., as that the liberty of the press ought not to be restrained."
65. *DHRC*, 10: 1326. Was Mason presaging the Alien and Sedition Laws of the late 1790s?
66. Ibid., 9: 951–952.

67. Storing, 3.3.14; *DHRC*, 13: 426.
68. Storing, 2.9.33; *DHRC*, 13: 529.
69. Storing, 3.11.42; *DHRC*, 2: 634.
70. Ibid., 10: 1394–1395. Henry, of course, was speaking in the wake of the Mississippi episode discussed above, Chap. 2, in text at n. 40.
71. *DHRC*, 10: 1536. The fear that the treaty power might be used not only to override state laws and constitutions but even to emasculate the provisions of the federal Constitution triggered the Bricker amendment initiatives in the 1950 s. See, on this topic, Louis Henkin, *Foreign Affairs and the Constitution* (New York: Norton, 1972), Chap. 5; also, Charles A. Lofgren, "*Missouri v. Holland* in Historical Perspective," *Supreme Court Review* (1975): 77–122.
72. Farrand, *Records*, 2: 640.
73. Storing, 4.13.28. Emphasis in original.
74. *DHRC*, 9: 1112; and see ibid., 9: 1135. See also the comment of Edmund Randolph, ibid., 10:1347.
75. Storing, 2.7.96.
76. Ibid., 2.9.8.
77. Ibid., 2.9.57.
78. Ibid., 2.9.141.
79. Ibid. In Brutus XII, he refers to the comments of Publius (presumably #33 and #44), as follows: "A voluminous writer in favor of this [constitutional] system, has taken great pains to convince the public, that this clause means nothing; for that the same powers expressed in this, are implied in other parts of the constitution." Ibid., 2.9.153.
    In the Virginia ratifying convention, Madison contended that the "dreaded" clause only defined "*how*" the powers shall be exercised. While the Constitution enumerated the powers that accrue to the General Government, it did not say "how" they were to be exercised. The "necessary and proper" clause answered that question, "but gives them no additional power." *DHRC*, 9: 1135.
80. Storing, 2.9.141.
81. *DHRC*, 9: 1046–1047.
82. Ibid., 3.3.12, 3.3.9. Emphasis in original.
83. Ibid., 3.3.12. Emphasis in original. In most instances, Antifederalists were wary of the judiciary, fearing that the court would join other branches of the federal government to override state interests. An Old Whig, however, highlighted the fact that a bill of rights without judicial supervision would be ineffective. Implicitly, all those calling for a bill of rights must have envisaged some judicial role to give meaning to the rights.
84. Ibid., 3.3.13. Quite clearly, An Old Whig accepted that the judiciary would have the power to invalidate legislation deemed to be in contravention of the Constitution. The addition of a bill of rights was considered vital, for only thus could legislation threatening rights be declared null and void.

CHAPTER 7

Three Ratification Contests: The Fate of the Union in the Balance

Massachusetts: "The Conciliatory Resolutions that Saved the Constitution."[1]

> The decision of Massachusetts is perhaps the most important event that ever took place in America, as upon her in all probability depended the fate of the Constitution.
>
> Edward Carrington to Henry Knox.[2]

> I should not forgive myself if I omitted the Occasion of congratulating with you on the Accession of Massachusetts to the new Constitution. This Event is in all Probability conclusive and gives to our Country the Chance for national Felicity.
>
> Gouverneur Morris to George Washington.[3]

By the time the Massachusetts Ratifying Convention got underway on January 9, 1788, Federalist strategy had paid off quite handsomely. The aim was to obtain early ratification in the states known to favor the Constitution (mainly the smaller ones) and to build up sufficient momentum so as to make it difficult, if not impossible, for the doubtful states to dissent.[4] Within 4 months of the Constitutional Convention, five state conventions, a majority of the required nine, had already approved the Constitution. These states were: Delaware, unanimously, on December 8, 1787; Pennsylvania on December 12; New Jersey, unanimously, on December 18; Georgia, unanimously, on January 2, 1788; and Connecticut on January 9.[5] Four of the five, being small states, had understandably acted with dispatch. They were intent on confirming the privileged standing they had secured at Philadelphia in such crucial matters as Senate membership and the Electoral College method of electing the President.

Given their desire to assure early entry into force of the Constitution, it is not surprising that the issue of a bill of rights did not arise in any of these states. The case of Pennsylvania, however, was different and, as noted earlier, a genuine fracas arose over various matters, and especially over the absence of a bill of rights. The issue was heatedly debated not only in the state legislature and the State Ratifying Convention, but also in the polemical essays that appeared in the press at that time and were distributed nationwide.

In contrast to Pennsylvania, where approval of the Constitution was attained by a lopsided vote, in the three other large states—Massachusetts, Virginia, and New York—the contest promised to be much tighter. Early rejection by any one of these large states could severely compromise the cause of ratification. While failure in Virginia might have been fatal to the Constitution, success in Massachusetts and Virginia would preserve the Union. Since Virginia and New York postponed their conventions to the summer, the contest in Massachusetts—scheduled for early January—was crucial. The question was whether the Bay State would come up with a solution for unqualified ratification even while promoting a bill of rights.

Broadsides and various publications in Massachusetts made it clear that there was a solid demand, not readily ignored, for a bill of rights.[6] Only two questions were at issue. Would the addition of a bill of rights need to be formulated in advance of—and as a condition for—ratification, or would Massachusetts accept a promise to append the document to the Constitution after ratification in the form of amendments? Second, would the bill of rights be directed only at protecting individual rights of conscience or would it also revise and restrict the scope of national authority vis-à-vis the states?

When the results of the election to the Massachusetts Ratifying Convention became known, it appeared that the Antifederalists had a decided edge.[7] The seriousness of the challenge facing the Federalists in Massachusetts is reflected in Madison's correspondence at the time. In a letter of January 20 to Randolph from New York, he wrote: "The intelligence from Massachts. begins to be rather ominous to the Constitution… the probabil[it]y is that the voice of that State will be in the negative."[8] Madison proceeded to assess the consequences of such a vote: "The decision of Massts, in either way, will decide the voice of this State [New York]." He also foresaw that the minority in Pennsylvania would be "emboldened" by a negative vote in Massachusetts and would seek a reversal of the affirmative vote in their state. In a message of January 23 to Madison, Rufus King, a leading Federalist in Massachusetts, wrote:

> Our prospects are gloomy, but hope is not entirely extinguished… We are now thinking of amendments to be submitted not as a condition of our assent & Ratification, but as the opinion of the Convention subjoined to their Ratification. This scheme may gain a few members, but the issue is doubtful.[9]

For his part, Madison was hoping that "even the project of recommendatory alterations" would be "dispensed with."[10] Given the mood and constellation of forces at the Massachusetts Convention, this expectation was not very realistic.[11]

The Massachusetts Federalists realized that there was little prospect of converting the rank-and-file Antifederalists to their cause. Their only hope lay in persuading the two most prominent men in the state, Samuel Adams and Governor John Hancock—both of whom were elected to the state Ratifying Convention and were regarded as harboring antifederal sentiments—to accept the Constitution as a fait accompli. This entailed, above all, convincing them that the wisest course was to work for appending a bill of rights subsequent to ratification rather than making ratification contingent on prior constitutional revision. At this stage, the Federalists argued, unconditional ratification was absolutely necessary. Otherwise the entire constitutional enterprise might be dislocated by an endless process of state amendments in favor of a multitude of diverse rights. A letter from Nathaniel Gorham to Madison, dated January 27, explained the Federalists' dilemma: "We shall loose [*sic*] the question, unless we can take of[f] some of the opposition by amendments. I do not mean those to be made the condition of the ratification—but recommendatory only. Upon this plan I flatter myself we may possibly get a majority of 12 or 15—& not more."[12] This meant that the Federalists would themselves have to come up with a list of rights to be submitted to the Massachusetts Ratifying Convention for its approval. The first step was to obtain the consent of the two leading figures in the state to openly support this procedure.

Samuel Adams was well known as a veteran fighter on behalf of American freedom. He had been one of the first to publicly protest British impositions on the colonies, and he helped found Boston's Sons of Liberty, which took a leading part in organizing opposition to British demands. At a later stage, Adams was prominent as a vigorous advocate of independence from Great Britain, and he signed the Declaration of Independence. By virtue of his zealous career in revolutionary America, he was known as "father of patriots,"[13] and "Firebrand of the Revolution."[14] Subsequently, he assumed a significant role as a member of the Massachusetts state convention that drafted the 1780 state constitution, famous for its enunciation, in the First Part, of a detailed Declaration of Rights. It is also noteworthy that Article IV of that constitution, in line with Article II of the Articles of Confederation, stressed that Massachusetts reserved to itself "every power, jurisdiction, and right," not "expressly" delegated to the federal government.[15] Although in the early 1780s, Adams saw the need to grant congress power over commerce, he held that a general overall revision of the Articles would result in "the artifices of a few designing men" destroying the liberty of the people. In this he was at one with Elbridge Gerry who, at that stage, opposed "a general Revision of the Confederation."[16] This negative attitude helps explain why Massachusetts never managed to participate in the 1786 Annapolis Convention, which had aimed at producing uniform commercial regulations for the United States. Many of the state appointees declined to attend, and when a Massachusetts delegation was finally strung together, it turned back shortly before reaching Annapolis, after learning from returning New York and New Jersey delegates that the Convention had been disbanded for lack of a quorum.[17]

It was Shays' Rebellion in the winter of 1786 that, as noted earlier, helped dramatically change public opinion in and outside Massachusetts regarding the urgent need to strengthen federal power.[18] Thus, even Rufus King, who previously had been opposed to a constitutional convention, came to see the wisdom of such an assembly. "Events are hurrying to a crisis," he told Gerry, and "prudent and sagacious men should be ready to seize the most favourable circumstances to establish a more permanent and vigorous government."[19] King had served as a Massachusetts delegate to the Constitutional Convention, and now, as a confirmed Federalist, was actively canvassing for his state's ratification of the Constitution.

Samuel Adams, it should be noted, had been proposed as a delegate to the Constitutional Convention. but had declined on the ground that the Convention seemed bent on concentrating too much power in the national government.[20] Upon receipt of a copy of the Constitution, he had declared: "As I enter the Building, I stumble at the Threshold. I meet with a National Government instead of a foederal Union of Sovereign States."[21] His skeptical attitude to ratification represented a serious hurdle to be overcome. Unless it was overcome, then—as his cousin John Adams warned—Samuel Adams "will draw many good Men after him, and I Suppose place himself at the head of an opposition."[22]

Governor John Hancock—whose signature, as the first and most distinctive on the Declaration of Independence earned him undying fame—was a close colleague of Samuel Adams and likely held the key to turning the tide in Massachusetts. A wealthy merchant whose business activities had brought him into conflict with the British authorities, he had taken a leading part in organizing Massachusetts' support for the Revolution, and he later competed for the role of commanding officer of the revolutionary forces. He was known to be politically opportunistic, and the state Federalists, led by Rufus King, sought to strike a deal with him. If Hancock could be won over, there was a good chance that enough convention delegates would follow suit and ensure ratification. Moreover, Samuel Adams would be less prone to stand and fight alone.

While Hancock may have sympathized with the Antifederalists, he had refrained all along from announcing his position on the matter of ratification. When he forwarded the draft of the Constitution to the state legislature, he refused to adopt a stand on the "momentous" issue.[23] At its first session, the state ratifying convention elected Hancock as its chairman, but he did not attend. He was laid up in bed with gout; and some claimed that his ailment would be cured only when he knew which way the majority at the Convention would vote. As Rufus King wrote: "As soon as the majority is exhibited on either side I think his Health will suffer him to be abroad [out of doors]."[24] To avoid being on the losing side, Hancock wished to make certain that whatever stand he took would prevail. His vacillation and calculating nature apparently led the Federalists to offer him a series of inducements to lure him to their side. For one thing, they were ready to pledge their support to him for a further term as governor. Moreover, in the event that George Washington would consent to run for President, they would support Hancock for the office of Vice-President. As a Northerner, he would be their candidate for balancing the ticket. And—the biggest prize of all—if Virginia failed to ratify the Constitution, thus disqualifying Washington as a candidate for President, the Federalists would be prepared to endorse Hancock for President. No man of ambition would dismiss such a generous offer blithely. The deal was apparently struck, and Hancock was ready to propose that the Convention endorse a list of rights to be attached to the Constitution as amendments, *after* its entry into force.[25]

Hancock appeared at the Convention for the first time on the morning of January 30. Still suffering from gout, he was carried into the hall with his feet wrapped in flannels.[26] The next day he rose, as President of the Convention, to submit a proposal for the Convention to "*assent to* and *ratify* the said *Constitution for the United States of America*." His motive, he said, arose from his earnest desire "that this Convention may adopt such a form of government, as may extend its good influences to every part of the United States, and advance the prosperity of the whole world."[27] Ratification, Hancock indicated, had to be absolute. However, given the fears and apprehensions of "many of the good people of this Commonwealth," and in order to "more effectually guard against an undue administration of the federal government," the Convention would also recommend that certain "alterations and provisions" be introduced into the Constitution. Hancock read out a list of nine draft amendments, in which the crucial ones proposed radical modification of various powers of the federal government. Matters relating to freedom of speech and, more generally, freedom of conscience, were not included.[28] Hancock gave the impression that the entire proposal originated with him.[29]

Samuel Adams, however, was different in temperament and character. He could not be so easily influenced by flattery or bribery, although, in the meantime, his antagonism had mellowed somewhat. Initially, as noted earlier, he had expressed strong opposition to the Constitution in its present form and had called for amendments as a condition for ratification. "Mr A[dams]," it was said, "will be indefatigable & constant in all ways & means to defeat the adoption of the proposed frame of *Government*."[30] Nonetheless, he tended to view the idea of subsequent amendments as an acceptable alternative: it appears that the wishes of many of his commercial supporters had helped change his attitude. Aware of Adams's negative approach, some 380 Boston tradesmen assembled on January 7, convention eve, and unanimously adopted a resolution describing opposition to the Constitution as "contrary to their best interest, the strongest feelings, and warmest wishes."[31] In the wake of this meeting, Adams objected to an Antifederalist attempt at the convention to have consideration of the Constitution speeded up. He explained that he, and assuredly others, desired "a full investigation of the subject"; and though, admittedly, "he had had difficulties and doubts respecting some parts of the proposed Constitution," he had "chosen rather to be an auditor, than an objector." Consequently, "we ought not ... to be stingy of our time, or the publick money, when so important an object demanded them."[32]

In light of this change of heart, it is not surprising that, following Hancock's presentation on January 31, Samuel Adams declared himself happy with the "conciliatory proposition" of the President of the Convention, which would tend to remove doubts and "conciliate the minds of the convention, and the people without doors."[33] This initiative of recommendatory amendments, Adams said, would undoubtedly evoke a positive response from other states that had yet to vote on the question of ratification. It would help unite the nation in the preservation of "their valuable rights and liberties." Adams correctly foresaw that the pattern of recommendatory amendments would pave the way for the other large states to ratify the Constitution, and enable it to enter into force. In any event, the fact that the proposal was endorsed by both Governor Hancock and Samuel Adams meant that it now stood every chance of being approved by a majority of the Massachusetts Convention. Rufus King, in a message to Madison, wrote: "We flatter ourselves that the weight of these two characters [Hancock and Adams] will insure our success, but the Event is not absolutely certain."[34]

The next day, February 1, Samuel Adams commented on some of the amendments proposed by Hancock for adoption by the incoming Congress.[35] His analysis of the first draft amendment warrants careful attention, since it highlights a crucial demand of the Constitution's opponents. The amendment read: "That it be explicitly declared that all powers not expressly delegated to Congress, are reserved to the several States, to be by them exercised." To ensure against federal invasion of state authority, Adams assumed that the courts would exercise judicial review. Hancock's first amendment, Adams said, constituted:

> a summary of a bill of rights, which, gentlemen are anxious to obtain; it removes a doubt which many have entertained respecting this matter, and gives assurance that if any law made by the federal government shall be extended beyond the powers granted by the proposed Constitution, and inconsistent with the Constitution of this State, it will be an errour, and adjudged by the courts of law to be void.[36]

Such a provision, he asserted, would be the counterpart of the second Article in the Articles of Confederation designed to prevent encroachments of power.[37] The fact that Hancock had placed this amendment at the head of his list, and that Adams referred to it as a "summary of a bill of rights," underscored the importance that both men attached to this proposition. It is not a coincidence that it appeared at the top of every list of draft amendments subsequently drawn up by Antifederalists in the various states.[38]

Upon conclusion of the debate, the Hancock proposal was sent to a 25-man committee, which approved it and—with insignificant changes—submitted it to the plenary. The first sign that a majority of the convention now favored ratification was the defeat of an Antifederalist attempt to adjourn the deliberations. As Benjamin Lincoln wrote to George Washington: "This was a damper upon the oposition [sic] and they had little hope after."[39] A newspaper headline captured the significance of the vote. It read: "*AUSPICIOUS OMEN.*"[40] The vote on ratification was set for the next day, February 6.

At this late stage, Samuel Adams introduced a proposal to add to the earlier list an amendment dealing with individual rights, including freedom of the press and freedom of assembly.[41] While his suggestion might have been expected to garner wide support, it was in fact strongly opposed,[42] apparently because it was seen as a misplaced attempt to delay the vote. According to one report, both Federalists and Antifederalists were "alarmed" by Adams's proposal, and "once he perceived the mischief he had made," he withdrew his motion.[43]

As noted earlier, the list of amendments recommended by Hancock appears to have been prepared by Theophilus Parsons, Rufus King, and the other Federalists. One would have thought that their list, like the one ultimately presented by Madison for congressional approval, would have concentrated on rights of conscience and would have omitted anything that bore on the powers of Congress. Instead, the Parsons–King draft dealt primarily with the powers of Congress and was directed principally at precluding a doctrine of implied powers. Besides a crippling limitation on tax power, the new congress, like the Confederation Congress, would be confined to those powers "expressly" enumerated in the Constitution. Why, it might be asked, were Massachusetts' leading Federalists willing to thus cripple the national government by denying it the full use of the necessary and proper clause? Why would they portray the reenactment of an Article II-type provision—the bugbear of the Federalists—as a Federalist victory? Presumably they were operating under constraints that, in their opinion, forced their hand.

In the final Convention tally, 187 of the 355 delegates present voted in favor and 168 against.[44] Clearly, the nineteen-vote margin was secured as a result of the conversion of Hancock and Adams to the Federalist cause; and their support was attained only thanks to the Federalist initiative in proposing specific amendments. In a letter to Washington, Madison expressed his pleasure with the "favorable result of the Convention at Boston." The amendments, he said, "are a blemish, but are in the least Offensive form."[45] Obviously, he did not approve of the contents of the proposed amendments, but he was relieved that the challenge of prior amendments had been defeated. Ratification was unconditional and a vital precedent was established.

The implications of the Massachusetts ratification were enormous. It was the critical turning point in the struggle for ratification, and the claim that the "Conciliatory Resolutions saved the Constitution" was no exaggeration.[46] Bernard Bailyn, assessing the significance of the crucial vote, wrote: "The outcome of the Massachusetts convention … was a decisive turning point in the adoption of the Constitution. If Massachusetts had not ratified when and how it did, the Constitution might not have been adopted."[47] Massachusetts was the first large state that endorsed the Constitution while overcoming the objections of the nominal Antifederalist majority at its convention. (In Pennsylvania it was never a contest.) The success of the Federalists in promoting the compromise notion of amendments to be added *after* ratification opened the way for this pattern to be repeated in the remaining two large states, Virginia and New York, in both of which there were, reputedly, Antifederalist majorities.

Nevertheless, the task of the Federalists in these two states remained formidable, especially since the opposition camp in each comprised some leading personalities determined to defeat the Constitution despite the groundswell for ratification. True, the way had been shown for overcoming the primary complaint—the absence of a bill of rights; and the objectors, now placed in a defensive position, were obliged to explain why the Massachusetts formula was unacceptable. Yet the type of amendments recommended by the Massachusetts Convention posed a serious problem for Federalist campaigners. They could hardly promote the "express" powers amendment without feeling that thereby they would be dangerously shackling the new government from the outset.

Since Massachusetts was the seventh state to ratify, only two more assents were needed to formally bring the Constitution into force. Of the six states in which the decision on ratification was still pending, however, Virginia and New York had a pivotal role. Without Virginia, the ratification campaign would almost certainly fail; without New York alone it would survive, but in an impaired condition. The key question was whether both of these states would fall into line and ratify, or whether they would seek to undermine the Constitution either by requiring prior amendments or—far more ominously—by insisting on the holding of a second constitutional convention.

Virginia: "The Battle Royal." Where Lies Dominion?

> I cast my eyes to the actual situation of America; I see the dreadful tempest, to which the present calm is a prelude, if disunion takes place. I see the anarchy which must happen if no energetic Government be established. In this situation, I would take the Constitution were it more objectionable than it is.
>
> Edmund Randolph at the Virginia Ratifying Convention, June 17, 1788.[48]

Virginia, even more than New York, held the key to the success of the entire ratification process. It was the largest state in the Union, both in size and population, and it was strategically situated between north and south. With Virginia, there was union; without it, there would likely be none.

The fact that both Virginia and New York—for one reason or another—decided to postpone their ratifying conventions until the spring or summer of 1788 had important consequences. By the time they deliberated, Massachusetts, Pennsylvania, and six smaller states had already ratified, and no state had rejected the Constitution. Only one ratification was now required before the Constitution could enter into force. Naturally, pressure mounted on the two remaining larger states to fall into line.

In contrast to the contest in Massachusetts, where the outcome turned on the attitudes of two key players, Virginia represented an arena in which a fierce clash took place between distinguished personalities arrayed on both sides of the ideological divide.[49] James Madison was confronted by Patrick Henry, and both had supporting casts. George Mason, William Grayson, and James Monroe sided with Patrick Henry, while Edmund Randolph, George Nicholas, John Marshall, and Henry Lee rallied to Madison's side. Nonetheless, the burden of the battle was borne by the leading protagonists. Matters between former governor Patrick Henry and current governor Edmund Randolph became so tense that, at one point, Henry was compelled to apologize for the insensitivity of his remarks.[50] In both Virginia and New York, the opponents of ratification demanded prior amendments; and their aim was to defeat, rather than improve, the Constitution. To meet their challenge, it became imperative to concede on the bill of rights issue. The Massachusetts formula—unconditional ratification with a pledge to secure subsequent amendments—supplied the margin, albeit narrowly, in favor of ratification. While the Antifederalists sought to demonstrate the danger which the Constitution, minus a bill of rights, posed to individual freedoms, the objective of the Federalists—in both the Virginia and New York Conventions—was to reduce the controversy to one fundamental question: Would the Union survive as one entity or disband?

When the Virginia Ratifying Convention opened on June 2, 1788, there were four matters that bore heavily on their deliberations. First, there was a great awareness that the crucial ninth ratification hung in the balance. Second, it appeared that the Federalists had secured, at least nominally, a slim majority of 86:80 when the Convention commenced its proceedings in Richmond.[51] Only if the Federalists held firm could they prevail; any backsliding in their ranks would doom their prospects of success. They needed to enlist a foremost Federalist spokesman qualified to counter effectively the powerful rhetoric of the leading Antifederalist, Patrick Henry. As a prime architect of the Constitution, James Madison was a logical choice for that role. Third, the absence of a bill of rights promised to be the most critical issue in the debate. After all, the subject had spawned an outpouring of vigorous conflicting arguments in the Virginia media ever since the Constitution had been presented to the American people for ratification.[52] Fourth, Antifederalists would have to explain why the Massachusetts formula for unconditional ratification was unsuited to the Old Dominion, especially in light of the numerous states that had already ratified. Conditional ratification by Virginia would require all those states to repeat the process with respect to a revised constitution—a daunting task.

Even before the Virginia Convention assembled, James Madison recognized that the debate in Virginia, no less than in Massachusetts, would revolve around the demand for a bill of rights and the corollary issue of conditional ratification. In a letter to Jefferson, dated April 22, 1788, he wrote:

> The preliminary question will be whether previous alterations shall be insisted on or not? Should this be carried in the affirmative, either a conditional ratification, or a proposal for a new Convention will ensue. In either event, I think the Constitution, and the Union will be both endangered.[53]

Those states that had already ratified, Madison said, could not be expected to accept "the alterations prescribed by Virga." And a second convention would simply be an invitation for opponents of a federal constitution to sow disunion by proposing alterations popular in some states but unacceptable to others.[54]

"It is as little to be expected that the same spirit of compromise will prevail in it [a second convention] as produced an amicable result to the first."[55]

It is noteworthy that the two leading Antifederalists at the Virginia Convention, Patrick Henry and George Mason, seemed—at least initially—to have had different goals in mind. In a letter to his Antifederalist colleague, Elbridge Gerry, Mason wrote on October 20, 1787: "It wou'd be fortunate for America, if the Conventions in the different States ... confining themselves to a few necessary amendments, & determining to join heartily in the System so amended, they might, without Danger of public Convulsion or Confusion, procure a general Adoption of the new Government."[56] Thus, while striving to gain the adoption of some important amendments, Mason acquiesced in the adoption of the Constitution. Henry, in contrast, was intent on denying the legal validity of the Constitution entirely and defeating ratification. As Edward Carrington observed in a letter to Jefferson, dated April 24, 1788: "Mr. H— does not openly declare for a dismemberment of the Union, but his Arguments in support of his opposition to the constitution, go directly to that issue."[57] In advance of the state-ratifying convention, Henry had revealed his true intention by asking the state Assembly to approve contingency funds for deputies to be sent to "a second Federal Convention."[58]

At the opening of the debate, Patrick Henry moved that the documents relating to the appointment of the state delegates to the Philadelphia Convention be read.[59] His aim was to demonstrate that the delegates to the Constitutional Convention had exceeded their powers in proposing a new constitution, making the whole enterprise ultra vires. The highly respected President of the state Convention, Judge Edmund Pendleton, countered that the purpose of the present assembly was to consider the Constitution, as is. If the Philadelphia Convention found the previous system so defective that it felt compelled to propose a new one, the present Convention's task was to acknowledge this fact and proceed accordingly.[60] Henry thereupon withdrew his motion.

The next day, however, he reverted to his fundamental complaint before proceeding to set forth his detailed critique of the Framers' handiwork. "That they exceeded their power is perfectly clear," he said. "The Federal Convention ought to have amended the old system—for this purpose they were solely delegated."[61] The Virginia Convention was entitled to learn "the reasons that actuated" the Federal Convention to propose "an entire alteration of Government." "What right," Henry asked, "had they to say ... *We, the People*, instead of *We, the States*."[62] "Were they not deputed [to go to Philadelphia] by States, and not by the people?"[63] The change in language connoted a shift from a confederation to a consolidated, national government which could threaten and destroy the liberties of the people, he said. "Here is a revolution as radical as that which separated us from Great Britain... The rights of conscience, trial by jury, liberty of the press, all your immunities and franchises, all pretensions to human rights and privileges, are rendered insecure, if not lost."[64] The new system of government, Henry argued, was the converse of a democracy, since even a majority of the people could not alter it if they found it oppressive.[65]

"There will be no checks, no real balances, in this Government: What can avail your specious imaginary balances, your rope-dancing, chain-rattling, ridiculous ideal checks and contrivances."[66] "Will the great rights of the people be secured by this Government?" "This Government is not a Virginian but an American Government. Is it not therefore a Consolidated Government?"[67] Henry feared especially the absolute federal power of taxation which would ruin the country. Why not retain, in the first instance, the system of requisitions, and authorize the federal government to impose direct taxes only if a state defaulted?[68] A bill of rights, Henry said, was "indispensably necessary." He then called for the addition of a provision comparable to Article II of the Articles of Confederation, so that implied powers would be precluded. "A general positive provision should be inserted in the new system, securing to the States and the people, every right which was not conceded to the General Government, and that every implication should be done away."[69] Minimizing the fact that eight states had already ratified, he declared that they "can hardly stand on their own legs"[70]; and even if twelve and a half states ratified, this would not be reason for Virginia to follow suit if the new system posed a danger.[71] "Unless the government be amended, we can never accept it," he concluded.[72]

The first to respond to Henry's criticism was Governor Edmund Randolph, who now felt bound to support the Constitution, despite the doubts which had led him to be a dissenter at Philadelphia. "I come hither … to repeat my earnest endeavours for a firm energetic government … and to concur in any practical scheme of amendments; but I never will assent to any scheme that will operate a dissolution of the Union," he stated.[73] "The only question has ever been, between previous and subsequent amendments," but "the postponement of this Convention, to so late a day, has extinguished the probability of the former without inevitable ruin to the Union … the anchor of our political salvation." He would rather assent to the lopping off of his arm, he said, "before I assent to the dissolution of the Union."[74] Randolph then launched into an explanation of why the Articles of Confederation were "totally inadequate" as a system of government. "Was it not a political farce, to pretend to invest powers, without accompanying them with the means of putting them in execution? This want of energy was not a greater solecism than the blending together, and vesting in one body, all the branches of Government."[75] A change in the system of government was a "necessity [that] was obvious to all America." He reminded his listeners that he had been a witness from the beginning, since he had attended both the Annapolis Convention and the Constitutional Convention. In conclusion, he declared: "I refused my signature [at Philadelphia], and if the same reasons operated on my mind, I would still refuse, but as I think that those eight States which have adopted the Constitution will not recede, I am a friend to the Union."[76]

Two days later, Randolph expanded on his initial remarks by analyzing why Virginia could not possibly go its own way and must remain part of the Union. The state was in dispute with its neighbors on numerous matters—borders, navigation rights, fisheries, western lands—and were Virginia to sever itself from the Union, its situation on all these matters would be perilous. Randolph admitted that Virginia, no less than the other states, had treated the federal government with contempt. "Every one of them has conspired against it," he said.[77] This was because "it cannot, perhaps with propriety, be denominated a Government—being void of that energy requisite to enforce sanctions." "We want Government, Sir—A Government that will have stability, and give us security. For our present Government is destitute of the one, and incapable of producing the other."[78] His conclusion was unequivocal. The Confederation "is too defective to deserve correction. Let us take farewell of it, with reverential respect, as an old benefactor. It is gone, whether this House says so, or not. It is gone, Sir, by its own weakness."[79] Randolph called on his colleagues to "catch the present moment—seize it with avidity and eagerness—for it may be lost—never to be regained."[80]

Randolph's change of heart invigorated the Federalists and dismayed the Antifederalists. George Mason confessed that he did not know what had induced his "honorable colleague in the late Convention ... [who] once saw as great danger in it as I do ... to alter his opinion." But now, said Mason, Randolph seemed intent "to raise phantoms, and to shew a singular skill in exorcisms, to terrify and compel us to take the new Government with all its sins and dangers." However, "in its present form we never can accede to it." He acknowledged that the Confederation had defects and required reforming, but the Constitution, without previous amendments, was pregnant with dangers.[81]

Exhibiting none of the flair and oratory of Patrick Henry, Madison undertook, in measured tones and systematic analysis, to answer Henry's diatribe.[82] At times, he spoke so low he could hardly be heard. Madison called on Henry to demonstrate the dangers he claimed to see in the Constitution.[83] If "any dangerous and unnecessary powers be given to the general Legislature, let them be plainly demonstrated, and let us not rest satisfied with general assertions of dangers, without examination. If powers be necessary, apparent danger is not a sufficient reason against conceding them."[84] Madison denied the charge that the national government would be a consolidated, rather than a federal, one. In fact, he said, it was a mixture, being neither entirely national or federal. "It is of a complicated nature, and this complication, I trust, will be found to exclude the evils of absolute consolidation, as well as of a mere confederacy." "Who are parties to it? The people—but not the people as composing one great body—but the people as composing thirteen sovereignties."[85] Rejecting the charge of consolidation, Madison declared that the Congress would be restrained from encroaching on state prerogatives, first by "the general limitation of their powers," and second "by the general watchfulness of the States."[86] To counter Henry's complaint that nine states could put the Constitution into effect, Madison reminded the Convention of the absurdity of the unanimity requirement of the Articles of Confederation, and how a single state—indeed the smallest—had repeatedly frustrated majority will. "Could any thing in theory, be more perniciously improvident and injudicious, than this submission of the will of the majority to the most trifling minority?"[87]

Madison staunchly defended the necessary and proper clause as a vital part of the Constitution. In Federalist #44 he had written:

> Few parts of the Constitution have been assailed with more intemperance than this:[88] yet on a fair investigation of it, no part can appear more completely invulnerable. Without the SUBSTANCE of this power, the whole Constitution would be a dead letter.[89]

In place of the necessary and proper clause, Madison listed four possible alternatives, all of which he proceeded to dismiss: (1) copying Article II of the Articles of Confederation; (2) enumerating in detail all possible powers possessed by the federal government; (3) enumerating all powers excluded from the scope of federal authority; and (4) remaining silent and leaving the issue of necessary and proper powers "to construction OR IMPLICATION."

If the Convention had adopted the first course, Madison explained, by prohibiting the exercise of any power "not EXPRESSLY granted," the government might readily be disarmed "of all real authority whatever," like its predecessor. Alternatively, it might be compelled to totally disregard the restrictive provision and act as if it did not exist. Neither of these choices was proper or desirable. "It would be easy to show if it were necessary, that no important power, delegated by the articles of Confederation, has been or can be executed by Congress, without recurring more or less to the doctrine of CONSTRUCTION or IMPLICATION." To attempt the second or third alternatives, by enumerating all powers or exceptions to powers, was to engage in "chimerical" tasks. This left the last option: remaining silent. But this, he concluded in *Federalist* #44, would have changed nothing:

> There can be no doubt that all the particular powers, requisite as means of executing the general powers would have resulted to the government, by unavoidable implication. No axiom is more clearly established in law, or in reason, than that wherever the end is required, the means are authorised; wherever a general power to do a thing is given, every particular power necessary for doing it is included.[90]

At the Virginia Convention, Madison adduced similar reasoning to overcome Henry's condemnation of the "sweeping clause." Henry had argued that the clause would allow Congress "to make *any law* that will enable them to carry their acts into execution." "It will be dangerous," he said, "to trust them with such unbounded powers."[91] The "terrors" Henry envisaged, Madison claimed, were exaggerated. "If that latitude of construction which he contends for, were to take place with respect to the sweeping clause, there would be room for those horrors." But the clause gives no supplementary power. It was merely explanatory, designating the means by which to exercise the delegated powers, and as such, it was "only a superfluity." "If the delegation of their powers be safe," their execution is equally safe. "For when any power is given, its delegation necessarily involves authority to make laws to execute it."[92]

Madison likewise dismissed the Antifederalist objection to the federal taxing power, an issue that generated much heat.[93] "If a Government depends on other Governments for its revenues," he argued, "its existence must be precarious. A Government which relies on thirteen independent sovereignties, for the means of its existence, is a solecism in theory, and a mere nullity in practice."[94]

In the course of the debate, Henry raised the sensitive issue of the right of passage on the Mississippi River—a subject which, in light of the Confederation Congress's handling of the matter in 1785–1786, aroused considerable apprehension among southerners generally, and Kentuckians in particular.[95] Henry obviously wished to induce as many Kentuckian delegates as possible to reject the Constitution; and he was handsomely supported by James Monroe who, as a member of the Confederation Congress, had been a leading opponent of the abortive effort to surrender US rights on the Mississippi. Madison reacted by arguing that the Constitution offered greater protection than the Articles of Confederation against undesirable concessions to foreign states, since it conditioned the entry into force of treaties on the assent of two branches of government—the President and two-thirds of the Senate.[96]

Although Jefferson was not at the Virginia Convention (he was the US ambassador in Paris), his position on the matter of the bill of rights became an issue of contention. Henry cited letters written by Jefferson to Madison and others in February 1788, in which he had recommended that nine states ratify the Constitution, thus bringing it into force for the ratifying states, while four states refrain from ratifying until a bill of rights was appended. "We shall thus have all it's [*sic*] good, and cure it's [*sic*] principal defect," he wrote to Madison.[97] At the Convention, on June 9, Henry referred to the correspondence to demonstrate that the great Jefferson was also insistent on rejecting the government until amendments were added to the Constitution.[98] In response, both Madison and Pendleton contended that it was improper to invoke the opinion of a person, however distinguished, who was not present at the Convention.[99]

As the debate wore on, it became increasingly apparent that the key disputed issue was the timing and status of amendments to be appended to the Constitution. While Madison had consistently hoped that amendments could be avoided altogether, he realized that—in order to preserve his slim majority—he needed to appear flexible and reasonable. He could "never ... consent to his [Henry's] previous amendments," he said, "because they are pregnant with dreadful dangers"[100]; but he could accept some amendments, provided they were additions subsequent to ratification. The purpose of these latter, as Madison explained, would be "to conciliate some individuals who are in general well affected, but have certain scruples drawn from their own reflexions, or from the temper of their Constituents."[101] "Such amendments as seemed in his judgment, to be without danger, he would readily admit, and ... he would be the last to oppose any such amendment as would give satisfaction to any Gentleman."[102] Henry completely dismissed the suggestion for subsequent amendments. "I should be led to take that man to be a lunatic, who should tell me to run into the adoption of a Government, avowedly defective, in hopes of having it amended afterwards. Were I about to give away the meanest particle of my own property, I should act with more prudence and discretion."[103] In like vein, George Mason stated: "Amendments after ratification, are delusive and fallacious—perhaps utterly impracticable."[104]

As agreed upon by both parties, the Convention thoroughly debated the Constitution, provision by provision; and by June 23, after some 3 weeks of deliberations, Madison felt that the time was ripe for a vote. Any further delay could only threaten his majority. The Federalists took the initiative, and George Wythe, distinguished Williamsburg law professor and tutor to Jefferson and Marshall,[105] was delegated to present a resolution the next day for the unconditional approval of the Constitution. Any necessary amendments, Wythe said, "would be easily obtained *after ratification* in the manner proposed by the Constitution."[106] As expected, Henry challenged the Wythe proposal and called for the adoption of prior amendments, saying that they were "necessary to procure peace and tranquility."[107] It was absurd, he said, to adopt a system and rely on the chance of getting it amended afterwards. Amendments, he said, "must be previous to adoption, or it will involve this country [Virginia] in inevitable destruction." To illustrate his point about the danger of implied powers, Henry went on to say: "Among ten thousand implied powers which they may assume, they may, if we be engaged in war, liberate every one of your slaves."[108]

Henry had prepared two sets of amendments to be attached to the Constitution. One set was drawn from—and largely copied—the Virginia Declaration of Rights authored by George Mason. Essentially, it encompassed procedural rights and rights of conscience. The second list, containing fourteen draft amendments, would have introduced a series of substantive changes in the Constitution designed to "ensure state supremacy in any conflict with national authority."[109] At the head of that list was a provision like the second article of the Confederation, limiting the federal government to "express" enumerated powers. The federal government would also have been deprived of the right of direct taxation, except when a state refused to fulfill its requisition. Legislation in matters of trade would require a two-thirds majority for adoption by Congress. (As will be recalled, one of Mason's principal complaints at the Constitutional Convention had been that the North might adopt navigation laws that would disadvantage the South. A two-thirds majority requirement would forestall any such eventuality.) Power to maintain an army in time of peace would be restricted, and the federal judiciary would be basically limited to one supreme court. Henry's aim was manifestly to cripple the national government and nullify the entire achievement of the Constitutional Convention.

Both Randolph and Madison argued strongly against Henry's conditional amendments proposal. However, in order to promote a spirit of compromise and reconciliation, and ensure that wavering Federalist delegates would find no cause for offence, Madison announced that many of Henry's amendments could be adopted once the Constitution was ratified. "As far as his [Henry's] amendments are not objectionable, or unsafe, so far they may be subsequently recommended. Not because they are necessary, but because they can produce no possible danger, and may gratify some Gentlemen's wishes."[110] There was more than a mite of dissembling in this statement by Madison, for in fact, as one writer has noted, Henry's amendments "were as dangerous as a match in a powder magazine," and Madison never had any real intention of approving them.[111] Thanks to Madison's conciliatory approach, the Federalist bloc remained solid. In the vote, Henry's proposition that, previous to ratification, a bill of rights and amendments "ought to be referred ... to the other States" for their consideration, was defeated 80:88.[112] The Constitution was then ratified unqualifiedly by a vote of 89:79.[113]

In the wake of the vote, two committees were set up to prepare lists of amendments. One committee drafted a Declaration of Rights to be added to the Constitution, covering all the rights of conscience, while the other committee prepared a list of structural amendments that the Congress should adopt. The latter list was headed by a provision reserving to each state every power not "expressly" granted the federal government, and included many of the other restrictive draft amendments referred to earlier by Henry. The Convention accepted both documents and ordered that they be submitted to the First Congress for adoption; and Virginia's Representatives were directed "to exert all their influence" to ensure their adoption. It is noteworthy that in the final formulation, the word "expressly" was dropped from the first of the substantive proposals, that relating to reserved powers. This was clearly done at Madison's behest. Those moving the original draft formula obviously intended an absolute restriction on the powers of Congress, something that would have extinguished implied powers. They were compelled to settle for a formula that merely confirmed that all powers not granted the federal government remained with the states.[114]

Virginia's accession to the list of ratifying states meant that, regardless of what the remaining three states might do, the constitutional edifice was firmly established and the Union was preserved. Even if New York, Rhode Island, and North Carolina opted to isolate themselves in dissent, the federal structure would remain unaffected and the machinery of a national government for the United States would begin to operate. As Edward Carrington wrote to Jefferson on May 14, 1788, in advance of the Virginia Convention: "Should Virga. adopt, we shall at once, have a Government."[115] On the surface, the Constitution was now secure. It had berthed in a safe harbor and there was no danger of shipwreck. Only two contingencies, were they to materialize, could mar this idyllic picture: Antifederalist control of the First Congress on the one hand and a powerful second convention movement on the other. For the moment, however, the dangers seemed remote, and did not much exercise either Madison or his Federalist colleagues.

New York: "Convinced by Circumstances." Antifederalists Come Face to Face with Reality

> Under these circumstances, can the State of N. York have hardiness eno' to refuse their Assent? – or will she consent to stand on the same Ground with our deluded Sister R. Island. I would fain hope, that shameless Prostitute will not be able to find an Associate in her Sins & Follies.
>
> Jonathan Trumbull to George Washington, June 20, 1788.[116]

Federalists in New York were justly concerned that they faced an uphill battle to secure sufficient pro-Constitution delegates in the state convention to ensure ratification. It was in light of this feeling that Hamilton, before the end of 1787, proposed to John Jay and James Madison to join him in publishing a series of articles both to explain the provisions of the Constitution and why it was essential to ratify it. This was the genesis of the *Federalist Papers*, renowned as the best work on the science and philosophy of government ever to appear in the United States.

Publication of the *Federalist Papers* offered Hamilton a further opportunity to explicate on the dangers of disunity among the states, to which he had referred earlier in his letters and at the Constitutional Convention. In #6 and #7 he spelled out in detail the harm that the United States would suffer if the states could not overcome their rivalries and jealousies and preserve the Union by ratifying the Constitution. His previous admonitions had been directed to a small circle, and sought to convince them to forego their prejudices and accept majority will in the formulation of the Constitution; now he was campaigning publicly on behalf of national unity in an effort to ensure state ratification of the Constitution. In *Federalist* #5, John Jay, who had served as Secretary of Foreign Affairs under the Confederation, outlined the dangers of foreign intervention in American affairs. It was probable, he wrote, that unless the states united, like "most other *bordering* nations, they would always be either envolved in disputes and war, or live in the constant apprehension of them." As a result, "weakness and divisions at home, would invite dangers from abroad." "Let candid men judge then whether the division of America into any given number of independent sovereignties would tend to secure us against the hostilities and improper interference of foreign nations."

In *Federalist* #6 and #7, Hamilton carried the argument a step further, contending that the dangers from disunity that arose on the domestic level were even more "alarming" than those that were likely to ensue "from the arms and arts of foreign nations":

> To look for a continuation of harmony between a number of independent, unconnected sovereignties, situated in the same neighborhood, would be to disregard the uniform course of human events, and to set at defiance the accumulated experience of ages.[117]

After reviewing the course of history, and how jealousy and rivalry between nations had led to countless wars, Hamilton enumerated the particular factors in America that would operate to produce strife and hostility between states, or groups of states. The vast area of the United States was fertile ground for territorial disputes, many of which had already arisen under the Confederation. The Western territory, he said, represented "an ample theatre for hostile pretensions, without any umpire or common judge to interpose between the contending parties." The competitions of commerce was another field inviting controversy. Similarly, the public debt of the Union would be a further cause of collision. And laws in violation of private contracts, since they amounted to "aggressions" on the rights of citizens of other states, were also probable sources of hostility between states or federations of states. In conclusion, reverting to the dangers of alliances with foreign nations, Hamilton declared:

> America, if not connected at all, or only by the feeble tie of a simple league, offensive and defensive, would by the operation of such opposite and jarring alliances be gradually entangled in all the pernicious labyrinths of European politics and wars; and by the destructive contentions of the parts into which she was divided, would be likely to become a prey to the artifices and machinations of powers equally the enemies of them all.[118]

Whether arguments based on the dangers of discord between the states influenced the selection of delegates to the state ratifying conventions is open to question, no less than the question of the measure of influence of the *Federalist Papers* generally in the struggle over ratification, immortal as the collection became.[119] In the debate at the state conventions, however, the threat of war between the states was resoundingly adverted to, and, as demonstrated, would seem to have played a crucial role in securing majority support for ratification in certain instances.

After the New York Ratifying Convention had been in session for some two weeks, Hamilton summed up the situation in a letter to Madison: "Our arguments confound, but do not convince. Some of the leaders however appear to me to be convinced *by circumstances* and to be desirous of a retreat. This does not apply to the Chief, who wishes to establish *Clintonism* on the basis of *Antifoederalism.*"[120] In light of Hamilton's assessment, it is worth tracing how the New York Convention came to retreat from its earlier stand and ratify the Constitution.

When the Convention opened in Poughkeepsie on June 17, 1788, the Antifederalists outnumbered the Federalists by more than two-to-one–46 delegates to 19.[121] The Antifederalists, led by Governor Clinton, were poised to condition ratification on the adoption of substantive changes in the Constitution or on the holding of a second constitutional convention. Within 2 weeks, however, they realized they had blundered. Their strategy had miscarried badly.

Initially, when the state legislature met in January 1788 to schedule a ratifying convention, both parties had found the June date for the Poughkeepsie Convention convenient. The Federalists were anxious to delay matters in order to gain time for convincing the state's voters to select delegates supporting ratification. Moreover, they assumed that by June, the Constitution would likely have been ratified by nine states, making it that much more difficult for New York to object to ratification. For their part, the Antifederalist majority wanted to act while avoiding the stigma of Constitution-doomers—in view, especially, of the flak from other states encountered by Clinton and his supporters when New York rejected the impost under the Confederation.[122] They anticipated that by June, one or more other states would have voted against ratification, and New York would be in a position simply to join the opposition camp. However, during the first week of the New York Convention, word arrived that a ninth state, New Hampshire, had ratified, allowing the Constitution to enter into force. This, in itself, was not fatal to Antifederal maneuvering; but when, a week later, the news of Virginia's ratification arrived, the cards became critically stacked against those seeking prior revision of the Constitution as a condition for ratification. The United States would have a federal government regardless of what New York decided. New York could determine what its position would be vis-à-vis the Union, but it could no longer settle the fate of the Union itself. As Rufus King reported to Madison, should New York vote against ratification, "the character of the Constitution will not thereby be injured."[123] The New York delegates ultimately had to come to terms with a Hobson's choice situation.

When the Convention opened its deliberations, both Federalist and Antifederalist delegates agreed that before any votes were taken the Constitution should be debated extensively, clause by clause, and proposals for amendments would be entertained at each stage. Evidently, the same considerations that had prompted them to postpone the Convention to June also led them to desire an exhaustive debate. By the time the three-week discussions ended on July 7, the Convention delegates had been bombarded by a battery of amendments proposed by the Antifederalists for addition to the Constitution. At this point, however, the Antifederalists began to falter and to begin to negotiate the terms of their surrender. Although the surrender was never all-encompassing—with Governor Clinton and other diehards remaining steadfast in their opposition to the Constitution—enough critics (led by Melancton Smith) were prepared to relent. The Antifederalist campaign progressed from a defiant demand for prior amendments, to a willingness to bargain, and ultimately to accepting unconditional ratification. Accompanying this acceptance, however, was a unanimously endorsed circular letter from the Convention. It was addressed to all the other states and urged them to join in applying to Congress for a second constitutional convention to be held in the near future—an ominous prospect!

Unlike the Virginian arena, where giants battled and the opposing positions were elaborately and eloquently presented, at Poughkeepsie the campaign against the Constitution was somewhat desultory both in content and presentation. The Antifederalist camp lacked champion debaters of the caliber of a Patrick Henry, or even of a George Mason. Since it was agreed that amendments could be proposed at every stage of the debate, the Antifederalists got bogged down in arguing on minutiae in one draft amendment after another, and they never succeeded in presenting a broad and substantive challenge to the Constitution. Governor Clinton, President of the Convention and head of the Antifederalists, was not a great orator, and he kept his interventions to a minimum. The leading spokesmen for the Antifederalists were Melancton Smith and John Lansing Jr. Lansing, it will be recalled, had been one of the three delegates representing New York at the Constitutional Convention, but together with his colleague, Robert Yates, he had left Philadelphia early to protest the nationalist program promoted by the majority. The rhetoric of Smith and Lansing never matched that of Hamilton.[124] Though Hamilton may not have succeeded in persuading the opposition, his arguments were impressive. John Jay, the leader of the Federalists, spoke less frequently and more tersely than Hamilton. However, by adopting a more conciliatory tone than Hamilton—whose remarks sometimes appeared rather strident—it was Jay who paved the way for some sort of rapprochement with the opposition forces.[125]

The defiant attitude that the Antifederalists adopted at the beginning of the Convention is well illustrated by the response of John Lansing to the address of the first speaker, Robert R. Livingston, the state Chancellor. Livingston urged the delegates to seize the opportunity for New York to join the national union. The Confederation had been proven defective, since "it operated upon states in their political capacity, and not upon individuals."[126] It was necessary, he said, that Congress be capable not only of forming laws, but also of carrying them "into effect." He warned his fellow delegates of the dangers inherent in a breakup of the Union. To this, Lansing answered: "However much I may wish to preserve the Union, apprehensions of its dissolution ought not to induce us to submit to any measure which may involve in its consequences the loss of civil liberty."[127] "A consolidated government" exercising control over "the inhabitants of the extensive territory of the United States," he said, "could not preserve the essential rights and liberties of the people." Therefore, despite "the pain" with which he might contemplate "a possible dissolution," this was no reason to abandon the existing Confederation.[128] He differed from those who maintained that the Articles were "incapable of amelioration." With provision of "a power to raise men and money," the Confederation would answer to all needs of the United States.[129]

In contrast to Lansing, Melancton Smith assumed a much more reasonable posture. He would not "now say that the adoption of the Constitution would endanger our liberties; because that was the point to be debated." He was "as strongly impressed with the necessity of a Union as any one could be" and "would seek it with as much ardor." To this end, "he was disposed to make every reasonable concession." However, he foresaw that the powers of the federal government would extend "to every thing dear to human nature." And "that power which had both the purse and the sword had the government of the whole country, and might extend its powers to any and every object."[130] His first objection was directed to the insecurity of rights owing to the inadequate number of Representatives in the lower House.

The tendency to become mired in details was never better illustrated than in the debate on representation. Discussion of the ideal composition of the national legislature extended for a week. The small number of Representatives, it was argued, meant that they were prone to corruption. Government would "fall into the hands of the few and the great" and become oppressive.[131] Melancton Smith moved that the number of Representatives in the first Congress be doubled.[132] To make the Senators more responsible to the states they represented, an amendment was moved to limit them to one term of six years in twelve, and to make them subject to recall.[133]

The open-ended nature of the powers of Congress was a matter of acute anxiety to the Antifederalists. Thus, John Williams observed that the power "to provide for the common defence, and the general welfare" were "indefinite, undefinable terms"[134] which, when combined with the necessary and proper clause, meant that "the Legislature … may pass any law which they think proper."[135] The taxing power would also be "undefinable" and potentially limitless.[136] "If we adopt this Constitution," he warned, "it is impossible, absolutely impossible to know what we give up, and what we retain."[137] Support of the government would fall upon the poor; they will be made "beasts of burthen to the rich."[138] He therefore moved an amendment according to which requisitions would first be levied upon the states, and only if these failed, would the federal government have power to impose direct taxes.[139] "Unless some certain specific source of revenue is reserved to the states," Melancton Smith declared, "their governments, with their independency, will be totally annihilated."[140]

The absence of a bill of rights was not particularly stressed in the Convention debates. The issue, however, was raised in various New York publications, and was stressed in an address that was apparently prepared for delivery at the Convention, but never presented. It subsequently appeared as an article, and was attributed by Elliot to Thomas Tredwell. "This government," he declared, was "founded in sin, and reared up in iniquity. The foundations are laid in a most sinful breach of public trust, and the top-stone is a most iniquitous breach of public faith."[141] If it were to go into operation, he said, "we shall be justly punished with the total extinction of our civil liberties." Tredwell rejected the Federalist argument that the national government, with defined and limited powers, could not threaten the rights of citizens. He pointed to the various rights expressly protected in the Constitution to demonstrate that the reserved powers doctrine was false. Summing up his fears regarding the rights of citizens, he declared:

> In this Constitution, sir, we have departed widely from the principles and political faith of '76, when the spirit of liberty ran high, and danger put a curb on ambition. Here we find no security for the rights of individuals, no security for the existence

of our state governments; here is no bill of rights, no proper restriction of power; our lives, our property, and our consciences, are left wholly at the mercy of the legislature, and the powers of the judiciary may be extended to any degree short of almighty.[142]

Since the issue of the absence of a bill of rights was not stressed in the Convention, Hamilton obviously had no need to argue why its absence was no blemish. In *Federalist* #84, in addition to presenting the Wilsonian thesis that the federal government could not threaten rights since it was a government of delegated and defined powers, Hamilton also contended that the Constitution itself was the best bill of rights that could be devised. By declaring and specifying "the political privileges of the citizens in the structure and administration of the government," the Constitution offered a sure means of preserving and protecting rights. The opening words of the Constitution, "We the people of the United States," provided "a better recognition of popular rights than volumes of those aphorisms ... which sound much better in a treatise of ethics than in a constitution of government," said Hamilton.[143] Apparently, the debate in Poughkeepsie focused primarily on the issue of federal powers, especially on that of excises and imposts, which New York stood to surrender to the federal government, and less on such matters as rights of conscience. Hamilton accordingly directed his main remarks to demonstrating that the system of requisitions had failed dismally, that the states retained the power to tax, and on denying that the powers of the national government threatened the sovereignty of the states.[144]

As impressive as were the counter-arguments of Hamilton, Jay, and other Federalists on these and other subjects, they failed to assuage the Antifederalists or to convince any of them to switch sides. Even the news of the New Hampshire and Virginia ratifications did not seem to make a dent in the Antifederalist phalanx. When the debate ended on July 7, the Antifederalists caucused for several days regarding the draft amendments they should propose for adoption. On July 10, Lansing presented a formal list of three types of amendments—explanatory, conditional, and recommendatory.[145] All in all, there were 55 proposed amendments,[146] and this from a state that was powerless to impose its will on the 10 states that had already ratified or to impede the entry into operation of the unamended Constitution! Lansing also proposed that an informal committee composed of fourteen members, equally divided between Federalists and Antifederalists, be formed to resolve matters relating to the final form of the proposed amendments.[147] John Jay led the Federalist team, from which Hamilton and Livingston—whose sharp rhetoric had not endeared them to the Antifederalists—were notably absent. The committee met immediately, but the issue of how to handle the question of amendments proved to be a major stumbling block to reaching a consensus between the two opposing camps.

Jay made it clear from the outset that the Antifederalists' idea of a conditional ratification would be totally unacceptable to Madison and the other

Federalists.[148] He submitted a motion to have the Convention ratify unconditionally, seek explanations for those parts of the Constitution not clearly understood, and recommend amendments that might be deemed useful or expedient.[149] Days went by as the Antifederalists tried to square the circle—to devise a formula that would denote conditional ratification, yet not be construed—and thus condemned—as rejection of the Constitution. Melancton Smith, who had led the fight on behalf of the Antifederalists, proposed that New York ratify with a right to secede if amendments were not adopted within a certain time frame; and until a convention was held to propose amendments, the Congress would refrain from imposing various laws and taxes on New York. In response, the Federalists argued that this suggestion was but another form of a conditional, rather than an actual, ratification.[150] Both sides were in a quandary, and even Hamilton, in writing to Madison, expressed his bewilderment at the state of affairs. "We are debating on amendments without having decided what is to be done with them. There is so great a diversity in the views of our opponents that it is impossible to predict any thing. Upon the whole, however, our fears diminish."[151]

The reason the Federalists remained hopeful was because the Antifederalists, despite their overwhelming numbers, were in a predicament. They could have overpowered the Federalists, but such action would have stamped them as rejecters of the Constitution, and it was fraught with consequences that they wished to avoid. The hopes of New York City to be selected as the capital of the United States would be dashed. Detaching the state of New York from the Union would also terminate New York's status as the leading port of the nation, while other ports would be serviced. In light of all this, New York City—a Federalist bastion—might well decide to secede from the state. The threat of secession, though not explicit, had been hinted at on various occasions and could not be entirely discounted.[152] Moreover, even if the state remained united, tension between supporters of the Constitution and its opponents might result in outbreaks of violence. Above all, could the state of New York afford to go it alone? As part of the federal Union, it could at least work to promote the adoption of the amendments that would "cure" the Constitution. By remaining outside, it would forfeit this advantage as well as other benefits of membership in the Union.

On July 19, when the Convention reassembled, Lansing submitted a resolution along the lines of Melancton Smith's proposal of conditional ratification, with a bill of rights prefixed. It was approved, and the Convention spent the next few days revising and formulating the amendments it desired.[153] The first draft amendment in the list dealt with elections and the second with the powers of Congress. According to the papers of Gilbert Livingston, a debate ensued about denying Congress the right to exercise implied powers. The relevant clause in Lansing's draft stipulated: "No power [was] to be exercised—but what is expressly given." Hamilton argued against the proposal, saying that Congress would be required to do countless things not expressly defined.[154] Nonetheless, when Lansing's draft Bill of Rights was adopted by the Convention for submission to Congress, the relevant clause in the preamble to the Bill of Rights contained the formula of his initial draft. Reflecting Antifederalist dominance, it was absolute, and read as follows:

> [E]very Power, Jurisdiction and right, which is not by the said Constitution *clearly* delegated to the Congress of the United States, or the departments of the Government thereof, remains to the People of the several States, or to their respective State Governments to whom they may have granted the same; And that those Clauses in the said Constitution, which declare, that Congress shall not have or exercise certain Powers, do not imply that Congress is entitled to any Powers not given by the said Constitution; but such Clauses are to be construed either as exceptions to certain specified Powers, or as inserted merely for greater Caution.[155]

The finale of the New York Ratifying Convention, which occurred several days later, was remarkable and dramatic. On July 23, Samuel Jones, a prominent Antifederalist from Queens County, who had been mulling over the dire implications for New York of a probable rejection by Congress of a conditional ratification, moved that the phrase "on condition" in Lansing's resolution be expunged and replaced by the term "in full confidence." This revolutionary motion, supported also by Melancton Smith and eleven other Antifederalists, was carried by the razor-thin majority of 30:27.[156] An attempt by Lansing to insert a right of secession by the state in the event that the desired amendments were not adopted was defeated 31:28.[157] The Federalists, however, paid a price for New York's approval. As part of the Antifederalist switch, it was agreed that a letter would be formulated calling upon the other states to apply to Congress to summon a second constitutional convention. Apparently the Federalists had so far committed themselves to this idea that they actively engaged in drafting the letter and ensuring that it would be supported unanimously. The text was formulated primarily by John Jay, with the support of John Lansing and Melancton Smith; and Alexander Hamilton worked arduously to convince the delegates to act with unanimity.[158] Thus, while New York, like other key states, endorsed a bill of rights, its price for becoming an integral part of the Union was, additionally, the call for a second constitutional convention.

New York's unqualified endorsement of the Constitution meant that the Federalists had made a clean sweep of the ratification process. Eleven states had accepted the Constitution without any reservations, and no state had rejected it.[159] The real coup lay in the endorsement of the last three states, Massachusetts, Virginia, and New York, all large states without whose participation the operation of the Union would have been adversely affected, if not undermined. Each of these states had attached a draft bill of rights for adoption by the First Congress, but in no way was this made a condition precedent for ratification, which was final and absolute in each case. On the surface, the Federalists had scored a great victory. This is obviously also the way John Jay and Alexander Hamilton viewed matters from the vantage point of New York state, where success had literally hung by a thread. Clearly enough, they saw no cause for concern in the resolution calling for a second constitutional convention which they had so avidly helped sponsor. For them, the call for a convention was no different from the demand for a bill of rights, which the other two large states had also presented. That the promotion of a bill of rights was defined and directed to Congress, while the convention call was directed to the states and open game for unlimited constitutional change, apparently did not occur to them. It did, however, occur to one Virginian Federalist, who found the implications of the circular letter to the states greatly alarming. In his view it placed in jeopardy the entire Federalist enterprise.

NOTES

1. The phrase is borrowed from Theophilus Parsons, Jr., who wrote: "These 'Conciliatory Resolutions' saved the Constitution." *Memoir of Theophilus Parsons.* (Boston, MA: Ticknor and Fields, 1859); cited in *DHRC*, 7: 1789.
   In an editorial note, Herbert Storing states that the Massachusetts formula "proved to be the compromise used to secure ratification in other states, tempering the opposition of the Anti-Federalists while maintaining the integrity of the Constitution." Storing, *Antifederalist*, 4:4.
   In an editorial note, Bernard Bailyn writes: "The outcome of the Massachusetts convention … was a decisive turning point in the adoption of the Constitution. If Massachusetts had not ratified when and how it did, the Constitution might not have been adopted." *Debate on Constitution*, Part 1: 1190.
   The appearance of Pauline Maier's monumental study, *Ratification: The People Debate the Constitution, 1787–1788* (New York: Simon & Schuster, 2010), has greatly expanded our knowledge of the critical nature of the contest in the three large states. My focus is on the outcome of the contest and how this paved the way for the ultimate adoption of the Bill of Rights. The Maier volume provides vast and fascinating background material.
2. March 13, 1788, *DHRC*, 16: 67; cited in John P. Kaminski, "Restoring the Grand Security: The Debate Over a Federal Bill of Rights, 1787–1788," 33 *Santa Clara Law Review*, 902 n. 139 (1993).
3. March 7, 1788, *DHC*, 4: 534; *GWP* 6: 147 (Confederation Series).
4. Edward Carrington, in a letter to Jefferson dated November 10, 1787, noted that the Virginia legislature had postponed the state convention until May, but he expressed doubts whether this would avail the Antifederalist cause: "The long postponement was occasioned by unfriendly intentions toward it [the Constitution], but I apprehend the rapidity of the movements of the other States in the business will, by that time, have brought so many into adoption, that even its enemies will see the *necessity* of joining." *TJP*, 12: 336. George Washington, in a letter to Madison dated January 10, 1788, wrote:

> Of all the arguments which may be used at this time, none will be so forcible, I expect, as that nine States have acceded to it. And if the unanimity, or majorities in those which are to follow, are so great as in those which have acted, the power of these arguments will be irrisistable. [*sic*] *JMP*, 10: 358.

5. See Chronology, *DHRC*, 7: xx. The vote in Pennsylvania was 46:23, and in Connecticut 128:40. For text of ratifications, see Tansill, *Documents*, 1009–1017.
   For an early account of the ratification struggle (before the full record published in the multi-volume *The Documentary History of the Ratification of the Constitution* became available), see Robert Allen Rutland, *The Ordeal of the Constitution: The Antifederalists and the Ratification Struggle of 1787–1788* (Norman: University of Oklahoma Press, 1966).
6. See essays by Vox Populi, in Storing, *Antifederalist*, 4.4.23–4.4.24; Agrippa, ibid., 4.6.71; and A Republican Federalist, ibid., 4.13.13–4.13.16.
7. See editorial comment, *DHRC*, 6: 1114ff. See also Melancton Smith to Abraham Yates, Jr., Jan. 28, 1788, ibid., 5: 1091, reporting that there were 201 against the Constitution and 119 for. Francis Baylies later said: "The weight of numbers was decidedly against it [the Constitution]." Ibid., 7: 1779.
8. Ibid., 5: 754; *JMP*, 10: 398–399. See also letter of Feb. 10 from Edward Carrington to Henry Knox, stating that the reports by Madison and Knox on Massachusetts "alarm me exceedingly." If that state, in conjunction with Virginia, should reject ratification, they might, he warned, "frustrate the measure altogether." *DHRC*, 5: 1102.
9. Ibid., 5: 1093–1094, *JMP*, 10: 411.
10. Letter to Washington, Feb. 8, 1788. Ibid., 10: 482.
11. Nathaniel Gorham, in a letter to Madison dated January 27, opined: "Never was there an Assembly in this State in possession of greater ability & information than the present Convention—yet I am in doubt whether they will approve the Constitution." Ibid., 435. And Francis Baylies described the period as being "of the most intense anxiety," adding: "It was thought throughout the States, that the rejection of the Constitution in Massachusetts, would be the precursor, not only of an entire dissolution of the Union, but of universal anarchy." *DHRC*, 7: 1779.
12. *JMP*, 10: 436.
13. See *DHRC*, 5: 642. For a fascinating and vivid account of the place of Samuel Adams in the pantheon of Founders, see Pauline Maier, *The Old Revolutionaries: Political Lives in the Age of Samuel Adams* (New York: Knopf, 1980), chap. 1. See ibid., 5, citing Thomas Jefferson's description of Adams as "the Man of the Revolution."
14. Alexander Winston, "Firebrand of the Revolution," *American Heritage Magazine*, April 1967.
15. Editor's introduction, *DHRC*, 4: xxvii.
16. Ibid., xxxiv.
17. Ibid., xxxv–xxxvii. On the Annapolis Convention, see above, Chap. 2, text at nn. 21–26.

18. On Shays' rebellion and its impact, see *DHRC*, 4: xxxix–xl, and see above, Chap. 2, text at nn. 26–36. For the influence of the rebellion on the Massachusetts Convention, see Richard D. Brown, "Shays' Rebellion and the Ratification of the Federal Constitution in Massachusetts" in Richard Beeman et al. (eds.), *Beyond Confederation: Origins of the Constitution and American National Identity* (Chapel Hill: University of North Carolina Press, 1987), 113–127. For short summaries of the event see Pauline Maier, *Ratification*, 15–17 and Beeman, Richard, *Plain, Honest Men: The Making of the American Constitution* (New York: Random House, 2010), 16–18.
19. Cited in *DHRC*, 4: xxxix.
20. See John J. Fox, "Massachusetts and the Creation of the Federal Union, 1775–1791" in Patrick T. Conley and John P. Kaminski (eds.), *The Constitution and the States: The Role of the Original Thirteen in the Framing and Adoption of the Federal Constitution* (Madison, WI: Madison House, 1988), 125.
21. Letter to Richard Henry Lee, Dec. 3. *DHRC*, 4: 349. This comment very much matches the comment Patrick Henry was due to make at the opening session of the Virginia Ratifying Convention. See below, text at nn. 59–63.
22. Letter from John Adams to Cotton Tufts, Jan. 23, 1788. *DHRC*, 5: 779.
23. See editor's comment, ibid., 6: 1117.
24. Ibid., 6: 1118.
25. This account is drawn basically from ibid., 6: 1118–1121.
26. Convention Journal, 30 Jan., ibid., 6: 1365.
27. Ibid., 6: 1381. Emphasis in the original.
28. Ibid., 6: 1381–1382. The nine proposed amendments were: (1) All powers not expressly delegated to Congress are reserved to the states. (2) There shall be one Representative for every thirty thousand persons. (3) Congress shall not prescribe rules for elections unless a state fails to do so. (4) Congress shall not impose direct taxes unless impost inadequate. (5) Congress shall not grant commercial monopolies. (6) No person to be tried for serious crime unless indicted by grand jury. (7) No jurisdiction to Supreme Court for claims by citizens of different states unless a major sum involved. (8) Disputes of fact between citizens of different states to be tried by jury. (9) Congress shall not be empowered to allow a citizen to accept any title from a foreign state.
29. The list had been drafted by the Federalists and conveyed to the Governor. See editor's introduction, ibid., 1120. However, he desisted from reading from the paper that they had prepared for him, lest this give the game away. He wished to convey the impression that the list was conceived and formulated by him alone. In fact, his secretary, James Sullivan, later Governor of Massachusetts, rewrote the complete draft, and it was from this paper, in the handwriting of his secretary, that Hancock read it to the assembled delegates. See letter of Josiah Quincy to Theophilus Parsons, April 23, 1857. Ibid., 7: 1794–1797. Parsons' father was regarded as one of the prime architects of the draft amendments. Quincy, formerly President of Harvard College, corrected Parsons' assumption that Hancock had read from the manuscript prepared by Parsons' father. Ibid., 1795. Quincy's description of the events of the Massachusetts convention is invaluable. See his account, ibid., 1795–1797.

   Hancock's biographer rejects this "simplistic" interpretation of his conduct. See William M. Fowler, Jr., *The Baron of Beacon Hill* (Boston, MA: Houghton, Mifflin, 1980), 272.

30. See letter of Christopher Gore to Rufus King, Jan. 6, on the eve of the state convention (emphasis in original). *DHRC*, 5: 627.
31. Ibid., 5: 632; and see editorial note, ibid., 5: 630–631.
32. Convention Debates, Jan. 24. Ibid., 6: 1335.
33. Ibid., 6: 1384.
34. Feb. 3, 1788. *JMP*, 10: 465.
35. *DHRC*, 6: 1394–1396.
36. Ibid., 6: 1395.
37. Ibid.
38. Adams also implicitly commended the Governor for not seeking, like others, to reinstate requisitions. Hancock had merely recommended that direct taxes not be imposed unless monies from the impost and excise prove "insufficient for the public exigencies." Thus, the matter was left to the discretion of Congress, and this body, Adams was sure, would not venture to impose such taxes unless the public exigency required it. Ibid., 1395–1396.
39. Feb. 6, ibid., 7: 1582.
40. Ibid., 6: 1452.
41. Ibid., 6: 1452–1454.
42. Ibid., 6: 1453.
43. Ibid., 6: 1452–1453. See letter of Jeremy Belknap to Ebenezer Hazard, Feb. 10, ibid., 7: 1583–1584.
44. Ibid., 6: 1467. The excitement in the gallery was so intense that it was reported that people remained glued to their seats all day, for fear of losing them if they dared move out. They ordered lunch to be brought to them there in the gallery. See letter of Henry Jackson to Henry Knox, Feb. 6. Ibid., 7: 1580.
45. Letter to George Washington, Feb. 15, 1788. *DHC*, 4: 505; *JMP*, 10: 510.
46. See letter of Henry Jackson to Henry Knox, Feb. 10, stating: "Governour Hancock has gained himself immortal Honor, in his conduct on this occasion—it is certain if he had not taken an active—indeed a very active part in favor of the adoption, we never should have gained a vote in favor of it." *DHRC*, 7: 1585. In contrast to the ill feeling created after the vote in Pennsylvania, in Massachusetts even those who had voted against ratification felt honor bound to respect the majority vote and pledged to support the Constitution thereafter and convince their electorates to do likewise. The goodwill exhibited at the conclusion of the Convention's deliberations was widely commented on in the newspapers and in private correspondence. See ibid., 6: 1487–1489, 1494–1497; and especially 7: 1645–1657, including a letter from George Washington to Benjamin Lincoln, dated Feb. 29, ibid., 1653.
47. Bernard Bailyn (ed.), *Debate*, Part 1, 1190.
48. *DHRC*, 10: 1353.
  For an insightful analysis of the Virginia Convention, see Jon Kulka, "A Spectrum of Sentiments: Virginia's Federalists, Antifederalists, and 'Federalists Who Are for Amendments,' 1787–1788," *Virginia Magazine of History and Biography*, 96 (1988): 276-296.
49. In a letter dated April 25, Washington wrote: "There will be a greater weight of abilities opposed to the system in the convention of this State [Virginia] than there has been in any other." Letter to John Armstrong, Sr., *DHRC*, 9: 760.

50. See ibid., 9: 1057–1058, 1081–1082, 1087, n. 1. Henry's biographer quotes an Antifederalist who compared the Convention to a ship with "one half the Crew hoisting sail for the land of Energy—and the other looking with a longing aspect on the Shore of Liberty." Henry Mayer, *A Son of Thunder: Patrick Henry and the American Republic* (Charlottesville: University Press of Virginia, 1991), 396–397.
51. See Alan V. Briceland, "Virginia: The Cement of the Union" in Conley and Kaminski, *Constitution and States*, 212.
52. On the demand in Virginia for a bill of rights, see George Mason's Objections to the Constitution, *DHRC*, 8: 43, 45; Madison's reference to Mason's criticism in his letter to Jefferson, Oct. 24, 1787 (reporting that Mason "considers the want of a Bill of Rights as a fatal objection"), ibid., 106; letter of Richard Henry Lee to Edmund Randolph, Oct. 16, 1787 (which Lee asked be publicized), ibid., 62, 65–66; Virginia Independent Chronicle, Oct. 31, ibid., 139; A True Friend, Dec. 6, 1787, ibid., 220; "The Impartial Examiner I," Feb. 20, ibid., 393–394, 462; letter of George Lee Turberville to Madison, April 16, 1788 (referring to the absence of a bill of rights as "the favorite Topic of the ablest Antifoederal declamers"), ibid., 9: 738; letter of Caleb Wallace to William Fleming, May 3, 1788, ibid., 782; "Brutus," May 14, 1788, ibid., 802; Observations of James Monroe, May 25, 1788, ibid., 859.
53. *JMP*, 11: 28.
54. Ibid. A similar argument was made by Washington to John Armstrong, Sr, April 25, *DHRC*, 9: 759.
55. At the Virginia Ratification Convention, in arguing against prior amendments, Madison pointed out the impossibility of getting unity on the subject with those states that had already ratified, if there was so much diverse opinion even among the proposers of the amendments. Ibid., 10: 1500ff. See also his comments in Federalist #38.
56. *DHRC*, 8: 86. Henry Lee, in a letter to Madison dated December 20, 1787, wrote:

> Three sets of men are to be found on the question of Government. One opposed to any system, was it even sent from heaven which tends to confirm the union of the states. Henry is leader of this band. Another who would accept the new constitution from conviction of its own excellence, or any foederal system, sooner than risk the dissolution of the confederacy, & a third who dislike the proposed Government, wish it amended, but if this is not practicable, would adopt it sooner than jeopardize the Union. Mason may be considered as the head of this set.

JMP, 10: 339.
57. *DHRC*, 9: 755.
In a letter to Madison dated April 8, 1788, George Nicholas wrote:

> Mr. Henry is now almost avowedly an enemy to the union, and therefore will oppose every plan that would cement it. His real sentiments will be industriously concealed, for so long as he talks only of amendments, such of the freinds [*sic*] to the union, as object to particular parts of the constitution will adhere to him, which they would not do a moment, if they could be convinced of his real design. *JMP*, 11: 9.

Madison recognized that there was a difference between Henry and Mason, but he felt that the latter's frustration was impelling him into the former's camp. See his comment to Jefferson, April 22: "The adversaries take very different grounds of opposition. Some are opposed to the substance of the plan; others to particular modifications only. Mr. H—y is supposed to aim at disunion. Col. M—n is growing every day more bitter, and outrageous in his efforts to carry his point; and will probably in the end be thrown by the violence of his passions into the politics of Mr. H—y." Ibid., 11: 28.
58. See Jack N. Rakove, *Original Meanings: Politics and Ideas in the Making of the Constitution* (New York: Knopf, 1966), 122. In the end, the Assembly only approved the costs of communicating with other states. Ibid.
59. *DHRC*, 9: 917.
60. Ibid.
61. Ibid., 9: 931.
62. Ibid., 9: 930. Emphasis in original.
63. Ibid., 9: 958.
64. Ibid., 9: 951.
65. Ibid., 9: 956.
66. Ibid., 9: 959.
67. Ibid., 9: 960. This, of course, was the converse of the declaration he had made in 1774, as the Revolution got underway: "The distinctions between Virginians, Pennsylvanians, New Yorkers, and New Englanders are no more. I am not a Virginian, but an American." Cited in Mayer, *Son of Thunder*, 212–213.
68. *DHRC*, 9: 962, 1045; ibid., 10: 1535. Similarly, James Monroe contended that the direct taxing power was "unnecessary, impracticable under a Democracy, and if exercised, as tending to anarchy, or the subversion of liberty." It was unnecessary, he said, "because exigencies will not require it." Current demands were a result of the war, but there was no danger of war. Consequently, "our necessities will therefore in a short time be greatly diminished." Ibid., 9: 1109. See also remarks of George Mason on the topic of taxation and requisitions, ibid., 936–938, 940. For the response of Madison, see ibid., 9: 996–997, 9: 1033, 10: 1202–1205, 1222; and of Randolph, ibid., 9: 1016–1023. See also below, text at nn. 91–92.
69. *DHRC*, 9: 1046–1047. As Mayer says, Henry's term for implied powers, "constructive reasoning," itself became the issue. Mayer, *Son of Thunder*, 427.
70. *DHRC*, 9: 966.
71. Ibid., 9: 951.
72. Ibid., 9: 967.
73. Ibid., 9: 932.
74. Ibid., 9: 933.
75. Ibid., 9: 934.
76. Ibid., 9: 936. In a letter to the Speaker of the Virginia House of Delegates, dated October 10, 1787, Randolph stated that at Philadelphia he had become persuaded "that the confederation was destitute of every energy which a constitution ought to possess." The current state of affairs, he said, dictated that "the new powers must be deposited in a new body, growing out of a consolidation of the union, as far as the circumstances of the states will allow." In conclusion, he expressed a "fervent prayer" for "the establishment of a firm, energetic government; that the most inveterate curse, which can befal us, is a

dissolution of the union; and that the present moment, if suffered to pass away unemployed, can never be recalled." Ibid., 8: 262, 268, 274.
77. Ibid., 9: 986.
78. Ibid., 9: 985.
79. Ibid., 9: 987.
80. Ibid., 9: 988.
81. Ibid., 9: 1162–1163.
82. Ibid., 9: 989. See letter of James Breckinridge to John Breckinridge, June 13, in which he refers to Henry's "eloquence and oratory," for which Madison's "plain, ingenious, & elegant reasoning" is hardly a match for convincing the Kentucky members at the Convention. Ibid., 10: 1621. Even Jefferson was skeptical about Madison's prospects. In a letter to William Carmichael, dated Dec. 15, 1787, he wrote: "Genl. Washington will be for it, [the Constitution] but it is not in his character to exert himself much in the case. Madison will be it's [sic] main pillar: but tho an immensely powerful one, it is questionable whether he can bear the weight of such a host. So that the presumption is that Virginia will reject it." *TJP*, 12: 425. But see the comment of John Marshall on Madison's eloquence cited in Editorial Note, *JMP*, 11: 75.
Gouverneur Morris, who happened to be in Richmond when the Virginia Convention sat, wrote the following interesting comment to Hamilton, on June 13, 1788:
> Matters are not going so well in this State as the Friends of America could wish… Altho Mr. Henry is most warm and powerful in Declamation being perfectly Master of Action Utterance and the Power of Speech to stir Men's Blood yet the weight of Argument is so strong on the Side of Truth as wholly to destroy even on weak Minds the Effects of his Eloquence… My Religion steps in where my Understanding falters and I feel Faith as I loose [sic] Confidence. Things will yet go right, but when and how I dare not predicate.

DHC, 4: 704–705; *AHP*, 5: 7.
83. The following comment by one observer sums up the nature of the contest revealed in the debate: "Nothing can exceed the teeming violence with which Mr. Henry and Col. Grayson combat the constitution, except the ability with which Mr. Maddison and Governor Randolph advocate it." Letter by John Brown Cutting to Jefferson, July 24, 1788, *DHC*, 4: 818; *TJP*, 13: 403.
84. *DHRC*, 9: 989–990.
85. *DHRC*, 9: 995–996. In Federalist #39, Madison had written: "The proposed Constitution therefore is, in strictness, neither a national nor a federal constitution, but a composition of both"; and he proceeded to illustrate how the Constitution partook of both categories.
86. *DHRC*, 9: 941. It is noteworthy that Madison did not refer to the judiciary as a guarantee against federal encroachment. He was never a great believer in judicial review, and most certainly not with respect to federal legislation. See his Observations on Jefferson's Draft for a Constitution for Virginia, *JMP*, 11: 293, and the Editorial Comments, ibid., 11: 284–285. But cf. Federalist #44, where Madison wrote: "In the first instance, the success of the usurpation will depend on the executive and judiciary departments, which are to expound and give effect to the legislative acts." And subsequently, in introducing the draft bill of rights to Congress, Madison did refer to judicial review as a means of protecting

rights. See *JMP*, 12: 206–207. On Madison and judicial review, see Ralph Ketcham, "James Madison and Judicial Review," *Syracuse Law Review*, 8 (1956–1957): 158–165, and Editorial Comment, *JMP*, 11: 284–285. See also, Ralph A. Rossum, "The Courts and the Judicial Power" in Levy and Mahoney, *Framing and Ratification*, 222–241, and Shlomo Slonim, "Federalist No. 78 and Brutus' Neglected Thesis on Judicial Supremacy," *Constitutional Commentary*, 23 (2006): 29–30.
87. *DHRC*, 9: 991. As noted earlier (Chap. 1, at nn. 3–7), in his pre-Constitutional Convention memorandum "Vices of the Political System of the United States," Madison had thought it indisputable "that a unanimous and punctual obedience of 13 independent bodies, to the acts of the federal Government, ought not be calculated on." *JMP*, 9: 351.
88. In *Federalist* #33, Hamilton wrote: "These two clauses [the necessary and proper clause, and the supremacy clause] have been the sources of much virulent invective and petulant declamation against the proposed Constitution. They have been held up to the people in all the exaggerated colours of misrepresentation as the pernicious engines by which their local governments were to be destroyed and their liberties exterminated; as the hideous monster whose devouring jaws would spare neither sex nor age, nor high nor low, nor sacred nor profane."
89. Emphasis in original. The essayist, entitled A Native of Virginia, had written in a similar vein: "This regulation is necessary; as without it the different States might counteract all the laws of Congress, and render the Federal Government nugatory." *DHRC*, 9: 675. According to Randolph, the clause was inserted "for greater caution, and to prevent the possibility of encroaching upon the powers of Congress." Ibid., 9: 1102.
90. *Federalist*, 304–305.
91. Ibid., 10: 1321–1322. Emphasis in original. James Monroe had earlier charged that the necessary and proper clause was a "very dangerous" provision. This power was subject to "no limits." As a result, the members of Congress "are not restrained or controuled from making any law, however oppressive in its operation, which they may think necessary to carry their powers into effect." They could abolish trial by jury, and infringe upon liberty of the press, and every other right "not expressly secured, or excepted from that general power." In the face of "such unlimited powers," he concluded, it was essential that the matter be rectified by one of two courses: appending a bill of rights or incorporating an Article II-type provision. It was immaterial to him "in which of these two modes rights are secured." Ibid., 9: 1112.
92. Ibid., 10: 1323.
93. Henry, Mason, and Monroe all spoke forcefully against the federal tax power, except as a last resort. See above, n. 68 and accompanying text.
94. *DHRC*, 9: 1028.
95. At the time, Kentucky was still part of Virginia; nonetheless, the area was treated by all commentators as a district having particular interests. See the lengthy index entry under "Kentucky: and Navigation of Mississippi" in *DHRC*, 10: 1846–1847.

On the Mississippi episode, see above, Chap. 2, text accompanying nn. 39–42. Regarding Henry's introduction of the issue, Henry Lee remarked: "I trust he is come to judge and not to alarm." *DHRC*, 9: 949.

96. For background on this topic, see Editor's Note, ibid., 10: 1179–1183. See also letter from Hugh Williamson to Madison, June 2, 1788, *Documentary History of Constitution*, 4: 677–679; *JMP*, 11: 71–72. The discussion at the Convention extended for 2 days, June 12 and 13. *DHRC*, 10: 1184–1258.
97. Letter to Madison, Feb. 6, 1788, *TJP*, 12: 569–570. He made the same point to William Stephens Smith, Feb. 2, ibid., 12: 558, and to Alexander Donald, Feb. 7, ibid., 12: 570–571. It is not known how a copy of the letter reached Henry, but it certainly did not come via Madison. Both James Monroe, on July 12, and Madison, on July 24, informed Jefferson that Henry had invoked his name in the debate. Ibid., 13: 352–353, 412–413.
98. *DHRC*, 9: 1051–1052, 1088, n. 7. See also June 12, ibid., 10: 1210.
99. Ibid., 10: 1201–1202, 1223. Madison said that if the names of "important character[s]" were to be mentioned, he could also "adduce a character equally great on our side," referring, of course, to George Washington. Ibid.
Unknown to the contending sides, Jefferson had, in the meantime, changed his mind and had come to favor the Massachusetts model of subsequent amendments. See his letter to Edward Carrington, May 27, 1788, *TJP*, 13: 208. The same letter would also seem to indicate that he had retreated from his earlier (12: 440) endorsement of an Article II-type amendment, since "it will do too much in some instances and too little in others. It will cripple the federal government in some cases where it ought to be free, and not restrain it in some others where restraint would be right." Madison's correspondence may have been the key factor in producing this change of heart.
100. *DHRC*, 10: 1504.
101. Cited in Briceland, "Virginia: Cement of Union," 218.
102. *DHRC*, 10: 1507.
103. Ibid., 9: 1072.
104. Ibid., 9: 1163.
105. Briceland, "Virginia: Cement of Union," 212.
106. *DHRC*, 10: 1474. Emphasis added.
107. Ibid., 10: 1478.
108. Ibid., 10: 1475–1476.
109. See Briceland, "Virginia: Cement of Union," 219. While the actual text of Henry's draft amendments has not been located, it is believed to be similar to the one defeated by the Convention on June 25. See editor's comments, *DHRC*, 10: 1512–1515. See also ibid., 1547–1550.
110. Ibid., 10: 1504.
111. Briceland, "Virginia: Cement of Union," 220.
112. *DHRC*, 10: 1538.
113. Ibid., 10: 1540.
114. As Henry's biographer explains, the initial draft had given "pride of place" to an Article II provision which included the word "expressly," but the word was eliminated in the shuffle. Mayer, *Son of Thunder*, 413. See the contrast between

the initial draft and the final version, *DHRC*, 10: 1548 and 1553. The difference is also noted ibid., 1550 n. 1. The editor points out other differences that were introduced in the final version. Ibid., 1547.

In the Convention debate on the necessary and proper clause, Madison, as noted, had strenuously objected to any Article II-type provision.

115. May 14, 1788. Ibid., 9: 796.
116. *GWP*, 6: 345.
117. *Federalist* #6.
118. *Federalist* #7.
119. In a letter to General Armstrong, dated April 25, 1788, George Washington wrote:

> Upon the whole I doubt whether the opposition to the Constitution will not ultimately be productive of more good than evil; it has called forth, in its defence, abilities (which would not perhaps have been otherwise exerted) that have thrown new lights upon the science of Government, they have given the rights of man a full and fair discussuon, and have explained them in so clear and forcible a manner as cannot fail to make a lasting impression upon those who read the best publications on the subject, and particularly the pieces under the signiture of Publius.

GWP, Confederation Series, 6: 226.

120. July 2, 1788. *JMP* 11: 185. Emphasis in original.
121. See the discussion in Linda Grant De Pauw, *The Eleventh Pillar: New York State and the Federal Constitution* (Ithaca, NY: Cornell University Press, 1966), 112–117. The De Pauw work, as Jack Rakove has noted, was indispensable for an understanding of the New York Ratifying Convention prior to the appearance of the relevant *DHRC* volumes. Now that volumes 22 and 23 have appeared they, naturally, have the last word. But see also Schechter, *Reluctant Pillar*, and especially Kaminiski, "New York" ibid., 48–117.
122. See above Chap. 1, text at nn. 37–46.
123. July 20, 1788, *JMP*, 11: 190.
124. Thus, at one point in the debate, Melancton Smith conceded that the Federalists had "the advantage of Abilities and habit of public speaking." And Governor Clinton noted that while the representatives of the country counties "were men of sound judgment," they were "not used to public speaking." Cited by De Pauw, *Eleventh Pillar*, 196. Robert Yates, it should be noted, spoke hardly at all at the State Convention. On this ground alone, the assumption that he wrote the Brutus series of essays that appeared in New York seems quite unreasonable. The essays are regarded as the most brilliant challenge to the Constitution presented by the Antifederalists (see, for example, above Chap. 6 at n. 75ff.), and it is highly unlikely that a master debater like its author would have found little to say throughout the Convention. Nor can Yates's minimal participation in the debates be attributed to a change in his anti-Constitution stance, since he voted consistently against ratification. See also the introductory comment to the Essays of Brutus, Storing, 2:358. It appears that Yates was also very reticent at the Constitutional Convention. See the comment of William Pierce, delegate of Georgia, in Farrand, *Records*, 3: 90.

125. See De Pauw, *Eleventh Pillar*, 202 and 220.
126. *DHRC*, 22: 1686.
127. Ibid., 22: 1707.
128. Ibid.
129. Ibid., 22: 1705.
130. Ibid., 22: 1712, 1717.
131. Ibid., 22: 1751.
132. Ibid., 22: 1754.
133. Ibid., 22: 1838.
134. Ibid., 22: 1917.
135. Ibid., 22: 1918.
136. Ibid.
137. Ibid., 22: 1936
138. Ibid., 22: 1937.
139. Ibid., 22: 1920.
140. Ibid., 22: 1926.
141. *Elliot's Debates*, II:405. This comment, and the following one, are taken from Elliot's entry for July 2, and are attributed to an address delivered on that date by Thomas Tredwell. The *DHRC* editor states that, in fact, it is drawn from an address possibly prepared for delivery, but never delivered at the Convention; nor is it clear that Tredwell was the author. It first appeared in the Albany Register, under the name, "A Real Federalist," on January 5, 1789, some 5 months after the Convention concluded its work. *DHRC*, 23: 2549–2560.
142. *Elliot's Debates*, II, 401.
143. For two outstanding analyses of Hamilton's thesis, see Walter Berns, "The Constitution as Bill of Rights" in Robert A. Goldwin and William A. Schambra (eds.), *How Does the Constitution Secure Rights?* (Washington, DC: American Enterprise Institute, 1985), 50–73, and Ralph A. Rossum, *The Federalist's* Understanding of the Constitution as a Bill of Rights" in Charles R. Kesler (ed.), *Saving the Revolution: Federalist Papers and the American Founding* (New York: Macmillan, 1987), 219–233.
144. See *DHRC*, 22: 1722–1726, 1790–1791, 1613, 1864–1866, 1890–1894, and 1952–1960.
145. Ibid., 2118–2119.
146. De Pauw, *Eleventh Pillar*, 219.
147. Ibid., 220.
148. Ibid., 220–221.
149. See *DHRC*, 22: 2130 and De Pauw, *Eleventh Pillar*, 221–222.
150. Ibid., 223.
151. July 22, 1788, *AHP*, 5:187.
152. See letter from John Jay to George Washington, May 29, 1788, *DHC*, 4: 643, *GWP*, 6: 303, and letter from Hamilton to Madison, June 8, 1788, *DHC*, 4: 687, *JMP*, 11: 99. See also De Pauw, *Eleventh Pillar*, chap. 17. The territory of New York City might have extended as far north as West Point.
153. See *DHRC*, 23: 2233–2234.
154. Bernard Schwartz, *The Bill of Rights: A Documentary History*. (New York: McGraw Hill, 1971), 2:898. Livingston's cryptic note, according to Schwartz, records the following:

> Ham[ilton] – combats the propriety of the word "expressly" – [for] congress one [power is] to regulate trade – now they must do a thousand things not expressly given – Virginia [may] say not given... Yates—agrees – that in grantg genl powers – the powers to execute are implied. questn on the paragraph—agreed.

155. Tansill, *Documents*, 1035. Emphasis added.
156. *DHRC*, 23: 2280–2281; De Pauw, *Eleventh Pillar*, 241–245; and Kaminski, "Reluctant Pillar," 111–114. For an account of Melancton Smith's role in New York's ratification, see Robin Brooks, "Alexander Hamilton, Melancton Smith, and the Ratification of the Constitution in New York," *William and Mary Quarterly*, 24, Third Series (1967): 339–357. Brooks, incidentally, denies that the threat of secession by New York City was a key factor in persuading Antifederalists to endorse the Constitution. Ibid., 341–344; but cf. ibid., 350, 358.
157. *DHRC*, 23: 2290, 2301; De Pauw, *Eleventh Pillar*, 243–244; and Kaminski, "Reluctant Pillar," 112–113.
158. De Pauw, *Eleventh Pillar*, 244–245. For the text of the circular letter, see *DHRC*, 23: 2528–2529.
159. North Carolina and Rhode Island had not yet ratified, but their ratification was regarded as simply a matter of time. Neither state could fend for itself and remain interminably outside the Union as an independent state.

CHAPTER 8

Madison and the Threat of a Second Constitutional Convention

Madison reacted with great consternation to the letter circulated among the states by New York calling for a second constitutional convention. He did not understand how that state's Federalists could have joined hands with the Antifederalist delegates in composing and distributing a document that clearly was far more menacing than the Massachusetts or Virginia proposals regarding supplementary amendments. Those proposals, at least, were to be handled by the Congress, which could be expected to protect the Constitution from harmful tampering. The New York suggestion, however, was a loose cannon that could lead to numerous unforeseeable changes in the entire constitutional edifice. A review of Madison's correspondence at this period reveals the depth of his dismay.

Outright rejection of the Constitution by New York, he wrote to Washington, would have been preferable to ratification accompanied by such a "pestilent" communication as the circular letter. "If an Early General Convention cannot be parried," he "seriously … feared that the system which has resisted so many direct attacks may be at last successfully undermined by its enemies."[1] In his reply, Washington also worried about the "pernicious consequences" that might ensue from the circular letter, and he found it "surprizing" that it had received unanimous support in the New York Convention.[2] Madison assumed that the New York Federalists had endorsed the letter in order to obtain "an immediate ratification in any form and at any price" and thereby to promote New York City's prospects of housing the new Congress.[3]

The fact that Randolph welcomed the New York move did not add to Madison's peace of mind.[4] New York's round robin, he wrote to Randolph, was "a signal of concord & hope to the enemies of the Constitution every where, and will I fear prove extremely dangerous." Such an "*early*" convention would be "an unadvised measure," as "the offspring of party & passion, and will probably for that reason alone be the parent of error and public injury." It would probably satisfy only "the ambition of the State legislatures."[5]

In a letter to Thomas Jefferson, Madison observed that the object was "to effect an early Convention composed of men who will essentially mutilate the system, particularly in the article of taxation, without which in my opinion the system cannot answer the purposes for which it was intended." "An early Convention," he concluded, "is in every view to be dreaded in the present temper of America."[6] Writing to Jefferson a month later, Madison noted that the New York letter had "rekindled an ardor among the opponents of the federal Constitution for an *immediate* revision of it by another General Convention... Mr. Henry and his friends in Virginia enter with great zeal into the scheme." The Second Convention proposal, Madison wrote, would be opposed, not only by those objecting to any changes in the Constitution, but also by those who preferred "the other mode" provided for the adoption of amendments namely, by means of Congress. The latter procedure, in their view, would be "most expedient at present for introducing those supplemental safeguards to liberty agst. which no objections can be raised."[7] Madison made similar arguments in writing to Edmund Pendleton. An early convention was premature, he said, and threatened "discord and mischeif [*sic*]." "It will be composed of the most heterogenious [*sic*] characters—will be actuated by the party spirit reigning among their constituents—will comprehend men having insidious designs agst. the Union—and can scarcely therefore terminate in harmony or the public good. Let the enemies to the System wait until some experience shall have taken place, and the business will be conducted with more light as well as with less heat."[8]

To add to Madison's concern, North Carolina adopted a resolution on August 1, 1788, declaring that it would ratify the Constitution only if Congress would propose the adoption of a bill of rights or call for a convention to consider the matter.[9] The resolution of the North Carolina Ratifying Convention contained a twenty-paragraph Declaration of Rights for adoption and a twenty-six paragraph list of proposed amendments, the first of which was a reserved-powers clause copied from the Virginia ratifying formula.[10] Rhode Island—where Antifederalists predominated—had earlier voted down ratification, by means of a popular referendum.[11] Manifestly, the call for amendments and for a second convention was gathering momentum in several states.

In the meantime, on October 29, 1788, Patrick Henry introduced a draft resolution in the Virginia legislature requesting Congress to summon a second constitutional convention for proposing amendments to the Constitution. The Assembly approved the draft resolution and another dealing with Clinton's circular letter. An alternative resolution, for a bill of rights to be adopted in the form of a draft amendment by Congress, was overwhelmingly rejected.[12] By now, Jefferson, like Madison, felt that a second convention would be unwise. He had abandoned his previous suggestion that nine states should ratify while the remaining four held out for the adoption of a bill of rights. Although he still wished to have a bill of rights adopted, he wanted this to be done by Congress, so as to safeguard against "any dangerous innovation in the plan."[13]

In a letter to Jefferson dated December 8, 1788, Madison succinctly summed up the division in public opinion on the question of a second constitutional convention. The public was divided, first, about "the extent of the amendments that ought to be made to the Constitution," and second, about "the mode in which they ought to be made." Friends of the Constitution, while they were sympathetic to amendments, "wish the revisal to be carried no farther than to supply additional guards for liberty, *without abridging the sum of power transferred from the States to the general Government or altering previous to trial, the particular structure of the latter*."[14] Moreover, they favored the congressional route for the adoption of amendments. "Those who have opposed the Constitution, are on the other hand, zealous for a second Convention, and for a revisal which may either not be restrained at all, or extend at least as far as alterations have been proposed by any State." Some of those urging a second Convention, he said, do so "with the insidious hope, of throwing all things into Confusion, and of subverting the fabric just established, if not the Union itself." Madison proceeded to outline a course of action to defeat the "insidious" element among the Antifederalists. He wrote: "If the first Congress embrace the policy which circumstances mark out, they will not fail to propose of themselves, every desireable [*sic*] safeguard for popular rights; and by thus separating the well meaning from the designing opponents, fix on the latter their true character, and give to the Government its due popularity and stability."[15] Subsequently, Madison adopted this very strategy in Congress to derail and defeat the call for a second convention. Attainment of this goal, however, was dependent on fulfillment of two conditions. The Federalists would have to obtain a handsome majority in the first Congress so as to ensure passage of the amendments Madison favored and exclusion of those that he felt would jeopardize the Constitution. Moreover, Madison himself would have to gain membership in one of the two Houses of Congress.[16]

George Washington, in a letter to Madison dated September 23, 1788, raised the need to ensure a Federalist Congress:

> It behoves all the Advocates of the Constitution, forgetting partial & smaller considerations, to combine their exertions for collecting the wisdom & virtue of the Continent to one centre; in order that the Republic may avail itself of the opportunity for escaping from Anarchy, Division, and the other great national calamities that impended. To be shipwrecked in sight of the Port would be the severest of all possible aggravations to our misery – and I assure you I am under painful apprehensions from the single circumstance of Mr. H—[']s having the whole game to play in the Assembly of this State, and the effect it may have on others – It should be counter-acted if possible.[17]

Washington's final remark, about Patrick Henry's conniving in the Virginia Assembly to dislodge the Constitution, was fully confirmed by Henry's handling of candidacies for membership in Congress, including that of Madison. The legislature was to select the two Senators and write the laws governing the election of Representatives. In the words of one commentator: "Henry, who ruled this session like an absolute monarch ... was determined to embarrass the friends of the Constitution by keeping them out of the first Congress... His special target was JM who had bested him at the Richmond convention."[18]

Knowing the Antifederalist constellation in the state Assembly, Madison did not actively seek an appointment to the Senate.[19] He did aspire, however, to serve as a member of the lower House. Against his wishes, his name was placed in nomination in the Assembly for a Senate appointment. He lost, but ran a close third to the two Antifederalists, Richard Henry Lee and William Grayson, who were selected. Patrick Henry had warned the Assembly that Madison's election to the Senate would "terminate in producing rivulets of blood throughout the land."[20] A rumor was spread that Madison favored surrender of American navigation of the Mississippi, and this proved to be fatal. Not content with keeping Madison out of the Senate, Henry sought to exclude him from Congress altogether. To this end, he got the Virginia Assembly to gerrymander congressional districts in the state. The result was that Madison's district incorporated many more Antifederalist supporters than it would otherwise have had.[21] Furthermore, Henry succeeded in drafting an outstanding Antifederalist candidate to run against Madison—James Monroe, a veteran of the War of Independence. This was a surprising choice, since Madison and Monroe were personal friends and both were protégés of Jefferson. They were also business partners in a variety of development schemes.[22] However, it was all part of Henry's design to ensure that Madison not sit in the first Congress. While Madison had expected to avoid this kind of contest, he was compelled by circumstances to campaign actively for his election.

The greatest hurdle that Madison had to overcome was the common belief among many of the electors that he was opposed to a bill of rights. This assumption stemmed from the battle that Madison had led in opposition to prior amendments. Henry's lieutenants were now spreading the word that Madison, in fact, objected to a bill of rights completely—prior or subsequent to ratification! Madison's prospects of winning the election seemed to be seriously jeopardized. He could not expect support from Antifederalist voters, and if nominal Federalists felt that he objected to a bill of rights, his support in the district in which he was running could be significantly affected. Madison's friends in the Virginia district alerted him to the danger posed by Henry's tactics and called upon him to return immediately from New York—where he was serving in Congress—and engage in active canvassing on behalf of his candidacy.[23] Above all, he needed to refute the charge that he was opposed to amendments. Reluctant as Madison was to engage in personal electioneering, he felt he had no alternative, and returned from New York just over a month before February 2, 1789, the date set for the elections to take place.

Upon his return, Madison immediately set about correcting the false impression that prevailed by then among much of the electorate. He made personal appearances in different parts of his district and sent letters to acquaintances and prominent personalities in his district in the hope that his message would be widely disseminated among the voters. Perhaps the most important communication was that directed to George Eve, a Baptist minister, with considerable influence in his community and the region generally.[24] Madison opened his letter, dated January 2, 1789, by noting that reports had circulated that he was not only "opposed to any amendments whatever to the federal Constitution," but that he had "ceased to be a friend to the rights of Conscience." This was incorrect:

> I freely own that I have never seen in the Constitution as it now stands those serious dangers which have alarmed many respectable Citizens. Accordingly whilst it remained unratified, and it was necessary to unite the States in some one plan, I opposed all previous alterations as calculated to throw the States into dangerous contentions, and to furnish the secret enemies of the Union with an opportunity of promoting its dissolution. Circumstances are now changed. The Constitution is established on the ratification of eleven States and a very great majority of the people of America; and amendments, if pursued with a proper moderation and in a proper mode, will be not only safe, but may serve the double purpose of satisfying the minds of well meaning opponents, and of providing additional guards in favour of liberty.[25]

Under the changed circumstances, said Madison, it was his sincere opinion "that the Constitution ought to be revised," and that the first Congress "ought to prepare and recommend to the States for ratification, the most satisfactory provisions for all essential rights, particularly the rights of Conscience in the fullest latitude, the freedom of the press, trials by jury, security against general warrants &c."[26]

Madison went on to explain why he preferred the congressional method for amendments to that of a general convention. For one thing, it was the most expeditious mode, since a convention could meet only after two-thirds of the state legislatures submitted a request to Congress, while Congress itself could tackle the issue of proposing amendments by "March next." Second, it was a more certain mode, since some states might oppose a general convention and yet be in favor of individual amendments. And finally, it was the safest method. The Congress, "appointed to execute as well as to amend the Government," would probably be careful "not to destroy or endanger it." "A convention, on the other hand, meeting in the present ferment of parties, and containing perhaps insidious characters from different parts of America, would at least spread a general alarm, and be but too likely to turn every thing into confusion and uncertainty." Madison closed by noting a very important point: that the issue of a general convention was not one for the federal legislature to decide upon. "If 2/3 of the States apply for one, Congress can not refuse to call it," he observed.[27]

In a publicized letter of January 27, 1789, to a Resident of Spotsylvania County, Madison summed up, once again, the considerations that had led him to oppose previous amendments to the Constitution, "as opening a door for endless and dangerous contentions among the states, and giving an opportunity to the secret enemies of the union to promote its dissolution." Now that the Constitution had been adopted and entered into force, he was free to endorse amendments as will "guard essential rights, and will render certain vexatious abuses of power impossible."[28] His commitment to a bill of rights as outlined in this extract was published in the Fredericksburg *Virginia Herald* on January 29, 1789, just a few days before the elections were to take place.[29] Such publications and his presence in the electoral district prior to the election were crucial factors in the contest.[30]

Madison's efforts succeeded, and he was elected to Congress by a large majority.[31] In the meantime, Madison received another encouraging report—that the Congress would be overwhelmingly Federalist in composition. In a letter to Jefferson, dated March 29, 1789, he revealed that the Antifederalists would be limited to two or three in the Senate and a small number (around ten out of fifty-nine) in the House.[32] Thus he could feel assured that the Constitution was in no danger of radical change by way of congressional amendment, but there was no guarantee that the second convention movement was dead. Perhaps a sufficient number of state legislatures would yet join New York and Virginia, immediately or a little later, in presenting a request to Congress for summoning such a convention. This would explain why, despite the positive picture that was shaping up in Congress, Madison was prompted to confirm, in this same letter to Jefferson, that he anticipated the adoption of amendments by Congress. There was ground, he said, to "hope and expect that some conciliatory sacrifices will be made, in order to extinguish opposition to the system, or at least break the force of it, by detaching the deluded opponents from their designing leaders."[33] In this statement, Madison was reiterating the strategy that he had already outlined to Jefferson some four months earlier, at the beginning of December, for detaching the well-meaning friends of the Constitution from the ideological diehards, and thereby defeating the proponents of a second constitutional convention.[34]

On the issue of a bill of rights, it is instructive to contrast the pragmatic but equivocal approach of Madison with the more committed attitude of Jefferson. Madison accepted that a bill of rights needed to be adopted in order to quiet public concern over the scope of federal power, but he was skeptical regarding the necessity or efficacy of such a document as a foil against tyranny. Jefferson, on the other hand—even with the entry into force of the Constitution—remained a firm believer in the need to adopt a bill of rights. In his letter to Madison, dated July 31, 1788, he detailed the rights he felt should be approved, and expressed the hope that "a bill of rights will be formed to guard the people against the federal government, as they are already guarded against their state governments."[35] In his reply of October 17, 1788,[36] Madison conceded that "a constitutional declaration of the most essential rights" would probably be added to the Constitution, "though there are many who think such addition unnecessary, and not a few who think it misplaced in such a Constitution." "My own opinion," he stated, somewhat inscrutably, "has always been in favor of a bill of rights; provided it be so framed as not to imply powers not meant to be included in the enumeration." "At the same time," he continued, "I have never thought the omission a material defect, nor been anxious to supply it even by *subsequent* amendment,[37] for any other reason than that it is anxiously desired by others. I have favored it because I supposed it might be of use, and if properly executed could not be of disservice." For various reasons, it was not a matter that he had "viewed ... in an important light." First, he agreed in principle with James Wilson's argument that in a Constitution of delegated powers there was no basis for federal interference in the rights of citizens. Second, there was the difficulty of enumerating rights "in the requisite latitude." He was "sure that the rights of Conscience in particular, if submitted to public definition would be narrowed much more than they are likely ever to be by an assumed power." By way of illustration, Madison noted that some people in New England had objected that the prohibition of religious tests in the Constitution "opened a door for Jews, Turks, & infidels." Third, the jealousy of the states, coupled with the limited powers possessed by the federal government, afforded a better security than had previously existed. Fourth, "experience proves the inefficacy of a bill of rights on those occasions when its controul is most needed. Repeated violations of these parchment barriers have been committed by overbearing majorities in every State." Madison went on to explain why this was so. "Wherever the real power in a Government lies, there is the danger of oppression. In our Governments the real power lies in the majority of the Community, and the invasion of private rights is *cheifly* [*sic*] to be apprehended,[38] not from acts of Government contrary to the sense of its constituents, but from acts in which the Government is the mere instrument of the major number of the constituents."

Given his deep skepticism, Madison asked: "What use then ... can a bill of rights serve in popular Governments?" He suggested two purposes. First, there was the moral and educative role: "The political truths declared in that solemn manner acquire by degrees the character of fundamental maxims of free Government, and as they become incorporated with the national sentiment, counteract the impulses of interest and passion." Second, although in America the danger of oppression arose from the majority's treatment of the minority rather than from "usurped acts of the Government, yet there may be occasions on which the evil may spring from the latter sources, and on such, a bill of rights will be a good ground for an appeal to the sense of the community." Obviously, at this point, Madison did not envisage judicial enforcement of a bill of rights on behalf of minorities against the national government. In his perception, the role of a bill of rights was limited to its influence on public opinion, either as a direct restraining force or as a useful basis for rectifying governmental wrongdoing. His failure to see any connection between judicial review of federal legislation, the validity of which he queried, and a bill of rights, explains why he derisively spoke of "parchment barriers." As will be seen, it was Jefferson who alerted Madison to a potentially significant judicial role.

It is well recognized that Madison believed that the rights of individuals and minorities were best protected by ensuring that the society was of considerable size and composed of numerous contending groups, thereby precluding the ability of any group, or combination of groups, to dominate and violate the rights of the others. This principle, he claimed, operated successfully in the field of religion, where no sect was accorded a commanding position; and the same rule was applicable to civil society. He enunciated this doctrine in advance of the Constitutional Convention, at Philadelphia on several occasions, and in the *Federalist Papers* #10 and #51.[39] Thus, in *Federalist* #51, he wrote:

> Whilst all authority in it [the United States] will be derived from and dependent on the society, the society itself will be broken into so many parts, interests and classes of citizens, that the rights of individuals, or of the minority, will be in little danger from interested combinations of the majority. In a free government the security for civil rights must be the same as that for religious rights. It consists in the one case in the multiplicity of interests, and in the other in the multiplicity of sects. The degree of security in both cases will depend on the number of interests and sects; and this may be presumed to depend on the extent of country and number of people comprehended under the same government.[40]

In a small state such as Rhode Island, continued Madison, there was every probability of "reiterated oppressions" by "factious majorities." It was different with "the extended republic of the United States." Given "the great variety of interests, parties, and sects which it embraces, a coalition of a majority of the whole society could seldom take place on any other principles than those of justice and the general good." And justice, he stressed, "is the end of government. It is the end of civil society." In view of Madison's belief that the diversified complexion of a society rather than formal paper pledges provides the best protection for individual and minority rights, his ambivalent attitude to the utility of a bill of rights is the more comprehensible.[41]

Jefferson's reply to Madison's letter was dated March 15, 1789, and in it a bill of rights was the first subject broached.[42] Jefferson lauded Madison's "thoughts on the subject of the Declaration of rights," which he had "weighed with great satisfaction"; but there was, from Jefferson's perspective, a crucial omission:

> In the arguments in favor of a declaration of rights, you omit one which has great weight with me, the legal check which it puts into the hands of the judiciary. This is a body, which if rendered independent, & kept strictly to their own department merits great confidence for their learning & integrity.[43]

To underscore that confidence in the judiciary was justified, Jefferson cited such distinguished Virginian jurists as Wythe, Blair, and Pendleton, who would not be shaken in their execution of justice by "the frenzy of fellow-citizens bidding what is wrong."[44]

Jefferson was pleased that Madison, despite his objections, "was a friend to this amendment" of a bill of rights. He then proceeded to answer each of the points which Madison raised for discounting the utility of a bill of rights. (1) "That the rights in question are reserved by the manner in which the federal powers are granted." While in principle this was valid, in "a constitutive act which leaves some precious articles unnoticed, and raises implications against others," a declaration of rights was warranted. This was the case with the new federal constitution. "This instrument forms us into one state as to certain objects, and gives us a legislative & executive body for these objects. It should therefore guard us against their abuses of power within the feild [*sic*] submitted to them." (2) That certain rights might not be defined "in the requisite latitude." "Half a loaf is better than no bread." (3) The jealousy of the state governments affords a security. Such jealousy, said Jefferson, was "a precious reliance," but these governments need a text "whereon to found their opposition." It was required by the federal government also, to "try the opposition of the subordinate governments." (4) Experience proves the inefficacy of a bill of rights. No doubt this is true, answered Jefferson, but "it is of great potency always, and rarely inefficacious." The executive, he said, "is scarcely the principal object of my jealousy. The tyranny of the legislature is the more formidable dread at present, and will be for long years. That of the executive will come in it's [*sic*] turn, but it will be at a remote period." He was happy to learn that a declaration of rights was to be added to the Constitution, but he hoped it would be done in a way "which will not endanger the whole frame of the government, or any essential part of it."[45]

Manifestly, Jefferson hoped to induce Madison, tactfully and inoffensively, to alter his stand and promote a bill of rights in Congress. When Madison did, in fact, act resolutely as Jefferson desired, his actions surprised many people at the time; and the seeming paradox has continued to engage commentators and historians ever since. Most of Madison's contemporaries attributed everything to his pledge to the voters in his district. George Mason, in a letter to his son dated July 31, 1789, referred to this consideration to explain Madison's conduct.[46] "Mr. Madison [knew that he cou]'d not be elected, without making some such Promises. By them he carryed his Election; and in order to appear as good as his Word, he has made some Motions in Congress on the Subject; and to carry on the Farce, is now the ostensible Patron of Amendments." His amendments, Mason believed, would be no better than "Milk & Water Propositions ... to the State Legislatures by Way of th[r]owing out a Tub to the Whale." The latter remark was a reference to a practice described by Jonathan Swift, according to which a ship threatened by a whale would throw out a tub for the whale to entertain itself with, while the ship made its getaway. The notion of a "tub to the whale" was cited by numerous critics, both Federalist and Antifederalist members of Congress, as an explanation for Madison's persistence in promoting a bill of rights.[47] In brief, it was claimed that having made a pledge to his electorate, Madison recognized that, unless he fulfilled his promise to promote the adoption of a bill of rights, it might be difficult for him to win reelection in 1790. But none of the amendments would be meaningful, for they related exclusively to rights of conscience and individual liberties and included no structural changes in the Constitution. For the Federalists, the amendments were superfluous, because rights were never endangered, and for the Antifederalists, they were unsatisfactory since they did not relate to the critical issue—the overwhelming power of the federal government that threatened to annihilate the state governments.

Writers of a later generation, familiar with the Jefferson–Madison correspondence, have ascribed to Jefferson a major role in ultimately inducing Madison, his protégé, to become a genuine believer in the necessity of a bill of rights.[48]

With respect, neither of these theories—Jefferson's influence and Madison's concern about reelection—is entirely satisfactory or convincing. There is no indication that Madison became convinced about the necessity, or value, of a bill of rights. Moreover, as noted previously, as early as December 8, 1788 he had adverted to the strategy of promoting a bill of rights as a means of separating the well-meaning supporters of the Constitution who complained about the absence of a bill of rights from the ideological diehards who were intent on sinking the Constitution.[49] Jefferson's letter on the essentiality of a bill of rights arrived only on, or about, May 27, 1789; but Madison had already announced to the House weeks earlier, on May 4, that he planned to submit draft amendments for the consideration of Congress. Thus, he apparently resolved to promote a bill of rights, quite independently of Jefferson's arguments.[50] And as for the need to fulfill his promise to his constituents for purposes of reelection, he had not yet made any such pledge when he outlined his strategy. His first assurance was given to George Eve and was dated January 2, 1789, nearly a month after his letter to Jefferson.[51]

On the basis of the documentary evidence, it emerges that Madison's primary consideration in undertaking to draft and present a bill of rights to Congress was his determination to forestall, at all costs, the introduction of structural amendments into the Constitution—whether by Congress or by means of a second constitutional convention. Prior to New York's circular letter, perhaps he would have been content to let others take the initiative; afterwards, he was clearly bent on taking charge himself. Above all, he sought to thwart the drive for a second convention, which, he was convinced, could only spell disaster.[52]

Jefferson's letters may indeed have influenced Madison, but not because they persuaded him to alter his skeptical attitude toward the virtues or necessity of a bill of rights. There is no evidence that Madison ever experienced such a change of heart. Yet he may have feared that Jefferson's forceful advocacy of a bill of rights could well play into the hands of diehard Antifederalists, such as Patrick Henry and Richard Henry Lee, and enable them to launch a powerful drive for a second convention. Although Jefferson and Henry were hardly colleagues, the combination, even unwittingly, of the two would present a formidable challenge. Jefferson, it might be noted, was due to return from Paris to the United States, on leave, in 1789, and his presence could conceivably be exploited to promote the idea of a convention for a bill of rights. True, Jefferson had retreated from his earlier proposal of a convention, and he now favored amendments via Congress, as a safer route. Madison could have been concerned, however, that Jefferson's earlier stand might still inspire some advocates to press for state applications for a convention. As much as Madison admired, and even revered, Jefferson, he was wary of his occasionally bizarre ideas. Thus Madison, whose reaction to Shays'

Rebellion was, in Adrienne Koch's words, "close to horror at the overthrow of law and order,"⁵³ could scarcely appreciate Jefferson's weird claim that "a little rebellion now and then is a good thing, & as necessary in the political world as storms in the physical."⁵⁴ Jefferson's conviction that "the tree of liberty must be refreshed from time to time with the blood of patriots and tyrants" (and that "it is it's [sic] natural manure)",⁵⁵ surely violated every value and notion of stability for which Madison struggled. Little wonder that Jefferson's suggestion, in his "Notes on the state of Virginia," that two out of the three branches of government be empowered to call for a convention to amend the constitution, so appalled Madison that he devoted two numbers of the *Federalist Papers* to politely repudiating the suggestion of his mentor.⁵⁶

With Jefferson on record in several instances as favoring conventions to revise the provisions of a constitution, either for the purpose of adding a bill of rights or changing the pattern of government, Madison could have been understandably worried about Jefferson's imminent arrival. His zeal to introduce a bill of rights might become the vehicle for instituting a second convention, Madison's bête noire. In short, Jefferson may not have convinced Madison, but he may well have frightened him. More than Jefferson was the source of Madison's inspiration, he was possibly the source of his desperation—and his resultant decision to pressure Congress to enact a bill of rights immediately upon convening.

In 1970, Linda Grant De Pauw, author of a classic study of New York's travail in ratifying the Constitution, published an article in which she presents the thesis that the second convention movement was not a serious threat and just fizzled out. "The New York circular letter, which had appeared like a bombshell to anxious Federalists, proved a dud. Rather than being 'every where ... laid hold of as the signal for united exertions,' as Madison had feared, it died with a whimper for lack of attention."⁵⁷ Although Virginia and New York submitted applications to Congress for a second convention, "it was already clear," she writes, "that no further applications could be anticipated." This assessment of the second convention movement is rather surprising, since Madison's contemporaneous correspondence is full of concern regarding the promotion of such a convention. Moreover, her suggestion that Madison omitted to promote structural amendments only to avoid controversy fails to appreciate that Madison never had the slightest intention of touching anything substantive in the Constitution.⁵⁸ His whole purpose in moving amendments of conscience was to safeguard the provisions of the Constitution from the slightest modification.

Most scholars today concur in the view that Madison's drive to promote a bill of rights was designed primarily to defeat the second convention movement. The first, it appears, to have suggested that the Federalists' aim was to upset Antifederalist machinations to revise the Constitution was Leonard Levy, one of the most insightful and prolific writers on the origins of the Constitution. In a volume published in 1960, he wrote: "Our precious Bill of Rights was in the main the chance result of certain Federalists' having been reluctantly forced to capitalize for their own cause the propaganda that had been originated in vain by the Anti-Federalists for ulterior purposes."⁵⁹ In a widely publicized essay on the Bill of Rights, Levy expanded upon his earlier comment.[60] Madison's plan, he said, was to win over those Antifederalists who favored an effective Union, but desired a bill of rights. By persuading the first Congress to adopt "protections of civil liberties," the public's anxieties would be alleviated, thereby "providing popularity and stability for the government, and isolating those Antifederalists whose foremost objective was "subverting the fabric ... if not the Union itself."[61] Madison "understood that his amendments, if adopted, would thwart the passage of proposals aggrandizing state powers and diminishing national ones. He would not be put off; he was insistent, compelling, unyielding, and, finally, triumphant."[62] At a later date, in a brilliant article Herbert J. Storing analyzed Madison's successful campaign to undermine the strategy of the Antifederalists to introduce substantive changes into the Constitution.[63] Storing's article was a pathfinder for all subsequent writing on the subject. Two excellent articles,[64] one by Kenneth R. Bowling and the other by Paul Finkelman, and an outstanding book by Robert Goldwin,[65] have appeared in the past two decades, and their analyses have enriched our appreciation of Madison's central role in the adoption of the Bill of Rights. His contribution to the establishment of America's system of government, resting both on a constitution and a bill of rights, is preeminent. While each of the titles is revealing, that of the Goldwin book is particularly enlightening: *From Parchment to Power: How James Madison Used the Bill of Rights to Save the Constitution*. These studies confirm that Madison was not only the Father of the Constitution, but also the Father of the Bill of Rights. Quite simply, as Madison outlined to Jefferson and others in very clear terms, his key aim in proposing a bill of rights was to derail the campaign to promote amendments which would revamp the division of powers between national and state governments. Although he himself had never felt that a bill of rights was either effective or warranted, the adoption of a series of amendments devoted exclusively to enumerating rights of conscience and civil liberties would satisfy the vast majority of the critics and make a second convention pointless. This was Madison's own explanation for his conduct in becoming, in Mason's term, the "patron" of a bill of rights. And, of course, this strategy worked magnificently. With the adoption of the draft amendments by Congress, the bottom fell out of the Antifederalist drive to organize a second convention, and the Constitution plus Bill of Rights were set to become the fundamental and revered writ of government and liberty for the nation.

Two matters of importance not dealt with by earlier writers remain to be analyzed and assessed, from which a new perspective on Madison's motive to secure a bill of rights can be gained. The first relates to the urgency with which Madison pressured Congress to act on amendments. Given that he felt it was essential that the very First Congress had to adopt amendments for submission to the states, why the urgency to wrap it all up in the first half of the first session? After all, there are two years to every session, and if the draft amendments had been presented to Congress in the first year, why was it deemed so critical to have them formulated and adopted by the Congress before the year was out?

No one could have complained that Madison was failing to live up to his pledge if the draft amendments were approved by Congress in the second half of the first session. This question is particularly relevant, given the other urgent business with which Congress was grappling when Madison overcame the objections of his colleagues and insisted that it must put everything aside in order to complete its deliberation on the draft amendments and vote on them before the end of the first year. The issue of Madison's race against time forms the subject matter of Chap. 9.

The second issue relates to the critical place of the Tenth Amendment in the Bill of Rights. The Tenth is distinguished from the previous nine by being the only one to deal with powers rather than rights. It is also distinguished by the fact that it is the only amendment the drafting of which provoked a serious dispute. The Antifederalists sought to introduce the word "expressly" into the text so as to limit the federal government to powers "expressly enumerated" and deny it resort to implied powers, but were defeated. This issue of implied powers had been a central focus of the Antifederalist campaign throughout the ratification struggle, and the dispute was carried over into the first session of Congress. This topic is explored, and elaborated upon, in Chap. 10, which confirms the critical importance of the Tenth Amendment in preserving the Constitution intact.

NOTES

1. Letter of Aug. 11, 1788, *JMP*, 11: 230, and of Aug. 24. 1788, ibid., 240.
2. Aug. 17, 1788, ibid., 11: 234.
3. Letter to Washington, Aug. 24, 1788, ibid., 11: 240.
4. Randolph's letters to Madison, Aug. 13, 1788, ibid., 11: 231 and Sept. 3, 1788, ibid., 246.
5. Aug. 22, 1788, ibid., 11: 237. See also Madison's letters to George Lee Turberville, Nov. 2, 1788, and to Henry Lee, Nov. 30, 1788, ibid., 11: 331 and 372.
6. Aug. 23, 1788, ibid., 11: 238.
7. Sept. 21, 1788, ibid., 11: 257–258.
8. Oct. 20, 1788, ibid., 11: 307.
9. *Elliot's Debates*, 4: 242; Tansill, *Documents*, 1044. For an historical review of North Carolina's ratification, see Michael Lienesch, "North Carolina: Preserving Rights" in Michael Allen Gillespie and Michael Lienesch (eds.), *Ratifying the Constitution*. (Lawrence: University Press of Kansas, 1989), 343–367.
10. *Elliot's Debates*, 243–247; Tansill, *Documents*, 1044–1051.
11. For an historical account of Rhode Island's ratification, see John P. Kaminski, "Rhode Island: Protecting State Interests" in Gillespie and Lienesch, *Ratifying*, 368–390.
12. *JMP*, 11: 323–324, nn. 1 and 2.
13. Nov. 18; ibid., 11: 353–354.
14. Ibid., 11: 382. Emphasis added. This sentence captured the essence of the dispute over a second constitutional convention. The proponents of the convention wished to revise the division of powers between federal and state

governments instituted by the Constitution. Madison and the other Federalists opposed any modification of federal power.
15. Ibid., 11: 382–383.
16. See the letter from Tench Coxe to Madison dated Jan. 29, 1789, on the eve of the elections to Congress, expressing the hope that Madison would be safely returned to the House. Without capable leadership, Coxe feared, the House of Representatives might fall under Antifederalist influence. Madison's guidance there was critical "to prevent the most serious evils." Ibid., 11: 431–432.
17. Ibid., 11: 262.
18. Editorial Note, "Madison's Election to the First Federal Congress," ibid., 11: 301.
19. Madison's friends were, for a time, left in the dark as to whether Madison preferred to seek a seat in the House or the Senate. See the discussion of Madison's reticence and the dilemmas faced by his supporters, in Lance Banning, *The Sacred Fire of Liberty: James Madison and the Founding of the Federal Republic* (Ithaca, NY: Cornell University Press, 1995), 11: 269–271.
20. Letter from Henry Lee to Madison, Nov. 19, 1788, *JMP*, 11: 356.
21. See Editorial Note, ibid., 11: 302; and see Madison's letter to Jefferson, Dec. 8, 1788, ibid. 384.
22. From Madison's subsequent remarks, it does not appear that the contest affected personal relations between the two men. See ibid., 12: 37.
23. See letters from Burgess Ball, Dec. 8, 1788, ibid., 11: 385–386, and from Hardin Burnley, Dec. 16, 1788, ibid., 398–399.
24. Ibid., 11: 404–405. This letter does not seem to have been published, but its contents became widely known and had considerable influence. Ibid., 405, n. 2.
25. Ibid., 404.
26. Ibid., 404–405.
27. Ibid., 405.
28. Ibid., 11: 428–429.
29. Editorial comment, ibid., 303, 429 n.
30. See Madison's letter to Randolph dated March 1, 1789, ibid., 453.
31. The margin was 1308 to 972. See Editorial Note, ibid., 438, n. 1; Helen E. Veit, Kenneth R. Bowling, and Charlene Bangs Bickford (eds.), *Creating the Bill of Rights: The Documentary Record from the First Federal Congress* (Baltimore, MD: Johns Hopkins University Press, 1991), XIII.
32. *JMP*, 12: 38. Two states, South Carolina and Rhode Island, had not yet ratified the Constitution and were thus not represented in Congress. This explains the fifty-nine, rather than the sixty-five, that the Constitution designated for the House of Representatives in the First Congress.

    For a valuable analysis of the first Federal elections and the factors contributing to the failure of the Antifederalists to score heavily in these elections, see Steven R. Boyd, *The Politics of Opposition: Antifederalists and the Acceptance of the Constitution* (Millwood, NY: KTO Press, 1979), Chaps. 6 and 7. See also, David J. Siemers, *Ratifying the Republic: Antifederalists and Federalists in Constitutional Time* (Stanford, CA: Stanford University Press, 2002), Chaps. 2 and 3.
33. Ibid.
34. See text at nn. 14–15, above.
35. *JMP*, 11: 212–213.
36. Ibid., 295–300.

37. Emphasis in original.
38. Emphasis in original.
39. The two essays do not deal with the same subject. *Federalist* #10 deals with preventing the rise of factions in the national legislature; the second half of #51 relates to protecting the rights of individuals and minorities.
40. *Federalist* #51, 351–352
41. Madison's notion that a pluralistic society provides the best guarantee for individual rights is widely discussed in the literature. See, for example, the comprehensive discussion by Jack Rakove in his "Federalism" chapter in *Original Meanings*, 161–202, as also that by Charles R. Kesler, "*Federalist* 10 and American Republicanism" in Charles R. Kesler (ed.), *Saving the Revolution: The Federalist Papers and the American Founding*. (New York: Macmillan, 1987), 13–39; and the insightful essay by Bernard Bailyn, "The Federalist Papers" in his *To Begin the World Anew: The Genius and Ambiguities of the American Founders*. (New York: Vintage, 2003), Chap. 4, 100–125. On this topic, see also Shlomo Slonim, "The Federalist Papers and the Bill of Rights," *Constitutional Commentary*, 20 (2003): 151–161. According to Ralph A. Rossum, Madison believed that, in addition to the operation of a multiplicity of interests, such constitutional features as separation of powers and federalism contributed to securing rights. "The *Federalist*'s Understanding of the Constitution as a Bill of Rights" in Kesler, *Saving the Revolution*, 228–233. See also the valuable summary by Alan Gibson, "Inventing the Extended Republic: The Debate over the Role of Madison's Theory in the Creation of the Constitution" in John R. Vile (ed.), *James Madison: Philosopher, Founder and Statesman* (Athens: Ohio University Press, 2008), 63–87.
42. *JMP*, 12: 13–15.
43. Ibid., 13.
44. Ibid., 12: 13 and n. 1.
45. Ibid., 12: 13–15.
46. *GMP*, 3: 1164.
47. See the references in Kenneth R. Bowling, "'A Tub to the Whale': The Founding Fathers and Adoption of the Federal Bill of Rights," *Journal of the Early Republic*, 8 (1988): 223–225, 236–237, 241.
48. See, for example, Richard B. Bernstein and Jerome Agel, *Amending America* (New York: Random House, 1993), 36; Leonard W. Levy, *Jefferson and Civil Liberties: The Darker Side* (Cambridge, MA: Harvard University Press, 1963), 3 (who writes that Jefferson "converted Madison to the cause of adding a Bill of Rights to the new federal Constitution"); Robert A. Rutland, "How the Constitution Protects Our Rights: A Look at the Seminal Years" in Robert A. Goldwin and William A. Schambra, *How Does the Constitution Protect Rights?* (Washington, DC: American Enterprise Institute, 1985), 3–5.
    Bernstein and Agel attribute Madison's "about-face" to four factors: (1) the "admonishing and persuasive letters" of Jefferson; (2) the advisability of Madison's taking the lead, in order to place himself in the best position to deflect any proposed amendments that might go beyond a bill of rights; (3) the hope of heading off a second constitutional convention; and (4) concern to ensure reelection. Bernstein and Agel, *Amending America*, 36–37.
49. See text at n. 15, above.
50. See *JMP*, 12: 125, 185, and 196.
51. Ibid., 11: 404–405, and see text above at n. 15.

52. It is also true, of course, that once elected to Congress, Madison was obliged to think about a bill of rights if he wanted to be reelected; but as noted, his commitment to a bill of rights preceded the pledge to his electors.
53. Adrienne Koch, *Jefferson and Madison: The Great Collaboration* (London: Oxford University Press, reprint ed. 1973), 45.
54. Jan. 30, 1787, *TJP*, 11: 93. For a review of the philosophy underlying Jefferson's approach to Shays' Rebellion, see Paul A. Rahe, *Republics Ancient and Modern: Classical Republicanism and the American Revolution*. (Chapel Hill: University of North Carolina Press, 1992), 698–701.
55. Letter to William Stephens Smith, Nov. 13, 1787, *TJP*, 12: 356. Jack Rakove likewise maintains that Madison was very little amused by Jefferson's sympathetic attitude toward Shays' Rebellion. See Rakove, *Original Meanings*, 331.
56. See *Federalist* #49 and #50.
57. Linda Grant De Pauw, "The Anticlimax of Antifederalism: The Abortive Second Convention Movement, 1788–1789," *Prologue*, 2: 98–114, at 105. Prior to De Pauw's article, the only other article devoted to the topic was that of Edward P. Smith, "The Movement Towards a Second Constitutional Convention in 1788" in J. Franklin Jameson (ed.), *Essays in the Constitutional History of the United States in the Formative Period, 1775–1789* (Boston, MA: Houghton, Mifflin, 1889), 46–115. Smith surveys the struggle over ratification in the various states, and concludes that the possibility of a second convention "excited in the minds of the Federalists the liveliest alarm." Ibid., 111. "Madison saved the day by introducing a series of amendments into the First Session of Congress, which upon ratification, became the revered Bill of Rights."
58. De Pauw, "The Abortive Second Convention," 109.
59. Leonard W. Levy, *Legacy of Suppression: Freedom of Speech and Press in Early American History* (Cambridge, MA: Harvard University Press, 1960), 233.
60. See the essay "Bill of Rights" in Leonard W. Levy (ed.), *Essays on the Making of the Constitution*, 2nd ed. (New York: Oxford University. Press, 1987), 258–306, at 280–289. The essay originally appeared in Jack P. Greene (ed.), *Encyclopedia of American Political History*. (New York: Scribner's, 1984), 2: 104–125.
61. Levy, *Essays*, 1987, 280.
62. Ibid., 281.
63. Herbert J. Storing, "The Constitution and the Bill of Rights" in M. Judd Harmon (ed.), *Essays on the Constitution of the United States* (Port Washington, NY: Kennikat Press, 1978), 32–48; republished in numerous collections, including Goldwin and Schambra, *How Does the Constitution Secure Rights?* 15–35.
64. The article by Bowling is the aforementioned, "A Tub to the Whale," and the one by Finkelman is "James Madison and the Bill of Rights: A Reluctant Paternity," *The Supreme Court Review*, 9 (1990): 301–347.
65. Robert A. Goldwin, *From Parchment to Power: How James Madison Used the Bill of Rights to Save the Constitution* (Washington, DC: AEI Press, 1997). The more recent work, Richard Labunski, *James Madison and the Struggle for the Bill of Rights* (New York: Oxford University Press, 2006), provides a dramatic account of the contest between Madison and Patrick Henry in Virginia over the formulation and adoption of a bill of rights.

CHAPTER 9

The Bill of Rights in Congress: Madison's Race Against Time

In promoting a draft bill of rights in Congress, Madison faced three challenges. He had to make certain that his draft would be presented first, before the Antifederalists had a chance to preempt him with their own version. He also had to persuade enough of his Federalist colleagues to join him in according top priority to the matter of adding constitutional amendments. And finally, he needed to foil any Antifederalist attempt to insert wording that would undermine the strict formula of rights that he was advocating. Above all, Madison had to move with alacrity, since any delay was fraught with danger. Inaction by Congress could revive the second convention movement and render it irresistible. Failure by Congress to produce a draft bill of rights would allow the Antifederalists to assert that the road through Congress was blocked and use of the alternative method for adopting amendments was therefore essential. With the author of the Declaration of Independence and other prominent personalities endorsing the need for a bill of rights, one state legislature after another might petition Congress to summon a convention to draft such a document. Two leading states, Virginia and New York, had already adopted resolutions to that effect. What would it take to persuade enough other states to concur with Jefferson and others that a bill of rights was vital and endorse the call for a convention? (It is to be noted that North Carolina and Rhode Island were conditioning their entry into the Union on the adoption of a bill of rights). Were two-thirds of the state legislatures to petition Congress, it would be obliged, according to Article V of the Constitution, to summon such a convention.[1] Once such a convention met, it would be as free as the Philadelphia Convention itself had been to produce an entirely new instrument of government.[2] With a farsighted vision that few of his friends possessed, Madison recognized that a passive approach to the question of a bill of rights could breed a perilous situation easily exploited by the Antifederalists to enfeeble, or even destroy, the Constitution.

To add to Madison's woes, Edmund Randolph was now once again endorsing the idea of a second convention, as noted in the previous chapter—and this despite Madison's best efforts to demonstrate to him the risks inherent in such an exercise. Randolph's oscillations in support of, and in opposition to, the Constitution, were a troubling feature throughout the constitutional formulation and ratification process. As Governor of his state, he had been given the honor of presenting the nationalist Virginia Plan to the Constitutional Convention, and he had supported the plan vigorously. As the deliberations at Philadelphia progressed, however, he had apparently become fearful of the reception that awaited him at home from Patrick Henry and other states' rights advocates, and he had adopted an increasingly critical attitude toward the draft constitution until—in the end—he was one of three who refused to sign the completed document. At the closing stage of the Convention, on September 10, Randolph outlined his "objections to the System." Among his primary complaints was the power conveyed to the federal government by means of the necessary and proper clause, and "the want of a more definite boundary between the General & State Legislatures."[3] He could not support a plan, he said, "which he verily believed would end in Tyranny." He advocated summoning a second convention to deliberate upon alterations in the Constitution that might be recommended by the state legislatures, and presented a motion to that effect.[4]

The suggestion for a second constitutional convention had first surfaced some 10 days earlier, on August 31. It was then that George Mason, after declaring that he would rather chop off his right hand than sign the Constitution "as it now stands," had recommended certain changes, and alternatively, the convening of "another general Convention" on "the whole subject."[5] In endorsing the suggestion at this time, Randolph said that "State Conventions should be at liberty to propose amendments to be submitted to another General Convention which may reject or incorporate them."[6] For his part, Gouverneur Morris felt that a second convention might "have the firmness to provide a vigorous Government, which we are afraid to do."[7] His aim was the establishment of a stronger, less constrained central government—the exact opposite of what the two Virginians desired. At that point, no one moved a formal motion on the subject. As noted, Randolph's formal motion was presented on September 10; and surprisingly enough, it was seconded by Benjamin Franklin.[8] Mason and Gerry spoke in favor of the proposal. Pinckney warned that "nothing but confusion & contrariety could spring from the experiment" of a second convention. "The States will never agree in their plans."[9] Indeed, Randolph's motion was unanimously rejected by all the states at the Convention.[10]

In the interval between the close of the Philadelphia Convention and the convening of the Virginia Ratifying Convention, Randolph continued to press for a second convention. Only a promise of a second convention, he wrote to Madison on December 27, 1787, would "save the foederal government in any shape in Virginia."[11] Madison, seeking to disabuse Randolph of his obsessive belief that such a course would best unite the nation, retorted, in his letter of January 10, 1788, that a second convention would likely have catastrophic, divisive, consequences. It would "give a loose [rein] to human opinions, which must be as various and irreconcileable concerning theories of Government, as doctrines of Religion; and give opportunities to designing men which it might be impossible to counteract."[12] The diverse aims of the opposition groups in the various states confirmed this. Some groups favored dissolving the Union, others wished to patch up the Articles of Confederation, and still others desired "a reversal of the Revolution." Patrick Henry, Randolph was sure, was "driving at a Southern Confederacy," and was not really interested in amendments at all. "The multiplied inducements at this moment to the local sacrifices necessary to keep the States together, can never be expected to co-incide again."[13]

At the Virginia Ratifying Convention, despite his earlier dissent, Randolph battled strongly for ratification, arguing that the choice was Union or no Union, and he could not passively sit by and witness the disintegration of the country. His support was perhaps critical in securing victory for Madison and the Federalists. Now, however, in the wake of New York's initiative, he reverted to his former position and again welcomed state action to promote a second convention. He recognized that there was a danger in convening such a body, but even the adoption of one amendment by the convention, he thought, would "bear down all malcontents."[14] And if their decision leads to the Constitution being "enervated ... if such be the will of America, who can withstand it?"[15] He could not thwart a second convention merely because of the risks it entailed. Upon joining the state Assembly, Randolph voted for a second convention.[16] Francis Corbin summed up the effect of Randolph's meanderings: "He will injure his political Reputation by his doublings and turnings. He is *too Machiavellian* and not *Machiavellian Enough*."[17]

The inauguration of George Washington as first President of the United States took place on April 30, 1789—a time when the executive department was not yet established and, according to the editor of the *Madison Papers*, Madison was serving as Washington's close confidant, his ghostwriter, and effectively the country's prime minister.[18] Washington turned to him to compose the inaugural address to be presented to Congress, and Madison used this opportunity to promote the idea of adopting appropriate constitutional amendments to secure rights. Thus, in his address, Washington noted that "objections" had been "urged against the System," and that under Article V, Congress had the power to initiate amendments. He then stated: "I assure myself that whilst you carefully avoid every alteration which might endanger the benefits of an United and effective Government, ... a reverence for the characteristic rights of freemen, and a regard for the public harmony," would undoubtedly influence your deliberations in deciding "how far the former can be more impregnably fortified, or the latter be safely and advantageously promoted."[19] The reply of the House of Representatives to the President (also composed by Madison) assured Washington that Congress would devote to the subject of amendments "all the attention demanded by its importance."[20] Thus (thanks to the identical author), both the executive and the legislature were on record as affirming that amendments to "fortify" the "rights of freemen" should be taken up at the right time.

In Madison's eyes, the right time was very soon after Congress opened its First Session on April 8, 1789. Congress was heavily engaged in drafting legislation on such critical matters as the formation of the executive and judiciary departments, the ways and means to provide revenue for the federal government, and regulating matters of commerce. Another important topic on the congressional agenda was the question of the location of the nation's capital. Nonetheless, for Madison, the adoption of amendments was no less urgent, and he announced on May 4 that he would submit draft amendments for congressional approval 3 weeks later. The House of Representatives agreed to his motion.[21] By this move, Madison skillfully seized the initiative and preempted the Constitution's opponents. That this was his intention becomes clear from a letter that he later wrote to Richard Peters, on August 19, 1789 (to be discussed below).[22] Among the seven reasons that he cites to justify pressuring Congress to move expeditiously to consider a bill of rights, he observes (in Point 4): "If amends. had not been proposed from the federal side of the House, the proposition would have come *within 3 days*, from the adverse side. It is certainly best that they should appear to be the free gift of the friends of the Constitution rather than to be extorted by the address & weight of its enemies."[23]

Madison's announcement to the House naturally served as a signal for Antifederalists to enter the fray. The very next day, on May 5, Theodorick Bland of Virginia submitted the application from his state requesting Congress to call a convention. Bland urged that the request be referred to a committee of the whole House. "It would be advisable," he said, "to give it a consideration at the same time that the amendment to be moved by Mr. Madison ... should be brought forward."[24] Stressing that the address was from "a respectable state," he thought "it might be of weight in the decisions of the committee." His reference to "a respectable state" was intended, no doubt, as a hint to his fellow Virginian, and it presented Madison with a delicate diplomatic quandary. As a Representative from Virginia, Madison could not appear disrespectful of a decision of the state legislature. He overcame the difficulty by stressing that Congress had no role to play in applications for a convention, and it was therefore proper that the Virginia address be recorded in the minutes and "remain on the files of the house" until further applications came to hand. In short, it was not to be taken up in the forthcoming debate.[25]

Madison's presentation of a text to the House was delayed until June 8. During the interval he sifted through some 200 proposed amendments that the various state legislatures had included in their acts of ratification.[26] Many of their proposals were of a structural nature, designed to revise the division of powers between national and state governments so as to restore the latter to the preeminence they had exercised under the Articles of Confederation. Usually leading the list of proposals was the call for an amendment, like Article II of the Articles, limiting the federal government to those powers expressly enumerated in the Constitution.[27] Disregarding all of the amendments that would modify in any manner the grant of powers to the federal government, Madison included predominantly rights of conscience in the list of nine clauses that he presented to the House of Representatives.[28] The restrictions on government interference with the rights of the people were directed against the national government, with one exception. The fifth provision declared: "No state shall violate the equal rights of conscience, or the freedom of the press, or the trial by jury in criminal cases." Two provisions were added to discount the fears of Antifederalists, as noted in the *Federalist Papers* (mainly #84), on the danger of attempting to enumerate rights. To preclude any argument that unenumerated rights were unprotected, the last sentence of the fourth amendment read: "The exceptions here or elsewhere in the constitution, made in favor of particular rights, shall not be so construed as to diminish the just importance of other rights retained by the people." It was also deemed necessary to counter the argument that by stipulating certain rights, the Constitution would implicitly acknowledge that Congress possessed powers in all the spheres to which the enumerated rights related. In order to avoid such an implication and to stress that the Constitution was one of delegated powers, the list ended with this provision: "The powers not delegated by this constitution, nor prohibited by it to the states, are reserved to the states respectively."[29] This reserved powers formula was designed neither to add to, nor subtract from, the powers accorded the federal government. It merely restated, in summary form, the basic principle of the Constitution—that the national government was one of enumerated powers, and powers not conveyed remained with the states.

When Madison rose in the House on June 8 to present and discuss his list of draft amendments, he ran into a maelstrom of opposition. It was the timing rather than the principle of appending a bill of rights that aroused fierce criticism. Why, it was asked, could the matter not wait until the second half of the First Congressional Session, when the government would be operative and Congress would be better able to debate the issue with due deliberation? After all, the Constitution had not even been tried and its defects had not yet been fully revealed. Was it not, then, more logical to wait, especially since so many matters connected with the establishment of the government and its financing demanded more urgent Congressional attention? Revenue was "daily escaping us," they complained. "Is it not of immense consequence to compleat the [revenue] system?[30] James Jackson of Georgia was vehement in his criticism. "Without revenue the wheels of government cannot move. I am against taking up the subject [of rights] at present, and shall therefore be totally against the amendments, if the government is not organized, that I may see whether it is grievous or not." He proposed that the subject be postponed for a year, until March 1790.[31]

In response, Madison stressed that, several times, he had postponed presenting the subject of amendments so as to allow other pressing business to be handled, but further delay, he insisted, was not proper. This was particularly so, since he was not suggesting that the House "enter into a full and minute discussion of every part of the subject" at this point. His purpose was to demonstrate to "our constituents" that "we pay a proper attention to a subject they have much at heart." Refusing to consider the topic now, he said, "may occasion suspicions, which, though not well founded, may tend to inflame or prejudice the public mind, against our decisions."[32] "He thought it necessary that Congress should commence the enquiry, and place the matter in such a train as to inspire a reasonable hope and expectation, that full justice would eventually be done to so important a subject."[33] Actually, Madison thought that it would have been salutary to make the issue of amendments the very first item of the House: "It would stifle the voice of complaint [against the Constitution], and make friends of many who doubted its merits."[34] Putting the government into operation justifiably took priority, but it was time to place the matter of amendments on the agenda for appropriate action. "I hold it to be my duty," he said, "to unfold my ideas, and explain myself to the house in some form or other without delay."[35]

Madison, it might be noted, was always discreet about his true aims in promoting a bill of rights. Only obliquely did he suggest that the adoption of amendments would avert modification of the Constitution and that it would stymie a second convention movement. But he never spelled out the latter consideration in clear terms. Where Madison was circumspect, his fellow Member of the House of Representatives, Virginian John Page, was blunt and candid. Given that Congress was reluctant to even give Madison an opportunity to present his list of amendments, Page warned the House of the repercussions:

> Putting myself into the place of those who favor amendments, I should suspect Congress did not mean seriously to enter upon the subject; that it was vain to expect redress from them; I should begin to turn my attention to the alternative contained in the fifth article [of the Constitution], and think of joining the legislatures of those states which have applied for calling a new convention. How dangerous such an expedient would be, I need not mention, but I venture to affirm, that unless you take early notice of this subject, you will not have power to deliberate. The people will clamor for a new convention, they will not trust the house any longer; those therefore, who dread the assembling of a convention, will do well to acquiesce in the present motion, and lay the foundation of an important work.[36]

In order to avoid further delay, Madison withdrew his motion for the House to form itself into a Committee of the Whole, and suggested instead that a select committee be created to consider which amendments should be proposed to the states for them to ratify as part of the Constitution. By this means, he said, the subject of amendments could be dealt with in committee while the House continued to attend to the critically urgent matters relating to the establishment of the government. This suggestion was accepted[37]; and Madison proceeded to explain, in a major address, the considerations that prompted him to submit his proposal and the significance of the series of amendments he was proposing for inclusion in a bill of rights.[38]

Some critics of the Constitution, he said, claimed that in its pristine form the document would "lay the foundation of an aristocracy or despotism." Many of these critics were "respectable for their talents, their patriotism, and respectable for the jealousy they have for their liberty, which, though mistaken in its object, is laudable in its motive."[39] The adoption of appropriate amendments would allay their suspicions without inflicting any injury on the Constitution. If all power is subject to abuse, then safeguards against abuse by the general government was also warranted, so long as the legitimate exercise of power was in no way harmed. Therefore, he would not propose any amendment that was not certain to command widespread support in Congress and in the states. This would exclude all structural changes that had been suggested, since these would endanger the Constitution.[40]

Madison cited the array of arguments that the Federalists had marshaled during the ratification struggle to dismiss the need for a bill of rights, but indicated that these arguments were inconclusive. The incorporation of rights into the Constitution, he stressed, would allow "independent tribunals of justice" to act as "the guardians of those rights" in striking down every improper assumption of power. With this concession to judicial review, he postulated that the liberty of the people would be enhanced without any undermining of federal authority.[41]

The select committee presented its report on July 28. After Madison overcame further delaying tactics, the report was taken up by the Committee of the Whole on August 13. Madison's list of amendments was reworked and revised there until it numbered seventeen distinct articles, together with a lengthy preamble outlining the basic principles of constitutional government—that all power derives from the people, that government should be exercised for their benefit, and that the people can change their system of government whenever they desire to do so.[42] In the subsequent House debate, numerous Antifederalist proposals to alter the amendments were rejected. Among these, significantly, were two attempts to revise the reserved powers clause by adding the word "expressly," so that, like Article II of the Articles of Confederation, all powers not "expressly delegated" would have been reserved to the states.[43] The House then took a step which, while it did not affect the character of the amendments, radically altered their location in relation to the Constitution, and thereby preserved them for posterity as a distinct corpus. Under Madison's scheme, the amendments would have been woven, at suitable places, into the fabric of the Constitution.[44] Roger Sherman of Connecticut moved that the amendments, in their entirety, be attached as a supplement to the Constitution.[45] Some of the House members who supported the motion felt that Madison's scheme tended to denigrate the importance of the original Constitution. Sherman's proposal was initially rejected, but ultimately approved.[46] The final version of the seventeen amendments was sent up to the Senate on August 24. The latter tightened the House formulation, and reduced the number of amendments to twelve. Various Antifederalist moves were defeated, including again an attempt to insert the word "expressly" in the reserved powers provision.[47] The Senate did add two phrases to that amendment; they are (in italics): "The powers not delegated *to the United States* by the Constitution, nor prohibited by it to the States, are reserved to the States respectively, *or to the people*."[48] In the process, the provision binding the states to various rights of conscience was eliminated. Madison deeply deplored the latter step, since he regarded this provision as the most important of his proposed amendments. Obviously, the members of the Senate—the body representing the states—were reluctant to approve a rights provision initiated by Congress and binding on the states. This tends to confirm the validity of John Marshall's conclusion in *Barron v. Baltimore* (1833), that the federal bill of rights was meant to bind the federal government exclusively.[49] The revised version was approved by both houses, and the text, composed of twelve draft amendments, was submitted to the states for approval on September 25, 1789.[50]

Many writers point to the arguments employed by Madison, derived from Jefferson's correspondence, as confirming Jefferson's influence in persuading him that a bill of rights was essential. In particular, they cite as evidence of Madison's change of heart his reference to Jefferson's suggestion that judicial review would operate as a means of restraining the violation of rights.[51] This deduction is unwarranted, since Madison could well have employed Jefferson's arguments without in any way being personally convinced. As Edward Dumbauld has said: "Although it was to satisfy the scruples of others rather than his own that Madison took the initiative in proposing amendments, he diligently set himself to the task of pushing them through the legislative treadmill in spite of the inertia and opposition of his colleagues."[52] Robert Goldwin has shown persuasively that in Madison's address to the House, he demonstrated no personal support for a bill of rights, or for any of the rights individually.[53]

Madison aimed to convince the members of Congress that the draft amendments would satisfy and please masses of people who had been skeptical about the Constitution. Detached from the ideological diehards, broad elements of the public would join the camp supporting the Constitution; the original text would be preserved intact; and the second convention movement, which Madison so dreaded, would, he believed, die a natural death. And so it did.

That Madison's zeal in rushing to secure the adoption of a bill of rights was tactical, to head off the threat of a second convention, is amply confirmed by a review of some contemporaneous private correspondence, the full significance of which, curiously, has gone largely unnoticed. His letter of August 19, 1789 to Richard Peters, a Pennsylvanian with whom Madison had served in the Continental Congress, is especially revealing. It helps explain why Madison deemed it so essential that the drafting of the bill of rights be launched and, if possible, completed by Congress before the end of the first year of its First Session. As noted earlier, various supporters of the amendments appealed to Madison to postpone consideration of the issue to the second year of the First Session and allow Congress to attend first to the most pressing matter of establishing the governmental apparatus. He still could have claimed then that he had faithfully fulfilled his pledge to have amendments adopted during the First Session of Congress.[54] Why did Madison so adamantly refuse to brook such an ostensibly reasonable delay in the amendment process? Why was he so unrelenting even about leaving the completion of the process to the second year, and so anxious to have the draft amendments completed and adopted by Congress within the very first year? The key can be found in his response to Peters.

Peters had expressed skepticism about the need for a bill of rights. A short period of experience with the Constitution, he was sure, would effectually dispel all the complaints of the Antifederalists; and promotion of a bill of rights only magnified the importance of the critics. He penned a poem comparing the urge to amend the Constitution to the actions of malcontents who found fault with a delicious soup and whose diverse complaints led, in the end, to its being spoiled.[55] In his reply, Madison enumerated seven reasons for promoting a bill of rights, and for doing so without delay.[56] In his opening sentence, he referred to the task of gaining the adoption of a bill of rights as "the nauseous project of amendments." It was clearly the task of overcoming congressional lethargy and resistance, rather than the amendments themselves, that were repulsive to him. Nevertheless, his choice of expression surely reveals his determination to extract a bill of rights from Congress immediately at all costs, despite the measure of personal discomfort it entailed. Madison proceeded to enumerate the following reasons for promoting a bill of rights:

1. "A constitutional provision in favr. of essential rights is a thing not improper in itself and was always viewed in that light by myself." It may be less necessary in a republic, especially a federal one, than in a monarchy, but in some degree it was "rational in every Govt., since in every Govt. power may oppress, and declarations on paper, tho' not an effectual restraint, are not without some influence." What is remarkable about this statement is its negative, understated character. Madison exhibits no great enthusiasm about the virtues of a bill of rights; he concedes faintly that it can have a "rational" purpose in preventing government oppression, at least nominally.
2. The Constitution was adopted in many state-ratifying conventions only "under a tacit compact" that it would be supplemented with the adoption of a bill of rights. "In Virga. It would have been *certainly* rejected" had no such assurances been given. "As an honest man *I feel* my self bound by this consideration."
3. In Virginia, it was only the promise by candidates to work for amendments that enabled Federalists to be elected to the House of Representatives. Otherwise, the state would have been represented "almost wholly by disaffected characters." He was, of course, implicitly stating that he himself would not now be in Congress, had he not pledged to work for a bill of rights.

4. If amendments had not been proposed in the House by Federalists when they were, "*within three days*" Antifederalists would have submitted their own proposals for amendments. "It is certainly best that they should appear to be the free gift of the friends of the Constitution rather than to be extorted by the address & weight of its enemies."
5. "It will kill the opposition every where, and by putting an end to the disaffection to the Govt. itself, enable the administration to venture on measures not otherwise safe." Otherwise, said Madison, "those who hate the Govt." would always be able to join with opponents of particular legislation to defeat it.
6. Unless amendments were proposed, Antifederalists would be able to turn to the people, and say:

> We advised you not to adopt the Constn. with[ou]t. previous amendts. You listened to those who told you that subsequent securities for your rights would be most easily obtained – We urged you to insist on a Convention as the only effectual mode of obtaining these – You yielded to the assurances of those who told you that a Convention was unnecessary, that Congs. wd. be the proper channel for getting what was wanted, &c. &c. Here are fine texts for popular declaimers who wish to revive the antifedl. cause, *and at the fall session of the [state] Legisla[tu]res. to blow the Trumpet for a second Convention*. In Virga. a majority of the Legislature last elected, is bitterly opposed to the govt. and will be joined, if no amendts. be proposed, by great nos. of the other side who will complain of being deceived.[57] (Emphasis supplied.)

7. Some amendments were essential for North Carolina to be encouraged to join the Union.

The sixth paragraph, and especially the italicized sentence, underscores what was probably the central reason for Madison's race against time. It was crucial, he felt, to derail the second convention movement before it built up steam. Madison was obviously tormented by the thought that, in the absence of immediate action by Congress to promote amendments, the Antifederalists would seize the initiative and, in the fall session of the state legislatures (1789–1790), would secure sufficient state resolutions calling on Congress to convene a second constitutional convention. According to Article V of the Constitution, Congress would then have no option but to summon such a convention; that assembly would be free to draft an entirely new constitution; and even if it did not, it might well adopt amendments that would maim—and effectively bury—the existing constitution.

Madison's success in expediting congressional endorsement of a bill of rights in the first half of the First Session was highly praised by Judge Edmund

Pendleton, who had served as President of the Virginia Ratifying Convention. In a letter to Madison dated September 2, 1789, Pendleton wrote:

> I congratulate you upon having got through the Amendments to the Constitution, as I was very anxious that it should be done before y'r adjournment, since it will have a good effect in quieting the minds of many well meaning Citzens, tho' I am of opinion that nothing was further from the wish of some, who covered their Opposition to the Government under the masque of umcommon zeal for amendments, & to whom a rejection or a delay as a new ground of clamour, would have been more agreeable.[58]

Of course, Madison's achievement did not bear on the question of his lack of conviction on the inherent necessity of a bill of rights. For in sum, there is no evidence that he ever became enamored of a bill of rights, Jefferson's best efforts notwithstanding. Either because he considered it an inefficacious method of protecting rights, or because he believed that rights could be better protected by other means, Madison was not a committed convert to the cause. He was driven to present a bill of rights to Congress only because he was fearful that the Antifederalists would take advantage of congressional irresolution and promote the cause of a second convention in the state legislatures. With Jefferson campaigning for a bill of rights, and with Patrick Henry and other prominent Antifederalists demanding a second convention, the call for such a convention would have become irresistible. The upshot would be a convention that would, in one way or another, virtually destroy the Constitution and undermine all hope of maintaining in the United States a model system of federal government. Anarchy and chaos would ensue and the Union would be threatened with disintegration. The adoption of a draft bill of rights at the very beginning of Congress's deliberations preempted the diehard Antifederalists and left them without a fighting cause. By satisfying all those desiring protection of freedom of conscience, and of fundamental civil liberties, Madison's initiative frustrated the demand for a second convention and saved the Constitution from disfigurement and dismemberment.

If, as noted, the essence of the Federalist Revolution was the drive to provide the United States with an effective national government operating under a "federal constitution adequate to the exigencies of Government & the preservation of the Union," then Madison's promotion of a bill of rights, including the Tenth Amendment, completed that Revolution. The twin goals were now fulfilled: An effective national government was in operation and the Union was preserved.

Notes

1. As noted earlier, during the Constitutional Convention, Madison had already sensed the danger of allowing states to initiate the summoning of a convention for the adoption of amendments. After all, in defiance of explicit provisions in the Articles of Confederation and all instructions, the Philadelphia Convention had acted in a revolutionary manner and drafted a new constitution. Madison sought to eliminate the convention clause from Article V, but he was foiled each time by George Mason's insistence that the amendment procedure not be left exclusively to congressional initiative. See discussion above, Chap. 4.
2. In the 1970s, a debate arose among law professors whether it was possible to restrict a convention to a defined agenda and thereby prevent it from becoming a "runaway" convention. The question arose at that time because over 30 states had applied to Congress to summon a convention for the express purpose of amending the Constitution to require a balanced federal budget. Since the required number of state applications was never reached, the movement collapsed; but the validity of single-topic applications continued to be a matter of controversy. Some argued that even if Congress had no right to impose limitations, the state legislatures could designate the exact topic, or topics, upon which the convention might draft amendments. Recommendations outside the defined sphere would be deemed *ultra vires* of the convention and hence null and void. See William W. Van Alstyne, "Does Article V Restrict the States to Calling Unlimited Conventions Only?—A Letter to a Colleague," *Duke Law Journal*, 27 (1979): 1295–1306. Others contended that Article V does not allow for the imposition of any advance restrictions by Congress or the state legislatures. The convention is completely free to set its own agenda. In fact, any attempt by a state legislature to include such a limitation in its application to Congress would disqualify the application and require Congress to disregard it. See Charles L. Black, "Amending the Constitution: A Letter to a Congressman," *Yale Law Journal*, 82 (1972): 189–215; Walter E. Dellinger, "The Recurring Question of the 'Limited' Constitutional Convention," *Yale Law Journal*, 88 (1979): 1623–1640; Bruce Ackerman, "Unconstitutional Convention," *The New Republic* (Mar. 3, 1979); Gerald Gunther, "The Convention Method of Amending the United States Constitution," *Georgia Law Journal*, 14 (1979): 1–25; and Michael Stokes Paulsen, "A General Theory of Article V: The Constitutional Lessons of the Twenty-Seventh Amendment," *Yale Law Journal*, 103 (1993): 677–789. See also Michael Kammen, *A Machine that Would Go of Itself: The Constitution in American Culture* (New York: Random House, 1986), 390.
3. Farrand, *Records*, 2: 563–564.
4. Ibid., 2: 556, 564.
5. Ibid., 2: 479.
6. Ibid., 2: 479, 561.
7. Ibid., 2: 479.
8. Ibid., 2: 556, 564.
9. Ibid., 2: 632.
10. Ibid., 2: 633, 634.
11. *JMP*, 10: 347.
12. Ibid., 10: 356. George Washington similarly endeavored to disabuse Randolph of his preconceptions with regard to a second constitutional convention. In a

letter dated January 8, 1788, he wrote: "To my Judgement, it is more clear than ever, that an attempt to amend the Constitution which is submitted, would be productive of more heat, & greater confusion than can well be conceived ... [T]his [constitution], or a dissolution of the Union awaits our choice, & are the only alternatives before us—Thus beliving [*sic*], I had not, nor have I now any hesitation in deciding on which to lean."
GWP, 6: 17–18.
13. *JMP*, 10: 355–356.
14. Sept. 3, 1788. Ibid., 11: 246–247.
15. Aug. 13, 1788. Ibid., 11: 231.
16. Letter from Edward Carrington, Nov. 18, 1788. Ibid., 11: 352. Initially, it was thought Randolph would be the one to present the proposal for a second convention to the Assembly, but it turned out that Patrick Henry submitted it.
17. Oct. 21, 1788. Ibid., 11: 311. Emphasis in original.
18. See Editorial Note, *JMP.*, 12: 120–121.
19. President's Address, April 30, 1789. Ibid., 12: 123.
20. Address of House of Representatives to President, May 5, 1789. Ibid., 12: 133.
21. See ibid., 12: 55–57; Helen E. Veit, Kenneth R. Bowling, and Charlene Bangs Bickford (eds.), *Creating the Bill of Rights: The Documentary Record from the First Federal Congress* (Baltimore, MD: Johns Hopkins University Press, 1991), 5.
For background to the adoption of the Bill of Rights see Robert Allen Rutland, *The Birth of the Bill of Rights, 1776–1791*, rev. ed. (Boston, MA: Northeastern University Press, 1983) and Leonard W. Levy, *Origins of the Bill of Rights* (New Haven, CT: Yale University Press, 1999).
22. See text following n. 53.
23. *JMP*, 12: 347. Emphasis in original.
24. *The Daily Advertiser*, May 6, 1789; Veit, *Creating*, 57.
25. Ibid., 57–62. The following day, May 6, John Laurance of New York presented his state's application for a convention. But Laurance was a Federalist, and following the precedent with the Virginia application, the New York application was also ordered to be filed. See reference in Robert A. Goldwin, *From Parchment to Power: How James Madison Used the Bill of Rights to Save the Constitution* (New York: Oxford University Press, 2006), *Parchment*, 77.
26. See Editorial Note, *JMP*, 12: 58.
27. See Tansill, *Documents*, 1018, 1023, 1025, 1031, 1035, 1047, 1052, 1056.
28. Veit, *Creating*, 11–14.
29. Ibid.
30. Ibid., 63–64.
31. Ibid., 71–72.
32. Ibid., 72–73.
33. Ibid., 65.
34. Ibid., 73.
35. Ibid.
36. Ibid., 75. Akhil Amar aptly describes the situation as follows: "If the First Congress failed to act, political pressure for such a convention might begin to build, and a new political bandwagon might start to roll. If the bandwagon were to gain momentum, who could tell whether Congress could halt or detour it?" Akhil Reed Amar, *America's Constitution: A Biography* (New York: Random House, 2005), 318.

37. It would appear, that it was only because of the high regard in which the members of Congress held Madison that his campaign for a bill of rights was given a hearing, and ultimately succeeded. No one felt it would be right to stymie the efforts of a major architect of the Constitution, although they were suspicious of his motives. See Veit, *Creating*, xv.
38. Ibid., 77–86.
39. Ibid., 78. One wonders if Madison was not alluding to Jefferson here.
40. Ibid., 79.
41. Ibid., 83–84.
42. Ibid., 11–12.
43. Ibid., 33, n. 33; 193, n. 27; and 197.
44. The Australian constitution, it might be noted, follows Madison's preference and incorporates amendments in the appropriate section of the text.
45. Ibid., 105, 108–109, 117–118, 125–126.
46. Ibid., 197–198. At this point, Madison's preamble to the draft Bill of Rights was also eliminated. See ibid., 29 and 37.
47. Ibid., 41, n. 21.
48. The significance of the two additions has been noted by Charles Hobson: "The final wording explicitly recognized the constituent elements in the new American federalism—the United States, the states and the people." Hobson also points out: "Fittingly, too, this change meant that a document that opened with "We the people" now concluded with "the people." Charles F. Hobson, "The Tenth Amendment and the New Federalism of 1789" in Jon Kukla, *The Bill of Rights: A Lively Heritage* (Richmond: Virginia State Library, 1989), 162. See also Goldwin, *Parchment*, 184.
49. 32 U.S. (7 Pet.) 243, 247–248 (1833). On this topic, see the discussion in Charles F. Hobson, "James Madison, the Bill of Rights, and the Problem of the States," *William and Mary Law Review*, 31 (1990): 273.
50. For the text of the twelve draft amendments submitted to the states, see Edward Dumbauld, *The Bill of Rights and What It Means Today* (Norman: University of Oklahoma Press, 1957), 220–222.
    The process of ratification took just over 2 years; the number of states needed to bring the amendments into force reached the required three-quarters on December 15, 1791. The last ratification was provided by Virginia, but not until a vigorous debate on the amendments ensued in the state Assembly.
    Of the twelve draft amendments only ten were ratified and they constitute the Bill of Rights. The first two draft amendments failed of adoption. The first dealt with the composition of the House of Representatives, and the second denied members of Congress a raise in salary until an election had intervened. The latter draft amendment was finally approved by the requisite number of states in 1992, and entered into force that year as Amendment 27 to the Constitution.
51. See, for instance, Alpheus Thomas Mason, *The States Rights Debate: Antifederalism and the Constitution* (Englewood Cliffs, NJ: Prentice-Hall, 1964), 97, 104–105, n. 178.
52. Edward Dumbauld, *The Bill of Rights*, 38.
53. Goldwin, *Parchment*, Chap. 4. See also the comment of Ralph A. Rossum: "It is significant that in this crucial speech, Madison never argued on behalf of these amendments in his own name." "The *Federalist*'s Understanding of the Constitution as a Bill of Rights" In: Charles R. Kesler (ed.), *Saving the*

Revolution: The Federalist Papers and the American Founding (New York: The Free Press, 1987), 229.
54. See the comment of James Jackson, Federalist from Georgia, June 8, 1789, Veit, *Creating*, 89.
55. July 20, 1789. *JMP*, 12: 301–303; *Veit, Creating*, 264–266.
56. Ibid., 281–282; *JMP*, 12: 346–348. See also the response of Peters, Aug. 24, 1789, ibid., 353–356.
57. *JMP*, 12: 347.
58. Ibid., 12: 368–369.

CHAPTER 10

The Tenth Amendment: Nation Over State Preserved

In Madison's campaign to forestall a second constitutional convention, the Tenth Amendment was pivotal. The battle between Federalists and Antifederalists with respect to a bill of rights revolved, most acutely, around the wording of this Amendment. Formulated one way, the provision would represent a Federalist triumph in the adoption of the Constitution; formulated the other way, it would spell the failure of the Federalist Revolution. Madison managed, ingeniously, to secure widespread support for a sanitized bill of rights capped at the end with an amendment that preserved intact the Constitution as it had been adopted at Philadelphia. The Tenth Amendment thus fulfilled a dual purpose, for as much as it reserved the powers of the states, it preserved the powers of the federal government. This dual purpose was Madison's primary objective in promoting a bill of rights. By serving as the Father of the Bill of Rights, Madison became the Father of the Constitution; for it was only when the Tenth Amendment was safely positioned in the Bill of Rights that the Federalist design was confirmed, and the Federalist Revolution was completed.[1] Clearly enough, for Madison the struggle was not over until the Bill of Rights—with the Tenth Amendment—was ratified in 1791.[2]

Madison's success in securing an inoffensive bill of rights was, as could be expected, the cause of deep frustration for the committed Antifederalists. Their sense of outrage and despair at having failed to obtain their desired structural

---

In writing this chapter I have been greatly aided by the valuable insights provided by Charles F. Hobson's, "The Tenth Amendment and the New Federalism of 1789" in Jon Kukla, (ed.), *The Bill of Rights: A Lively Heritage* (Richmond, VA: Virginia State Library, 1989), 152–163. Moreover, for further excellent publications relating to this topic, see Walter Berns, "The Meaning of the Tenth Amendment" in Robert A. Goldwin, (ed.), *A Nation of States: Essays on the American Federal System* (Chicago: Rand McNally, 1961), 126–148; Charles A. Lofgren, "The Origins of the Tenth Amendment: History, Sovereignty, and the Problem of Constitutional Intention" in Ronald K.L. Collins (ed.), *Constitutional Government in America* (Durham, NC: Carolina Academic Press, 1980), 331–357; Mark R. Killenbeck, "Pursuing the Great Experiment: Reserved Powers in a Post-Ratification Compound Republic," *Supreme Court Review* (1999): 81–140; and Mark R. Killenbeck (ed.), *The Tenth Amendment and State Sovereignty: Constitutional History and Contemporary Issues* (Lanham, MD: University Press of America, 2002).

amendments was evinced in their comments during the congressional debate, and even more in subsequent correspondence. Thus, in the House debate, Representative Aedanus Burke of South Carolina, decrying Madison's proposed amendments, declared:

> [They] are very far from giving satisfaction to our constituents; they are not those solid and substantial amendments which the people expect; they are little better than whip-syllabub, frothy and full of wind, formed only to please the palate, or they are like a tub thrown out to a whale, to secure the freight of the ship, and its peaceable voyage.[3]

It was all a waste of time, said Burke, and he advocated dropping the subject of amendments and concentrating instead on the organization of the government. The amendments were also scornfully dismissed by Representative Samuel Livermore of New Hampshire. They merely "secure[d] rights never in danger," and were worth no more "than a pinch of snuff."[4]

Senator Richard Henry Lee of Virginia, in a letter he later wrote to Patrick Henry, lamented the fact that, despite his best efforts, the draft amendments as adopted by Congress were a far cry from "the wishes of our [Virginia] Convention."[5] "We might as well have attempted to move Mount Atlas upon our shoulders," he said. "The most essential danger from the present System arises ... from its tendency to a Consolidated government, instead of a Union of Confederated States." The history of the world, he thought, confirmed that a territory as extensive as the United States could never be governed in freedom, and that standing armies and despotism would follow automatically. It was, therefore, essential that "the friends of liberty" maintain "perfect vigilance" against every invasion of rights "that belong to the sta[tes]." There was a need to persist in efforts "for so amending the federal Constitution as to prevent a Consolidation by securing the due Authority of the States." Before long, he anticipated, enough states would be found to call for a second convention.[6]

In their formal letter submitting proposed amendments to the Speaker of the Virginia House of Delegates, Lee and his Senate colleague, William Grayson, noted that "nothing on our part has been omitted to procure the success of those Radical Amendments proposed by the [state] Convention." Consolidation and "the annihilation of the State Government" were inevitable, they said, if no further amendments were adopted.[7] Similar sentiments were voiced by Samuel Adams in two letters that he addressed to members of Congress in that period. In a letter to Representative Elbridge Gerry, dated August 22, 1789, he stressed the need "to see a Line drawn as clearly as may be, between the federal Powers vested in Congress and the distinct Sovereignty of the several States upon which the private and personal Rights of the Citizens depend." He warned that "without such Distinction there will be Danger of the Constitution issuing imperceptibly, and gradually into a Consolidated Government over all the States."[8] And to Richard Henry Lee he wrote that he wished to convey "how deeply I am impressed with a sense of the Importance of Amendments; that the good People may clearly see the distinction, for there is a distinction, between the *federal* Powers vested in Congress, and the *sovereign* Authority belonging to the several States, which is the Palladium of the private, and personal rights of the Citizens."[9]

Had the Antifederalist campaign for substantive, structural amendments succeeded, the Constitutional design instituted at Philadelphia would have been radically transformed. The federal government would have been limited to the express powers enumerated in the Constitution, and implied powers would have been proscribed, even as they had been under Article II of the Articles of Confederation. Throughout, the Antifederalists strove to get a similar provision incorporated in a revised constitution. The desired amendment would be proposed either by Congress directly or by a second constitutional convention that Congress would summon on the basis of state applications. With one stroke, the states would then regain the superior, sovereign status that they had forfeited to the nation with the adoption of the Constitution.

Were such an amendment to be adopted, many Antifederalists felt, a bill of rights might readily be dispensed with. For example, at the Virginia Ratifying Convention, after analyzing the dangerous scope of the necessary and proper clause, James Monroe said: "Our great unalienable rights ought to be secured from being destroyed by such unlimited powers, either by a Bill of Rights, or by an express provision in the body of the Constitution. It is immaterial in which of these two modes rights are secured."[10] William R. Davie, who had served in the Constitutional Convention as a delegate from North Carolina, wrote a letter to Madison on June 10, 1789, outlining what his countrymen (refusing to ratify the Constitution until a bill of rights was appended) preferred in the way of amendments: "Instead of a Bill of rights attempting to enumerate the rights of the indivi[du]al or the State Governments, they seem to prefer some general negative confining Congress to the exercise of the powers particularly granted, with some express negative restriction in some important cases."[11] And at the Massachusetts Ratifying Convention, Samuel Adams said of the Massachusetts draft amendment that would reserve to the states all powers not expressly granted to the federal government: "This appears to my mind to be a summary of a bill of rights." It gives assurance, he said, "that if any law made by the federal government shall be extended beyond the powers granted by the proposed Constitution, and inconsistent with the Constitution of this State, it will be an errour, and adjudged by the courts of law to be void." The provision was "consonant with the second article in the present Confederation."[12] Even some nominal Federalists were not averse to the adoption of this kind of provision. Charles Jarvis, for one, found the Massachusetts draft provision "very agreeable" to him. "When we talk of our wanting a bill of rights to the new Constitution," he said, "the first article proposed must remove every doubt on this head – as by positively securing what is not expressly delegated, it leaves nothing to the uncertainty of conjecture, or to the refinements of implication."[13] And Samuel Spencer proposed a similar amendment at the North Carolina Ratifying Convention, explaining that "such a clause ... would have superseded the necessity of a bill of rights."[14] Even Jefferson thought an amendment along the lines of the one proposed by Massachusetts, would "in some degree ... answer" the need for a bill of rights.[15]

In the ratification struggle, much clamor was raised about the scope of the federal tax power, with Patrick Henry, in particular, stressing the need to reinstate requisitions.[16] However, the impact of a general "express powers" amendment obviously would have been far greater than any revised provision relating to the taxing power or any other single federal power. It would have affected the entire gamut of federal power and reconstructed much of the pre-Philadelphia federal-state nexus.[17] Unsurprisingly, therefore, the Antifederalists sought to get Congress to propose a sweeping "reserved powers" amendment; but their plans were foiled by Madison's strategy. As Alpheus Mason has said: "Those who feared federal encroachment had to be content with a constitutional tranquilizer, an empty declaration – the Tenth Amendment."[18]

Madison succeeded in fashioning and guiding his amendments through Congress, precisely to frustrate any thought of introducing structural amendments into the Constitution. Only one amendment dealt with powers, the Tenth, and this had been carefully crafted to do no more than confirm the basic principle of the Constitution—that the federal government was a government of enumerated powers, whilst all other powers were reserved for the states. Significantly, Madison, unlike the Antifederalists, placed the reserved powers clause at the end—rather than at the head—of the list of amendments. This placement did not connote any diminution, in Madison's mind, of the legal status of the last amendment; but it did reflect an intention to avoid attributing to it a constitution-modifying effect. Nothing was to be changed with the adoption of a bill of rights. The presence in the Constitution of the "necessary and proper" and supremacy clauses confirmed that the federal government could dispose also of implied powers. And by successfully working to defeat every attempt in Congress to insert the word "expressly" in the Tenth Amendment, Madison ensured that those implied powers would not be eliminated or diminished. Representative Elbridge Gerry's August 22 attempt to have the word "expressly" added evoked the following illuminating response from Madison:

> Mr. Madison objected to this, as confining the government within such limits as to admit of no implied powers, and I believe, that no government ever existed which was not necessarily obliged to exercise powers by implication. This question was agitated in the Convention of Virginia; it was brought forward by those who were opposed to the Constitution, and was finally given up by them.[19]

Clearly, Madison had no desire to return to the paralytic condition of the central government under the Articles of Confederation—a condition that had so largely furnished the impetus for the Federalist Revolution in the first place.

Madison's attempts to withstand the Antifederalist thrust might well have failed but for the support of the camp of moderate Antifederalists, whose sole complaint had been the failure of the Constitution to protect essential rights, and who were greatly pleased with Madison's draft amendments.[20] In their view, by safeguarding what had previously been unguarded, these amendments had effectively converted the Constitution into a charter of liberty. Even George Mason viewed the amendments with favor and thought that only a few more would perfect the system.[21] Madison's strategy of detaching the well-wishers of the Constitution from the hard-core die-hard ideological opponents worked exactly as he had planned. Members of the latter group—among whom Patrick Henry featured prominently—were not mollified by amendments which, in their perception, were of the meaningless "milk and water" variety and failed utterly to grapple with the central issue of federal-state distribution of powers.[22] In Merrill Jensen's words: Henry "looked upon the passage of the Bill of Rights as a political defeat which would make it impossible to block the centralization of all power in the national government."[23] In contrast, Jefferson was generally pleased with the result of Madison's endeavors, even though some amendments that he had endorsed were omitted. He still entertained the hope that several more would be adopted.[24] Above all, the second convention movement was killed, and its primary goal of restructuring the division of national and state powers, was frustrated. The Federalist Revolution had triumphed.

As noted earlier, the Tenth Amendment served to confirm without qualification, the full range of federal power, including implied powers. It sealed the Bill of Rights, and thereby saved the Constitution from tampering. The road to a further convention, whose aim would be to delineate more clearly the dividing line between national and state authority, was effectively barred. The Federalist Revolution had now attained the goals to which its organizers had aspired—the establishment of a federal government endowed with sufficient energy and supremacy to "render the federal constitution adequate to the exigencies of Government & the preservation of the Union."

Omission of any of the other amendments in the Bill of Rights, important as they may have been, would not have been really critical. The absence of other guarantees might have aroused protest which, however, would not likely have been widespread enough to spark a second convention movement. But a reserved powers clause in the form of the Tenth Amendment was different. Robert Goldwin has demonstrated incisively how, in the course of American history, the Tenth Amendment—even without the word "expressly"—was viewed by Antifederalists, and even by some Federalists, as if that term were an inherent part of the provision.[25] Viewed in this light, the danger that anyone could obtain sufficient support—two-thirds of the state legislatures—to apply for a convention merely to add the word "expressly" was very remote.

The Federalist Revolution succeeded in drafting a constitution that would establish an effective national government within a federal framework. By allowing amendments to be adopted by less than unanimous consent of either Congress or the states, the Constitution eschewed the inflexible system of government of the colonies' original experiment in constitution-making. No less significantly, it permitted the evolution and application of a doctrine of implied powers. The supremacy clause, as Justice Oliver Wendell Holmes once declared, was the "linchpin" of the Constitution. So too, it may be said, was the "necessary and proper clause." For, as Leonard Levy has said, this clause "was the most formidable in the array of national powers, therefore the most controversial, and the one most responsible later for the demand for a bill of rights to ensure that the United States did not violate the rights of the people or of the states."[26] However, as its history reveals, the Tenth Amendment was no less pivotal in preserving the full scope of federal power as devised at Philadelphia. A reversion to a form of the earlier Confederation model was a threat repeatedly resisted both during the early struggles over ratification and subsequently in Congress, and it was effectively scotched only when the threat of a second constitutional convention was finally averted. It is no exaggeration to state that the absence of a necessary and proper clause in the Articles of Confederation was the reason for the adoption of an entirely new constitution, and the presence of the necessary and proper clause in the Constitution was the reason for the adoption of the Bill of Rights. The issue of a doctrine of implied powers was a central feature in the struggle surrounding the formation of the founding documents of the American system of government. The interpretation of the necessary and proper clause remains a matter of controversy to the present day, and will continue as such for as long as the Constitution remains the governing document of the United States.

Madison was clearly the mastermind of the strategy of resistance. At Philadelphia, his initial concept of a unitary national government had been rejected in favor of a truly federal arrangement. Thereafter, he worked to preserve at all costs the remarkable division of national and state authority consecrated in the new Constitution, and to remove the threat of a second constitutional convention which would likely have undone the Framers' handiwork. The early adoption of a Bill of Rights, and within it a Tenth Amendment formulated so as to secure reserved powers to the states without impinging on a federal doctrine of implied powers, formed an essential part of Madison's successful strategy. Preservation of the doctrine of implied powers was the master-stroke of the Federalist Revolution.

An incidental product of this study is a further refutation, if such were needed, of the Beardian and neo-Beardian theses of the origin of the Constitution. Beard claimed that the Constitutional Convention represented a giant conspiracy to impose on the American people a system of government that would serve to protect the economic class interests of the Founders. The neo-Beardians, such as Merrill Jensen and Gordon Wood, have contended that the Framers met to devise a constitution that would protect the aristocratic values they felt were being undermined by the outburst of liberty released by the 1776 Revolution. One looks in vain in the published record of the Constitutional Convention and the ratification debates for evidence in support of these social-economic theses. The documentary record confirms the validity of the earlier perception of the Framers as devoted patriots whose central aim was to provide effective national government for the United States and save it from anarchy and dismemberment.

The battle between proponents and opponents of the Constitution in the debates did not revolve around the wish to protect the interests of the propertied class or their aristocratic mores by denying democracy to the American people. It centered on the question how far federalism should qualify the national design. In light of the paucity of evidence to sustain the Beardian approach, it is quite remarkable that this unsubstantiated thesis, in its various forms, was able to dominate the landscape of American historical writing for so long.

Viewed in detailed historical context, the entire saga of the adoption of the Bill of Rights calls for a reassessment of some of the earlier accepted wisdom and leads to some paradoxical conclusions. It has often been claimed that while the Federalists gave America its Constitution, the Antifederalists provided it with a bill of rights.[27] Underlying this assertion is the assumption that the Antifederalists demanded a bill of rights and the Federalists—perhaps reluctantly—complied. The true picture was different, more complex, and shot through with no small measure of irony.

Left to their own devices, most Federalists would have done nothing to promote a bill of rights. As Edward Dumbauld wrote: "In sponsoring amendments, Madison received little help from his colleagues. The Federalists did not wish amendments at all; the Anti-Federalists desired more than Madison offered, and knew that adoption of his amendments would kill the prospect of any radical changes in the future."[28] Even those Federalists who favored appending a bill of rights saw no need to expedite its adoption before the new governmental machinery was firmly in place. The Antifederalist demand could thus have been parried. It was pure chance that the last critical ratification, that of New York, produced the circular letter calling for a second constitutional convention. And it was the threat of such a convention that galvanized Madison to work for an immediate bill of rights. From all indications, the circular letter, in turn, was inspired by New York Federalists Jay and Hamilton, intent on enlisting sufficient votes to secure New York's ratification of the Constitution in the state Ratifying Convention. If so, then the Bill of Rights—no less than the Constitution—might be said to be derived, in the immediate sense, from a Federalist initiative. It was the Federalist-inspired, or at least Federalist-formulated, round robin that set in motion the process of speedy formulation in Congress of a draft bill of rights.

Ironically, and perhaps counter-intuitively, the struggle between the Federalists and the most committed Antifederalists revolved less around rights than around powers. In promoting a bill of rights, both the Federalists and the hard-core ideological Antifederalists had ulterior motives, and the emergence of a bill of rights was something of an accident of history.[29] The Antifederalists sought to create a channel for restoring state power to its former primacy; and the Federalists, under Madison's prompting, strove to prevent the Antifederalists from achieving this goal. For Madison preserving the federal compact exactly as instituted at Philadelphia was the primary achievement of the Tenth Amendment. In the end, the major issue between the two camps hinged on a single word—"expressly." Its presence or absence in the Tenth Amendment determined whether implied powers would be denied or confirmed.

In sum, it was only thanks to Madison's innovative tactics that the Antifederalist campaign was roundly defeated, and the full scope of federal power, including implied powers, remained unimpaired, even while state sovereignty was preserved. His acceptance of the need for a bill of rights turned the tables on the Antifederalist effort to promote a second convention, and saved the Philadelphia formula from modification.[30] As Herbert Storing has said: "Madison's insistent sponsorship of amendments has to be seen ... as the final step in the strikingly successful Federalist strategy to secure an effective national government."[31] The Bill of Rights was the price the Federalists paid to the Antifederalists for ratification of the Constitution; and Madison's version of the Tenth Amendment was the price the Antifederalists paid to the Federalists for a bill of rights. The Bill of Rights saved the Constitution, and the Tenth Amendment saved them both.

Notes

1. Helen E. Veit, Kenneth R. Bowling, and Charlene Bangs Bickford (eds.), *Creating the Bill of Rights: The Documentary Record from the First Federal Congress* (Baltimore, MD: Johns Hopkins University Press, 1991), 175.
2. The question is often asked: When did the Federalist Revolution come to an end? Various answers are provided. Some say it ended with the signing of the Constitution at Philadelphia in September 1787. Others claim that the crucial date was when the Confederation Congress, a year later, arranged for elections to be held for the office of President and for the Congress. Still others believe it was only consummated with the institution of the new government. The thesis presented in this work is that the Revolution was only completed when the Bill of Rights, including the Tenth Amendment, came into force on December 15, 1791, with the ratification by the state of Virginia. It was only then that the Constitution was safely harbored, and the risk of having a second constitutional convention that would revise the federal character of the Constitution was removed. But cf. the view of Richard Leffler, "The Constitution of the United States: The End of the Revolution" in Stephen L. Schechter, (ed.), *The Reluctant Pillar: New York and the Adoption of the Federal Constitution* (Troy, NY: Russell Sage College, 1985), 47.
3. Veit, *Creating*, 175.
4. Ibid., 210. This comment and the following one are also cited by Herbert J. Storing, "The Constitution and the Bill of Rights" in Robert A. Goldwin, and William A. Schambra (eds.), *How Does the Constitution Secure Rights?* (Washington, DC: American Enterprise Institute, 1985), 20–21.
5. Veit, *Creating*, 295–296.
6. Ibid., 295.
7. Ibid., 299.
8. Ibid., 284–285.
9. Ibid., 286.
10. *DHRC*, 9: 1112.
11. Veit, *Creating*, 246; June 10, 1789. See also the letters of Richard Parker to Richard Henry Lee, July 6, 1789, and of Henry Gibbs to Roger Sherman, July 16, 1789, ibid., 260, 263.
12. *DHRC*, 6: 1395.

13 Ibid., 6: 1426. This citation and the next are cited by Lofgren, "Origins of Tenth Amendment," 345.
14 Elliot, 4: 163; also cited in Schwartz, *Bill of Rights*, 2: 945.
15 Letter to Edward Carrington, May 27, 1788, *TJP*, 13: 208. Jefferson had reservations, however, since in some cases it may not go far enough and in others too far.
The Massachusetts Bill of Rights of 1780 contained a clause paralleling Article II of the Articles of Confederation and reserving to the state "every power, jurisdiction, and right, which is not ... expressly delegated to the United States." The New Hampshire Bill of Rights of 1784 incorporated a similar clause.
16 See *DHRC*, 10: 1215–1216, 1221–122, 1535. See also D. Stuart to George Washington, Sept. 12, 1789. "The success of amendments will leave but a few scattering opponents... Mr. Henry is the only one of the party, I have heard of, who disapproves of it – he still thinks too that the single amendment proposed in our [Virginia] convention, respecting direct taxes, worth all the rest." Cited in Robert A. Goldwin, *From Parchment to Power: How James Madison Used the Bill of Rights to Save the Constitution* (Washington, DC: AEI Press, 1997), 199, n. 6. See also Randolph letter to Madison, Aug. 18, 1789, Veit, *Creating*, 281.
Madison had varied opinions on the key target of the Antifederalists in their campaign against the Constitution. In a letter to Jefferson, dated October 17, 1788, he included a pamphlet that presented, one by one, the text of the draft amendments proposed in the various state conventions. He wrote: "Various and numerous as they appear they certainly omit many of the true grounds of opposition. The articles relating to Treaties – to paper money, and to contracts, created more enemies than all the errors in the System positive & negative put together." *JMP*, 11: 297. Notably absent here is any reference to the taxing power. Yet in an earlier letter to Tench Coxe, dated July 30. 1788, he wrote: "The conspiracy agst. direct taxes is more extensive & formidable than some gentlemen suspect. It is clearly seen by the enemies to the Constitution that an abolition of that power will re-establish the supremacy of the State Legislatures, the real object of all their zeal in opposing the system." Ibid., 210. The broad aim of the Antifederalists, as Madison said, was the restoration of state authority by means of a revision of the federal-state equation. This was the central aim of the reserved powers clause that they promoted, invariably placed at the head of their respective lists of amendments.
17 For Patrick Henry's remarks on a reserved powers clause see, *DHRC*, 10: 1215–1216, 1322, 1329. For those of George Mason, see ibid., 1326.
18 Alpheus Thomas MasonHall, *The States Rights Debate: Antifederalists and the Constitution* (Englewood Cliffs, NJ: Prentice-Hall, 1964), 5.
19 Veit, *Creating*, 193.
20 See, for example, the letter of Edward Carrington to Henry Knox, Aug. 3, 1789, ibid., 271, and his letter to Madison, Sept. 9, ibid., 292–293; see also the letter of Rhode Island Governor, John Collins, to the President and Congress, Sept. 26, ibid., 298.
21 See Mason's letter to Samuel Griffin, Sept. 8, 1789, *GMP*, 3: 1172.
22 In a letter, dated Aug. 28, 1789, to Richard Henry Lee, Henry wrote: "As to my opinion of the Amendments, I think they will tend to injure rather than to serve the Cause of Liberty... For Right without her Power & Might is but a Shadow... While impediments are cast in the Way of those who wish to retrench

the exorbitancy of Power granted away by the Constitution from the People." Veit, *Creating*, 289–290.
23 Jensen, *Making*, 149.
24 See Jefferson's letter to George Mason, June 13, 1790. *GMP*, 3: 1201–1202.
25 Robert Goldwin, *Parchment to Power*, 198, n. 4.
26 Leonard W. Levy, "Bill of Rights" in *Essays*, 1987, 262.
27 See, for example, Herbert J. Storing, "The Constitution and the Bill of Rights", 16.
28 Dumbauld, Edward, *The Bill of Rights and What It Means Today* (Norman: University of Oklahoma Press, 1957), 34.
29 According to Merrill Jensen, the Bill of Rights was "the product of eighteenth century politics" in which the motives of the politicians were simply "cynical." Merrill Jensen, *The Making of the American Constitution* (Malabar, FL: Krieger, 1979), 150. And, in the words of Leonard Levy: "Our precious Bill of Rights was in the main the chance result of certain Federalists having been reluctantly forced to capitalize for their own cause the propaganda that had been originated in vain by the Anti-Federalists for ulterior purposes." Leonard W. Levy, *Legacy of Suppression: Freedom of Speech and Press in Early American History* (Cambridge, MA: Harvard University Press, 1960), 233. Most historians agree with this assumption, that the adoption of the Bill of Rights was an accident of history. See the comment of Charles Hobson: "Its adoption was largely a historical accident, an unintended consequence of the debate over the ratification of the Constitution." "James Madison, the Bill of Rights, and the Problem of the States." *William and Mary Law Review*, 31 (1990): 268. On the other hand, one prominent historian, Robert Rutland, author of *The Birth of the Bill of Rights*, differs. He maintains that "the Bill of Rights would be in place whether Madison had been present or not." "The Trivialization of the Bill of Rights," ibid., 287.
30 Levy, "Bill of Rights," 289.
31 Storing, "The Constitution and the Bill of Rights," 18.
    While Madison's version of the Tenth Amendment saved the Constitution from tampering, it did not end the dispute about the federal character of the Union. As Richard Ellis observed: "The bill of rights, as finally adopted did not lay to rest the concerns of many Antifederalists about the kind of central government created by the United States Constitution. As a result, the question of how power was to be distributed between the state and federal governments was to remain the central constitutional and political issue in American history until the Civil War." Richard E. Ellis, "The Persistence of Antifederalism after 1789" in Beeman et al. (eds.), *Beyond Confederation: Origins of the Constitution and American National Identity* (Chapel Hill: University of North Carolina Press, 1987), 299. Other, more recent writers would go further and say that the tug of war between center and periphery is a perennial issue that is inherent in the structure of the American political system. Nevertheless, the fact is that the Framers sought to establish a powerful central government that would dominate the states. And despite all the concessions to the smaller states and slave states, the inclusion of the supremacy clause represented the fulfillment of this purpose. See further, below, Postscript.

CHAPTER 11

Postscript: Federalism Tested: Madison v. Marshall and the Antifederalist Revival

This review briefly examines the course of federalism in the early Republic in relation to the following topics:

1. Madison's Embrace of Antifederalist Ideology
2. Madison's Legal Theses: How Tenable?
3. The Implications of the Emergence of a Democratic-Republican Party
4. Antifederalists: Co-Founders of the Constitution?
5. Marshall's Federalism, Dual Federalism, and the New Federalism

The entry into office of the Washington administration in early 1789 symbolized the success of the Federalist Revolution and the primacy of nation over state. At the same time, it also signaled the end of the age of constitutional formation and the beginning of the era of constitutional interpretation. Given the vast expanse of the United States, it was only natural that the provisions of the Constitution would evoke different interpretations in diverse geographical areas. North and south, east and west were divided in economic interests, in products, in labor forces, in markets, and in means of communication. Differences of interpretation arose early, but all this was expected and was no cause for surprise. What did provoke surprise, indeed astonishment, was the radical change that occurred in Madison's approach to constitutional interpretation. From being an exponent of the greatest measure of national authority, he became a strict constructionist in defining the scope of federal power. Under the Articles of Confederation, Madison had claimed that even without a necessary and proper clause, the Articles provided for the exercise of a sweeping doctrine of implied powers according to which the national authority was empowered to exact requisitions from the states at the force of a gun.

In writing on this topic, I found Forrest McDonald, *States' Rights and the Union: Imperium in Imperio 1776–1876* (Lawrence: University Press of Kansas, 2000) to be immensely useful and informative.

A delinquent state, he claimed, could be subjected to a naval blockade of its ports or a military siege of its lines of communication on land, until it surrendered the sum due.[1] Now, with a Federalist government in office, Madison contended that the necessary and proper clause did not even permit the government to establish a national bank. This turn-about was breathtaking. It puzzled contemporaries and has intrigued historians for generations. From being a strong nationalist and critic of "factions," Madison was transformed into a powerful critic of the Federalist government and the progenitor of an opposition party designed to restrict the powers of the federal government. In contrast to his previous stance in vigorously promoting nation over state, he now equally firmly advocated state over nation. His approach was virtually indistinguishable from that of his erstwhile opponents, the Antifederalists. In turn, this inspired sharp disputes between North and South, ultimately paving the way, according to some authorities, to secession and the Civil War.

Madison's Embrace of Antifederalist Ideology

In January 1790, Secretary of the Treasury Alexander Hamilton submitted to Congress the first part of his national economic program dealing with settlement of foreign and domestic debts that had been incurred during the War of Independence. Virginia had paid off its domestic loans and was not inclined to bear the burden of funding the debts owed by other states that had not yet settled their obligations. Moreover, Madison claimed it was not fair to pay the ultimate owners of securities rather than the original owners who had sold their certificates, in most instances, for a pittance. Hamilton said it would be an impossible task to discover those original owners. Despite the differences, the matter of the national and state debts was attended to as part of a bargain whereby the capital of the nation was earmarked to rise in Virginia on the shores of the Potomac River, and the debt crisis was resolved to Hamilton's satisfaction.[2]

The most divisive issue that pitted Hamilton against Madison and Jefferson was the creation of the Bank of the United States. The issue of the legitimacy of the bank was the first serious dispute that erupted between members of George Washington's cabinet, and the contours of that controversy reflect the never-ending debate about the proper scope of national and state authority under the Constitution. No sooner had the federal government begun to operate, and the same arguments that had engaged Federalists and Antifederalists in the ratification struggle over the range of federal power—and especially on the scope of the necessary and proper clause—now surfaced between colleagues in what was, ostensibly, a Federalist government. Whereas Thomas Jefferson was never a Federalist and had always espoused a narrow gauge for national power, Madison's about-face in joining Jefferson in a vehement campaign against the bank was another matter altogether.[3]

Hamilton conveyed the bank proposal to Congress in December 1790, and the Senate endorsed the bill shortly thereafter. When the House of

Representatives began debating the subject on February 2, 1791, Madison opposed the measure on the ground that the federal government lacked constitutional authority to create corporations.[4] He recalled that a suggestion for providing for such a power was proposed at the Philadelphia Convention but "rejected."[5] Under which clause of the Constitution, asked Madison, could the power be found? It was not a tax bill, nor did it purport to borrow money on the credit of the United States. The only possible basis was the necessary and proper clause. Madison denied the bank was necessary; "at most it could be but convenient."[6] Adopting a very strict construction, he argued that the clause relates only to the "technical means" of executing one of the enumerated powers. It could not be interpreted to give "an unlimited discretion to Congress."[7] "If implications, thus remote and thus multiplied, can be linked together, a chain may be formed that will reach every object of legislation, every object within the whole compass of political economy."[8] Madison stressed that the Constitution had been ratified on the expectation that the federal government would not roam too far in its search for energy. "He considered the enlightened opinion and affection of the people the only solid basis for the support of this government."[9] Notably, Madison made no mention of a doctrine of implied powers.

Madison's address was startling. The editor of the *Madison Papers* cites an article by Kenneth R. Bowling,[10] according to which the opposition of Madison, Jefferson, and others might also have reflected a fear that stationing the bank in New York or Philadelphia might scuttle plans for the capital to be located on the banks of the Potomac.[11] Elkins and McKitrick, authors of the magisterial work *The Age of Federalism*,[12] also cite this thesis as a possible explanation for Madison's radical about-face from an expansive to a narrow perspective of federal authority. They note that he had reportedly approached the Pennsylvanians with a suggestion that the bank charter last 10 years, rather than twenty, so that its date of expiration would coincide with the proposed move of the capital from Philadelphia to the Virginia site in 1800. "When this move failed, the only device that remained was to oppose the bank on grounds of constitutionality."[13]

It should be recalled that in *Federalist* #44, as noted above,[14] Madison had written that even if the Constitution had been silent on such matters, the necessary and proper clause "would have resulted to the government, by unavoidable implication. No axiom is more clearly established in law, or in reason, than that wherever the end is required, the means are authorized; wherever a general power to do a thing is given, every power necessary for doing it, is included." In light of this commitment to a doctrine of implied powers, it is difficult to comprehend how Madison could have performed such a policy somersault in the space of such a short period. Despite occasional flexibility, he never really retreated from the antifederalist philosophical stance that he adopted at this time.

The Tenability of Madison's Legal Theses

In support of his claim that the administration was not authorized to create a bank, Madison posited several legal theories that are open to serious question.[15] On various occasions, he contended that the Constitution as it emerged from Philadelphia was merely a proposal, and its meaning must be ascertained from the state ratifying conventions. Addressing the House of Representatives in 1796, he said:

> As the instrument came from them [the Framers] it was nothing more than the draft of a plan, nothing but a dead letter, until life and validity were breathed into it by the voice of the people, speaking through the several State Conventions. If we were to look, therefore, for the meaning of the instrument beyond the face of the instrument, we must look for it, not in the General Convention, which proposed, but in the State Conventions, which accepted and ratified the Constitution.[16]

Madison's reasoning is not easy to follow. To ascertain the meaning of a legal document, the contemporaneous comments of its drafters are regularly and justifiably given greater weight than later second thoughts and suggestions that do not alter the text. At Philadelphia, the delegates had been free to adopt, modify, or reject the drafts before them. The state conventions, on the other hand, were presented with the Constitution as a fait accompli, and bidden to accept or reject that document as is. They had no opportunity to revise anything, and their remarks—even assuming that they paralleled those of delegates in other states—were not legally binding. They did not affect the meaning imparted to the document by its authors at its birth. They effected no changes in the text of the Constitution; they only succeeded in extracting a promise for the addition of constitutional amendments—which became the Bill of Rights. But, as noted earlier, in proposing the Bill of Rights, Madison declared categorically that it in no way modified any part of the Constitution. Even the Tenth Amendment, he insisted, added nothing new, and only reaffirmed the relationship that was instituted between federal and state powers under the Constitution. As Bernard Bailyn aptly observed: "How the Antifederalists' views explain the Constitution that was adopted over their objections has not been made clear."[17]

There are also technical considerations that Madison seems to have overlooked in arguing that only the debates in the state ratifying conventions determine the meaning of the provisions of the Constitution. It is illuminating to examine his original statement, as recorded in his *Papers*, made in the House of Representatives on February 2, 1791. In opposing the administration's bill on the establishment of the Bank of the United States, he stated[18]:

> The powers not given were retained; and ... those given were not to be extended by remote implications... The explanations in the state conventions all turned on the same fundamental principle, and on the principle that the terms necessary and proper gave no additional powers to those enumerated. (Here he read sundry passages from the debates of the Pennsylvania, Virginia, and North-Carolina

conventions, shewing the grounds on which the constitution had been vindicated by its principal advocates against a dangerous latitude of its powers, charged by its opponents.)

To which states and debates was Madison referring? In accordance with Article VII, the Constitution came into force on June 21, 1788, when New Hampshire became the ninth state to ratify. Of those nine states, six—Delaware, Pennsylvania, New Jersey, Georgia, Connecticut, and Maryland—had ratified without any proposals for amendments. The suggestion for amendments arose only at the Massachusetts Convention, which "recommended" a series of amendments. Throughout the ratification campaign, no state was allowed to make its ratification subject to conditions. New York tried countless times to introduce a variety of conditions but was rebuffed each time.[19] Madison made it absolutely clear that ratification had to be unqualified. Each of the remaining seven states came up with "recommended" amendments. The key amendment that they sought was one on reserved powers. Five of the seven recommended that the word "expressly" be stipulated in this amendment, so that the federal government would be limited to those powers "expressly" enumerated in the Constitution. Virginia and North Carolina made no such stipulation, Madison having categorically rejected any such proposal, just as he would later reject it in Congress during the debate over the draft amendment slated to be the reserved powers amendment. Both Houses of Congress adopted the Madisonian version, and this is the formula that was ratified by the number of states required for its entry into force as the Tenth Amendment.

Madison's reference to the debate in the states of Pennsylvania, Virginia, and North Carolina is particularly problematic. Pennsylvania ratified without any proposal for amendments. Virginia and North Carolina ratified *after* the Constitution had gone into effect with ratification by nine states. How, then, can it be said that the Constitution was adopted subject to the conditions enunciated in their ratifying conventions? Granted, Virginia's ratification was crucial to the future of the Union, but the Constitution was already in force, so what effect does belated accession by one or two states have on constitutional interpretation? And who was qualified to commit the United States to anything? In drawing up his draft bill of rights for approval by two-thirds of Congress, Madison disregarded 80 or 90% of the state proposals, and especially those designed to modify federal power that the proponents had stamped as vital; the ones that he did incorporate were only those, including the Tenth, which would in no way affect the Constitution.

What is one to make of this whole saga? Six states, a clear majority of the nine required for entry into force of the Constitution, ratified without any amendments. The appeals for amendments by the other seven states were only suggestions, and they certainly could not bind the initial six. Five of the seven states proposed the term "expressly," but on Madison's insistence that was deliberately excluded in the proposed list of amendments presented by the two other states. Thus, eight states had abjured requiring inclusion of the term "expressly" in the text of the Tenth Amendment. Madison had denied any suggestion that the Tenth Amendment was a repeat of Article II of the Articles of Confederation. In sum, the Tenth Amendment, as Madison emphasized in the congressional debate, merely confirmed the existing state of affairs under the Constitution, and did not in any way modify any of the powers of Congress. Thus, it preserved the full scope of the necessary and proper clause which was clearly designed to expand, not contract, congressional powers. An implied powers doctrine was thus a fundamental part of the Constitution.

No clear expression of opinion regarding the provisions of the Constitution emerges from all, or even the majority, of the state conventions, and it is vain to search for a common interpretation of any particular provision. We know what the Antifederalists wanted and we know that they voted against ratification, even with Madison's promises. We do not know how many delegates to the ratifying conventions would have voted for ratification even without any promises. So how relevant are the supposed "commitments"? As Kasavan and Paulsen have argued, "How can one rely on particular utterances in the Virginia ratifying convention, unknown to those in all preceding ratifying conventions?"[20] And as for the Tenth Amendment, the only thing that was common to those recommending a reserved powers clause was the demand for inclusion of the term "expressly," and this was repudiated by Madison himself.[21] The entire thesis of attaching a gloss enunciated by the Antifederalist opposition in the Virginia Ratifying Convention onto the necessary and proper clause, was fanciful, and lacking any legal force.

Regardless of the foregoing weaknesses in Madison's theories, his constitutional objections apparently impressed the President enough to prompt him to request Madison to prepare a veto statement in the event that he should decide to cancel the bank law. He also turned to Attorney-General Edmund Randolph and Secretary of State Thomas Jefferson for their opinions of the bill. Randolph, in a rather rambling memorandum, recommended vetoing it.

Jefferson opened his critique by quoting the Tenth Amendment (although it had not yet been ratified so as to enter into force) and declared that "to take a single step beyond the boundaries thus specially drawn around the powers of Congress, is to take possession of a boundless field of power, no longer susceptible of any definition."[22] The incorporation of a bank, Jefferson argued, was not delegated to the United States by the Constitution. It did not come under either the power to lay taxes, to borrow money, or to regulate commerce. If the measure was regarded as an exercise of the commerce clause "it would be void, as extending as much to the internal commerce of every state, as it is external." Nor could it be said that the authority to lay taxes "for the general welfare of the United States" validated the bill, since the provision only related "*to laying taxes*" for the general welfare, and it was not a grant "*to do anything they please*, to provide for the general welfare." "Certainly no such power was meant to be given them. It was intended to lace them up straightly within the enumerated powers, and those without which, as means, these powers could not be carried into effect." He also asserted (thanks to information from Madison) that the very power to establish corporations was rejected by the Constitutional Convention. (This is open to divergent interpretation, as noted earlier in n. 5.) Jefferson then considered the meaning of the necessary and proper clause. Necessary, he said, does not mean convenient, for if convenience were to be the criterion, then the enumeration of powers would be "completely useless." The whole instrument would be reduced to a single phrase of doing "whatever would be for the good of the United States." But the Constitution limited the government to "those means without which the grant of power would be nugatory." All the enumerated powers could be carried into execution without a bank, so its creation could not be regarded as necessary. "Nothing but a necessity invincible by other means, can justify such a prostration of laws, which constitute the pillars of our whole system of jurisprudence." He called on the President to veto the bank bill.

In sum, Madison and Jefferson built their case against the bank on two central arguments: First, the Constitution did not provide for establishing corporations. In the absence of a reference to an express power to create corporations, the federal government could not incorporate a bank. Nor could it assume such a power as being inherent in the very nature of a sovereign entity such as a state. The sovereignty of the federal government was of a limited nature, as defined by the powers enumerated in Article 1, Sect. 8, and, therefore, it could not invoke sovereignty as a basis for fashioning new powers. Second, the government could not rely on the necessary and proper clause to furnish an implied power. In order to apply that constitutional clause it was essential that it be in the service of some express power. Possible references to financial or administrative provisions are insufficient to sustain a right to imply a power to make a bank. If it were sufficient, there would be no limit to such a doctrine of implied powers, and the federal government would possess sweeping authority to do anything it pleased. The whole notion of a government of defined and limited powers would be emasculated, and the United States would become a consolidated national state.

In response, Hamilton pointed out in his brief to the President, that Jefferson's argument "was founded on a general denial of the authority of the United States to erect corporations."[23] But the United States, Hamilton observed, was a sovereign state with sovereign powers. Every power vested in a government was *sovereign* and even without a necessary and proper clause, includes "by *force* of the *term* a right to employ all the *means* requisite and fairly *applicable* to the attainment of the *ends* of such power." "It is unquestionably incident to *sovereign power* to erect corporations, and consequently to *that* of the United States, *in relation to the objects* entrusted to the management of government." Citing the supremacy clause, Hamilton declared that "the power which can create *a supreme law of the land*, is doubtless sovereign as to such a case." In other words, a power to create a corporation was simply *incidental* to the fact of a national government being a sovereign entity. There was no need for an express power. In the same manner that the several states could create corporations and banks, if desired, because of their sovereign nature, so could the federal government.

Besides the reasoning based on the sovereign character of the federal government, there was a second argument derived from a doctrine of implied powers. It could not be denied, Hamilton contended, "that there are implied as well as express powers" accruing to the federal government by virtue of the necessary and proper clause. In rejecting Jefferson's narrow interpretation of the word "necessary" in the clause, which limited it to those means without which the power would be nugatory, he averred: "It is essential to the being of the national government, that so erroneous a conception of the meaning of the word *necessary* should be exploded." Both in the grammatical and popular sense, necessary simply meant "*needful, requisite, incidental, useful, or conducive to...*" To adopt a restrictive interpretation was also contrary to sound construction since powers that concern the affairs of a country "ought to be construed liberally in advancement of the public good." Hamilton saw great danger in Jefferson's approach: "Principles of construction like those espoused by the Secretary of State ... would be fatal to the just and indispensable authority of the United States." In sum: "If the end be clearly comprehended within any of the specified powers, and if the measure have an obvious relation to that end, and is not forbidden by any particular provision of the Constitution, it may safely be deemed to come within the compass of the national authority."

Washington accepted Hamilton's argument for a broad interpretation of the Constitution, and signed the bank bill into law on February 25, 1791. As Forrest McDonald noted, this "was arguably the most important decision on domestic policy he made during his presidency, and certainly the most important constitutional decision."[24] By this act, the President gave meaning to, and confirmed, the national ideology and aims that underlay the Federalist Revolution. He set the United States on a course of broad national development and growth, and ensured that the United States would be more than just one common market in which the federal government would be able to foster industry and commerce. Hamilton's brief empowered that government to contend with nationwide problems, although they were only domestic, and promote—in the words of the preamble to the Constitution—"the general welfare" of the nation. It imparted nationhood to the separate powers conveyed to the federal government so that, in implementing national policies, the government would be able to treat the United States as a single polity. In time, that brief would facilitate the emergence of the United States as a global power, firmly united under a central authority. It has justly been said that "No state paper written by Hamilton had larger consequences than his opinion on the constitutionality of the bank."[25] Little wonder that Washington was persuaded to sign.

The struggle over the scope of federal authority and the fear of national consolidation did not end with the formation of the Bank of the United States in 1791. The bank functioned for the 20 years of its charter, but the attempt in Congress to create a second such bank was vetoed by President Madison in

1815. A year later, with technical changes in the charter, he accepted the legislation establishing the Second Bank of the United States. On this occasion, he was led to waive the question of congressional power to create a bank "as being precluded in my judgment by repeated recognitions under varied circumstances of the validity of such an institution in acts of the legislative, executive, and judicial branches of the Government."[26] The operation of this Second Bank in the State of Maryland occasioned a constitutional controversy that led to the seminal Supreme Court decision in the 1819 case *McCulloch v. Maryland*.[27] The Maryland state government sought to bar operation of the bank within its territory by imposing a heavy tax.

Chief Justice John Marshall, in a unanimous decision, adopted Hamilton's reasoning confirming the validity of the bank law on the basis of a broad interpretation of congressional powers even as they relate to domestic affairs. He adhered closely to Hamilton's two-pronged argument: one based on the sovereignty of the federal government and the other on the existence of a doctrine of implied powers. Marshall opened his analysis by rejecting Maryland's argument that the Constitution was the creation of the sovereign states so that the powers of the general government must be exercised in subordination to the states. The people of the United States, not the sovereign states, had ratified the Constitution and put it into force, said Marshall. The creation of a corporation is an incidental power of a sovereign entity. It could not be denied that the federal government was sovereign, and the formation of a corporation simply a means of exercising the power it possesses. "The power of creating a corporation is never used for its own sake, but for the purposes of effecting something else. No sufficient reason is therefore perceived why it may not pass as incidental to those powers which are expressly given if it be direct mode of executing them."[28] As such, creating a corporation was simply an attribute of sovereignty, whether this involved a national, state, or local authority. But the Constitution did not leave it just to "general reasoning;" it included a specific provision, the necessary and proper clause, to confirm the right of the government to select the means most appropriate in each case to execute its powers. Thus, the opinion confirmed the existence and legitimacy of a doctrine of implied powers. Where the Constitution wanted to restrict something to what was "absolutely necessary," it said so, as in Article 1, Sect. 10. The absence of any such qualifying adjective in the necessary and proper clause meant that the term "necessary" should be given its normal meaning, as something required and desirable. In dismissing a narrow interpretation of the necessary and proper clause, Marshall closely paralleled Hamilton's definition by declaring, in an oft-quoted passage, "Let the end be legitimate, let it be within the scope of the constitution, and all means which are appropriate, which are plainly adapted to that end, which are not prohibited, but consist with the letter and spirit of the constitution, are constitutional."[29] He also pointed out that the Tenth Amendment did not contain the term "expressly," limiting the federal government to those powers expressly enumerated in Article 1, Sect. 8. This, he said, contrasted with the formula of

Article II in the Articles of Confederation. Given the supremacy clause that imparted primacy to federal law over state law, the attempt to tax the bank was declared unconstitutional.

By confirming the doctrine of implied powers, Marshall's opinion—besides demolishing Madison's thesis by reference to the sovereign status of the federal government—provided the imprimatur to an expansive interpretation of federal powers and assured federal supremacy wherever it encountered contrary state legislation. The decision did not impel the federal government to institute national policies that might impinge on state sovereignty, but *McCulloch* provided the necessary license if the matter fell within the purview of any of the federal powers broadly defined. The states were not at liberty to impede national policies. Their representation and status in both houses of the national legislature, as the Opinion made clear, offered them the opportunity to object to policies that they regarded as inimical to state interests. In light of Marshall's pronouncement, henceforth, even during eras when the federal government avoided the application of broad national policies in domestic development, the arm of the law was available to sustain long-standing national programs that were yet in operation. And when a new spirit moved a successor government to initiate some new national program, as in the period of the New Deal, the legal sanction enunciated in *McCulloch* furnished legitimization for the exercise of federal power.

THE CREATION OF THE DEMOCRATIC-REPUBLICAN PARTY

Whatever else Madison's about-face achieved, it gave rise to the creation of a new political configuration in the United States. The men who had banded together to produce a new constitution for the United States were no longer united under the Federalist banner. As Gordon Wood explained in his outstanding work on the first years of the republic, while Jefferson was consistent with his earlier Antifederalist views, Madison, "for reasons that are still disputed ... had become fearful of the very government he had done so much to create."[30] With the change in Madison's political outlook, it was natural that he would join forces with Jefferson in opposing government policies, particularly economic ones; and beyond that, he would also find common ground with the Antifederalists, the very elements he had battled in order to secure ratification of the Constitution.[31] Their primary complaint against the Constitution was based on the expandable nature of the necessary and proper clause operating in conjunction with the supremacy clause to give the national government complete mastery over the states in establishing a consolidated government, if it so desired. Belatedly, Madison had become distressed at the potential Leviathan that these provisions of the Constitution afforded, and sought to nip in the bud any pattern of sweeping interpretation. So long as George Washington was President, the opposition had to walk gingerly so as not to arouse his ire. However, upon Washington's announcement in 1796 that he would not run for a third term, the way was cleared for a fully fledged battle between the two political parties, the Federalists and the Democratic Republicans. The latter had come to realize that influence in Congress alone, without control of the executive department, was insufficient to guide national policy. The rival candidates for the office of President that year were the Federalist Vice-President, John Adams, and Thomas Jefferson, former Secretary of State. Adams won by a vote of 71:68 in the Electoral College.

If differences over economic matters during Washington's term had been sufficient to engender the birth of an opposition party, under Adams clashes over the conduct of foreign affairs raised tensions to new heights. The French Revolution, the Reign of Terror, and the outbreak of war between England and France pitted the two parties into a fully fledged controversy over questions of war, peace, and neutrality. The Jay Treaty, which had settled differences between the United States and Britain, became a central subject of dispute. Madison and Jefferson accused Hamilton of having capitulated to the British in order to preserve economic ties with London, and had done so at the price of abandoning the Power that had helped save America's independence. The vigorous domestic debate that ensued became particularly complicated when the French ambassador became personally involved. In an attempt to prevent matters from getting out of hand, Congress passed the Alien and Sedition laws in 1798, which made it a crime to slander and deride government policy or policymakers, and authorized the government to deport aliens regarded as threats to national security.[32] The Sedition Law paralleled the common law of England, but was more liberal in accepting the truth of the supposed libel as a valid defense. Far from subduing controversy, this furnished the opposition with new ammunition to charge that the legislation, by penalizing freedom of speech and press, represented a blatant violation of the First Amendment to the Constitution. This prompted Madison and Jefferson to draft the Virginia and Kentucky Resolutions, in which they decried the impositions the laws prescribed. Moreover, in terms that reflected a strongly Antifederalist ideology, the Resolutions urged the states to interdict implementation of the laws and stem the tide of "monarchist absolutism." The Resolutions even hinted at a right on the part of the states to nullify the unconstitutional measures by threat of secession. Abandoning his strong endorsement of the opening words of the Constitution that attributed its formation to "the people of the United States," Madison now claimed that the nation was formed by the states, and that the action of the federal government endangered both state sovereignty and the civil liberties of their populace. In light of this development, Jefferson and Madison were now asserting a right to adopt an appropriate states' rights stand, and even to nullification of these laws within the precincts of their states. If not for Madison, Jefferson was posed to announce a right of disunion. As Alpheus Mason has indicated, Jefferson's Kentucky Resolution imperiled the Union.[33]

Curiously enough, despite their use of extreme terminology, the authors of these Resolutions were not harshly condemned for the intemperance of their remarks. In fact, their invocation of the First Amendment was taken at face value, and aided them significantly in their popular campaign to secure the executive office. In the 1800 Electoral College contest, Jefferson beat Adams by 73:65. Elkins and McKitrick, in their classic work, *The Age of Federalism*, indicate that the election was "exceedingly close."[34] The crucial state was New York, and the difference there was a mere 250 votes which, had they gone the other way, would have made Adams the victor over Jefferson for a second time. Adams also suffered from some bad luck. The quasi-war that had been going on with France was settled at around the time of the election, but news of the signing of the treaty of Montenfontaine reached America too late to influence the election.[35] Had the document been signed a few weeks earlier, and news thereof arrived in time, this master-stroke by Adams for avoiding hostilities would assuredly have swung votes in his favor. Furthermore, the feud within the Federalist party between the President and Hamilton did not help his cause. Adams had dismissed the Hamiltonians from his cabinet just months before the 1800 elections. The personal enmity between Adams and Hamilton, according to Elkins and McKitrick, was greater than any "comparable enmity." A letter by Hamilton on the eve of the election attacking Adams as totally incompetent was publicized, and it had disastrous effects on the outcome.[36] Obviously, public display of the turmoil in the Federalist Party did not inspire confidence in the Federalist candidate.[37]

When one examines the unbridled, even reckless, conduct of three of the leading protagonists on the eve of the election—Madison, Jefferson, and Hamilton—Adams emerges as the only sober figure intent on saving the United States from war against either side in the European conflict, even at the price of his losing the domestic contest. Only Adams displayed national responsibility in a period of national and international crisis. One can only speculate what a second Adams administration might have achieved. Would he have taken the reins of power in hand and exercised executive authority with vigor, or would he have repeated the pusillanimity of his first term? Had he been returned to office, he might have revived the Federalist Party, and thereby forestalled the Republican sweep for the next decade or more. Elkins and McKitrick analyze the prospects of a revived Federalist party, but conclude that the party was demoralized beyond repair. They accept Jefferson's verdict that the "revolution of 1800" was an "authentic one," and that "the American people had spoken" in favor of Jeffersonian republicanism.[38] If the vote was as close as they describe, it appears difficult to assert that the American people had resolved the matter with finality. Moreover, given the fact (which they do not note), that Jefferson won only thanks to the three-fifths increment that the slave states enjoyed in the Electoral College, one cannot say that "the American people" decided anything. The repeated claim of the Republicans that everything done in Jefferson's first term was action taken in accordance with American public opinion is open to question given the fragile source of his majority in the Electoral College. If the Federalists had won in 1800, they might well have dominated the scene for some time. A second failure for Jefferson to gain the office of Chief Executive could have seriously injured the Democratic Republican Party, even as the loss of the election fatally injured the Federalist Party. After all, in the United States, unlike Britain and other parliamentary states, the party out of office has no acknowledged leader to rally and reorganize it. No doubt this was a big factor in the decline of the Federalists, and if the outcome of 1800 had been reversed, it might well have affected future prospects for the Republicans with dramatic consequences for the course of American history.

As it is, the Democratic Republicans swept into office for successive presidencies, and the Federalist Party went into decline and oblivion. The year 1800 was truly a major turning point in American history. It resulted in an eclipse of the Federalist Revolution that had united the nation under one powerful central government, poised to lead the United States into the industrial age that was dawning at the advent of the nineteenth century. Strangely enough, federalism assumed an Antifederalist image with strict interpretation of the constitutional text. Perhaps the high point of self-denial of the sovereign status of the federal government was reflected in the dilemma that President Jefferson faced when he was presented with the opportunity of the Louisiana Purchase by Napoleon Bonaparte in 1803. The Constitution did not contain a specific power that would authorize purchase of territory by the federal government, and Jefferson felt it could not be effected without a constitutional amendment. Only the fear that the whole deal might fall apart if he tarried brought him to throw himself on the mercy of Congress to provide the necessary funds and validate the purchase. Even after the purchase had been completed, he still sought to get an amendment to ratify the deal retroactively. Had he acknowledged the validity of the Hamilton/Marshall thesis that the federal government representing a sovereign state was competent to buy and sell, the whole question of a formal power would never have arisen. No less than the creation of a bank that Jefferson opposed so vigorously, the purchase of territory was simply a concomitant of sovereignty.

The Jeffersonian era is noteworthy for the Antifederalist image that federalism assumed, with one President after another vetoing congressional legislation designed to establish either a national bank or expend funds for internal improvements.[39] Even though two branches of the federal government, Congress and the judiciary, validated schemes for national development, executive vetoes just as frequently stymied such proposals. Thus, Madison, as the final act of his presidency in 1816, vetoed the bill that had provided for an extensive program of canal and road development. Similarly, President Monroe vetoed the Cumberland Road bill of 1822 and blocked every congressional attempt to build canals. He adhered firmly to the narrow constitutional ideology of his predecessor. However, neither Jefferson, Madison, nor Monroe matched Jackson's fierce opposition to anything involving federal participation in economic proposals for internal improvements. Whereas his predecessors refrained from interfering with a functioning institution, Jackson not only vetoed new schemes but also removed all government funds from the second Bank of the United States, with the aim of bringing about the collapse of the bank. He regarded it as the plaything of the wealthy, intent on despoiling the poor. However, despite his intense states' rights ideology, Jackson acted vigorously in 1832 to quash South Carolina's defiant move toward nullification, and he stamped it as an act of treason. States' rights was not to be a prescription for shattering and undermining the Union.

The restrictive policy of these Presidents meant that national development was not part of the Democratic-Republican platform. Industrialization progressed in the United States, but it did so despite the federal government, not because of it. Remarkably, the rearguard philosophy of Jefferson and Madison, which deemed the agricultural productivity of Virginia—and the south generally—to be the lifeblood of the nation, seized public imagination in presidential elections. Yet Congress, which repeatedly voted for internal improvements, was obviously not always impressed with the restrictive ideology embraced by residents of the White House. Perhaps that restrictive philosophy was never really overcome until the industrial and economic demands of the Civil War imposed themselves on both sides of the Mason–Dixon Line.

Antifederalists: Co-founders of the Constitution?

With the absorption of the Antifederalists into the Democratic-Republican Party, history was somehow revised to give credit to the Antifederalists for their contribution to the formation and design of the Constitution, when, in fact, they had fiercely opposed ratification. In the wake of the strong objections of other states to the 1798 Virginia and Kentucky Resolutions, Madison drafted a major paper—known as the Report of 1800—which he submitted to the Virginia legislature for adoption. The Report was meant to deflect the widespread criticism of the Resolutions by explaining that, in referring to the states as the parties to the Constitution, it meant the people of the states rather than the state governments. Nonetheless, the Report highlighted the sovereign status of the states in the federal compact, and argued that this entitled them to protest as they did. Implicitly, this formulation of the meaning of the Resolutions was intended to revise the earlier hints of a right of secession. The Report is important as a summation of Antifederalist ideology, which Madison now endorsed in opposing the Federalist position. It warned of the danger of consolidation, which tended "to transform the republican system of the United States into a monarchy," and which could only be overcome by a theory of strict interpretation of the constitutional text. As Saul Cornell, in his work *The Other Founders* has said: "The original Anti-Federalist critique of the Constitution was elevated [by the Report] to new prominence as part of the original public debate that defined the terms under which the people had ratified the Constitution."[40]

With the progress of time, the claim that the Antifederalists had shared in the formation and adoption of the Constitution was so well believed that former President Martin Van Buren could write that "the Anti-Federalist mind represented the core values of Revolutionary constitutionalism that defined the nation's political identity."[41]

Van Buren admitted that "America's institutions were crafted by Federalists," but he "believed its spirit was shaped by Anti-Federalists,"[42] presumably by their criticism of the Constitution. According to Van Buren, Antifederalists constituted a majority of the population at the time of the ratification of the Constitution. He contended "that it was the Anti-Federalists, not the Federalists, who represented the spirit of American politics and constitutionalism. The Anti-Federalist mind was the mind of America." Cornell asserts that "the New Deal coalition, historians now recognize, was extremely fragile and began to unravel by the middle of the 1960s… The faith in centralized government associated with the New Deal legacy was a temporary anomaly in American politics, not a permanent realignment in attitudes… The distinguishing characteristic of [American] politics is the intensity of localism, not support for strong central government."[43] All this leads Cornell to conclude that the recent "explosion of interest among legal scholars" in Antifederalist writings is evidence that the Antifederalists are now justly "counted among the ranks of America's founders."[44]

This is an amazing conclusion to an extraordinary chapter of history. It dismisses Marshall's decision in *McCulloch v. Maryland* as obsolete and views as valid Madison's thesis that the Constitution was an empty shell, only to be filled by the Antifederalist criticism at the Virginia Ratifying Convention. It is highly doubtful if many legal scholars would concur with such a conclusion. *McCulloch v. Maryland* stands today as unchallenged as ever, and—as noted earlier—Madison's theses were completely discredited in that immemorial opinion by Chief Justice Marshall.

Little wonder that one writer has pointed out that "Anti-Federalists are sometimes called 'Other Founders,' but they did not draft the Constitution, nor influence its drafting, and they opposed the fixed written document when they got to see it."[45] And to quote another prominent writer: "Americans are fortunate that the antifederalists were the failed, defeated, would-be founders of what would have been a very different nation."[46]

And finally, the assertion that the New Deal, with its revolution in government policy designed to improve the economic condition of the lower classes in American society, is only a passing phenomenon, reflects a rather uncommon viewpoint in this day and age.

Marshall's Federalism, Dual Federalism, and the New Federalism

McCulloch v. Maryland is generally regarded as John Marshall's greatest decision. It confirmed that the Constitution had formed a nation out of the divergent states, and that the government established under this document was endowed with wide-ranging powers to promote both the welfare of the population and the might of the United States. Marshall's opinion established the principle that, although the powers of the federal government were enumerated and limited, they were subject to a supplementary gloss of implied powers. This is probably the central feature that most people recognize in connection with the case. In fact, however—as noted earlier—this is only part of the analysis presented in the opinion in favor of national power.

The difference between Federalist and Antifederalist doctrines revolved at base around the meaning and application of the term "sovereignty" under the Constitution. Although the word does not appear anywhere in the document, it underlies the divergent ideologies. According to the Antifederalists, the Union was composed of thirteen states, and ratification of the Constitution added another state-like entity, resulting in fourteen units in the Union. In this sense, the federal government was simply an additional sovereign-bearing entity, but one that was defined by the powers enumerated in Article 1, Sect. 8 of the Constitution. In the event of a dispute between a state and the national government, the national authority would prevail only if the issue was within one of the defined powers. Only then would the supremacy clause come into action. This arrangement also meant that the necessary and proper clause must be narrowly interpreted, because otherwise the national government would become master of the entire Union, rather than a limited partner.

In contrast, according to the Federalists, the sovereignty which the national government acquired upon the adoption of the Constitution, while limited by its terms, was fundamentally different from the sovereignty of the individual states. Each state had its own sovereignty but none of any other state's sovereignty. National sovereignty was distinct and unique by representing the sovereignty of each state plus its own distinctive sovereignty. It acted on behalf of the nation and was therefore stamped with a comprehensive and international character. This analysis underlies Marshall's argument in the first part of his opinion, before he discusses a doctrine of implied powers. Thus, he states:

> The power of creating a corporation is one appertaining to sovereignty, and is not expressly conferred on Congress. This is true. But all legislative powers appertain to sovereignty... The Government must, according to the dictates of reason, be allowed to select the means [to implement the power.]... If any one proposition could command the universal assent of mankind, we might expect it would be this – that the Government of the Union, though limited in its powers, is supreme within its sphere of action. This would seem to result from its nature. It is the Government of all; its powers are delegated by all; it represents all, and acts for all.[47]

On this basis, Marshall held that creation of a corporation was simply an *incidental* power arising naturally from the sovereignty appertaining to the federal government, and was an appropriate means for executing its vast powers in relation to economic, military, and untold other needs of the nation. Consequently, establishing a corporation for the establishment of the Bank of the United States was perfectly valid and consistent with the Constitution. It was here that Marshall also enunciated the doctrine of *implied* powers, supplementary to his thesis on *incidental* powers based on the sovereign character of the federal government.

I have spelled out this analysis of Marshall's opinion in order to identify the broad range of his concept of national powers even within the type of federal system of government that was instituted in the United States. According to Marshall, the unique sovereignty of the federal government imparts a distinct status to that government in its relations with the states. It has national responsibilities that no single state has, and it has commensurate national authority that no state possesses. So long as Marshall and his disciple Joseph Story dominated the Court, Federalist doctrine reigned supreme within the judiciary. Thus, the Court also established that its jurisdiction encompassed the state courts whenever a federal issue arose under the Constitution. This was a source of considerable contention with Virginia and its Chief Justice, but the view of the Marshall court prevailed. This fact did not prevent President Jackson from defying Marshall's opinions on several occasions. For Jackson, *McCulloch* was not law: Each branch of the federal government was entitled, and obliged, to judge constitutional issues according to its own lights. One of Jackson's final acts was the appointment of Roger B. Taney as Chief Justice to succeed Marshall in 1836. This appointment was to have major consequences for the character of federalism under the Court.

Gradually the Court moved to enunciate a new doctrine, that of Dual Federalism, which was to last for close to a century. Under this doctrine, the Court assumed that the national and state levels of government were coequal sovereignties, each supreme within its own sphere.[48] Dual Federalism placed particular stress on the Tenth Amendment as assuring the states that their reserved powers would be unfettered by federal regulation. Federal intervention in areas reserved for the states could not prevail over state legislation, since this would violate state sovereignty. The climax of Dual Federalism, according to most authorities, was reached in the *Hammer v. Dagenhart* decision of 1918,[49] which declared that a federal law barring interstate traffic in goods produced by child labor was unconstitutional. The purpose of the law, said the Court, was to forbid child labor and not the regulation of interstate commerce. Child labor was not an enumerated power of the national government and hence beyond the power of Congress. Justice William R. Day, author of the majority opinion, wrote: "The grant of authority over a purely federal matter [such as commerce] was not intended to destroy the local power always existing and carefully reserved to the States in the Tenth Amendment." In citing that amendment, he went on to misquote it by asserting that "the powers not expressly delegated to the National Government are reserved" to the states and the people. The word "expressly" does not appear in the Tenth Amendment, and its absence was highlighted in Marshall's *McCulloch* opinion as an indication that the Tenth Amendment was not intended to impinge in any manner on the doctrine of implied powers. The *Dagenhart* decision was sharply attacked as a demonstration of a politically minded Court. Nonetheless, when Congress attempted to reach the same goal by means of a tax imposed on goods produced by child labor, the Court, in the case of *Bailey v. Drexel Furniture Co.*,[50] once again pronounced the law unconstitutional. This law, the Court said, was not designed to raise revenue but to regulate child labor, a subject that was beyond congressional reach.

Matters reached a point of crisis when much of the New Deal legislation, designed to overcome the economic crisis that gripped the United States in the 1930s, was declared unconstitutional by a conservative majority that dominated the Supreme Court. With changes in the composition of the Court, the majority abandoned Dual Federalism and returned to Marshall's broad interpretation of federal powers and national supremacy and validated all the measures taken to restore life to the American economy.[51] The doctrine of implied powers was revived, while the Tenth Amendment was defanged and classified as a truism that added no new authority to the powers automatically reserved to the states by virtue of the federal character of the Constitution. State sovereignty was relegated to the margin as national schemes were accorded priority for their promotion of national and social welfare. Furthermore, once Congress adopts legislation under the commerce clause, the courts will not search beneath the surface of the law to determine how substantive an association with commerce there really is. In short, if Congress declares and demonstrates that the act is connected with commerce, the Court will not second-guess the accuracy of the congressional declaration. Little wonder that in the wake of these, and similar, decisions, the doyen of constitutional analysis at that time, Edward S. Corwin, was prompted to publish a law article entitled "The Passing of Dual Federalism."[52]

For some 40 years Congress had free rein, and the biblical verse "And the land lay quiet for forty years" may be said to have applied to federal affairs. During this period the federal government adopted numerous social welfare laws applicable throughout the country, designed to improve the life of American citizens. Rarely did a measure based on the commerce clause come before the Court during this period on the ground that it lacked constitutional license.

Change came to the Court in 1971 with the appointment of Associate Justice William H. Rehnquist, who strongly espoused a philosophy of states' rights. In 1986, he was appointed Chief Justice, and together with four other conservative Justices, instituted a new jurisprudence called The New Federalism.[53] According to this doctrine, it was the responsibility of the Court to supervise the application of federalism by striking down federal legislation that invaded the field of state sovereignty. It was, basically, a limited reapplication of the Dual Federalism of an earlier age. The analysis presented in this work, and at greater length in an article that I recently published,[54] queries the premises of The New Federalism doctrine.

This study has shown how the Federalist movement, at a critical moment in American history, seized the initiative and produced the Constitution that saved the United States from dismemberment. The nation formed under the Constitution instituted a federal system of government that preserved the status of the individual states, even while it provided for national domination of the Union. Madison was not responsible for the introduction of federalism into the

Constitution, but he certainly saved the final document from tampering, by promoting the adoption of a bill of rights that satisfied most Antifederalists who had opposed the Constitution.

But once the Constitution became operational, Madison shattered the national unity of the Federalist movement by joining Jefferson in creating the Democratic-Republican Party that adopted Antifederalist ideology. He, together with Jefferson, leveled charges that the Federalist policies of the government, designed to invigorate the American economy and reinforce national unity, were in fact meant to institute a monarchist regime in the United States. Without Madison at his side, it is quite doubtful whether Jefferson alone would have been able to launch a powerful Antifederalist political party. Madison was his ideologue and arch-strategist to defeat the Federalist Party. Unfortunately, the wild and exaggerated charges against the Federalists laid the groundwork for dissension, and even secession from the Union, with fateful consequences for the future of the American nation.

Federalism in action has not matched federalism in theory. Two fundamental ideologies have alternated in American history with regard to the meaning and implementation of federalism. While federalism started out as a means of preserving the states, even while the federal government would undertake national projects that individual states could not effect, it was replaced by a doctrine of narrow interpretation that frustrated national development. Only in the 1930s, with the adoption of the New Deal, was this arch-conservative pattern revised, once the court began cooperating with the other two branches to give full license under the necessary and proper clause to expand and implement national welfare programs. The recent birth of the New Federalism in the Supreme Court might be said to reflect the Dual Federalism of an earlier age. Not surprisingly, this jurisprudence has aroused concern about the scope of the revisionism envisaged.[55] Is it a temporary correction of expansive interpretation, or does it foreshadow a deeper and longer program of the overpowering of broad national projects by those pushing for greater attention to states' rights?[56]

NOTES

1. See above, Chap. 1 in text at nn. 21–23.
2. See Gordon S. Wood, *Empire of Liberty: A History of the Early Republic, 1789–1815* (New York: Oxford University Press, 2009), 141–142.
3. For recent works contending that Madison was, in fact, ideologically consistent throughout, see Drew R. McCoy, *The Last of the Fathers: James Madison and the Republican Legacy* (Cambridge: Cambridge University Press, 1989); Lance Banning, *The Sacred Fire of Liberty: James Madison and the Founding of the Federal Republic* (Ithaca, NY: Cornell University Press, 1995), and Gary Rosen, *American Compact: James Madison and the Problem of Founding* (Lawrence: University Press of Kansas, 1999). The leading biographers of Madison, including Irving Brant, Forrest McDonald, and Ralph Ketcham, all agree that Madison made a 180° turn in his campaign to defeat the creation of the bank.

In an important recent work that also reviews Madison's subsequent constitutional interpretation, Jeremy D. Bailey writes: He "often contradicted himself on whether the intention of the members of the Convention or the understanding of those at the state ratifying conventions was to be used." *James Madison and Constitutional Imperfection* (New York: Cambridge University Press, 2015), 155.

4. *JMP*, 13: 373–382, 383–388. The essential arguments of Madison, Jefferson, and Hamilton on the bank bill are conveniently reproduced in Philip B. Kurland and Ralph Lerner (eds.), *The Founders' Constitution: Major Themes*, 5 vol. (Chicago: University of Chicago Press, 1987), 3: 244–250.

5. *JMP*, 13: 374. The word "rejected," if Madison used that expression, is not fully accurate, since the matter, as such, never came up for a vote. Madison raised the proposal for empowering Congress "to grant charters of incorporation." Rufus King of Massachusetts "thought the power unnecessary." Madison's proposal was joined with one by Franklin empowering Congress to provide for cutting canals. The Convention voted separately on the suggestion to empower Congress to cut canals, and it was rejected. Madison's text reads: "The other part fell of course, as including the power rejected." Nothing further was done in relation to the power of incorporation. Thus, the question remains open whether the Convention's silence was dictated by opposition to such a power, or because, as King said, it was "unnecessary." Farrand, *Records*, 2: 615–616.

King's comment can be read in two ways—either that he thought the federal government should not have the power, or that the power is subsumed in the powers already given to Congress. Most people would probably read it in accordance with the latter meaning. King was a nationalist, and it is not likely that he would object to such a power being part of the federal government's arsenal. From a second comment, it appears that King feared that mention of a federal power to create corporations might excite unwelcome opposition in some states, to be avoided if possible. This second comment again points to an interpretation according to which he held that Congress had the power anyway and that it was not expedient to spell it out. The less said about the powers of Congress, the better. King also suggested that the Convention journal be destroyed or deposited with Washington, lest "a bad use would be made of them by those who would wish to prevent the adoption of the Constitution." Ibid., 2: 648. As a Senator, King voted for the establishment of the bank. See also Mark R. Killenbeck, *M'Culloch v. Maryland: Securing a Nation* (Lawrence: University Press of Kansas, 2006), 19–20.

6. Amazingly, he said, whatever deficiency occurred could be made up "by loans from individuals." *JMP*, 13: 380.
7. Ibid., 13: 376.
8. Ibid., 378.
9. Ibid., 386–387.
10. Ibid., 396, n. 1.
11. See, "The Bank Bill, the Capital City and President Washington," *Capitol Studies*, 1 (1972): 59–71.
12. Stanley Elkins and Eric McKitrick, *The Age of Federalism: The Early American Republic, 1788–1800* (New York: Oxford University Press, 1993), 229.
13. Ibid.
14. See above Chap. 7, in text at nn. 89–92.

15. The discussion of Madison's theses presented here is drawn from my article: "The Scheme of Enumeration: A Critical Analysis of the New Federalism in the U.S. Supreme Court," *Univ. of St. Thomas Law Review*, 12 (2015): 221–225.
16. Farrand, *Records*, 3: 374.
17. Bernard Bailyn, *To Begin the World Anew: The Genius and Ambiguities of the American Founders* (New York: Vintage, 2004), 128. Jack Rakove concurs with the view of his mentor: "He [Madison] never explained how criticisms of the Constitution could be transformed into interpretations of its meaning when the opposite inference was most logical." Jack Rakove, *Original Meanings: Politics and Ideas in the Making of the Constitution* (New York: Knopf, 1996), 363.
18. *JMP*, 13: 380.
19. Ibid., 11: 188–189.
20. Vasan Kasavan and Michael Stokes Paulsen, "The Interpretive Force of the Constitution's Secret Drafting History," *Georgetown Law Journal*, 91 (2003): 1113.
21. See Chap. 10.
22. *TJP*, 19: 275–280.
23. *AHP*, 8: 97–106.
24. *Novus Ordo Seclorum: The Intellectual Origins of the Constitution* (Lawrence: University Press of Kansas, 1985), 194.
25. Richard B. Morris, *Alexander Hamilton and the Founding of the Nation* (New York: Harper, 1957), 263.
26. Cited in Gerald Gunther and Kathleen M. Sullivan, *Constitutional Law*, 13th edition (Westbury, NY: Foundation Press, 1997), 104.
27. 17 U.S. (4 Wheaton) 316 (1819). The foremost author on the subject of *McCulloch v. Maryland* is Gerald Gunther. He published two major works in 1969 revealing that Marshall had anonymously published two series of articles defending his position in the decision from the onslaught of States' Rights critics, particularly those from Virginia. The works are: "*John Marshall's Defense of* McCulloch v. Maryland" (Stanford, CA: Stanford University Press, 1969), and "John Marshall, 'A Friend of the Constitution' in Defense and Elaboration of *McCulloch v. Maryland*," *Stanford Law Review*, 21 (1969): 449. For another invaluable work on the case, its history and impact, see Killenbeck, *M'Culloch v. Maryland*.
28. *McCulloch v. Maryland*, 411.
29. 17 U.S. (4 Wheaton) 316, 421 (1819).
30. Wood, *Empire of Liberty*, 148.
31. On the manner in which the Antifederalists were absorbed into the Republican Party, see article by Richard E. Ellis, "The Persistence of Antifederalism after 1789" in Beeman et al. (eds.), *Beyond Confederation: Origins of the Constitution and American National Identity* (Chapel Hill: University of North Carolina Press, 1987), 300–302. Ellis notes that the Antifederalists were delighted to shed the name Antifederalists and assume a much more engaging name, Democratic-Republicans.
32. For background to the adoption of the Alien and Sedition laws, see Wood, *Empire of Liberty*, 246–260.
33. Alpheus Thomas Mason, *The States Rights Debate: Antifederalism and the Constitution* (Englewood Cliffs, NJ: Prentice-Hall, 1964), 1.

For a different appreciation of the "Revolution of 1800", see Peter S. Onuf, *Jefferson's Empire: The Language of American Nationhood* (Charlottesville: University of Virginia, 2000), chap. 3.

34. Elkins and McKitrick, *The Age of Federalism*, 692. See also David McCullough, *John Adams* (New York: Simon & Schuster, 2001), 556.
35. See McCullough, *Adams*, 556–557 and Wood, *Empire of Liberty*, 275. In particular, see Bruce Ackerman, *The Failure of the Founding Fathers: Jefferson, Marshall and the Rise of Presidential Democracy* (Cambridge, MA: Belknap Press, 2005). "Adams believed—with a good deal of justice—that he had lost the election by placing the public good above partisan advantage in seeking peace with France." Ibid., 121.
36. See Wood, *Empire of Liberty*, 274–275.
37. See Wood, *Empire of Liberty*, 275 and McCullough, *Adams*, 556–557.
38. Elkins and McKitrick, *Age of Federalism*, 693.
39. On the topic of presidential opposition to internal improvements as part of Republican ideology, besides the Wood volume, I have relied heavily on the informative volume by Forrest McDonald, *States' Rights and the Union: Imperium in Imperio, 1776–1876*.
40. Saul Cornell, *The Other Founders: Anti-federalism & the Dissenting Tradition in America, 1788–1828* (Chapel Hill: University of North Carolina Press, 1999), 244.
41. Ibid., 301. Jeremy Bailey notes that, in 1828, Madison corrected Martin Van Buren for contending that the most important question at the Constitutional Convention was the "degree of power" granted to the national government. Madison declared that the real question was "the rule by which the states would be represented, with the smaller States insisting on the rule of equality." *Madison and Constitutional Imperfection*, 170, n. 106.
42. Ibid., 307.
43. Ibid., 304.
44. Ibid., 306. See the works cited above in n. 3 for the view that Madison was consistent and that his support for an ideology based on localism accorded with the spirit of the broader American public.

    One recent work expounds an interesting thesis. It maintains that the United States had two Foundings, the Articles of Confederation and the Constitution, and that the history of America is the account of the alternating ideologies that have dominated the federal government at different times. One camp strives to reinstate the "hands off" policy of the Articles, while the other seeks to resolve all problems, national and state, by directives from Washington. Both approaches are intrinsically American. See Elvin T. Lim, *The Lovers' Quarrel: The Two Foundings & American Political Development* (New York: Oxford University Press, 2014).
45. Calvin H. Johnson, *Righteous Anger at the Wicked States: The Meaning of the Founders' Constitution* (New York: Cambridge University Press, 2005), 133.
46. Paul Finkelman, "Turning Losers into Winners: What Can We Learn, If Anything, From the Antifederalists?," *Texas Law Review*, (2001): 854.
47. *McCulloch*, 405, 411.
48. For a concise summary of Dual Federalism, see C. Herman Pritchett, *The American Constitution* (New York: McGraw Hill, 1959), 66. The foremost authority on the subject, Edward S. Corwin, defined the doctrine in terms of

four postulates. (1) The national government is one of enumerated powers only, (2) The purposes it may constitutionally promote are few, (3) Within their respective spheres the federal and state governments are sovereign and hence equal; (4) Relations between the two centers is one of tension rather than collaboration. "The Passing of Dual Federalism," *Virginia Law Review*, 36 (1950): 4. See also the excellent analysis of Dual Federalism in the final chapter of Alpheus Thomas Mason's wonderful work, *The States Rights Debate*.
49. 247 U.S. 251 (1918).
50. 259 U.S. 20 (1922).
51. See *U.S. v. Darby*, 312 U.S. 100 1941, and *Wickard v. Filburn*, 317 U.S. 111 1942.
52. *Virginia Law Review*, 36 (1950): 1–24.
53. Gerald Gunther and Kathleen M. Sullivan labeled the New Federalism "the Modern Antifederalist Revival." See Gunther and Sullivan, *Constitutional Law*, 113.
54. See citation above in n. 15.
55. Compare the views of two authors:

> The purpose [of the Senate] was not just to protect the interests of small states such as Delaware and Rhode Island, but also to protect all of the states from the national government. The continued existence of states as quasi-independent sovereigns is crucial to the preservation of individual liberty. The Court is correct to reinvigorate its institutional role in maintaining the constitutional balance between the federal and state governments.

> John Choon Yoo, "Federalism and Judicial Review," in Killenbeck, *The Tenth Amendment and State Sovereignty*, 143, 172, 132.
> Antifederalists today would turn the clock back; they would scuttle the Constitution and return us to the monstrous imperium in imperio, so convincingly discredited in the years before and after 1776.
> Alpheus Thomas Mason, *The States Rights Debate*, 193.

56. In this regard, see the dissenting opinion of Justice Clarence Thomas in the *Obamacare* case, *National Federation of Independent Business v. Sibelius*, 567 U.S.—(2012).

CHRONOLOGY

1776 July 4	The United States declares its independence from Great Britain.
1777 November 15	The Continental Congress adopts the Articles of Confederation and submits them to the states for ratification.
1780 September	Even before Articles are ratified, Hamilton suggests convention to draft new constitution.
1781 March 1	The Articles of Confederation enter into force with ratification by Maryland, the last of the 13 states to ratify.
1783–1786	All attempts by the Continental Congress to amend the Articles are frustrated by need for unanimous approval of states.
1786 September	Annapolis Convention for commercial reform among states fails for lack of quorum. Meeting adopts a resolution for Congress to propose holding a convention in Philadelphia in May 1787.
1786 Fall	Shays' Rebellion in Massachusetts alarms men of property and commerce.
1787 February 21	Continental Congress recommends that states send delegates to convention to meet in Philadelphia in May to propose alterations to Articles, so as to "render the federal constitution adequate to the exigencies of Government & the preservation of the Union."
1787 March–April	Madison, in letters to Jefferson, Randolph, and Washington, outlines major reforms he proposes, including a national veto on all state legislation.
1787 May 14	Lack of quorum delays opening of Constitutional Convention.

1787 May 25	Convention begins deliberation with arrival of majority of state delegates. George Washington is elected as Chairman.
1787 May 29	Gov. Edmund Randolph submits Virginia Plan to plenum.
1787 June 15	Wm Paterson submits New Jersey Plan to plenum.
1787 June 19	By vote of 7:3, one divided, convention adopts Virginia Plan over New Jersey Plan as working document.
1787 July 12	By vote of 6:2, two divided, convention accepts proportional representation for both lower house of national legislature and for direct taxation, according to population and three-fifths of slave population.
1787 July 16	By vote of 5:4, one divided, convention adopts Connecticut Compromise for equality of representation for states in upper house of legislature.
1787 July 17	Convention rejects Madison's scheme for national veto over state legislation.
1787 September 6	Convention adopts Electoral College system for electing President.
1787 September 17	Convention adopts Constitution signed by delegates from all 12 states present; Massachusetts delegate Elbridge Gerry, and Virginia delegates George Mason and Edmund Randolph, decline to sign.
1787–1788	During fall and winter, Hamilton, Madison, and Jay, publish 85 essays of the *Federalist Papers* in New York newspapers, to rally support for Constitution.
1787–1790	Ratification by 9 states is required for Constitution to enter into force between ratifying states. Ultimately all 13 states ratify. The following is the sequence of ratification:
1787 December 7	Delaware, unanimous ratification.
1787 December 12	Pennsylvania, 46:23.
1787 December 18	New Jersey, unanimous ratification.
1788 January 2	Georgia, unanimous ratification.
1788 January 9	Connecticut, 128:40.
1788 February 6	Massachusetts, 187:168, with recommendation, but not on condition, that bill of rights be appended to Constitution. This formula of ratification serves as model for other states.
1788 April 28	Maryland, 63:11.
1788 May 23	South Carolina, 149:73, with recommendatory amendments.
1788 June 21	New Hampshire, 57:47, with recommendatory amendments. This ratification allows the Constitution to enter into force between the nine ratifying states.

1788 June 26	Virginia, 89:79, with recommendatory amendments.
1788 July 26	New York, 30:27, with recommendatory amendments, plus a round-robin to the other states proposing a second constitutional convention to revise parts of Constitution.
1789 November 21	North Carolina, 194:77, with recommendatory amendments.
1790 May 29	Rhode Island, 34:32, with recommendatory amendments.
1788 July 2	Continental Congress acknowledges that Constitution was ratified by required number of states to enter into force.
1788 September 13	Continental Congress adopts resolution for putting Constitution into operation, with election of President by Electoral College scheduled for February 1789.
1789 February	Electoral College unanimously elects George Washington as first President of the United States.
1789 March 4	Congress opens proceedings under Constitution.
1789 April 30	George Washington takes oath as first President of the United States.
1789 September 28	First Congress adopts resolution submitting 12 draft amendments to the states for ratification. These amendments constitute a bill of rights. Madison, who rushed resolution through Congress, rejects every attempt to limit Congress to powers expressly enumerated in Constitution.
1790 December	Hamilton submits Bank Bill to Congress.
1791 February 2	Madison opposes Bank Bill in House of Representatives.
1791 February 25	President Washington signs Bank Bill into law.
1791 December 15	Bill of Rights comes into force with ratification of 10 of the amendments by required number of states when Virginia adds its ratification.
1796 April 6	Madison enunciates novel thesis that only commentary (largely Antifederalist) at state ratifying conventions offers valid interpretation of provisions of Constitution.
1798	Jefferson and Madison formally establish Democratic-Republican Party as opposition to Federalist Party.
1799	In opposing Alien and Sedition Laws, Madison issues the Virginia Resolution, and Jefferson the Kentucky Resolution, according to which an individual state is qualified to nullify a federal law which it deems violates the Constitution. Resolutions have fateful consequences for American history.
1800	Jefferson defeats Adams in close election, thanks to three-fifths slave increment in Electoral College.

1803	Jefferson in constitutional dilemma over purchase of Louisiana Territory.
1808	Madison elected President.
1816 April	After originally opposing renewal of national bank, Madison signs renewal bill.
1819	Chief Justice John Marshall, in historic unanimous opinion in *McCulloch v. Maryland*, rules that creation of national bank is valid and Maryland attempt to tax bank unconstitutional. Opinion endorses implied powers doctrine by adopting broad interpretation of necessary and proper clause, as outlined by Hamilton. Madison's narrow thesis is dismissed.
1847	Chief Justice Roger Taney enunciates concept of Dual Federalism in *License Cases*. This doctrine dominates Supreme Court jurisprudence for close to a century.
1933–1936	President Franklin D. Roosevelt launches New Deal program to revive American economy. Program stymied by conservative Supreme Court jurisprudence.
1941–1942	With change in composition of Court, Chief Justice Harlan Stone invokes, in two cases (*U.S. v. Darby* and *Wickard v. Filburn*), Marshall's federal jurisprudence of *McCulloch v. Maryland*, to validate New Deal legislation. Tenth Amendment deemed a mere truism.
1976	Chief Justice William Rehnquist, in his decision in *National League of Cities v. Usery*, enunciates New Federalism doctrine, which represents revival of Dual Federalism.

Appendix 1: The Constitution of The United States of America 1787

Preamble

We the People of the United States, in Order to form a more perfect Union, establish justice, insure domestic Tranquility, provide for the common defense, promote the general Welfare, and secure the Blessings of Liberty to ourselves and our Posterity, do ordain and establish this Constitution for the United States of America.

Article I

Section 1. All legislative powers herein granted shall be vested in a Congress of the United States, which shall consist of a Senate and House of Representatives.

Section 2. The House of Representatives shall be composed of members chosen every second year by the people of the several states, and the electors in each state shall have the qualifications requisite for electors of the most numerous branch of the state legislature.

No person shall be a Representative who shall not have attained to the age of twenty five years, and been seven years a citizen of the United States, and who shall not, when elected, be an inhabitant of that state in which he shall be chosen.

Representatives and direct taxes shall be apportioned among the several states which may be included within this union, according to their respective numbers, which shall be determined by adding to the whole number of free persons, including those bound to service for a term of years, and excluding Indians not taxed, three fifths of all other Persons. The actual Enumeration shall be made within three years after the first meeting of the Congress of the United States, and within every subsequent term of ten years, in such manner as they shall by law direct. The number of Representatives shall not exceed one for every thirty thousand, but each state shall have at least one Representative; and until such enumeration shall be made, the state of New Hampshire shall be entitled to chuse three, Massachusetts eight, Rhode Island and Providence Plantations one, Connecticut five, New York six, New Jersey four, Pennsylvania eight, Delaware one, Maryland six, Virginia ten, North Carolina five, South Carolina five, and Georgia three.

When vacancies happen in the Representation from any state, the executive authority thereof shall issue writs of election to fill such vacancies.

The House of Representatives shall choose their speaker and other officers; and shall have the sole power of impeachment.

Section 3. The Senate of the United States shall be composed of two Senators from each state, chosen by the legislature thereof, for six years; and each Senator shall have one vote.

Immediately after they shall be assembled in consequence of the first election, they shall be divided as equally as may be into three classes. The seats of the Senators of the first class shall be vacated at the expiration of the second year, of the second class at the expiration of the fourth year, and the third class at the expiration of the sixth year, so that one third may be chosen every second year; and if vacancies happen by resignation, or otherwise, during the recess of the legislature of any state, the executive thereof may make temporary appointments until the next meeting of the legislature, which shall then fill such vacancies.

No person shall be a Senator who shall not have attained to the age of thirty years, and been nine years a citizen of the United States and who shall not, when elected, be an inhabitant of that state for which he shall be chosen.

The Vice President of the United States shall be President of the Senate, but shall have no vote, unless they be equally divided.

The Senate shall choose their other officers, and also a President pro tempore, in the absence of the Vice President, or when he shall exercise the office of President of the United States.

The Senate shall have the sole power to try all impeachments. When sitting for that purpose, they shall be on oath or affirmation. When the President of the United States is tried, the Chief Justice shall preside: And no person shall be convicted without the concurrence of two thirds of the members present.

Judgment in cases of impeachment shall not extend further than to removal from office, and disqualification to hold and enjoy any office of honor, trust or profit under the United States: but the party convicted shall nevertheless be liable and subject to indictment, trial, judgment and punishment, according to law.

Section 4. The times, places and manner of holding elections for Senators and Representatives, shall be prescribed in each state by the legislature thereof; but the Congress may at any time by law make or alter such regulations, except as to the places of choosing Senators.

The Congress shall assemble at least once in every year, and such meeting shall be on the first Monday in December, unless they shall by law appoint a different day.

Section 5. Each House shall be the judge of the elections, returns and qualifications of its own members, and a majority of each shall constitute a quorum to do business; but a smaller number may adjourn from day to day, and may be authorized to compel the attendance of absent members, in such manner, and under such penalties as each House may provide.

Each House may determine the rules of its proceedings, punish its members for disorderly behavior, and, with the concurrence of two thirds, expel a member.

Each House shall keep a journal of its proceedings, and from time to time publish the same, excepting such parts as may in their judgment require secrecy; and the yeas and nays of the members of either House on any question shall, at the desire of one fifth of those present, be entered on the journal.

Neither House, during the session of Congress, shall, without the consent of the other, adjourn for more than three days, nor to any other place than that in which the two Houses shall be sitting.

Section 6. The Senators and Representatives shall receive a compensation for their services, to be ascertained by law, and paid out of the treasury of the United States. They shall in all cases, except treason, felony and breach of the peace, be privileged from arrest during their attendance at the session of their respective Houses, and in going to and returning from the same; and for any speech or debate in either House, they shall not be questioned in any other place.

No Senator or Representative shall, during the time for which he was elected, be appointed to any civil office under the authority of the United States, which shall have been created, or the emoluments whereof shall have been increased during such time: and no person holding any office under the United States, shall be a member of either House during his continuance in office.

Section 7. All bills for raising revenue shall originate in the House of Representatives; but the Senate may propose or concur with amendments as on other Bills.

Every bill which shall have passed the House of Representatives and the Senate, shall, before it become a law, be presented to the President of the United States; if he approve he shall sign it, but if not he shall return it, with his objections to that House in which it shall have originated, who shall enter the objections at large on their journal, and proceed to reconsider it. If after such reconsideration two thirds of that House shall agree to pass the bill, it shall be sent, together with the objections, to the other House, by which it shall likewise be reconsidered, and if approved by two thirds of that House, it shall become a law. But in all such cases the votes of both Houses shall be determined by yeas and nays, and the names of the persons voting for and against the bill shall be entered on the journal of each House respectively. If any bill shall not be returned by the President within ten days (Sundays excepted) after it shall have been presented to him, the same shall be a law, in like manner as if he had signed it, unless the Congress by their adjournment prevent its return, in which case it shall not be a law.

Every order, resolution, or vote to which the concurrence of the Senate and House of Representatives may be necessary (except on a question of adjournment) shall be presented to the President of the United States; and before the same shall take effect, shall be approved by him, or being disapproved by him, shall be repassed by two thirds of the Senate and House of Representatives, according to the rules and limitations prescribed in the case of a bill.

Section 8. The Congress shall have power to lay and collect taxes, duties, imposts and excises, to pay the debts and provide for the common defense and general welfare of the United States; but all duties, imposts and excises shall be uniform throughout the United States;

To borrow money on the credit of the United States;

To regulate commerce with foreign nations, and among the several states, and with the Indian tribes;

To establish a uniform rule of naturalization, and uniform laws on the subject of bankruptcies throughout the United States;

To coin money, regulate the value thereof, and of foreign coin, and fix the standard of weights and measures;

To provide for the punishment of counterfeiting the securities and current coin of the United States;

To establish post offices and post roads;

To promote the progress of science and useful arts, by securing for limited times to authors and inventors the exclusive right to their respective writings and discoveries;

To constitute tribunals inferior to the Supreme Court;

To define and punish piracies and felonies committed on the high seas, and offenses against the law of nations;

To declare war, grant letters of marque and reprisal, and make rules concerning captures on land and water;

To raise and support armies, but no appropriation of money to that use shall be for a longer term than 2 years;

To provide and maintain a navy;

To make rules for the government and regulation of the land and naval forces;

To provide for calling forth the militia to execute the laws of the union, suppress insurrections and repel invasions;

To provide for organizing, arming, and disciplining, the militia, and for governing such part of them as may be employed in the service of the United States, reserving to the states respectively, the appointment of the officers, and the authority of training the militia according to the discipline prescribed by Congress;

To exercise exclusive legislation in all cases whatsoever, over such District (not exceeding ten miles square) as may, by cession of particular states, and the acceptance of Congress, become the seat of the government of the United States, and to exercise like authority over all places purchased by the consent of the legislature of the state in which the same shall be, for the erection of forts, magazines, arsenals, dockyards, and other needful buildings;—And

To make all laws which shall be necessary and proper for carrying into execution the foregoing powers, and all other powers vested by this Constitution in the government of the United States, or in any department or officer thereof.

Section 9. The migration or importation of such persons as any of the states now existing shall think proper to admit, shall not be prohibited by the Congress prior to the year one thousand eight hundred and eight, but a tax or duty may be imposed on such importation, not exceeding ten dollars for each person.

The privilege of the writ of habeas corpus shall not be suspended, unless when in cases of rebellion or invasion the public safety may require it.

No bill of attainder or ex post facto Law shall be passed.

No capitation, or other direct, tax shall be laid, unless in proportion to the census or enumeration herein before directed to be taken.

No tax or duty shall be laid on articles exported from any state.

No preference shall be given by any regulation of commerce or revenue to the ports of one state over those of another: nor shall vessels bound to, or from, one state, be obliged to enter, clear or pay duties in another.

No money shall be drawn from the treasury, but in consequence of appropriations made by law; and a regular statement and account of receipts and expenditures of all public money shall be published from time to time.

No title of nobility shall be granted by the United States: and no person holding any office of profit or trust under them, shall, without the consent of the Congress, accept of any present, emolument, office, or title, of any kind whatever, from any king, prince, or foreign state.

Section 10. No state shall enter into any treaty, alliance, or confederation; grant letters of marque and reprisal; coin money; emit bills of credit; make anything but gold and silver coin a tender in payment of debts; pass any bill of attainder, ex post facto law, or law impairing the obligation of contracts, or grant any title of nobility.

No state shall, without the consent of the Congress, lay any imposts or duties on imports or exports, except what may be absolutely necessary for executing its inspection laws: and the net produce of all duties and imposts, laid by any state on imports or exports, shall be for the use of the treasury of the United States; and all such laws shall be subject to the revision and control of the Congress.

No state shall, without the consent of Congress, lay any duty of tonnage, keep troops, or ships of war in time of peace, enter into any agreement or compact with another state, or with a foreign power, or engage in war, unless actually invaded, or in such imminent danger as will not admit of delay.

Article II

Section 1. The executive power shall be vested in a President of the United States of America. He shall hold his office during the term of four years, and, together with the Vice President, chosen for the same term, be elected, as follows:

Each state shall appoint, in such manner as the Legislature thereof may direct, a number of electors, equal to the whole number of Senators and Representatives to which the State may be entitled in the Congress: but no Senator or Representative, or person holding an office of trust or profit under the United States, shall be appointed an elector.

The electors shall meet in their respective states, and vote by ballot for two persons, of whom one at least shall not be an inhabitant of the same state with themselves. And they shall make a list of all the persons voted for, and of the number of votes for each; which list they shall sign and certify, and transmit sealed to the seat of the government of the United States, directed to the President of the Senate. The President of the Senate shall, in the presence of the Senate and House of Representatives, open all the certificates, and the votes shall then be counted. The person having the greatest number of votes shall be the President, if such number be a majority of the whole number of electors appointed; and if there be more than one who have such majority, and have an equal number of votes, then the House of Representatives shall immediately choose by ballot one of them for President; and if no person have a majority, then from the five highest on the list the said House shall in like manner choose the President. But in choosing the President, the votes shall be taken by States, the representation from each state having one vote; a quorum for this purpose shall consist of a member or members from two thirds of the states, and a majority of all the states shall be necessary to a choice. In every case, after the choice of the President, the person having the greatest number of votes of the electors shall be the Vice President. But if there should remain two or more who have equal votes, the Senate shall choose from them by ballot the Vice President.

The Congress may determine the time of choosing the electors, and the day on which they shall give their votes; which day shall be the same throughout the United States.

No person except a natural born citizen, or a citizen of the United States, at the time of the adoption of this Constitution, shall be eligible to the office of President; neither shall any person be eligible to that office who shall not have attained to the age of thirty five years, and been fourteen years a resident within the United States.

In case of the removal of the President from office, or of his death, resignation, or inability to discharge the powers and duties of the said office, the same shall devolve on the Vice President, and the Congress may by law provide for the case of removal, death, resignation or inability, both of the President and Vice President, declaring what officer shall then act as President, and such officer shall act accordingly, until the disability be removed, or a President shall be elected.

The President shall, at stated times, receive for his services, a compensation, which shall neither be increased nor diminished during the period for which he shall have been elected, and he shall not receive within that period any other emolument from the United States, or any of them.

Before he enter on the execution of his office, he shall take the following oath or affirmation:—"I do solemnly swear (or affirm) that I will faithfully execute the office of President of the United States, and will to the best of my ability, preserve, protect and defend the Constitution of the United States."

Section 2. The President shall be commander in chief of the Army and Navy of the United States, and of the militia of the several states, when called into the actual service of the United States; he may require the opinion, in writing, of the principal officer in each of the executive departments, upon any subject relating to the duties of their respective offices, and he shall have power to grant reprieves and pardons for offenses against the United States, except in cases of impeachment.

He shall have power, by and with the advice and consent of the Senate, to make treaties, provided two thirds of the Senators present concur; and he shall nominate, and by and with the advice and consent of the Senate, shall appoint ambassadors, other public ministers and consuls, judges of the Supreme Court, and all other officers of the United States, whose appointments are not herein otherwise provided for, and which shall be established by law: but the Congress may by law vest the appointment of such inferior officers, as they think proper, in the President alone, in the courts of law, or in the heads of departments.

The President shall have power to fill up all vacancies that may happen during the recess of the Senate, by granting commissions which shall expire at the end of their next session.

Section 3. He shall from time to time give to the Congress information of the state of the union, and recommend to their consideration such measures as he shall judge necessary and expedient; he may, on extraordinary occasions, convene both Houses, or either of them, and in case of disagreement between them, with respect to the time of adjournment, he may adjourn them to such time as he shall think proper; he shall receive ambassadors and other public ministers; he shall take care that the laws be faithfully executed, and shall commission all the officers of the United States.

Section 4. The President, Vice President and all civil officers of the United States, shall be removed from office on impeachment for, and conviction of, treason, bribery, or other high crimes and misdemeanors.

Article III

Section 1. The judicial power of the United States, shall be vested in one Supreme Court, and in such inferior courts as the Congress may from time to time ordain and establish. The judges, both of the supreme and inferior courts, shall hold their offices during good behaviour, and shall, at stated times, receive for their services, a compensation, which shall not be diminished during their continuance in office.

Section 2. The judicial power shall extend to all cases, in law and equity, arising under this Constitution, the laws of the United States, and treaties made, or which shall be made, under their authority;—to all cases affecting ambassadors, other public ministers and consuls;—to all cases of admiralty and maritime jurisdiction;—to controversies to which the United States shall be a party;—to controversies between two or more states;—between a state and citizens of another state;—between citizens of different states;—between citizens of the same state claiming lands under grants of different states, and between a state, or the citizens thereof, and foreign states, citizens or subjects.

In all cases affecting ambassadors, other public ministers and consuls, and those in which a state shall be party, the Supreme Court shall have original jurisdiction. In all the other cases before mentioned, the Supreme Court shall have appellate jurisdiction, both as to law and fact, with such exceptions, and under such regulations as the Congress shall make.

The trial of all crimes, except in cases of impeachment, shall be by jury; and such trial shall be held in the state where the said crimes shall have been committed; but when not committed within any state, the trial shall be at such place or places as the Congress may by law have directed.`

Section 3. Treason against the United States, shall consist only in levying war against them, or in adhering to their enemies, giving them aid and comfort. No person shall be convicted of treason unless on the testimony of two witnesses to the same overt act, or on confession in open court.

The Congress shall have power to declare the punishment of treason, but no attainder of treason shall work corruption of blood, or forfeiture except during the life of the person attainted.

Article IV

Section 1. Full faith and credit shall be given in each state to the public acts, records, and judicial proceedings of every other state. And the Congress may by general laws prescribe the manner in which such acts, records, and proceedings shall be proved, and the effect thereof.

Section 2. The citizens of each state shall be entitled to all privileges and immunities of citizens in the several states.

A person charged in any state with treason, felony, or other crime, who shall flee from justice, and be found in another state, shall on demand of the executive authority of the state from which he fled, be delivered up, to be removed to the state having jurisdiction of the crime.

No person held to service or labor in one state, under the laws thereof, escaping into another, shall, in consequence of any law or regulation therein, be discharged from such service or labor, but shall be delivered up on claim of the party to whom such service or labor may be due.

Section 3. New states may be admitted by the Congress into this union; but no new states shall be formed or erected within the jurisdiction of any other state; nor any state be formed by the junction of two or more states, or parts of states, without the consent of the legislatures of the states concerned as well as of the Congress.

The Congress shall have power to dispose of and make all needful rules and regulations respecting the territory or other property belonging to the United States; and nothing in this Constitution shall be so construed as to prejudice any claims of the United States, or of any particular state.

Section 4. The United States shall guarantee to every state in this union a republican form of government, and shall protect each of them against invasion; and on application of the legislature, or of the executive (when the legislature cannot be convened) against domestic violence.

Article V

The Congress, whenever two thirds of both houses shall deem it necessary, shall propose amendments to this Constitution, or, on the application of the legislatures of two thirds of the several states, shall call a convention for proposing amendments, which, in either case, shall be valid to all intents and purposes, as part of this Constitution, when ratified by the legislatures of three fourths of the several states, or by conventions in three fourths thereof, as the one or the other mode of ratification may be proposed by the Congress; provided that no amendment which may be made prior to the year one thousand eight hundred and eight shall in any manner affect the first and fourth clauses in the ninth section of the first article; and that no state, without its consent, shall be deprived of its equal suffrage in the Senate.

Article VI

All debts contracted and engagements entered into, before the adoption of this Constitution, shall be as valid against the United States under this Constitution, as under the Confederation.

This Constitution, and the laws of the United States which shall be made in pursuance thereof; and all treaties made, or which shall be made, under the authority of the United States, shall be the supreme law of the land; and the judges in every state shall be bound thereby, anything in the Constitution or laws of any State to the contrary notwithstanding.

The Senators and Representatives before mentioned, and the members of the several state legislatures, and all executive and judicial officers, both of the United States and of the several states, shall be bound by oath or affirmation, to support this Constitution; but no religious test shall ever be required as a qualification to any office or public trust under the United States.

Article VII

The ratification of the conventions of nine states, shall be sufficient for the establishment of this Constitution between the states so ratifying the same.

APPENDIX 2: THE BILL OF RIGHTS

Amendments to the US Constitution

Amendment I
Congress shall make no law respecting an establishment of religion, or prohibiting the free exercise thereof; or abridging the freedom of speech, or of the press; or the right of the people peaceably to assemble, and to petition the Government for a redress of grievances.

Amendment II
A well regulated Militia, being necessary to the security of a free State, the right of the people to keep and bear Arms, shall not be infringed.

Amendment III
No Soldier shall, in time of peace be quartered in any house, without the consent of the Owner, nor in time of war, but in a manner to be prescribed by law.

Amendment IV
The right of the people to be secure in their persons, houses, papers, and effects, against unreasonable searches and seizures, shall not be violated, and no Warrants shall issue, but upon probable cause, supported by Oath or affirmation, and particularly describing the place to be searched, and the persons or things to be seized.

Amendment V
No person shall be held to answer for a capital, or otherwise infamous crime, unless on a presentment or indictment of a Grand Jury, except in cases arising in the land or naval forces, or in the Militia, when in actual service in time of War

or public danger; nor shall any person be subject for the same offence to be twice put in jeopardy of life or limb; nor shall be compelled in any criminal case to be a witness against himself, nor be deprived of life, liberty, or property, without due process of law; nor shall private property be taken for public use, without just compensation.

Amendment VI
In all criminal prosecutions, the accused shall enjoy the right to a speedy and public trial, by an impartial jury of the State and district wherein the crime shall have been committed, which district shall have been previously ascertained by law, and to be informed of the nature and cause of the accusation; to be confronted with the witnesses against him; to have compulsory process for obtaining witnesses in his favor, and to have the Assistance of Counsel for his defence.

Amendment VII
In Suits at common law, where the value in controversy shall exceed 20 dollars, the right of trial by jury shall be preserved, and no fact tried by a jury, shall be otherwise re-examined in any Court of the United States, than according to the rules of the common law.

Amendment VIII
Excessive bail shall not be required, nor excessive fines imposed, nor cruel and unusual punishments inflicted.

Amendment IX
The enumeration in the Constitution, of certain rights, shall not be construed to deny or disparage others retained by the people.

Amendment X
The powers not delegated to the United States by the Constitution, nor prohibited by it to the States, are reserved to the States respectively, or to the people.

BIBLIOGRAPHY

Abraham, Henry J. *Justice, Presidents and Senators: A History of the U.S. Supreme Court Appointments from Washington to Clinton.* Lanham, MD: Rowman and Littlefield, 1999.
Ackerman, Bruce. Unconstitutional Convention. *The New Republic,* March 3, 1979.
Ackerman, Bruce. *We the People, Vol. 1: Foundations.* Cambridge, MA: Harvard University Press, 1991.
Ackerman, Bruce. *We the People, Vol. 2: Transformations.* Cambridge, MA: Harvard University Press, 1998.
Ackerman, Bruce. *The Failure of the Founding Fathers: Jefferson, Marshall, and the Rise of Presidential Democracy.* Cambridge, MA: Harvard University Press, 2005.
Ackerman, Bruce and Neal Katyal. Our Unconventional Founding. *University of Chicago Law Review,* 62 (1995): 492–498.
Adair, Douglass. *Fame and the Founding Fathers: Essays by Douglass Adair,* ed. Trevor Colbourn. New York: W.W. Norton, 1974.
Amar, Akhil Reed. Of Sovereignty and Federalism. *Yale Law Journal,* 96 (1987): 1425–1520.
Amar, Akhil Reed. *The Bill of Rights: Creation and Reconstruction.* New Haven, CT: Yale University Press, 1998.
Amar, Akhil Reed. *America's Constitution: A Biography.* New York: Random House, 2005.
Anderson, Thornton. *Creating the Constitution: The Convention of 1787 and the First Congress.* University Park: Pennsylvania State University Press, 1993.
Arkes, Hadley. *Beyond the Constitution.* Princeton, NJ: Princeton University Press, 1990.
Baer, Judith A., Lloyd N. Cutler et al. *Politics and the Constitution: The Nature and Extent of Interpretation.* Washington, DC: American Studies Center, 1990.
Bailey, Jeremy D. *James Madison and the Constitutional Imperfection.* New York: Cambridge University Press, 2015.
Bailyn, Bernard. *Faces of Revolution: Personalities and Themes in the Struggle for American Independence.* New York: Knopf, 1990.
Bailyn, Bernard. *The Ideological Origins of the American Revolution.* Cambridge, MA: Harvard University Press, 1992.
Bailyn, Bernard (ed.). *The Debate on the Constitution: Federalist and Antifederalist Speeches, Articles and Letters During the Struggle over Ratification, Parts I & II.* New York: Library of America, 1993.
Bailyn, Bernard. *To Begin the World Anew: The Genius and Ambiguities of the American Founders.* New York: Vintage Books, 2004.

Ballagh, James Curtis (ed.). *The Letters of Richard Henry Lee*. New York: Macmillan, 1914.

Banning, Lance. *The Jeffersonian Persuasion: Evolution of a Party Ideology*. Ithaca, NY: Cornell University Press, 1978.

Banning, Lance. The Hamiltonian Madison. *Virginia Magazine of History and Biography*, 92 (1984): 3–28.

Banning, Lance. Jeffersonian Ideology Revisited: Liberal and Classical Ideas in the New American Republic. *William and Mary Quarterly*, 43 (1986): 3–19.

Banning, Lance. *The Sacred Fire of Liberty: James Madison and the Founding of the Federal Republic*. Ithaca, NY: Cornell University Press, 1995.

Barber, Sotirios A. Defending Dual Federalism: A Self-Defeating Act. Paper Delivered at APSA Annual Meeting, Seattle, WA, 2011.

Barber, Sotirios A. and James E. Fleming. *Constitutional Interpretation: The Basic Questions*. New York: Oxford University Press, 2007.

Barnett, Randy E. *Restoring the Lost Constitution: The Presumption of Liberty*. Princeton, NJ: Princeton University Press, 2004.

Barrow, Clyde W. *More than a Historian: The Political and Economic Thought of Charles A. Beard*. New Brunswick, NJ: Transaction, 2000.

Beard, Charles A. *An Economic Interpretation of the Constitution of the United States*. New York: Free Press, 1986.

Beeman, Richard. *Plain, Honest Men: The Making of the American Constitution*. New York: Random House, 2010.

Beeman, Richard, Stephen Botein, and Edward C. Carter II (eds.). *Beyond Confederation: Origins of the Constitution and American National Identity*. Chapel Hill: University of North Carolina Press, 1987.

Belz, Herman. *A Living Constitution or Fundamental Law? American Constitutionalism in Historical Perspective*. Lanham, MD: Rowman and Littlefield, 1998.

Belz, Herman et al. (eds.). *To Form a More Perfect Union*. Charlottesville: University Press of Virginia, 1992.

Bemis, Samuel Flagg. *Pinckney's Treaty*. Baltimore, MD: Johns Hopkins, 1926.

Bemis, Samuel Flagg. *A Diplomatic History of the United States*, 5th ed. New York: Holt, Rinehart and Winston, 1965.

Berger, Raoul. 'Original Intention' in Historical Perspective. *George Washington Law Review*, 54 (1986): 296–337.

Berns, Walter. *The First Amendment and the Future of American Democracy*. New York: Basic Books, 1976.

Berns, Walter. *Taking the Constitution Seriously*. New York: Simon & Schuster, 1987.

Berns, Walter. The Constitution as Bill of Rights. In Robert A. Goldwin and William A. Schambra (eds.), *How Does the Constitution Secure Rights?* Washington, DC: American Enterprise Institute, 1985, 50–73.

Bernstein, Richard B. and Jerome Agel. *Amending America*. New York: Random House, 1993.

Bestor, Arthur. Respective Roles of Senate and President in the Making and Abrogation of Treaties The Original Intent of the Framers of the Constitution Historically Examined. *Washington Law Review*, 55 (1979): 1–135.

Bilder, Mary Sarah. *Madison's Hand: Revising the Constitutional Convention*. Cambridge, MA: Harvard University Press, 2015.

Billias, George Athan. *Elbridge Gerry: Founding Father and Republican Statesman*. New York: McGraw-Hill, 1976.

Black, Charles L. Amending the Constitution: A Letter to a Congressman. *Yale Law Journal*, 82 (1972): 189–215.
Bork, Robert H. *The Tempting of America: The Political Seduction of the Law*. New York: Free Press, 1990.
Bowling, Kenneth R. The Bank Bill, the Capital City and President Washington. *Capitol Studies*, 1 (1972): 59–71.
Bowling, Kenneth R. 'A Tub to the Whale': The Founding Fathers and Adoption of the Federal Bill of Rights. *Journal of the Early Republic*, 8 (1988): 223–225, 236–237, 241.
Boyd, Steven R. *The Politics of Opposition: Antifederalists and the Acceptance of the Constitution*. Millwood, NY: KTO Press, 1979.
Brant, Irving. *James Madison, Father of the Constitution: 1787–1800*. Indianapolis, IN: Bobbs-Merrill, 1950.
Brant, Irving. *James Madison, Father of the Constitution The Bill of Rights: Its Origin and Meaning*. New York: Mentor Books, 1967.
Broadwater, Jeff. *George Mason: Forgotten Founder*. Chapel Hill: University of North Carolina Press, 2006.
Brooks, Robin. Alexander Hamilton, Melancton Smith, and the Ratification of the Constitution in New York. *William and Mary Quarterly*, 24, Third Series (1967): 339–357.
Brown, Robert E. *Charles Beard and the Constitution: A Critical Analysis of "An Economic Interpretation of the Constitution"*. Princeton, NJ: Princeton University Press, 1956.
Burnett, Edmund Cody. *The Continental Congress*. New York: Macmillan, 1941.
Burns, James McGregor. *The Deadlock of Democracy*. Englewood Cliffs, NJ: Prentice-Hall, 1963.
Carey, George W. The Federalist: *Design for a Constitutional Republic*. Urbana: University of Illinois Press, 1989.
Chitwood, Oliver Perry. *Richard Henry Lee: Statesman of the Revolution*. Morgantown: West Virginia University Library, 1967.
Choper, Jesse H. *Judicial Review and the National Political Process*. Chicago: University of Chicago Press, 1980.
Cochrane, Thomas C. *New York in the Confederation: An Economic Study*. Port Washington, NY: Kennikat Press, 1932.
Cogan, Neil H. (ed.). *The Complete Bill of Rights: The Drafts, Debates, Sources, and Origins*. New York: Oxford University Press, 1997.
Combs, Jerald A. The Jay Treaty: Political Battleground of the Founding Fathers. Berkeley: University of California Press, 1970.
Commager, Henry Steele (ed.). *Documents of American History*, 7th ed. 2 vol. New York: Appleton-Century-Crofts, 1963.
Conlan, Timothy J. and François Vergniolle de Chantal. The Rehnquist Court and Contemporary American Federalism. *Political Science Quarterly*, 116 (2001): 253–275.
Conley, Patrick T. and John P. Kaminski (eds.). *The Constitution and the States: The Role of the Original Thirteen in the Framing and Adoption of the Federal Constitution*. Madison, WI: Madison House, 1988.
Cornell, Saul. *The Other Founders: Anti-Federalism & the Dissenting Tradition in America, 1788–1828*. Chapel Hill: University of North Carolina Press, 1999.
Dahl, Robert. Pluralist Democracy in the United States: Conflict and Consent. Chicago: Rand McNally, 1967.

Dahl, Robert. *A Preface to Democratic Theory*. Chicago: University of Chicago Press, 1977.
De Pauw, Linda Grant. *The Eleventh Pillar: New York State and the Federal Constitution*. Ithaca, NY: Cornell University Press, 1966.
De Pauw, Linda Grant. The Anticlimax of Antifederalism: The Abortive Second Convention Movement, 1788–1789. *Prologue*, 2 (1970): 98–114.
Dellinger, Walter E. The Recurring Question of the 'Limited' Constitutional Convention. *Yale Law Journal*, 88 (1979): 1623–1640.
Diamond, Martin. Democracy and *The Federalist*: A Reconsideration of the Framers' Intent. *American Political Science Review*, 53 (1959): 52–68.
Diamond, Martin. The Federalist, 1787–1788. In Strauss, Leo and Joseph Cropsey (eds.). *History of Political Philosophy*. 3rd ed. Chicago: University of Chicago Press, 1987, 659–679.
Dietz, Gottfried. The Federalist: *A Classic on Federalism and Free Government*. Baltimore, MD: Johns Hopkins University Press, 1960.
Documentary History of the Constitution of the United States of America 1786–1870. 5 vol. Washington, DC: Dept. of State, 1894–1905.
Dumbauld, Edward. *The Bill of Rights*. Norman: University of Oklahoma Press, 1957.
Documentary History of the Constitution of the United States of America. The Bill of Rights and What It Means Today. Norman: University of Oklahoma Press, 1957.
Dunn, Susan (ed.). *Something That Will Surprise the World: The Essential Writings of the Founding Fathers*. New York: Basic Books, 2006.
Edling, Max M. *A Revolution in Favor of Government: Origins of the Making of the U.S. Constitution and the Making of the American State*. Oxford: Oxford University Press, 2003.
Eidelberg, Paul. *The Philosophy of the American Constitution: A Reinterpretation of the Intentions of the Founding Fathers*. New York: Free Press, 1968.
Elkins, Stanley and Eric McKitrick. The Founding Fathers: Young Men of the Revolution. *Political Science Quarterly*, 76 (1961): 181–216.
Elkins, Stanley and Eric McKitrick. *The Age of Federalism: The Early American Republic, 1788–1800*. New York: Oxford University Press, 1993.
Ellis, Joseph J. *Founding Brothers: The Revolutionary Generation*. New York: Vintage Books, 2002.
Ellis, Joseph J. *The Quartet: Orchestrating the Second American Revolution, 1783–1789*. New York: Knopf, 2015.
Ellis, Richard E. "The Persistence of Antifederalism after 1789" in Beeman et al. (eds.), *Beyond Confederation: Origins of the Constitution and American National Identity*. Chapel Hill: University of North Carolina Press, 1987, 295–314.
Epstein, David F. *The Political Theory of* The Federalist. Chicago: University of Chicago Press, 1984.
Estes, Todd. *The Jay Treaty Debate, Public Opinion, and the Evolution of Early American Political Culture*. Amherst, MA: University of Massachusetts Press, 2006.
Farrand, Max. *The Framing of the Constitution of the United States*. New Haven, CT: Yale University Press, 1913.
Farrand, Max. (ed.). *The Records of the Federal Convention of 1787*. Revised edition, 4 vol. New Haven, CT: Yale University Press, 1913, 1966.

Alexander Hamilton, James Madison, John Jay. *Federalist.* Jacob E. Cooke. (ed.). Middletown, CT: Wesleyan University Press, 1982.
Federalist Society. *The Great Debate: Interpreting Our Written Constitution.* Washington, DC: Federalist Society, 1986.
Finkelman, Paul. The Constitution and the Intentions of the Framers: The Limits of Historical Analysis. *Univ. of Pittsburgh Law Review,* 50 (1989): 349–398.
Finkelman, Paul. James Madison and the Bill of Rights: A Reluctant Paternity. *The Supreme Court Review,* 9 (1990): 301–347.
Finkelman, Paul. *Slavery and the Founders: Race and Liberty in the Age of Jefferson,* 2nd ed. New York: E. M. Sharpe, 2001.
Ford, Paul Leicester. *Essays on the Constitution of the United States: Published During Its Discussion by the People, 1787–1788.* Brooklyn, NY: Historical Printing Club, 1892.
Fowler, William M. Jr. *The Baron of Beacon Hill.* Boston, MA: Houghton, Mifflin, 1980.
Friedman, Lawrence M. and Harry N. Scheiber (eds.). *American Law and the Constitutional Order: Historical Perspectives.* Cambridge, MA: Harvard University Press, 1988.
Frisch, Morton J. *The Hamilton-Madison-Jefferson Triangle.* Ashbrook Essay no. 4. Ashland, OH: John M. Ashbrook Center for Public Affairs, 1992.
Gibson, Alan. "Inventing the Extended Republic: The Debate over the Role of Madison's Theory in the Creation of the Constitution" in Vile et al. (eds.), *James Madison: Philosopher, Founder, and Statesman.* Athens: Ohio University Press, 2008, 63–87.
Gibson, Alan. *Interpreting the Founding: Guide to the Enduring Debates over the Origins and Foundations of the American Republic.* 2nd ed. Lawrence: University Press of Kansas, 2010.
Gibson, Alan. *Understanding the Founding: The Crucial Questions.* 2nd ed. Lawrence: University Press of Kansas, 2010.
Gillespie, Michael Allen and Michael Lienesch (eds.). *Ratifying the Constitution.* Lawrence: Univ. Press of Kansas, 1989.
Goldwin, Robert A. (ed.). *A Nation of States: Essays on the American Federal System.* Chicago: Rand McNally, 1961.
Goldwin, Robert A. *From Parchment to Power: How James Madison Used the Bill of Rights to Save the Constitution.* Washington, DC: AEI Press, 1997.
Goldwin, Robert A. and William A. Schambra (eds.). *How Does the Constitution Secure Rights?* Washington DC: American Enterprise Institute, 1985.
Greene, Jack P. (ed.). *The Ambiguity of the American Revolution.* New York: Harper & Row, 1968.
Greene, Jack P. (ed.). *Encyclopedia of American Political History.* New York: Scribner's, 1984.
Greene, Jack P. (ed.). *The American Revolution: Its Character and Limits.* New York: New York University Press, 1987.
Greene, Jack P. *Understanding the American Revolution: Issues and Actors.* Charlottesville: University Press of Virginia, 1995.
Greve, Michael S. *The Upside-down Constitution.* Cambridge, MA: Harvard University Press, 2012.
Gunther, Gerald (ed.). *John Marshall's Defense of McCulloch v. Maryland.* Stanford, CA: Stanford University Press, 1969.
Gunther, Gerald. The Convention Method of Amending the United States Constitution. *Georgia Law Journal,* 14 (1979): 1–25.

Gunther, Gerald and Kathleen M. Sullivan. *Constitutional Law*, 13 ed. Westbury, NY: Foundation Press, 1997.

Gutzman, Kevin R.C. *James Madison and the Making of America*. New York: St Martin's Griffin, 2012.

Hamilton, Alexander. *The Papers of Alexander Hamilton*. Edited by Harold C. Syrett and Jacob E. Cooke. 27 vols. New York: Columbia University Press, 1961–1979.

Harmon, M. Judd (ed.). *Essays on the Constitution of the United States*. New York: Kennikat Press, 1978.

Hartz, Louis. *The Liberal Tradition in America*. New York: Harcourt, Brace and World, 1955.

Hendrickson David C. *Peace Pact: The Lost World of the American Founding*. Lawrence: University Press of Kansas, 2003.

Henkin, Louis. *Foreign Affairs and the Constitution*. New York: Norton, 1975.

Hill, Helen. *George Mason: Constitutionalist*. Gloucester, MA: Peter Smith, 1966.

Hobson, Charles F. "The Negative on State Laws: James Madison, the Constitution, and the Crisis of Republican Government," *William and Mary Quarterly*, 36, Third Series (1979): 214–435.

Hobson, Charles F. "James Madison, the Bill of Rights, and the Problem of the States," *William and Mary Law Review*, 31 (1990): 267–274.

Hobson, Charles F. *The Great Chief Justice: John Marshall and the Rule of Law*. Lawrence: University Press of Kansas, 1996.

Holmes, Oliver W. "Law and the Court," *Collected Legal Papers*. New York: Harcourt Brace, 1921.

Hutson, James H. *Supplement to Max Farrand's The Records of the Federal Convention of 1787*. New Haven, CT: Yale University Press, 1987.

Jameson, J. Franklin (ed.). *Essays in the Constitutional History of the United States in the Formative Period, 1775–1789*. Boston, MA: Houghton, Mifflin, 1889.

Jay, John. *The Correspondence and Public Papers of John Jay*. Edited by Henry P. Johnston. 4 vols. New York: G.P. Putnam's, 1890–1895.

Jefferson, Thomas. *The Papers of Thomas Jefferson*. Edited by Julian P. Boyd et al. 27 vols. to date. Princeton, NJ: Princeton University Press, 1950–.

Jensen, Merrill. *The Articles of Confederation: An Interpretation of the Social-Constitutional History of the American Revolution, 1774–1781*. Madison: University of Wisconsin Press, 1940.

Jensen, Merrill. "The Idea of a National Government during the American Revolution," *Political Science Quarterly*, 58 (1943): 372–373–.

Jensen, Merrill. *The Making of the American Constitution*. Malabar, FL: Krieger, 1979.

Jensen, Merrill, John P. Kaminski and Gaspare J. Saladino (eds.). *The Documentary History of the Ratification of the Constitution*. 27 vols. to date. Madison, WI: State Historical Society of Wisconsin, 1976–.

Johnson, Calvin H. *Righteous Anger at the Wicked States: The Meaning of the Founder's Constitution*. New York: Cambridge University Press, 2005.

Kaminski, John P. Restoring the Grand Security: The Debate Over a Federal Bill of Rights, 1787–1792. *Santa Clara Law Review*, 33 (1993): 887–930.

Kaminski, John P. *A Necessary Evil? Slavery and the Debate Over the Constitution*. Madison, WI: Madison House, 1995.

Kaminski, John P. and Richard Leffler (eds.). *Federalists and Antifederalists: The Debate Over the Ratification of the Constitution*. Madison, WI: Madison House, 1989.

Kammen, Michael. *A Machine that Would Go of Itself: The Constitution in American Culture.* New York: Random House, 1986.

Kelly, Alfred H., Winifred A. Harbison, and Herman Belz. *The American Constitution, Its Origins and Development.* 6th ed. New York: Norton, 1983.

Kenyon, Cecelia M. Men of Little Faith: The Anti-Federalists on the Nature of Representative Government. *William and Mary Quarterly,* 12 (1955): 3–43.

Kenyon, Cecelia M. (ed.). *The Antifederalists.* Boston, MA: Northeastern University Press, 1985.

Kesavan, Vasan and Michael Stokes Paulsen. "The Interpretive Force of the Constitution's Secret Drafting History,"*Georgetown Law Journal,* 91 (2003): 1113–1214.

Kesler, Charles R. (ed.). *Saving the Revolution: The Federalist Papers and the American Founding.* New York: Free Press, 1987.

Ketcham, Ralph. James Madison and Judicial Review. *Syracuse Law Review,* 8 (1956–1957): 158–165.

Ketcham, Ralph. *James Madison: A Biography.* Charlottesville: University Press of Virginia, 1992.

Ketcham, Ralph.. *Framed for Posterity: The Enduring Philosophy of the Constitution.* Lawrence: University Press of Kansas, 1993.

Killenbeck, Mark R. Pursuing the Great Experiment: Reserved Powers in a Post-Ratification Compound Republic. *Supreme Court Review* (1999): 81–140.

Killenbeck, Mark R. (ed.). *The Tenth Amendment and State Sovereignty: Constitutional History and Contemporary Issue*s. Lanham, MD: Rowman & Littlefield, 2002.

Killenbeck, Mark R. In(re)Dignity: The New Federalism in Perspective. *Arkansas Law Review,* 57 (2004): 1–68.

Killenbeck, Mark R.. *M'Culloch v. Maryland: Securing a Nation.* Lawrence: University Press of Kansas, 2006.

Koch, Adrienne. *Jefferson and Madison: The Great Collaboration.* London: Oxford University Press, 1973.

Kramer, Larry D. Madison's Audience. *Harvard Law Review,* 112 (1999): 611–679.

Kramer, Larry D. Putting the Politics Back Into the Political Safeguards of Federalism. *Columbia Law Review,* 100 (2000): 215–293.

Kramer, Larry D. *The People Themselves: Popular Constitutionalism and Judicial Review.* New York: Oxford University Press, 2004.

Kukla, Jon (ed.). A Spectrum of Sentiments: Virginia's Federalists, Antifederalists, and 'Federalists Who Are for Amendments,' 1787–1788. *Virginia Magazine of History and Biography,* 96 (1988): 276–296.

Kukla, Jon. *The Bill of Rights: A Lively Heritage.* Richmond: Virginia State Library, 1989.

Kurland, Philip B. and Ralph Lerner (eds.). *The Founders' Constitution.* 5 vols. Chicago: University of Chicago Press, 1987.

Kyvig, David E. *Explicit and Authentic Acts: Amending the U.S. Constitution, 1776–1995.* Lawrence: University Press of Kansas, 1996.

Labunski, Richard. *James Madison and the Struggle for the Bill of Rights.* New York: Oxford University Press, 2006.

Levinson, Sanford. 'Veneration' and Constitutional Change: James Madison Confronts the Possibility of Constitutional Amendment. *Texas Tech Law Review,* 21 (1990): 2443–2460.

Levinson, Sanford. *Our Undemocratic Constitution: Where the Constitution Goes Wrong (And How We the People Can Correct It)*. New York: Oxford University Press, 2006.

Levinson, Sanford. *Framed: America's 51 Constitutions and the Crisis of Governance*. New York: Oxford University Press, 2012.

Levinson, Sanford. The Twenty-First Century Rediscovery of Nullification and Secession in American Political Rhetoric: Frivolousness Incarnate or Serious Arguments to be Wrestled With? *Arkansas Law Review*, 67 (2014): 17–80.

Levy, Leonard W. *Legacy of Suppression: Freedom of Speech and Press in Early American History*. Cambridge, MA: Harvard University Press, 1960.

Levy, Leonard W. *Jefferson and Civil Liberties: The Darker Side*. Cambridge, MA: Harvard University Press, 1963.

Levy, Leonard W.(ed.). Essays *on the Making of the Constitution*, 2nd edition. New York: Oxford University Press, 1987.

Levy, Leonard W. *Original Intent and the Framers' Constitution*. New York: Macmillan, 1988.

Levy, Leonard W. *Origins of the Bill of Rights*. New Haven, CT: Yale University Press, 1999.

Levy, Leonard W. and Dennis J. Mahoney (eds.). The Framing and Ratification of the Constitution. New York: Macmillan, 1987.

Lim. Elvin T. *The Lovers' Quarrel: The Two Foundings and American Political Development*. Oxford: Oxford University Press, 2014.

Lofgren, Charles A. "Missouri v. Holland in Historical Perspective. 1975 *Supreme Court Review* 77–122.

Lofgren, Charles A. The Origins of the Tenth Amendment: History, Sovereignty, and the Problem of Constitutional Intention. In Ronald K.L. Collins (ed.), *Constitutional Government in America*. Durham, NC: Carolina Academic Press, 1980, 331–357.

Lutz, Donald S. The Relative Influence of European Writers on Late Eighteenth-Century American Political Thought. *American Political Science Review*, 78 (1984): 189–197.

Madison, James. *The Papers of James Madison*. Edited by William T. Hutchinson, William M.E. Rachal, Robert A. Rutland, Charles F. Hobson et al. 17 vols. to date. 1–10: Chicago: University of Chicago Press., 1962–1977; Vols. 11–: Charlottesville: University of Virginia Press, 1978.

Maier, Pauline. *The Old Revolutionaries: Political Lives in the Age of Samuel Adams*. New York: Knopf, 1980.

Maier, Pauline. *Ratification: The People Debate the Constitution, 1787–1788*. New York: Simon & Schuster, 2010.

Main, Jackson Turner. *The Antifederalists: Critics of the Constitution, 1781–1788*. Chapel Hill: University of North Carolina Press, 1961.

Mansfield, Harvey C., Jr. *America's Constitutional Soul*. Baltimore, MD: Johns Hopkins University Press, 1991.

Mason, Alpheus Thomas. *The States Rights Debate: Antifederalism and the Constitution*. Englewood Cliffs, NJ: Prentice-Hall, 1964.

Mason, George. *The Papers of George Mason, 1725–1792*. Edited by Robert Allen Rutland. 3 vols. [Chapel Hill]: University of North Carolina Press, 1970.

Matthews, Richard K. *The Radical Politics of Thomas Jefferson*. Lawrence: University Press of Kansas, 1984.

Matthews, Richard K. *If Men Were Angels: James Madison and the Heartless Empire of Reason*. Lawrence: University Press of Kansas, 1995.

Mayer, Henry. *A Son of Thunder: Patrick Henry and the American Republic.* Charlottesville: University Press of Virginia, 1991.
McClendon, R. Earl. Origin of the Two-Thirds Rule in Senate Action Upon Treaties. *American Historical Review,* 36 (1931): 768–772.
McCloskey, Robert G. Revised by Sanford Levinson, *The American Supreme Court.* 4th ed. Chicago: University of Chicago Press: 2005.
McCoy, Drew R. *The Last of the Fathers: James Madison and the Republican Legacy.* Cambridge: Cambridge University Press, 1989.
McDonald, Forrest. *We the People: The Economic Origins of the Constitution.* Chicago: University of Chicago Press, 1958.
McDonald, Forrest. *E Pluribus Unum: The Formation of the American Republic, 1776–1790.* Cambridge, MA: Riverside Press, 1965.
McDonald, Forrest. *Confederation and Constitution: 1781–1789.* New York: Harper & Row, 1968.
McDonald, Forrest. *Alexander Hamilton: A Biography.* New York: W.W. Norton, 1979.
McDonald, Forrest. *Novus Ordo Seclorum: The Intellectual Origins of the Constitution.* Lawrence: University Press of Kansas, 1985.
McDonald, Forrest. *States' Rights and the Union: Imperium in Imperio, 1776–1876.* Lawrence: University Press of Kansas, 2000.
McDowell, Gary L. The Politics of Original Intention. In Robert A. Goldwin and William A. Schambra (eds.). *The Constitution, the Courts, and the Quest for Justice.* Washington, DC: American Enterprise Institute, 1989, 1–24.
McDowell, Gary L. and Colleen A. Sheehan (eds.). *Friends of the Constitution: Writings of the "Other" Federalists 1787–1788.* Indianapolis, IN: Liberty Fund, 1998.
McLaughlin, Andrew C. *A Constitutional History of the United States.* New York: Appleton-Century-Crofts, 1935.
McLaughlin, Andrew C. *Foundations of American Constitutionalism.* Greenwich, CT: Fawcett, 1961.
McLaughlin, Andrew C. *The Confederation and the Constitution: 1783–1789.* New York: Crowell-Collier, 1962.
Monaghan, Frank. *John Jay: Defender of Liberty.* New York: Bobbs-Merrill, 1935.
Monaghan, Henry Paul. Stare Decisis and Constitutional Adjudication. *Columbia Law Review,* 88 (1988): 723–773.
Monaghan, Henry Paul. We the People[s], Original Understanding, and Constitutional Amendment. *Columbia Law Review* 96 (1966): 121.
Morgan, Robert J. *James Madison on the Constitution and the Bill of Rights.* New York: Greenwood Press, 1988.
Morris, Richard B. *Seven Who Shaped Our Destiny: The Founding Fathers as Revolutionaries.* New York: Harper & Row, 1973.
Morris, Richard B. *Witnesses at the Creation: Hamilton, Madison, Jay, and the Constitution.* New York: Henry Holt, 1985.
Murphy, William P. *The Triumph of Nationalism: State Sovereignty, the Founding Fathers, and the Making of the Constitution.* Chicago: Quadrangle, 1967.
Murrin, John M. 1787: The Invention of American Federalism. In David E. Narrett and Joyce S. Goldberg, (eds.). *Essays on Liberty and Federalism: The Shaping of the U.S. Constitution.* College Station: Texas A & M University Press, 1988.
Onuf, Peter S. *The Origins of the Federal Republic: Jurisdictional Controversies in the United States, 1775–1787.* Philadelphia: University of Pennsylvania Press, 1983.

Onuf, Peter S. James Madison's Extended Revolution: *The Federalist Symposium. Texas Tech Law Review*, 21 (1990): 2375–2388.
Onuf, Peter S. *Jefferson's Empire: The Language of American Nationhood*. Charlottesville: University of Virginia Press, 2000.
Pancake, John S. *Thomas Jefferson & Alexander Hamilton*. Woodbury, NY: Barron's Educational Series, 1974.
Paulsen, Michael Stokes. A General Theory of Article V: The Constitutional Lessons of the Twenty-Seventh Amendment. *Yale Law Journal*, 103 (1993): 677–789.
Paulsen, Michael Stokes and Luke Paulsen. *The Constitution: An Introduction*. New York: Basic Books, 2015.
Peterson, Paul C. The Problem of Consistency in the Statesmanship of James Madison. In Ralph Rossum and Gary L. McDowell (eds.). *The American Founding: Politics, Statesmanship, and the Constitution*. Port Washington, NY: Kennikat Press, 1981, 122–134.
Powell, H. Jefferson. The Original Understanding of Original Intent. *Harvard Law Review*, 98 (1985): 885–948.
Prakash, Saikrishna Bangalore. Field Office Federalism. *Virginia Law Review*, 79 (1993): 1957–2037.
Rahe, Paul A. *Republics Ancient and Modern: Classical Republicanism and the American Revolution*. Chapel Hill: University of North Carolina Press, 1992.
Rakove, Jack N. *The Beginnings of National Politics: An Interpretive History of the Continental Congress*. New York: Knopf, 1979.
Rakove, Jack N. Solving a Constitutional Puzzle: The Treatymaking Clause as a Case Study. *Perspectives in American History*, 1, New Series (1984): 233–281.
Rakove, Jack N. Mr. Meese, Meet Mr. Madison. *Atlantic Monthly* (Dec. 1986): 77–86.
Rakove, Jack N. *Original Meanings: Politics and Ideas in the Making of the Constitution*. New York: Knopf, 1996.
Rakove, Jack N. Making a Hash of Sovereignty, Parts 1 and 2. *Green Bag* 2d. (1998): 2:35 & 51.
Rakove, Jack N. *James Madison and the Creation of the American Republic*. New York: Pearson-Longman, 2007.
Rakove, Jack N. *Revolutionaries: A New History of the Invention of America*. New York: Houghton Mifflin Harcourt, 2010.
Rehnquist, William H. *The American Constitutional Experience: Stress and Strain among the Three Branches of Government*. [London]: Institute of United States Studies, University of London, 2000.
Robinson, Donald L. (ed.). *Reforming American Government: The Bicentennial Papers of the Committee on the Constitutional System*. Boulder, CO: Westview Press, 1985.
Rosen, Gary. *American Compact: James Madison and the Problem of Founding*. Lawrence: University Press of Kansas, 1999.
Rossiter, Clinton. *1787: The Grand Convention*. New York: W.W. Norton, 1987.
Rossum, Ralph A. and Gary L. McDowell (eds.). *The American Founding: Politics, Statesmanship, and the Constitution*. Port Washington, NY: Kennikat Press, 1981.
Rutland, Robert Allen. *George Mason: Reluctant Statesman*. Charlottesville: University Press of Virginia, 1961.
Rutland, Robert Allen. *The Ordeal of the Constitution: The Antifederalists and the Ratification Struggle of 1787–1788*. Norman: University of Oklahoma Press, 1966.
Rutland, Robert Allen. *The Birth of the Bill of Rights: 1776–1791*. Boston, MA: Northeastern University Press, 1983.
Rutland, Robert Allen.(ed.). *James Madison and the American Nation, 1751–1836: An Encyclopedia*. New York: Simon & Schuster, 1994.

Samples, John (ed.). *James Madison and the Future of Limited Government.* Washington, DC: Cato Institute, 2002.
Schechter, Stephen L. (ed.). *The Reluctant Pillar: New York and the Adoption of the Federal Constitution.* Troy, NY: Russell Sage College, 1985.
Scheiber, Harry N. Federalism and the Constitution: The Original Understanding. In Lawrence M. Friedman and Harry N. Schieber (eds.). *American Law and the Constitutional Order: Historical Perspectives.* Cambridge, MA: Harvard University Press, 1978, 85–98.
Schwartz, Bernard. *The Bill of Rights: A Documentary History.* New York: McGraw Hill, 1971.
Schwartz, Herman (ed.). *The Rehnquist Court: Judicial Activism on the Right.* New York: Hill and Wang, 2002.
Shalhope, Robert E. Republicanism and Early American Historiography. *William and Mary Quarterly,* 39 (1982): 334–356.
Sheehan, Colleen A. The Politics of Public Opinion: James Madison's 'Notes on Government'. *William and Mary Quarterly,* 49 (1992): 609–627.
Sheehan, Colleen A. *James Madison and the Spirit of Republican Self-Government.* Cambridge, MA: Cambridge University Press, 2009.
Sheehan, Colleen A. *The Mind of James Madison: The Legacy of Classical Republicanism.* New York: Cambridge University Press, 2015.
Sheehan, Colleen A. and Gary L. McDowell (eds.). *Friends of the Constitution: Writings of the "Other" Federalists 1787–1788.* Indianapolis, IN: Liberty Fund, 1998.
Siemers, David J. *Ratifying the Republic: Antifederalists and Federalists in Constitutional Time.* Stanford, CA: Stanford University Press, 2002.
Slonim, Shlomo. Congressional–Executive Agreements. *Columbia Journal of Transnational Law,* 14 (1975): 434–450.
Slonim, Shlomo. The Electoral College at Philadelphia: The Evolution of an Ad Hoc Congress for the Selection of a President. *Journal of American History,* 73 (1986): 35–58. Republished in Slonim, *Framers'Construction/Beardian Deconstruction,* chap. 1.
Slonim, Shlomo. Securing States' Interests at the 1787 Constitutional Convention: A Reassessment. *Studies in American Political Development,* 14 (2000): 1–19.
Slonim, Shlomo. *Framers'Construction/Beardian Deconstruction: Essays on the Constitutional Design of 1787.* New York: Peter Lang, 2001.
Slonim, Shlomo. The Federalist Papers and the Bill of Rights. *Constitutional Commentary,* 20 (2003): 151–156
Slonim, Shlomo. Federalist No. 78 and Brutus' Neglected Thesis on Judicial Supremacy. *Constitutional Commentary,* 23 (2006): 7–31.
Slonim, Shlomo. The Scheme of Enumeration: A Critical Analysis of the New Federalism in the U.S. Supreme Court. *University of St. Thomas Law Review,* 12 (2015): 178–227.
Stockwell, Mary. Madison and Hamilton: The End of a Friendship. In Vile et al. (eds.), *James Madison: Philosopher, Founder, and Statesman.* Athens: Ohio University Press, 2008, 175–192.
Storing, Herbert J. *What the Anti-Federalists Were For.* Chicago: University of Chicago Press, 1981.
Storing, Herbert J. (ed.). *The Complete Anti-Federalist.* 7 vols. Chicago: University of Chicago Press, 1981.
Storing, Herbert J. The Constitution and the Bill of Rights. In Robert A. Goldwin and William A. Schambra (eds.), *How Does the Constitution Secure Rights?* Washington, DC: American Enterprise Institute, 1985, 15–35.

Stourzh, Gerald. *Alexander Hamilton and the Idea of Republican Government*. Stanford, CA: Stanford University Press. 1970.

Tansill, Charles C. *Documents Illustrative of the Formation of the Union of the American States*. Sewanee, TN: Spencer Judd, 1984.

Urofsky, Melvin I. and Paul Finkelman. *A March of Liberty: A Constitutional History of the United States, Vol. 1: From the Founding to 1890*, 2nd ed. New York: Oxford University Press, 2002.

Utley, Robert L., Jr. (ed.). *Principles of the Constitutional Order: The Ratification Debates*. Lanham, MD: University Press of America, 1989.

Van Alstyne, William W. Does Article V Restrict the States to Calling Unlimited Conventions Only?—A Letter to a Colleague. *Duke Law Journal*, 27 (1978): 1295–1306.

Veit, Helen E., Kenneth R. Bowling and Charlene Bangs Bickford (eds.). *Creating the Bill of Rights: The Documentary Record from the First Federal Congress*. Baltimore, MD: John Hopkins University Press, 1991.

Vile, John R., William D. Pederson and Frank J. Williams (eds.). *James Madison: Philosopher, Founder, and Statesman*. Athens: Ohio University Press, 2008.

Warren, Charles. *The Making of the Constitution*. Boston, MA: Little, Brown and Company, 1928; reprinted: Littleton, CO: Fred B. Rothman, 1993.

Washington, George. *The Papers of George Washington, Confederation Series*. Dorothy Twohig et al. (eds.). 6 vols. Charlottesville: University Press of Virginia, 1987.

Wechsler, Herbert. *Principles, Politics, and Fundamental Law*. Cambridge, MA: Harvard University Press, 1961.

White, G. Edward. *The Constitution and the New Deal*. Cambridge, MA: Harvard University Press, 2000.

Whittington, Keith E. *Constitutional Interpretation: Textual Meaning, Original Intent, and Judicial Review*. Lawrence: University Press of Kansas, 1999.

Wills, Garry. *Explaining America: Inventing America: Jefferson's Declaration of Independence*. London: Athlone, 1980.

Wills, Garry. *The Federalist*. London: Athlone Press, 1981.

Winston, Alexander. Firebrand of the Revolution. *American Heritage Magazine* (April 1967).

Wood, Gordon S. *The Creation of the American Republic, 1776–1787*. New York: W.W. Norton, 1969.

Wood, Gordon S. *The Confederation and the Constitution: The Critical Issues*. Lanham, MD: University Press of America, 1973.

Wood, Gordon S. Democracy and the Constitution. In: Robert A. Goldwin and William A. Schambra (eds.). *How Democratic Is the Constitution?* Washington, DC: American Enterprise Institute, 1980, 1–17.

Wood, Gordon S. *Revolutionary Characters: What Made the Founders Different*. New York: Penguin Press, 2006.

Wood, Gordon S. *Empire of Liberty: A History of the Early Republic, 1789–1815*. Oxford: Oxford University Press, 2009.

York, Neil L. (ed.). *Toward a More Perfect Union: Six Essays on the Constitution*. Provo, UT: Brigham Young University, 1988.

Zuckert, Michael P. Federalism and the Founding: Toward A Reinterpretation of the Constitutional Convention. *Review of Politics*, 48 (1986): 166–210.

INDEX

A

Ackerman, Bruce: on John Adams'search for peace, 226n.35
Adams, John: lauds Constitution as creating nation, vi, 23, 130; becomes President by defeating Jefferson in 1796 election, 215; succeeds in avoiding war, but loses 1800 election, 215–217
Adams, Samuel, 7; critical role in securing Massachusetts ratification, with bill of rights to follow adoption of Constitution, 129–134; seeks Article II amendment as alternative to bill of rights, 131, 132, 197; relies on judicial review to forestall federal expansionism, 132
Alien and Sedition laws: adopted by Federalists to forestall U.S. involvement in Napoleonic war, 215; condemned by Antifederalists and exploited as campaign issue in 1800 election, 215–216
Amar, Akhill Reed: on Tenth Amendment, 82n.77; on second constitutional convention, 191n.36
Amending Constitution: formulation of provision, 72–76; convention method of amendment worries Madison, 73–75; and 1970's debate over restricted or open-ended agenda for convention, 190n.2
American nation: product of Constitution reversing primacy of states, xvi–xvii, 75; and Antifederalist diehards' drive to restore state sovereignty, xvii, 197–198; and Madison's success in preserving national paramountcy, xvii–xviii, 173–174, 198–199
Anarchy: fear of, sparked by Shays' Rebellion, 21, 152n.11; danger of, if Constitution falls, 7, 18, 21, 37, 96, 156n.68, 189; Randolph favors Virginia ratification, since alternative would be calamitous, 134
Annapolis Convention 1786: background, 19–20; proposes 1787 Philadelphia convention, 20
Antifederalists: diehards' aim to defeat ratification of Constitution, 106–107, 108–110, 119; charge that implied powers doctrine threatens state sovereignty, 105; demand bill of rights or Article II provision, 105, 111–112; dismiss Wilson's thesis on superfluity of bill of rights, 108–110, 117–119; Madison's strategy of wooing moderates by offering mild bill of

rights, xvii–xix, 94–95, 97–98, 107, 119, 132, 136–137, 140, 141, 173–174, 198–199
Antifederalist ideology: in ratification contests, Chapter 6, 105–125; in Democratic-Republican Party, 214–215, 217–218; *see also* Madison, about-turn
Appointments: joint involvement of President and Senate, but unlike treaties, 41–49
Armstrong, John, 160n.119
Article V of Constitution. *See* Amending Constitution
Articles of Confederation, 88; state over nation, difficulty in formulation, 4; unanimity requirement, 6; reasons for failure, xvi–xviii, 1–4; proposals for reform, 4–6, 8–9, 16, 19, 23–26; abandonment of reform, 9–10, 15–17; Article II preserving state sovereignty, xvi, 72, 92; absence of Article II in Constitution, deplored, 111, 112, 119; attempts to insert, rejected, 159n.114, 185, 197

B

Bailey v. Drexel Furniture Co., as epitome of dual federalism doctrine, 221
Bailyn, Bernard: on Virginia Plan as creating a "*Machstaat*", 33; on slavery as northern concession to preserve Union, 39; deems Massachusetts ratification "decisive turning point in adoption of Constitution", 133, 151n.1; wonders how views of Antifederalists can be used to interpret constitution they opposed, 208
Bank of United States, 17; Hamilton submits proposal to Congress, 206; background, 206–207; Madison objects, 207–209; *McCulloch v Maryland* validates, 213–214

Barron v. Baltimore, 186
Baylies, Francis, 152n.11
Beard, Charles, 12n.23; economic thesis refuted, 200–201
Bedford, Gunning: warns larger states to concede equality in one House, 35, 36; proposes expansion of federal power, 63–64; criticizes legislative veto, 68
Bilder, Mary Sarah, xxn.5
Bill of Rights: omission from Constitution decried by dissenters at Philadelphia, 85–86, 95; primary demand of Antifederalists in ratification debates, 105–110; necessity of, reluctantly accepted by Madison, 140–142; Massachusetts' consent to post-ratification adoption of, 140–142; Madison's rejection of proposals to revise nation-state formula, 142, 164–165; adoption of, as accident of history, 204n.29; Antifederalist criticism of lack of structural changes in Constitution, 195–198
Blair, John, member of Virginian delegation at Constitutional Convention, 32
Bland, Theodorick, 96; submitted Virginia's application for second constitutional convention, 182
Bonaparte, Napoleon: offer to sell Louisiana territory to United States, 217
Bowling, Kenneth R., 174
Brearley Committee on Unfinished Parts: formulates Electoral College provision, 40–41; raises majority required in Senate for treaties to two-thirds, 46
Bricker Amendment: 1950s' movement to prevent using treaty power to override Constitution, 125n.71
Breckinridge, James: compares Madison's arguments to Henry's eloquence, 157n.82
Brutus: on essentiality of bill of rights, 116, 117; critical of supremacy

clause, 122n.18; Robert Yates' authorship doubted, 98, 160n.124
Burnett, Edmund C.: credits Hamilton with initiating 1787 Constitutional Convention, 18
Butler, Pierce: South Carolina delegate, opposed unlimited power of national government, 61–62
Bryan, Samuel: author of Antifederalist *Centinel* series, 106, 107, 114, 117
Burke, Aedanus, 196

C
Carrington, Edward, 17; on Federalist strategy on ratifications, 120n.4, 151n.4; on Massachusetts ratification as most important event in American history, 127; on Henry's aim to defeat the Constitution, 136; that Virginian ratification meant the United States had a government, 142
"Cassius II": argues that bill of rights unnecessary and dangerous, 122n.20
"Centinel": *see* Bryan, Samuel
Chase, Samuel: alias CAUTION, warns Maryland against attempt to stampede ratification, 120n.4
Child labor: *see Hammer v. Dagenhart*
Choper, Jesse: representation in national institutions protects states' interests, 49
Clinton, George, Governor of New York, 19; early proponent, and later opponent, of greater federal power, 6–9; fought against New York's ratification of Constitution, 145–146
Coercion of states: proposed by 1781 Hartford Convention, 4–5; endorsed by Madison, 5
Collins, John, Governor of Rhode Island, 203n.20
Committee of Detail, 89; composition and pattern of operation, 64–66,
79n.33; enumeration of congressional powers, unilaterally determined by, 64–66; criticized by Hueston for disregarding Plenary instructions and weakening Congress, 65; on addition of necessary and proper clause, 73; on convention method for adopting amendments, 73–74
Committee of the Whole, 33, 68, 54n.53; endorses Article 6 of Virginia Plan, 61; rejects legislative veto, 67–68
Confederacy, 4, 27, 51n.6, 88, 181; malaise affecting, 22
Congress, U.S.: role of federalism in creation of, xv–xviii, 33–39; defining powers, 59–66; Madison for heads of power, 61; slave states and enumeration of powers, 61–66
Connecticut Compromise: resolves Convention deadlock and introduces federalism into Constitution, 34–36, 40–41, 43, 62
Consolidation: in planning for Convention, Madison rules out as impractical, 26; at Convention, Mason, Gerry, and Randolph alarmed by scope of federal power, 91, 95; Henry charges Constitution creates American, hence consolidated, government, 137; Madison's response, 138; with adoption of Bill of Rights criticism muted; *see also* Antifederalists; implied powers, 73, 105, 119
Constitution of U.S.: enters into force with ratification of ninth state, New Hampshire, 209
Constitutional Convention 1787: formulation of new constitution contra directives of Congress and states, 22, 136; smaller states' demand for equality federalizes

nationalist scheme, 33–39, 71–72; nation over state within federal framework, 39–49

Constitutional interpretation: subject of Jefferson-Hamilton debate, 210–212; Washington opts for broad interpretation, 212; Madison's thesis questioned, 205–210; C.J. Marshall adopts Hamilton argument, 213–214; New Federalism reopens issue, 222

Constitutional flexibility: absent in Articles of Confederation, 3–4, 9–10; confirmed in Constitution by necessary and proper clause or formal amendment, 72–75; necessity of, expounded upon in *Federalist* and Virginia ratification convention, 139; Madison's concern over convention method of amending Constitution, 74–75; Madison's turn-about restricts flexibility, 217–218

Conventions, *see* State Conventions for Amendments

Continentalist, The: articles by Hamilton calling for strengthening Articles of Confederation, 18

Corbin, Francis: comment on Randolph's meanderings, 181

Cornell, Saul, 121n.15; on Madison's Report of 1800, 218; on obsolescence of *McCulloch v. Maryland*, 219; on New Deal as temporary anomaly in American politics, 219; on Antifederalists as cofounders of Constitution, 219

Corwin, Edward, S.: on passing of Dual Federalism, 222, 227n.48

Coxe, Tench: fears Antifederalist domination of Congress unless Madison elected, 176n.16

Cumberland Road Bill: vetoed by President Monroe, 217

Cutting, John Brown: on Madison's ability to overcome Henry's rhetoric, 157n.83

D

Davie, William Richardson: North Carolina delegate; on states' insistence that Senate, as agency of states, be accorded role on treaties, 46; strove to introduce Article II amendment, 197

Day, William R., Supreme Court Justice: author of *Hammer v. Dagenhart*, 221; misquoted Tenth Amendment by adding "expressly", 221

Dayton, Jonathan, 38

Delaware, 209; first state to ratify Constitution, 127

"A Democratic Federalist", 111

Democratic-Republican Party: launched by Madison and Jefferson, 214–218

DePauw, Linda Grant, 174

Dickinson, John: warns Madison against pressing Virginia Plan on smaller states, 35

Donald, Alexander, 159n.97

Dual Federalism, xix, 221–222

Duane, James, 36; solicits letter from Hamilton on how to remedy U.S. political system, 15

Dumbauld, Edward: on Madison's struggle for a bill of rights due to apathy of colleagues, 186, 201

E

Elkins, Stanley and McKitrick, Erick: authors of The *Age of Federalism*, 207, 216

Electoral College: concession to small and slave states, xvi, 39–41

Elliot, Jonathan, 147

Ellis, Richard: on Civil War as confirming national dominance, 204n.29; on absorption of Antifederalists into Democratic Republican party, 225n.31

Ellsworth, Oliver, Connecticut delegate: member of Committee of Detail, 64; objects to legislative veto, 70; favors coercion of law on individuals, 77n.3

Energy, need for, in Government, 15–16, 18, 21, 25, 27
Epstein, David, 122n.18; on Wilson's thesis, 123n.37
Europeanization, danger of, 19; large states arguments, 34–36; small states response, 35–36; significance of debate analyzed by Peter Onuf, 36–37
Eve, George: Baptist minister to whom Madison wrote favoring a bill of rights, 166–167
Executive: selection of; *see* Electoral College
Export taxes: banning of, as part of north-south agreement, 47

F

Fairfax Resolves: drafted by Mason in 1774, enumerating complaints against British, 86, 90
Farrand, Max: editor of minutes of Constitutional Convention, 39, 65, 89
Federal Convention 1787: *see* Constitutional Convention
A Federal Farmer: describes how tax power can pose threat to freedom of speech and press, 115
Federal power: formulation of, 59–66
Federalism: purposely excluded from Virginia Plan, 32–33; imposed on larger states by small state-slave state alliance, xv–xviii, 32, 36, 39, 49, 78; reflected in formation of all branches of government, 49, 71–73
Federalism thesis of Wechsler, Choper, and Kramer: on securing state interests primarily by state participation in national governmental bodies, rather than by judicial review, 49–51
Federalist Papers: xv-xvi, 19, 31, 77, 173; #14, vii; #15, 1–2; #6 and #7, 143–144; #10 and #51, 170, 177n.39, 41; #38, 155n.55; #43, 75; #44, 139, 157–158n.86, 207; #84, 108, 122n.64
Federalist Party: victor in 1796; suffers eclipse in 1800 election, leading to dissolution of party, 216–217
Federalist Revolution: movement promoting convening of 1787 conclave to formulate new constitution, 199, 202, 222; debate over date of termination, 202n.2
Finkelman, Paul, 174; details northern concessions on slavery, 38–39; on Antifederalists as opponents of Constitution, 219
Foreign relations: state neglect of treaty obligations, 23; freedom of passage on Mississippi, 24, 140; Adams' avoidance of war with either England or France, 215–216
Founding Fathers: desire strong national government that would dominate states completely, xvi, 32–33; nationalist scheme frustrated by joint demands of smaller states and slave states, 34–36
Franklin, Benjamin: endorses motion for second convention, 180; proposes that Congress have power to cut canals, 224n.5; calls on all delegates to sign completed Constitution, 95–96
Freedom of the press, 114–116, 215
French Revolution, 215

G

de Gardoqui, Diego, 24
Georgia: insisted on preservation of slave trade, 38; endorses compromise for abandoning navigation laws in return for twenty more years of slave trade, 89
Gerry, Elbridge, Massachusetts delegate, 44, 198; background, 91–93; republican but critical of democracy, 91–92; primary concern to restrict exercise of power, 92–93; fearful of standing

army, 92, 101n.44; proposal for bill of rights to be included in Constitution fails, 85; one of three who refuse to sign Constitution, 95–96

Goldwin, Robert A.: reveals how Madison used Bill of Rights to save Constitution, 174; notes widely held wrong belief that Tenth Amendment limits federal government to "express powers,", 199, 221

Gorham, Nathaniel (*also* Ghorum), Massachusetts delegate, 62, 152n.11

Grayson, William: ally of Henry in opposing ratification, 134; selected as Senator over Madison, 166; promotes amendments for substantive revisions in Constitution, 196

Great Compromise: *see* Connecticut Compromise

Gunther, Gerald: authored works revealing that Marshall anonymously published series of articles defending *McCulloch* decision, 225n.27

H

Hamilton, Alexander: background, 15–16, 97, 146, 148, 149, 201; outlines scheme to strengthen Confederal government, 15–17; warns against Europeanization, 36, 143–144; enunciates doctrine of implied powers, 17, 19; first to propose constitutional convention to replace Articles, 15–19; as solitary New York delegate at Constitutional Convention unable to vote, 97; initiates Federalist Papers, 143–144; campaigns vigorously to secure New York ratification, 146; contends that Constitution itself best bill of rights, 148; as Secretary of Treasury, institutes national bank, 206–207; debates Jefferson on need for broad interpretation of Constitution, 210–212; thesis accepted by Washington and Marshall, 212–214; sharply criticizes John Adams as president, thereby contributing to his failed re-election bid in 1800, 216

Hammer v. Dagenhart: as epitome of dual federalism doctrin, 221

Hancock, John, Governor of Massachusetts: background, 130; persuaded to accept formula for bill of rights to follow ratification, 7, 130–131; succeeds in swinging majority to endorse ratification, 131; Massachusetts vote as real turning point in ratification of Constitution, 133

Harrison, Benjamin, Governor of Virginia: obdurate in passport controversy, 3

Hartford Convention 1780: proposes use of force against states failing to pay requisitions, 4–5

Henkin, Louis: on different Senate vote for appointments and treaties, 54n.50; on Bricker amendment, 125n.71

Henry, Patrick, 6, 20, 117, 146, 198, 199; as states' righter, opposes ratification of Constitution, 119, 134–135; charges Constitutional Convention with exceeding authority, 136; debates Madison on impact of "sweeping clause", 139; charges that government under Constitution is not a Virginian, but an American, hence consolidated, government, 137; demands Article II provision or bill of rights prior to ratification, 137, 141; warns that implied powers would enable federal government to free slaves, 114, 141; favors reinstatement of requisitions, 137; vigorously promotes second constitutional convention, 164–165; conspires to limit Virginia's congressional representation to Antifederalists, 165–166; succeeds in keeping Madison out of Senate, 166; gerrymanders Madison's congressional district and induces Monroe to run against him, 166

Hobson, Charles: on National Legislative Veto, 80n.44; comment on wording of Tenth Amendment, 192n.48; deems Bill of Rights an accident of history, 204n.29

Holmes, Oliver Wendell, Supreme Court Justice: on supremacy clause, 200

Howell, David: explains Rhode Island's refusal to support 1781 impost, 6

Hueston, John C.: charges Committee of Detail with deliberately weakening federal power, 65–66; Rutledge, Committee chairman, aimed to protect slavery from federal intervention, 65–66

I

Imperia in imperio: [divided government], 76

Implied powers doctrine: not part of Articles of Confederation, 3, 10; Hamilton, Madison, Jefferson, claim doctrine implicit under Articles of Confederation, 16–17; in Constitution under necessary and proper clause, xvi–xviii, 66, 73, 75, 96–97, 105, 198, 199, 200, 213; Antifederalists charge that doctrine endangers state sovereignty, 105, 112, 117–119; focus of dispute between Federalists and Antifederalistis in ratification contests, 96–97, 117–119, 139; Madison declares doctrine axiomatic in every grant of power, 10, 105, 117–119; Antifederalist complaint remedied by adoption of bill of rights, 198–199; after ratification, Madison and Jefferson demand narrow interpretation, 207–208, 210–211; Hamilton presents broad interpretation, 211–212; Washington, accepting Hamilton interpretation, signs bank bill, 212; Marshall, in *McCulloch v. Maryland*, confirms doctrine as inherent element in Constitution, 213–214

Impost proposals: 1781, 1783, 5–9

J

Jackson, Andrew: on right of executive to reject *McCulloch v. Maryland*, 217; on vetoing domestic improvement schemes, 217–218; on quashing South Carolina's nullification drive, 218

Jarvis, Charles: nominal Federalist, favors clause limiting Congress to express powers, 197

Jay, John: Secretary for Foreign Affairs, 146, 148, 201; views Shays' Rebellion as serious threat to stable government, 22; deplores state violations of treaties, 23, 29n.37; on Mississippi negotiations, 24; contributes to *Federalist*, 143; leads campaign for New York to ratify, 146; drafts round-robin urging states to petition Congress to summon second convention, 150–151

Jay Treaty: Washington denies background papers to House of Representatives, 49; subject of dispute between Hamilton-Washington and Jefferson-Madison, 215

Jefferson, Thomas, 6, 20; endorses implied powers doctrine, 17; unusual comment on Shays' Rebellion, 186; dismisses Wilson's thesis, 111; contends that people entitled to bill of rights against every government, 111; initially favors withholding ratification until bill of rights enacted, 140; later endorses ratification of Constitution with bill of rights to follow, 159n.99; retreats from endorsing Article II provision, 159n.99; debates Hamilton on implied powers doctrine, 210–212; organizes Democratic-Republican opposition party, 214–216; Kentucky Resolution interposition implies right of secession, 215; as President equivocates over Louisiana Purchase, 217

Jeffersonian era: as reflection of Antifederalist ideology, 217–218

Jensen, Merrill: maintains Articles of Confederation were operating successfully, 12n.23; contends Constitutional Convention a *coup d'etat* by nationalist aristocrats, 12n.23; labels Bill of Rights as expedience of "eighteenth century politics", 204n.29; his socio-economic view unsupported by published record, 200

Johnson, Calvin H.: on Antifederalists as opponents, not "Other Founders," of the Constitution, 219

Jones, Samuel: moves that New York ratify Constitution, 150

Judiciary, national: with rejection of National Legislative Veto, becomes umpire of federal-state equation, 71–72

Judicial review: essentiality of, to protect rights, 71–72, 118–119

Jury trial: omitted from Constitution in civil cases, 106; Wilson justifies, 109; Jefferson dismisses Wilson argument, 123n.36

K

Kaminski, John, 8; confirms lack of bill of rights as most important ratification issue, 121n.15

Kasavan, Vasan, and Paulsen, Michael Stokes: Virginia Antifederalist arguments irrelevant for interpreting Constitution, 210

Kentucky: targeted by Henry over vulnerability of Mississippi River, 140

Kentucky Resolution: drafted by Jefferson, imperils Union by implying that state secession valid, 215

Killenbeck, Mark: author of works, *M; Culloch v.Maryland*; and *The Tenth Amendment*, 224n.5, 225n.27

King, Rufus, Massachusetts delegate, a leading Federalist: engineered deal with Hancock at state ratifying convention, 130; sharply critical of slavery, 37; but voted for continuance of slave trade, 83; dismisses New York vote on ratification as irrelevant, 145; on federal power of incorporation, 224n.5; as Senator, voted for Bank of United States, 224n.5

Knox, Henry (General): message on Shays' Rebellion alarms Washington, 21

Koch, Adrienne: contrasts Jefferson's view of Shays' Rebellion with those of Madison, 172–173

Kramer, Larry D.: joins Wechsler and Choper in arguing that state representation in federal government is primary safeguard of states' interests, 50–51

L

Langdon, John, New Hampshire delegate: dismisses national legislative veto, 70

Lansing, John, New York delegate, 97, 146, 148, 149, 150; quits Convention because it aims to create consolidated government, 97; opposes New York ratification, 146–148; his proposal for conditional

ratification found unacceptable, 149–150; assists Jay in formulating round-robin for second constitutional convention, 150–151
Lee, Henry: diverse opinions on adoption of Constitution, 155n.56; on Henry's raising Mississippi issue at Virginia convention, 158n.95
Lee, Richard Henry: Antifederalist, 19; opposes granting powers to Confederation, 6–7; declines to attend Constitutional Convention, 6; selected as Senator, 166; fears national consolidation, 196; decries Madison's Bill of Rights, 196
Legislative veto: Madison's scheme to allow Congress to veto all state legislation. *See* National legislative veto
Levy, Leonard W.: on necessary and proper clause as leading to Bill of Rights, 73, 105; on Madison's promoting bill of rights to defeat second convention movement, 173–174; on Bill of Rights as accident of history, 173–174, 204n.29
Lim, Elvin T.: presents novel thesis that America experienced two foundings, 226n.44
Livermore, Samuel: Antifederalist, decries Bill of Rights as worth no more "than a pinch of snuff", 196
Livingston, Gilbert, 149
Livingston, Robert R, Chancellor of New York: urges delegates to vote to join national union, 146, 148
Lofgren, Charles A.: on role of judiciary in national system, 81n.63; on Bricker amendment, 125n.71
Louisiana Purchase: Jefferson's equivocation over the offer, 217

M
McClurg, James, Virginia delegate, 32
McCulloch v. Maryland: adoption of Constitution confirms formation of American nation, 219; United States as a sovereign power, 220–221; on implied powers, 219; on right of federal government to create bank, 219–220
on federal supremacy, 220
McDowell, Gary L.: on Richard Henry Lee and search for constitutional liberty, 13n.33
McKean, Thomas, Justice: employs Wilson's thesis to reject Antifederalist demand for bill of rights, 110
McLaughlin, Andrew C.: on failure of Confederacy, 2–3
Madison, James, 149, 198; as nationalist, xv; advocates use of force against delinquent Confederal states, 4–5; endorses implied powers doctrine, 5, 9–10; reaction to Shays' Rebellion and disarray in America's foreign relations, 22–24; prepares two studies, Ancient & Modern Confederacies and Vices of U.S. Political System, 24–25; draws conclusions about necessity of national paramountcy, 24–27; authors Virginia Plan for establishing powerful central government able to veto state legislation, 25–26; dismisses southern objections to national powers under Virginia Plan, 61; presents sectionalist argument, 5; regards Convention as failure for rejecting legislative veto, 76–77; opposes all attempts to qualify ratification with conditions, 148; succeeds in deflecting Henry's

rhetoric, 157n.82, 83; rejects Henry's claim that implied powers threaten rights of states and individuals, 139; rejects clause limiting federal government to express powers, 142, 198; in *Federalist* writes on extended republic and on axiomatic nature of implied powers, 139, 169–173, 186; appalled by New York's call for second constitutional convention, xvii, 163–164; analyzes motives of promoters of second constitutional convention, 163–165; accepts need for bill of rights, 168, 173–174, 202; defeats Monroe in race for Congress, 168; succeeds in separating mild critics from diehards, 186, 189; explains urgency for Congress to endorse draft bill of rights, 182, 186–188; enumerates draft bill of rights, 182, 185; rejects all attempts to limit Congress to express powers, 139, 142, 198; as Father of Bill of Rights earns title of Father of Constitution, xviii, 195; as Prime Minister for Washington, pressures Congress to approve draft bill of rights, 181–182; initially hesitant, but later endorses judicial review, 157n.86, 185–186

Madison about-turn: surprises Washington and erstwhile colleagues, xix, 205–207; opposes bank bill with Antifederalist arguments, 206–210; empty vessel thesis, that Constitution to be filled by Antifederalist interpretations from ratification conventions, 208–210; thesis lacks historical basis, 208–210; thesis demolished by *McCulloch v. Maryland*, 212–214; joins Jefferson in creating Democratic-Republican party, 214–216; as President, vetoes bill for national improvements, 217

Madison-Jefferson correspondence: on implied powers, 5; on National Legislative veto, 25–26; on bill of rights, 168–171; on judicial review, 168–173; on Constitution as failure to secure effective national government, 76–77

Maier, Pauline, 120n.3, 151n.1; on Martin, Lansing, Yates, 99; on Martin, 102n.84

Main, Jackson Turner: on New York's refusal to endorse impost, 8

Marshall, John, Chief Justice: sustains Hamilton's broad interpretation of Constitution and confirms doctrine of implied powers in *McCulloch v. Maryland*, 213–214

Martin, Luther, Maryland delegate: states' rightist, opposes national powers, 98; opposes National Legislative Veto, 69; authors supremacy clause, 69; quits Constitutional Convention, 98; in lengthy diatribe, opposes Maryland ratification, 98

Maryland: withholds ratification of Articles, 4; ratifies Constitution overwhelmingly, 98–99

Mason, Alpheus Thomas: Antifederalists awakened only slowly to consolidating tendency of Constitution, 99n.1; Jefferson's Kentucky Resolution imperiled the Union, 215; on danger of current Antifederalist drive to turn clock back, 227n.55

Mason, George, Virginia delegate: background, 70, 85–86, 146, 199; slave owner, with liberal and democratic ideas, 86–87; condemns slavery, 37, 89–90; insists on two-thirds vote for navigation (trade) laws, 89–91; outraged by agreement to permit slave trade in return for cancellation of navigation restriction, 90–91; raises issue of bill of rights, 85, 91, 95; refuses to sign Constitution, 95; recommends second convention, 95, 97; though allied with Henry, opposes undermining Union, 155n.57; insists that states be able to initiate amendments, 83n.90; Madison's draft bill of rights reconciles him to Constitution, 199

Massachusetts: alarmed by Shays' Rebellion, 20–21; need recognized for powerful central government, 21; Federalist strategy to secure state ratification, 129; support of Governor Hancock and Samuel Adams crucial, 129–133; state convention ratifies without requiring prior bill of rights, 133–134; pattern of ratification, with later amendments, saves Constitution, 133–134

Mississippi River Debate: freedom of navigation for U.S. vessels jeopardized, 24; issue raised by Henry at Virginia convention, 140

Mitchell, James: member of committee to study ways to implement Confederal decisions, 5

Monroe, James: veteran and Antifederalist, 166; joins Henry at Virginia convention in reporting on Mississippi River proposal, 140; claims that national taxing power not needed, tends "to anarchy", 156n.68; condemns necessary and proper clause for lack of "limits", 112; insists on bill of rights or Article II amendment, 112, 197; induced by Henry to run for Congress against Madison, 166; as President, vetoes domestic development schemes, 217

Morris, Gouverneur, Pennsylvania delegate, 63; condemns state sovereignty, xvi; opposes small state demands for equality, 34–36; severely condemns slavery and objects to three-fifths rule, 37–38; opposes federalism, 35–36; favors national domination of states, 34–35; criticizes National Legislative veto, 68–69; on Massachusetts ratification, as turning point in creating nation, 127

Morris, Robert, Pennsylvania delegate: as Confederation Superintendent of Finance, requested charter for national bank, 28n.10; Madison objection that Articles did not permit it, 28n.10

Mount Vernon 1785 conference: Virginia and Maryland agreement on waterways, 19

Murrin, John H: on passport issue, 3

N

Nation over State: goal of Federalist Revolution, xvii–xix, 189, 199–202

National bank: *see* Bank of United States

National legislature: *see Congress, U.S.*

National Legislative Veto, xviii; Madison's key proposal for national domination of states; in pre-Convention correspondence, 25–26, 66–68; modified in Virginia caucus, 67; practical difficulties of veto, 68–70; veto totally rejected by Convention, 69–72; Madison deems omission fatal to national authority, 76–77

Navigation (trade) laws: over Mason's objections, simple majority fixed for all laws, 89–91; major factor in Mason's refusal to sign Constitution, 95

Necessary and proper clause: basis of implied powers, xvi–xvii, 66; Wilson, probable author, 82n.76; central issue in ratification contest, 139; deemed by Madison in *Federalist # 44* as implicit in every grant of power, 139, 199–200

Necessary and Proper clause combined with supremacy clause: Antifederalist argument that joint operation could impose national consolidation, xvi–xvii, 117–119, 147; Madison's response, xvii, 138–139

New Deal: reflection of federal supremacy, as per *McCulloch v. Maryland*, 222

New England states: compromise with slave states in return for cancellation of navigation laws, 45–47, 89–91

New Federalism, xviii–xix, 221–223

New Hampshire: ninth state to ratify, bringing Constitution into force between ratifying states, 230

New Jersey: sponsor of small states New Jersey Plan, based on state equality, 34

New York: supports impost and then retracts, 7–9; departure of Yates and Lansing from Convention deprives New York of vote, 97; Antifederalist stronghold under Clinton, 143; confronts dilemma of ratification when Constitution already in force, 148; falls into line and ratifies by narrow margin, 150; ratification seals Federalist triumph of adoption of Constitution, 150; round robin letter for second constitutional convention, as price of New York victory, 150–151

New York City: hints that it might secede from state if ratification rejected, 149

Newfoundland fisheries: factor for two-thirds requirement in Senate for treaties, 47

Nicholas, George: describes Patrick Henry as "enemy" to Union, 155n.57

North Carolina: declines to ratify Constitution until Congress adopts draft bill of rights, 164

O

Old Whig: treaty power threatens rights, 116; judicial review essential to protect rights, 118; necessity of bill of rights, 118

Onuf, Peter: on provisional character of Articles of Confederation, 4; on danger of Europeanization of American scene, 36–37; on views of Luther Martin, 98; on Maryland ratification, 99

P

Page, John, Congressman: warns colleagues they must act on bill of rights, 184

Passports: issue in dispute between Confederal Congress and Governor of Virginia, 3

Paterson, William, New Jersey delegate: presents New Jersey Plan to Plenum, 34

Pendleton, Edmund, 27, 28n.10, 164, 170; serves as President of Virginia Ratifying convention, 136; congratulates Madison on early adoption of draft bill of rights, 188–189

Pennsylvania: Federalists employ overbearing tactics to schedule early ratification convention, 106; absenting representatives publish opposing *Address*, 106–107;

Wilson's thesis in response to *Address*, 108–109
Peters, Richard: Madison's letter explains urgency for draft bill of rights, 182, 186–188
Philadelphia Convention: *see* Constitutional Convention
Pierce, William: Georgia delegate, 78n.9, 98, 160n.124
Pinckney, Charles, South Carolina delegate: attributed failure of Articles to the unanimity requirement, 1; advises giving equal vote to smaller states and they will support system, 31; praises larger states for accepting Connecticut Compromise, 36; supported Madison's absolute legislative veto scheme, 70, 90; favored two-thirds vote for navigation laws, 90; opposed second constitutional convention scheme, 180
Pinckney, Charles Cotesworth (General), South Carolina delegate, 62, 63; highlights large state concession to save Union, 36; claims that Constitution does not enable federal government to interfere with slavery, 66
Pinckney Plan, submitted May 29, but did not emerge as a major factor in the deliberations, 79n.33

Q

Quincy, Josiah: describes the events at the Massachusetts ratifying convention, 153n.29

R

Rahe, Paul A., on impact of Shays' Rebellion, 23
Rakove, Jack N.: rejects view that the President was expected to be agent of Senate on treaties, 55n.84; accepts that enumeration of congressional powers intended from beginning, 79n.34; Madison shaken by Jefferson's view of Shays' rebellion, 178n.55; questions Madison's claim that Antifederalist criticism of Constitution could serve as basis for interpretation, 225n.17
Randolph, Edmund, Governor of Virginia, former Attorney-General: on passport issue, 3; presents Virginia Plan to Convention, 32–33; acknowledges large state retreat on equality in one House, 36; denies granting national government unlimited power, 61, 64; explanation for his retreat from Federalist position, 96; refuses to sign completed Constitution, 94–96; fears scope of necessary and proper clause, 96–97; even after ratification, favors second constitutional convention, 95, 97, 179; critical help to Madison to secure Virginia ratification, 181; fears anarchy from breakup of Union if Constitution rejected, 134, 137, 156n.76
Ratification of Constitution: entry into force upon ratification by nine states as per Article VII; Federalists' strategy to build up momentum and thus compel larger states to ratify, 127; smaller states hasten to ratify, 127–128; fate of Union in hand of three large states, 128; key issue is whether bill of rights to precede or follow ratification, 128; Massachusetts sets precedent with unqualified ratification, bill of rights to follow, 133–134; Virginia adheres to precedent, 141–142; New York left with no viable alternative, 150–151
Rehnquist, William H., Chief Justice: instituted New Federalism that seeks to protect state sovereignty, 222;

premises of New Federalism doctrine, questioned, 222–223

"A Republican": notes that federal copyright power could be used to threaten freedom of the press, 115

"A Republican Federalist": labels necessary and proper clause an "omnipotent" provision, 117

Requisitions: oft unfulfilled under Articles of Confederation, 1; Henry argues for requisitions in the first instance, 137; dismissed by Madison as a nullity, 140

Reserved powers clause: *see* Tenth Amendment

Rhode Island: opposes 1781 impost, 6; labeled as "shameless prostitute" state, 143; referendum votes down ratification, 164; condition ratification on adoption of bill of rights, 179

Rossiter, Clinton: describes Article 6 of Virginia Plan as "too large a dose of nationalism", 77

Rossum, Ralph A.: notes that Madison, in presenting rights, never argued for them in his own name, 192n.53

Rush, Benjamin: distinguishes between American war and American Revolution, 1; warmly supports exclusion of bill of rights from Constitution, 110

Rutland, Robert: failure of Federalists to include bill of rights in Constitution imperiled ratification, 99n.1, 107; rejects thesis that Bill of Rights was accident of history, 204n.29

Rutledge, John (*also* Rutlidge), South Carolina delegate: issues ultimatum that larger states must concede equality in one house, 36; insists on enumeration of powers of Congress, 61–62; chairman of Committee of Detail that delimits federal powers, 64–65; rejects legislative veto, 70

S

Schuyler, Philip: father-in-law and political ally of Hamilton, 18

Second constitutional convention movement, 142, 144; initiated by Randolph's motion at end of Philadelphia meeting, 95; supported by Mason and Gerry, but unanimously rejected, 95, 97; proposal revived by New York round robin to other states, 150; Madison appalled by proposal which could wreck Constitution, 163–165; Madison's strategy, to undercut movement by hastening bill of rights through Congress, 165; plan dependent on securing Federalist majority in Congress and election of Madison, 165; Henry strives to defeat Madison by drafting James Monroe as counter-candidate, 166; by stressing his endorsement of bill of rights, Madison prevails, 173–175; Madison strategy succeeds and the second convention movement defeated, 202

Sedition Law: *see* Alien and Sedition laws

Senate: role of federalism in formation of, 33–39; equal state representation federalizes Constitution, 37, 49; "advice and consent" of, on appointments and treaties, as products of federalism, 41–49

Shays, Daniel (Captain): led Massachusetts farmers to prevent courts from issuing eviction notices, 20

Shays' Rebellion: widely regarded as breakdown of authority; stimulates calls for new constitution to maintain law and order, 20–23; reaction of George Washington, 21

Sherman, Roger, Connecticut delegate: opposes slave trade but accepts agreement with deep south, 38; seeks clear line separating national from state powers, 63, 65; opposes legislative veto, 68–69; House accepts his proposal to keep bill of rights amendments as one corpus, 185

Slave states: secure two-thirds rule in lower house representation, 37–39; reject popular election of executive, 40; object to Virginia Plan's Article 6, granting absolute authority to national government, 49–64; succeed in securing enumeration of national powers, 64–66

Slave trade: in return for modification of navigation laws, import of slaves permitted until 1808, 38; critical factor in Mason's opposition to Constitution, 89–91

Slavery: condemned by northern delegates, but accepted to preserve Union, 37–39

Smaller states: secured a role in each branch of government: in Congress by equality in Senate; in Executive, by Electoral College; and in Judiciary, by advice and consent of Senate, 49, 75

Smith, Melancton: leader of Antifederalists at New York ratification convention, 146; committed to preserving Union and more reasonable than diehard colleague, Lansing, 146–147; proposal for conditional ratification rejected, 147–148; concern regarding survival of state independence, 147; supports unconditional ratification, 150; helps in formulation of round-robin, 150

South Carolina: and enumeration of congressional powers. *See also* Hueston, 61–65

Sovereignty: of states; under Articles of Confederation, 3–4, 16–17; of nation, under Constitution, 16–18, 25–27, 211, 212, 213–214

Spencer, Samuel, 197–198

State conventions for Amendments: debate over limiting agenda to one topic, 190n.2

State over Nation: basic thesis of Articles of Confederation, reversed with adoption of Constitution, xvii–xix, 189, 199–202

States' rights: underlying thesis of Antifederalists, 136–137; reflected in philosophy of Democratic-Republican party, 215; approach adopted in New Federalism, 222

Storing, Herbert J.: on Massachusetts formula as model for securing ratification in other states, 151n.1; on Madison's strategy to foil Antifederalist designs to alter Constitution, 174; credits Madison's sponsorship of amendments as final step in establishing effective national government, 202

Story, Joseph, Supreme Court Justice: adhered to Marshall's Federalist ideology, 221

Stuart, D.: notifies Washington that Bill of Rights satisfies nearly all, except Henry, 203n.16

Sullivan, James: on Hancock's decision to opt for ratification, 153n.29

Supreme Court: espousing diverse ideologies; Federalist under Marshall; Dual Federalism under Taney; Federalist under Stone; New Federalism under Rehnquist, 221–223

Supremacy clause, proposed by Luther Martin, 69; linchpin of Constitution as per Justice Holmes, 200

"Sweeping clause": Henry's title to necessary and proper clause, 139

Swift, Jonathan: "a tub to the whale", 196

T

Taney, Roger B., Chief Justice of U.S. Supreme Court: launches Dual Federalism doctrine, 221

Taxation: debate between Henry and Madison, 137, 140, 203n.6

Tenth Amendment: pivotal nature of, xvii, 195; formulation of, determines fate of Federalist Revolution, 195, 198; different from Article II, 210, 214; fulfills dual purpose, safeguards state powers while preserving federal implied powers, 198–200; Madison succeeds in excluding structural changes to Constitution, 195, 197; Antifederalist frustration at Madison's version, 195–196; focus of Federalist v. Antifederalist versions, 201; serves questionably as basis for Dual Federalism and New Federalism, 221; defined as truism by New Deal court, 222

Thompson, Samuel (General): cites Job to establish need for bill of rights, 111

Three-fifths rule: in House of Representatives; northern concession on slavery to preserve Union, 34, 38; helped swing Electoral College for election of southern presidents, 38

Treaties: failure of states under Articles to observe terms, 23; federalism accorded role for both President and Senate, differently from appointments, 41–49; Antifederalist argument that treaties facilitate expansion of national power, 116–117

Tredwell, Thomas: absence of bill of rights stamps Constitution as sinful, 147

Trumbull, Jonathan: hopes that New York will not join Rhode Island in failing to ratify, 143

Tyler, John: on Virginia Plan as consolidating, 51n.6; on implied power to ban slave trade, 124n.53

V

Van Buren, Martin, former President: Antifederalists shaped America's spirit, even while its institutions were crafted by Federalists, 219

Vices of Political System of United States: Madison's memorandum in advance of Convention, 25

Virginia: initiates call for constitutional convention, 22; prominence of delegation, 32; split at signing ceremony, 95; battle royal at ratifying convention, 134–142; Madison v. Henry, 134; Henry claims Constitutional Convention exceeded authority, 136; Randolph declares issue is Union or no-Union, 137; Madison concedes bill of rights, 140; Madison's tactic succeeds and majority endorses ratification, 142; Constitution already in force when Virginia ratifies, 209, 231

Virginia Plan: formulated by Virginia's delegation on Madison outline, 32; scheme for national paramountcy over states, 32–33; challenged by smaller states, with New Jersey Plan demanding state equality in one house, 34; Convention opts for Virginia Plan, 43; smaller states unrelenting until Connecticut Compromise, 43

Virginia Plan's Article 6 on powers of Congress: Madison's linchpin of Constitution, 25–26, 59–60, 66–68; south objects to unlimited authority granted national government, 59–64;

consequences of enumeration in place of heads of power, 71–72
Virginia Ratifying Convention: Madison v. Henry, 134; Henry charges Constitutional Convention with exceeding authority in proposing new constitution, 136; Randolph rallies support for ratification by declaring, issue is Union or no-Union, 137; Madison concedes bill of rights to conciliate mild critics, 140; Madison's tactic succeeds and majority endorses ratification, 142; Constitution already in force when Virginia ratifies, 209, 231
Virginia's Declaration of Rights, 1776: authored by Mason, 85–86
Virginia and Kentucky Resolutions: Madison and Jefferson assert right of state to interdict federal laws, 215

W

Warren, Charles: on triumph of drafting Constitution, xix
Washington, George: Shays' Rebellion prompts his call for alterations in government to maintain law and order, 21–22; attends constitutional convention, 32; praises *Federalist*, 160n.119; opposes second constitutional convention and promotes a Federalist Congress, 163, 165; hails entry into force of Constitution, 152n.4; inaugurated as President, April 30, 1789, 181; employs Madison as Prime Minister, 181; astonished at Madison's about-turn, 205; signs bank bill, 212
Wechsler, Herbert; thesis on federalism, 31, 49
Wechsler-Choper-Kramer thesis that federalism designed to protect state interests without Supreme Court intervention, 49–51
Whipple, William (General), 7
Whitehill, Robert: illustrates threat to freedom of speech by reference to copyright power, 115
Williams, John: critical of open ended powers, 147
Williamson, Hugh: on Mississippi, 48
Wilson, James, delegate from Pennsylvania: declaims against small state demands, 35; in State House Yard address dismisses need for bill of rights, 108–110; enumeration of powers prevents violation of rights, 108–110; sovereignty resides in people not state governments, 109; defends absence of jury trial requirement in civil cases, 109; favors clear line separating national from state powers, 63–65; member of Committee of Detail that enumerated powers of Congress, 64
Wood, Gordon, 200; contending arguments over sovereignty, 123n.38
Wythe, George, delegate of Virginia: distinguished jurist; moved resolution for Virginia to ratify, 141

Y

Yates, Robert, New York delegate, 146; quits Convention on ground it promotes consolidated government, 97; reputed to be author of Brutus Antifederalist papers; authorship doubted, 98
Yeates, Jasper: attempts to explain why certain rights are included in Constitution, 113
Yoo, John Choon: on the New Federalism, as vital to preserve federal balance, 227n.55

The manufacturer's authorised representative in the EU is Springer Nature Customer Service Centre GmbH, Europaplatz 3, 69115 Heidelberg, Germany. If you have any concerns regarding our products, please contact ProductSafety@springernature.com

Printed and bound by CPI Group (UK) Ltd, Croydon, CR0 4YY
23/03/2026
02076662-0017